HISTORICAL DICTIONARIES OF RELIGIONS, PHILOSOPHIES, AND MOVEMENTS

Jon Woronoff, Series Editor

Orthodox Church, by Michael Prokurat, Alexander Golitzin, and Michael D. Peterson, 1996
Civil Rights Movement, by Ralph E. Luker, 1997
Catholicism, by William J. Collinge, 1997
North American Environmentalism, by Edward R. Wells and Alan M. Schwartz, 1997
Taoism, by Julian F. Pas in cooperation with Man Kam Leung, 1998
Gay Liberation Movement, by Ronald J. Hunt, 1999
Islamic Fundamentalist Movements in the Arab World, Iran, and Turkey, by Ahmad S. Moussalli, 1999
Cooperative Movement, by Jack Shaffer, 1999
Kierkegaard's Philosophy, by Julia Watkin, 2001
Slavery and Abolition, by Martin A. Klein, 2002
New Religious Movements, by George D. Chryssides, 2001
Prophets in Islam and Judaism, by Scott B. Noegel and Brannon M. Wheeler, 2002
Lesbian Liberation Movement: Still the Rage, by JoAnne Myers, 2003
Descartes and Cartesian Philosophy, by Roger Ariew, Dennis Des Chene, Douglas M. Jesseph, Tad M. Schmaltz, and Theo Verbeek, 2003
Witchcraft, by Michael D. Bailey, 2003
Unitarian Universalism, by Mark W. Harris, 2004
New Age Movements, by Michael York, 2004
Organized Labor, Second Edition, by James C. Docherty, 2004
Utopianism, by James M. Morris and Andrea L. Kross, 2004
Feminism, Second Edition, by Janet K. Boles and Diane Long Hoeveler, 2004
Jainism, by Kristi L. Wiley, 2004
Wittgenstein's Philosophy, by Duncan Richter, 2004
Schopenhauer's Philosophy, by David E. Cartwright, 2005
Seventh-day Adventists, by Gary Land, 2005
Methodism, Second Edition, by Charles Yrigoyen Jr. and Susan E. Warrick, 2005
Sufism, by John Renard, 2005
Sikhism, Second Edition, by W. H. McLeod, 2005
Kant and Kantianism, by Helmut Holzhey and Vilem Mudroch, 2005
Olympic Movement, Third Edition, by Bill Mallon with Ian Buchanan, 2006
Anglicanism, by Colin Buchanan, 2006
Welfare State, Second Edition, by Bent Greve, 2006
Feminist Philosophy, by Catherine Villanueva Gardner, 2006
Logic, by Harry J. Gensler, 2006
Leibniz's Philosophy, by Stuart Brown and Nicholas J. Fox, 2006
Non-Aligned Movement and Third World, by Guy Arnold, 2006
Salvation Army, by Major John G. Merritt, 2006

Judaism, Second Edition, by Norman Solomon, 2006
Epistemology, by Ralph Baergen, 2006
Bahá'í Faith, Second Edition, by Hugh C. Adamson, 2006
Aesthetics, by Dabney Townsend, 2006
Socialism, Second Edition, by Peter Lamb and James C. Docherty, 2007
Marxism, by David M. Walker and Daniel Gray, 2007
Nietzscheanism, Second Edition, by Carol Diethe, 2007
Medieval Philosophy and Theology, by Stephen F. Brown and Juan Carlos Flores, 2007
Shamanism, by Graham Harvey and Robert Wallis, 2007
Ancient Greek Philosophy, by Anthony Preus, 2007
Puritans, by Charles Pastoor and Galen K. Johnson, 2007
Green Movement, Second Edition, by Miranda Schreurs and Elim Papadakis, 2007
Husserl's Philosophy, by John J. Drummond, 2008
Existentialism, by Stephen Michelman, 2008
Zionism, Second Edition, by Rafael Medoff and Chaim I. Waxman, 2008
Coptic Church, by Gawdat Gabra, 2008
Jehovah's Witnesses, by George D. Chryssides, 2008
Hume's Philosophy, by Kenneth R. Merrill, 2008
Shakers, by Stephen J. Paterwic, 2008
Native American Movements, by Todd Leahy and Raymond Wilson, 2008
Mormonism, Third Edition, by Davis Bitton and Thomas G. Alexander, 2008
Hegelian Philosophy, Second Edition, by John W. Burbidge, 2008
Ethics, by Harry J. Gensler and Earl W. Spurgin, 2008
Environmentalism, by Peter Dauvergne, 2009
Bertrand Russell's Philosophy, by Rosalind Carey and John Ongley, 2009
Baptists, Second Edition, by William H. Brackney, 2009
Islam, Second Edition, by Ludwig W. Adamec, 2009
Homosexuality, by Brent L. Pickett, 2009
Buddhism, by Carl Olson, 2009
Holiness Movement, Second Edition, edited by William Kostlevy, 2009
Reformed Churches, Second Edition, by Robert Benedetto and Donald K. McKim, 2010
The Reformation and Counter-Reformation, by Michael Mullett, 2010
Heidegger's Philosophy, Second Edition, by Frank Schalow and Alfred Denker, 2010
Jesus, by Daniel J. Harrington, S.J., 2010
Metaphysics, by Gary Rosenkrantz and Joshua Hoffman, 2011
Shinto, Second Edition, by Stuart D. B. Picken, 2011
The Friends (Quakers), Second Edition, by Margery Post Abbott, Mary Ellen Chijioke, Pink Dandelion, and John William Oliver Jr., 2011
Lutheranism, Second Edition, by Günther Gassmann with Duanne H. Larson, and Mark W. Oldenburg, 2011
Hinduism, New Edition, by Jeffery D. Long, 2011

Historical Dictionary of Hinduism

New Edition

Jeffery D. Long

The Scarecrow Press, Inc.
Lanham • Toronto • Plymouth, UK
2011

Published by Scarecrow Press, Inc.
A wholly owned subsidiary of The Rowman & Littlefield Publishing Group, Inc.
4501 Forbes Boulevard, Suite 200
Lanham, Maryland 20706
http://www.scarecrowpress.com

Estover Road
Plymouth PL6 7PY
United Kingdom

British Library Cataloguing in Publication Information Available

Library of Congress Cataloging-in-Publication Data

Long, Jeffery D.
Historical dictionary of Hinduism / Jeffery D. Long. -- New ed.
p. cm. -- (Historical dictionaries of religions, philosophies, and movements)
Updated and revised ed. of: The A to Z of Hinduism / Bruce M. Sullivan.
Includes bibliographical references.
ISBN 978-0-8108-6764-2 (cloth : alk. paper) -- ISBN 978-0-8108-7960-7 (ebook)
1. Hinduism--Dictionaries. I. Sullivan, Bruce M., 1951- A to Z of Hinduism. II. Title.
BL1105.S847 2011
294.503--dc22 2011013053

∞™ The paper used in this publication meets the minimum requirements of American National Standard for Information Sciences—Permanence of Paper for Printed Library Materials, ANSI/NISO Z39.48-1992.

Printed in the United States of America

For Billy

Contents

Editor's Foreword

Hinduism is the world's third-largest religion and still growing, with about 900,000,000 adherents at present. It is also the oldest major religion, with a tradition reaching back not just centuries but millennia, with many notable peaks and periods of glory. It has influenced and been affected by other world religions, including Islam and Buddhism as well as Christianity. Yet, despite repeated attempts to contain it, it has maintained an exceptional vigor and boasts a rich spiritual culture with celebrated thinkers and teachers and an extensive literature. Nonetheless, it is rather poorly known outside of India and the surrounding region, and the fascination in the West with some aspects has perhaps been less enlightening than mystifying. We are familiar with things like caste, guru, karma, meditation, ashram (āśrama), and even the sacred cow. But we know pitifully little about its basic writings and principal beliefs and practices. Gradually, as more Hindus move to the West, that is changing, but the change is slow because, among other things, Hinduism is not particularly easy to understand, especially when coming from another horizon.

This *Historical Dictionary of Hinduism* should contribute to a greater understanding—or at least less misunderstanding—by presenting the religion in very comprehensible terms. This means, among other things, providing biographical sketches of particularly significant persons as well as further information on the movements, schools, and communities they founded. Other entries deal with the basic writings, doctrines, and practices. But inevitably many more have to clearly explain the basic concepts, some of these best conveyed by the Sanskrit term and others, more or less effectively, by an English translation. This is embedded in a chronology reaching back four and a half millennia that then focuses on an impressively active past century or so. The introduction covers this long period as well, showing how Hinduism has evolved and grown, emphasizing many highlights and turning points. Although this volume already contains an amazing amount of information, quite enough for those who are casually interested, specialists and those with more precise interests can find ample additional reading in the bibliography.

This completely new edition of the *Historical Dictionary of Hinduism* is particularly useful for various reasons. Certainly one is that its author, Jeffery D. Long, himself originally came from another horizon, Catholicism, so he first saw Hinduism from outside before getting to know it better from inside. Moreover, he has spent the past decade explaining it to students at the Department of Religious Studies at Elizabethtown College, where he has been working as an associate professor and as department chair. Over the years, he has written substantially on Hinduism, starting with his doctoral dissertation at the University of Chicago's Divinity School and continuing with several dozen articles and reviews as well as two recent books, *A Vision for Hinduism: Beyond Hindu Nationalism* and, on a related religious current, *Jainism: An Introduction*. In addition, he has served as chair of the steering committee of the Dharma Academy of North America and is currently cochair of the North American Hinduism Consultation of the American Academy of Religion. This permits him to present Hinduism to a broad public, including both initiates and those who are curious but have found it hard to get comprehensible answers to their questions elsewhere.

Jon Woronoff
Series Editor

Acknowledgments

I thank the following persons who have made it possible for me to complete this project.

First, Jon Woronoff, the editor of the Scarecrow Press series of Historical Dictionaries of Religions, Philosophies, and Movements, who invited me to write this book. I found Jon to be very kind and generous in regard to deadlines, and also most helpful and prompt in responding to my questions and concerns and in giving editorial suggestions.

I also thank my department colleagues and the administration of Elizabethtown College for granting me a one-year sabbatical (consisting of a reduced teaching load and a bare minimum of department chair–related duties) in order to help me complete this project.

I thank all of my teachers, colleagues, and fellow Hindus who, over the years, have added to my knowledge base and put me in a position to even contemplate taking on a project such as this. I hope this book is useful to you and to future generations of scholars in the field of Hindu studies.

A special word of gratitude goes to my wife and best friend, Mahua Bhattacharya, who has been, as always, encouraging and patient. I am sorry for all of the times we have had to forego seeing a movie or taking a drive because "I need to work on my *Historical Dictionary of Hinduism*!"

Readers of my previous two books, *A Vision for Hinduism* and *Jainism: An Introduction*, may recall my mentioning in the acknowledgments of those books my orange tabby cat, Billy, who was constantly at my feet during the writing of those books and was always a dear and supportive presence. During the writing of this book, Billy was diagnosed with, and eventually succumbed to, a very aggressive lymphoma. The *Bhagavad Gītā* and the Vedānta tradition that I practice tell me that the soul continues on, and I believe this to be true. But there is an empty space at my feet and sorrow in my heart as I share this news with my readers. I dedicate this book to Billy.

Reader's Note

The bulk of the terminology in this dictionary is in Sanskrit and other Indic languages. The scripts ("alphabets") of these languages are phonetic in nature—that is, each of the characters stands for exactly one sound, and there is a character for each sound. As a result, the Indic scripts have far more characters than the mere 26 of the Roman alphabet used in English and most western European languages—about 50, to be precise. In order to render words from Indic languages in the Roman script in an exact way that does not lend itself to mispronunciation, scholars have developed a system of diacritical marks in order to distinguish between, for example, the short "a" of Sanskrit (pronounced like the "u" in "bud") and the Sanskrit long "ā" (which is pronounced like the "a" in the English word "father"). The correct pronunciation of the Indic sounds, as depicted using the standard system, is as follows:

a This is pronounced "uh," as in "bud."
ā This is pronounced "ah," as in "father."
i This is pronounced like the "i" in "bit."
ī This is pronounced like the "ee" in "beet."
u This is pronounced like the "oo" in "book."
ū This is pronounced like the "oo" in "boot."
ṛ This is pronounced like the "ri" in "rig," with a slight roll of the tongue, though not as hard a roll as in Spanish "r."
e This is pronounced like "ay" in "say."
ai This is pronounced like "aye" or "eye."
o This is pronounced "oh," as in "Ohio."
au This is pronounced like "ow" in "how."

Consonants are pronounced as in English, but retroflex consonants (consonants with a dot under them, such as "ṭ") are pronounced with the tongue touching the roof of the mouth.

Aspirated consonants are immediately followed by an "h" (for example, "th," "dh") and include an exhalation—that is the "h" is pronounced, producing somewhat of a softening of the sound of the consonant. The "h" is *not* a separate syllable. So "dha" is pronounced "dha," and not "daha."

The "ś" and "ṣ" sounds are almost indistinguishable and are sometimes confused even by native speakers. The "ṣ" sound is pronounced with the tongue at the roof of the mouth, but "ś" is not. They both sound like the "sh" in "she."

The sound "ḥ," which is always preceded by a vowel, produces a slight echoing of that vowel. So "aḥ" is pronounced "aha." The sound "ṃ" is a slightly nasalized "m" which sounds almost like an "n" and bears some resemblance to the nasalized French "n."

I have used this system for most terms in this dictionary, except for most modern proper names that have a popular spelling (such as "Ramakrishna"). For the sake of consistency I have also tended to use Sanskrit terminology, even when the corresponding Hindi term is better known (so "avatāra" instead of "avatar").

This book is extensively cross-referenced. In the dictionary section, if there is an entry on a specific topic, this is shown by bolding it the first time it appears (with the exception of "Hindu" and "Hinduism"). Other related entries are listed as *See also*. If a topic does not have an entry of its own, but it appears under another heading or is amply discussed there, it is indicated by a *See*.

Acronyms and Abbreviations

BAPS	Bocāsanvāsī Akṣar Puruṣottam Swāmīnārāyaṇ Sansthā
BJP	Bhāratīya Janatā Party
DĀNAM	Dharma Academy of North America
HAF	Hindu American Foundation
ISKCON	International Society for Krishna Consciousness
RKM	Ramakrishna Mission
RSS	Rāṣṭrīya Svayamsevak Saṅgh
SRF	Self-Realization Fellowship
TM	Transcendental Meditation
VHP	Viśva Hindu Pariṣad

Chronology

All dates are CE (Common Era; AD) unless otherwise indicated. Most premodern dates are approximations, especially for the composition of texts. Most Hindu chronologies traditionally locate texts far earlier than does modern scholarship. The dates given here generally reflect the modern scholarly consensus. It should be noted, however, that texts were often transmitted orally for many generations before taking their current form. So it may be that the beginning of this process of composition and transmission extends back considerably further than modern scholarship, which focuses on the texts in their extant form, suggests.

c. 50,000 BCE Stone Age cultures arise in the Indian subcontinent.

c. 30,000 BCE Bhimbetka cave paintings drawn, including depictions of horses.

7000–5000 BCE Mixed pastoral and agricultural settlements, centered on Mehrgarh, emerge in what is today western Pakistan.

4000–3000 BCE Proto-Indo-European language breaks up into distinct languages.

c. 3000 BCE Pastoral nomadic societies are prominent in northern India.

c. 2700 BCE Large-scale urban societies emerge along the Indus and Sarasvatī Rivers, in continuity with the culture of Mehrgarh.

2600–1900 BCE Indus Valley/Indus-Sarasvatī Civilization, advanced urban phase.

2300–2000 BCE Indo-European speakers in the Ural region of Russia are the first to invent chariots with light spokes, as described in the *Ṛg Veda*.

c. 2200 BCE Sumerian texts mention trade with the land of *Meluhha*, possible reference to the Indus Valley Civilization.

c. 2100 BCE Indo-European speakers are living in Persia and Afghanistan.

1900–1800 BCE The Sarasvatī River dries up and the Indus River changes course, leading to massive disruption of the economy of the Indus-Sarasvatī

Civilization, with most of its cities being abandoned. A slow but major migration begins from the Indus-Sarasvatī region to the Ganges River Valley.

1900–1700 BCE Indo-European speakers are living in Northwestern India.

1900–1200 BCE Indus Valley Civilization gradually declines.

1700–1500 BCE Composition of *Ṛg Veda*. Horses and light-spoked chariots present in Northwestern India.

c. 1500 BCE Submergence of the stone port city of Dvārakā, on the coast of Gujarat, site associated with Kṛṣṇa, suggesting a possible date for the *Mahābhārata* war.

c. 1300 BCE Hittite inscriptions contain references to Vedic deities.

1200–1000 BCE Composition of *Yajur Veda* and *Sāma Veda*.

c. 1000 BCE The city of Kauśāmbi in Vatsa, in central India, is founded.

c. 950 BCE Date for the *Mahābhārata* battle preferred by most scholars.

c. 900 BCE Composition of *Atharva Veda*. Vedic peoples move more deeply into the Ganges Valley. City of Kāśi (Banaras) is founded.

850–750 BCE Life of Pārśvanātha, 23rd Tīrthaṅkara of Jainism.

800–600 BCE Composition of the *Brāhmaṇas*, early priestly commentaries on the *Vedas*.

600–500 BCE Composition of the *Āraṇyakas*, or "forest texts."

518 BCE Persians invade Northwest India, under Emperor Darius I.

c. 500 BCE *Śrauta Sūtras*, *Vedāṅgas*, and *Bṛhaddevatā* (Sanskrit commentaries upon Vedic rituals and deities) are composed. City of Pataliputra founded. Vedic peoples go south.

500–400 BCE *Bṛhadāraṇyaka*, *Chāndogya*, *Taittirīya*, and *Kauṣītaki Upaniṣads* are composed.

499–427 BCE Life of Vardhamāna Mahāvīra, 24th Tīrthaṅkara of Jainism.

490–410 BCE Life of Siddhārtha Gautama, the Buddha.

c. 400 BCE Pāṇini's *Aṣṭadhyāyī*, major work on Sanskrit grammar, composed.

400–300 BCE *Kaṭha*, *Śvetāśvatāra*, and *Muṇḍaka Upaniṣads* are composed.

350–283 BCE Life of Kauṭilya (Canakya), advisor to Candragupta Maurya, to whom the *Artha Śāstra*, a work of political science, is attributed.

327–325 BCE Alexander of Macedon invades Northwest South Asia.

320–293 BCE Reign of Candragupta Maurya, founder of the Mauryan Dynasty.

c. 300 BCE Greek ambassador Megasthenes travels to India.

300–200 BCE Composition of *Gṛhya Sūtras* (outlines of rituals for householders), Gautama's *Nyāya Sūtra*, Kaṇāda's *Vaiśeṣika Sūtra*, Jaimini's *Pūrvamīmāṃsā Sūtra* (the foundational documents, respectively, of the Nyāya, Vaiśeṣika, and Pūrva Mīmāṃsā *darśanas*, or systems of philosophy), and Kauṭilya's *Artha Śāstra*.

300 BCE–100 CE Composition of major *Dharma Śāstras*, or legal texts.

300 BCE–300 CE Composition of *Mahābhārata*.

268–233 BCE Reign of Aśoka, Mauryan emperor and renowned convert to Buddhism.

c. 250 BCE Third Buddhist Council takes place at Pataliputra, under Aśoka's auspices.

c. 200 BCE Bādarāyaṇa's *Vedānta Sūtras* composed, which summarize the philosophy of the *Upaniṣads*.

200 BCE–200 CE *Rāmāyaṇa* composed.

184 BCE Mauryan Dynasty ends. Hindu general Puśyamitra Śuṅga founds Śuṅga Dynasty.

166 BCE–78 CE Greeks, Scythians, Bactrians, and Parthians enter India.

c. 150 BCE Buddhist monuments of Bharhut and Sanchi are built during Śuṅga Dynasty.

150 BCE–100 CE Patañjali's *Mahābhāṣya*, a work of Sanskrit grammar, composed.

100 BCE–100 CE *Bhagavad Gītā* composed.

100 BCE–200 CE *Tirukkural* composed in southern India.

100 BCE–500 CE Patañjali's *Yoga Sūtra* composed.

73 BCE Hindu Śuṅga Dynasty ends, replaced by the Buddhist Kuṣāna Dynasty.

78–140 CE Central Asian Kuṣāna king Kaniṣka reigns and promotes Buddhism.

c. 100 Composition of *Manusmṛti*. Composition of Sangham poetry in southern India.

100–500 Expansion of Hinduism and Buddhism into Southeast Asia through trade.

250–1200 Major *Pūrāṇas* composed, texts consisting largely of tales of the deeds of Hindu deities, forming the basis of much of the theological writing of the Vaiṣṇava, Śaiva, and Śākta theistic traditions, which all become highly prominent during this period.

c. 300 Vātsyāyana composes the *Kāma Sūtra*.

320–550 Gupta Dynasty reigns over northern India from Pāṭaliputra, does much to promote Hinduism in period sometimes called "Hindu Renaissance."

375 Pallava Dynasty is founded in southern India.

c. 400 Kālidāsa writes Sanskrit plays and long poems; also the period of astronomer and mathematician Āryabhaṭṭa.

405–411 Chinese Buddhist pilgrim Faxian visits India.

c. 450 *Harivaṃśa* composed.

455–467 The Huns attack northern India.

460–477 The Vakataka Dynasty completes the caves at Ajanta in central India.

500–900 Period of the Nāyanār Śaiva Tamil poets.

550–575 Kalachuris create the cave of Śiva at Elephanta.

550–880 Cālukya Dynasty, based in Badāmi, Karnataka, thrives, controlling much of southern and central India.

570–632 Life of Prophet Muhammad, founder of Islam, in the Arabian Peninsula.

600–900 Period of the Āḷvār Vaiṣṇava Tamil poets.

606–647 Reign of Harṣa of Kanauj over much of northern India.

630–644 Chinese Buddhist pilgrim Xuanzang visits India.

650 Arab armies reach the Indus after conquering Persia.

650–800 Early Tantras are composed.

711–715 Arabs invade Northwestern India.

765–773 Rāja Kṛṣṇa I creates the Kailāsa temple to Śiva at Ellora in central India.

788–820 Life of Śaṅkara (Ādi Śaṅkarācārya), major exponent of Advaita Vedānta and founder of the Daśanāmi order of monks; born in Kerala, though he travels throughout India.

c. 800 Māṇikkavācakar composes the *Tiruvācakam* in southern India.

880–1200 Coḷa Empire dominates South India.

900–1150 The Chandellas build the temples at Khajuraho.

973–1048 Life of al-Bīrunī, Arab traveler, documents Hindu beliefs and customs.

950–1020 Life of Śaiva philosopher Abhinavagupta, in Kashmir.

1001 Mahmud of Ghazni (979–1030) raids north India.

1021 Ghaznavid (Turkish) Muslim capital established at Lahore.

1077–1157 Life of Rāmāṇuja, Śrīvaiṣṇava theologian and founder of the Viśiṣṭādvaita system of Vedānta, in Tamil Nadu.

1120–1145 Building of Angkor Wat in Cambodia, a major Hindu and Buddhist temple complex.

1192–1206 Muhammad of Ghor establishes Ghorid Muslim capital at Delhi.

c. 1200 Early orders of Sufis thrive in north India, Vīraśaivas (Basava) in the south. Jayadeva's *Gītāgovinda*, a major Vaiṣṇava devotional work is composed in Bengal.

1210–1526 The Delhi Sultanate is in power.

1238–1258 Narasiṃhadeva I builds the sun temple of Konārak in Orissa.

1238–1317 Life of Madhva, Vaiṣṇava theologian and founder of the Dvaita system of Vedānta, in Karnataka.

c. 1300 Śrīvaiṣṇavas split into Teṅkalai and Vaṭakalai sects.

1325–1351 Muhammad bin Tughluq reigns from Delhi.

1336–1565 Vijayānagara Empire is in its prime.

1440–1518 Life of Kabīr, major figure of the Sānt movement, which draws upon both Hinduism and Islam for inspiration.

1399 Timur, ruler of Central Asia, destroys Delhi.

1469–1539 Life of Guru Nānak, founder and first guru of Sikhism, in the Punjab.

1486–1533 Life of Caitanya, Vaiṣṇava saint and founder of Acintya Bhedābheda Vedānta, in Bengal; major inspiration for the Bengali Gauḍīya Vaiṣṇava tradition (and, in the modern period, for both Ramakrishna and ISKCON).

1498–1547 Life of Vaiṣṇava saint Mīrā Bai in Rājasthān.

1526 Babur founds the Mughal Empire.

1530–1556 Reign of Mughal Emperor Humayun.

1532–1623 Life of Tulsīdās, author of the *Rāmcaritmānas*.

1556–1605 Reign of Mughal Emperor Akbar.

1600 Queen Elizabeth I charters the British East India Company.

1605–1627 Reign of Mughal Emperor Jahangir.

1608–1649 Life of Vaiṣṇava saint Tukārām.

1627–1658 Reign of Mughal Emperor Shah Jahan, builder of the Taj Mahal.

1658–1707 Reign of Mughal Emperor Aurangzeb.

1713–1719 Reign of Mughal Emperor Farrukhsiyar.

1757 British defeat Muslim rulers in Bengal. First wave of British Rāj begins under the British East India Company.

1758–1828 Life of Charles "Hindoo" Stuart, first "white" Hindu of the modern period.

1772–1833 Life of Rām Mohan Roy, founder of the Brahmo Samāj.

1803–1882 Life of Ralph Waldo Emerson, American philosopher and a leading figure of the Transcendentalist movement, heavily influenced by early English translations of Hindu texts such as the *Bhagavad Gītā* and the *Upaniṣads*.

1824–1883 Life of Swāmī Dayānanda Sarasvatī, founder of the Ārya Samāj.

1828 Founding of Brahmo Samāj by Rām Mohan Roy.

1831–1891 Life of Helena Petrovna Blavatsky, founder of the Theosophical Society.

1836–1886 Life of Sri Ramakrishna, guru of Swāmī Vivekānanda, in Bengal.

1838–1894 Life of Bankim Chandra Chatterjee, major Bengali literary figure.

1847–1933 Life of Annie Besant, leader of the Theosophical Society and of the Indian National Congress.

1857–1858 The Rebellion, or War of Independence, known in British histories as the Sepoy Mutiny.

1858 Final phase of the British Rāj begins when the British viceroy officially replaces both Mughal rule and the East India Company.

1861–1941 Life of Rabindranath Tagore, Nobel laureate and Bengali cultural hero.

1863–1902 Life of Swāmī Vivekānanda, founder of the Ramakrishna Order, Vedānta Society, and Ramakrishna Mission.

1869–1948 Life of Mohandās K. (Mahātma) Gāndhī, leader of the nonviolent movement for Indian independence.

1872–1950 Life of Aurobindo Ghose, Hindu nationalist leader (in his early years) and Hindu sage and founder of Integral Yoga (in his later years).

1875 Founding of Ārya Samāj and Theosophical Society.

1879–1950 Life of Sri Ramana Maharshi, Hindu sage of southern India.

1888–1975 Life of Sarvepalli Radhakrishnan, philosopher and statesman.

1891–1956 Life of Bhīmrao Ambedkar, Dalit leader and author of the constitution of India.

1893 Swāmī Vivekānanda speaks at the Parliament of World Religions, in Chicago.

1893–1952 Life of Paramahāṃsa Yogānanda, founder of Self-Realization Fellowship (SRF).

1893–1976 Life of Swāmī Prabhavānanda, prominent monk of the Ramakrishna Order and founder of the Vedānta Society of Southern California whose disciples included Christopher Isherwood and Aldous Huxley.

1895–1983 Life of Vinoba Bhave, Gandhian activist.

1896–1977 Life of A. C. Bhaktivedānta Swāmī Prabhupāda, founder and *ācārya* of the International Society for Krishna Consciousness (ISKCON).

1896–1982 Life of Ānandamāyī Mā, female guru and Hindu saint.

1897 Founding of Vedānta Society in America by Swāmī Vivekānanda.

1916–1993 Life of Swāmī Chinmayānanda.

1918–2008 Life of Maharishi Mahesh Yogi, founder of Transcendental Meditation.

1919 Amritsar massacre takes place, helping turn the tide of world opinion against British rule of India.

1927–2001 Life of Satguru Sivaya Subramuniyaswami, founder of *Hinduism Today*.

1931–1990 Life of Bhagwan Shree Rajneesh (Osho), controversial Tantric guru.

1935 Birth of Swāmī Agniveśa, founder of the World Council of the Ārya Samāj.

1947 Independence and partition of India on 15 August.

1948 Assassination of Mohandās K. Gāndhī by Nathuram Godse on 30 January.

1951 Bhīmrao Ambedkar leads mass conversion of Dalits to Buddhism.

1953 Birth of Amma (Mātā Amritānandamayī), the "Hugging Saint."

1966 Founding of ISKCON in New York City.

1968 The Beatles travel to Rishikesh, India, to study Transcendental Meditation with the Maharishi Mahesh Yogi.

1970 Hindus in Europe, the United States, and Canada start building temples on a large scale.

1984 Massive Hindu–Sikh riots sparked by Indian army attack on the Golden Temple of Amritsar and assassination of Prime Minister Indira Gandhi. Many Sikhs immigrate to the United States, Canada, and the United Kingdom.

1992 Demolition of Babrī Masjīd in Ayodhyā, followed by Hindu–Muslim riots.

2002 Hindu–Muslim riots in Ahmedabad, Gujarat, claim hundreds of lives.

2004 Manmohan Singh elected first Sikh prime minister of India.

2009 President Barack Obama acknowledges Hinduism as a significant part of religious life in America in his inaugural address; later in the year, he sends Diwali greeting to Hindus, Jains, and Sikhs.

2010 Indian high court resolves Babrī Masjīd issue by dividing the land between Hindu and Muslim organizations. Though there are objections to the decision, the responses of both sides are nonviolent.

Introduction

Hinduism—the name evokes a topic so vast that one despairs of being able to cover it in an adequate fashion in a single volume. At the same time, this term does point to something distinctive—a tradition, or rather a family of traditions, that today commands the loyalty of over 900,000,000 human beings, making it the third-largest religion in the world, in terms of the numbers of its adherents, after Christianity and Islam. It is the fourth largest if one considers the category variously described as "nonreligious," "secular," "agnostic," or "atheist" to be something akin to a religion (or at least a distinct worldview and value system), which ranks third. It nearly ties with Islam, however, if one regards Buddhism, Jainism, and Sikhism—as many Hindus do—as part of the same family of traditions that is called *Hinduism*. (The reactions of Buddhists, Jains, and Sikhs to being perceived by at least some Hindus as, in some sense, fellow Hindus, vary greatly, ranging from a sharp rejection to indifference to acceptance.)

The Hindu community is today a global one, though the vast majority of Hindus reside in India and in countries immediately adjacent to it, such as Pakistan, Bangladesh, Nepal, and Sri Lanka. Contrary to one popular understanding, however, Hinduism is not limited only to people with an Indian or South Asian ethnic identity. There have been Hindus in Southeast Asia—that is, Hindus indigenous to Southeast Asia—for over a millennium and a half, and Bali, in Indonesia, continues to be home to a thriving Hindu community today. There is also a growing number of converts to Hinduism from Europe, North and South America, Australia, and Africa, as well as practitioners of traditions with a clear Hindu provenance—such as Siddha Yoga, Vedānta, and Transcendental Meditation—that do not necessarily identify themselves as *Hindu*. And there are those non-Hindus who observe Hindu practices and hold Hindu beliefs without necessarily realizing that this is what they are doing: vegetarians, practitioners of yoga, believers in reincarnation, and those who believe that there are many paths to salvation. Enough such people exist in the Western world to lead a recent commentator on religion to remark, "We're all Hindus now."[1]

But what is Hinduism? What is the history of this vast and internally varied tradition? It has become something of a truism among scholars of religion to say that "Hinduism does not exist." Although offensive to many Hindus (since no one likes to be told the tradition they practice and hold dear does not exist), the truth to which this claim, rather clumsily, points is that the term *Hinduism* has, historically, been imposed upon what are now called Hindu traditions by outsiders, many of whom were invested in the colonial exploitation of the Indian subcontinent. The terms *Hindu* and *Hinduism* were utterly foreign to most Hindus for most of history—a fact that can be expressed far less paradoxically in the form "There was no Hinduism for most of history, until 19th-century scholars created it." But this is also highly unsatisfactory, because those who do regard themselves as Hindus also see themselves and their traditions as being in continuity with a very ancient set of practices and beliefs that is as old as civilization itself.[2] In many works by Hindu authors, one frequently encounters the claim that Hinduism is the oldest of the world's religions.

The term *Hindu*—derived from a Persian mispronunciation of *Sindhu*, the river known to the Greeks as the *Indus*—was originally used by Persian and Arab travelers to refer to the people who lived beyond the Indus River. In other words, *Hindu*, originally just meant *Indian*. This usage continued into the period of the British Rāj, whose colonial scholars coined the term *Hinduism* to refer to the religious beliefs and practices native to India, in contrast with such non-indigenous Indian religions as Christianity, Islam, Zoroastrianism, and Judaism—all of which have been practiced in India for centuries, alongside the native Indian traditions. Over the course of time, as Western knowledge of the Indian traditions increased, a distinction was made between those traditions that professed the sanctity of an ancient set of religious texts called the *Vedas* and those that did not. *Hinduism* came to refer, then, to the subset of indigenous Indic traditions that observed the sanctity of the *Vedas*. The non-Vedic traditions—Buddhism, Jainism, and Sikhism—came to be defined as distinct and separate religions.

Hinduism, defined as the collective term for the Vedic traditions, is a term with a number of flaws and limitations. On the one hand, it obscures the many differences among these traditions—including the degree to which the *Vedas* are even relevant to their day-to-day practice. The daily rituals of a Smārta Brahmin, for example, are quite heavily shaped by Vedic injunctions and additional injunctions that are contained in a set of texts based on the *Vedas*—the *Smṛtis*—that this community takes to be authoritative. But such injunctions are altogether irrelevant to the spiritual life of a Vīraśaiva. And a member of the Aghorī sect will even deliberately invert them. On the other hand, the definition of *Hindu* as *Vedic* can also downplay the many close similarities between Vedic traditions and non-Vedic ones. The basic worldviews of a Vedāntin, a Buddhist, and a Jain, for example, are not all that different from each other on a host of religiously important topics. And if one goes to Sanjusangendo, a famous Buddhist temple in Kyoto, Japan, which enshrines 1,001 forms of the bodhisattva of compassion, Avalokiteśvara, one will find that these forms are guarded by images of all of the major Vedic deities. Not far from Kyoto, the Buddhist monks of the Shingon sect regularly perform a fire ceremony that is called *goma* and is clearly modeled on the Vedic *homa* ritual at their monastery on Mount Koya. The Jain community in India celebrates the holiday Dīwali by worshiping the goddess Lakṣmī. Numerous other examples of shared practices, deities, symbols, and concepts could be cited as well, not least being the cosmology of karma and rebirth and a soteriology centered on liberation from this process.

The understanding of *Hinduism*, however, as Vedic religion, with whatever inadequacies this understanding may have, is the one that is deployed by most mainstream scholarship on Hindu traditions. One must always remember that terms and categories are scholarly tools. They do not necessarily correspond precisely to what is "there" in terms of ground realities. Rather, they seek to clarify for us what is "there." Sometimes they are useful in doing this, and at other times they may need to be set aside in favor of other categories that may be more illuminating in particular situations.

With the understanding, therefore, that the terms *Hindu* and *Hinduism* are relatively new arrivals on the scene of world history and that our use of them to refer to ancient realities is an anachronism—referring actually to practices and beliefs with which those who today call themselves *Hindu* see their own traditions to be in historical continuity—we can turn to an overview of the history of Hinduism.

THE QUESTION OF ORIGINS: HINDUISM AND EARLY INDIAN CIVILIZATION

Unlike most of the world's religions, Hinduism does not originate from the teachings of a single founding figure. There is no equivalent, for all of Hinduism, to a Jesus, a Buddha, or a Prophet Muhammad. There are, instead, many such figures—founders of particular lineages or "subtraditions" that collectively make up what we now call Hinduism. And there are innumerable local traditions that have emerged in conversation with one another over the course of many centuries. Hinduism, one could say, is the ethos of a civilization. Presentations of the history of Hinduism, therefore, usually begin with a look at the earliest phases of civilization in the Indian subcontinent.

Human beings have been present in the Indian subcontinent almost as long as there have been human beings. One of the first waves of human migration out of Africa carried a group of early humans to southern Asia, and various groups of migrants have passed both in and out of the subcontinent ever since. Indian Stone Age culture is in evidence starting around 50,000 BCE. The

Bhimbetka cave paintings, traced to around 30,000 BCE and discovered in the central Indian state of Madhya Pradesh, depict human beings engaged in warfare, riding on horses and elephants, and deploying technologies such as spears and tents (probably made from the hides of animals).[3] The first settled, non-nomadic cultures began to appear in the region of Mehrgarh (a town in what is now Pakistan) around 7000 BCE. The people of Mehrgarh practiced a mix of pastoralism and agriculture.[4]

There is close continuity—a claim based on the artwork depicted on pottery—between this early community and the very highly developed Indus Valley Civilization, which was at its technological height from roughly 2600 to 1900 BCE. With planned cities and a very advanced knowledge of sanitation and irrigation, the people of the Indus Valley achieved one of the highest standards of living in the ancient world.[5]

Unfortunately, the writing system of this civilization has not yet been deciphered. This makes all claims about its religious beliefs and practices a matter of conjecture, based on interpretation of artifacts rather than on the direct statements of the Indus people. A good deal of evidence has been discovered, however, that indicates a number of continuities—though not necessarily a perfect correspondence—between beliefs and practices in the Indus Valley and those of later Hinduism. Examples include figures that appear to be practicing some form of yoga, figures with features in common with the Hindu deities Śiva and Śakti, large public baths and a broader cultural preoccupation with cleanliness and sanitation and a reverence for water that all resonate with Hindu practice, and figures making the traditional Hindu gesture of respect—or *añjali*—that consists of the palms of the hands being placed together. Other practices of the Indus civilization, not of a religious nature, that persist in later Indian culture include its highly developed system of weights and measures and a system of social organization based on occupation that has some resemblance to the later caste system. It is not clear if the occupational groups in the Indus civilization were arranged in a hierarchy. The different groups appear to have had segregated living arrangements, which suggests that they were endogamous, like the castes of later Indian society. But there is no discernible difference in the quality of their living arrangements, which suggests an egalitarian, rather than hierarchical, relationship. Interestingly, some contemporary Hindus do claim that the castes were originally on an equal footing.[6]

The Indus Valley Civilization entered a rather drastic period of decline around 1900 BCE due primarily to geological factors. A series of devastating earthquakes resulted not only in the destruction of many Indus cities but also in the Indus River changing its course, as a result of which some cities were flooded and others that had been prosperous trading ports were left high and dry.

Recent studies have also revealed that the Indus had a companion, the Sarasvatī—a river that, judging by the sheer number of settlements found along what used to be its banks, may have been more central to the life of the civilization than the Indus itself. Because of this, some scholars have argued that the civilization should be called not the Indus Valley Civilization, but the Indus-Sarasvatī Civilization (or even the Sarasvatī Civilization). The Sarasvatī River dried up completely in some places due to the same tectonic shifts that changed the course of the Indus, and in some places it went underground. What little of it that remains on the surface is a periodic stream—that is, a stream that is dry during part of the year and has running water during the rainy season—called the Gaggar-Hakra.

THE EARLY VEDIC PERIOD

According to mainstream scholarship, the next phase of Indian civilization, and so of the history of Hinduism, begins with the arrival in India of small waves of migrants from the area of Central Asia. Filtering gradually into the northwestern region of the subcontinent beginning around 1900 BCE, these migrants spoke an Indo-European language and used small, light chariots of a kind developed in southern Russia between 2300 and 2000 BCE. Settling in India and gradually blending into the indigenous population, the language and cultural practices of this community are preserved in the *Vedas*, the oldest extant texts of Hinduism. These texts were gradually compiled into four collections called the *Ṛg Veda*, *Sāma Veda*, *Yajur Veda*, and *Atharva Veda*. These texts date from roughly 1700 BCE (in the case of the oldest parts of the *Ṛg Veda*, the oldest of the Vedic texts) to 900 BCE (the approximate date of the *Atharva Veda*, the last of the Vedic collections, or *Saṃhitās*, to be compiled).

Geographic points of reference in the *Vedas* suggest that the texts were composed in the northwestern region of the Indian subcontinent, showing greatest familiarity with the area now known as Punjab. They also suggest that the community that composed them did not see themselves as newcomers to the region, there being no overt references to another homeland or to migration from such a homeland to India. Vedic Sanskrit, the language in which these texts were composed, also shows evidence of a non-Indo-European substrate, suggesting that this community was multilingual, or at least that it had already had a good deal of interaction with persons of another language group, adopting words and ways of speaking different from those of their Indo-European-speaking ancestors.

The *Vedas* and the religious practices and beliefs that they represent were not, therefore, imported *in toto* to the subcontinent from outside. They are, rather, the product of a long process of cultural hybridization of Indo-European and non-Indo-European elements that had already been underway for some time—at least two centuries, if current scholarship is correct—prior to the composition of these texts.

It was long believed by many scholars that Indo-European culture was brought to India in a sudden and violent invasion and that this invasion was the cause of the fall of the Indus Valley Civilization. But it is now known that this was not the case. The evidence points instead to the geological changes mentioned above as the chief culprit in the decline of the Indus culture. The Indo-European migrants did not cause the fall of, but rather filled a vacuum created by the already declining, Indus Valley Civilization.

It is also likely that the descendants of the Indo-European migrants helped to preserve the Indus culture. Vedic references, for example, to the Sarasvatī River in the present tense, as a wide, flowing river with many settlements on its banks, suggest that the *Vedas* are a repository not only of Indo-European culture but of indigenous Indus Valley Civilization cultural elements and other indigenous Indian elements as well—an idea that is consistent with the thesis that these texts are the product of centuries of cultural hybridization.

This picture of the past is a point of contention among some scholars today. An alternate view, according to which the *Vedas* predate the Indus Valley Civilization, being written at the time of the mixed pastoral and agricultural society that existed between 7000 BCE and the advanced urban phase of the Indus Valley that began around 2600 BCE, has been defended by a number of scholars—particularly Hindu scholars—who argue that this view is more consistent with traditional Hindu accounts of ancient Indian history and point to the highly conjectural nature of the dates assigned to the Vedic texts, as well as political misuses of early, racially tinged versions of the "Āryan Invasion Theory." This "Out of India" theory suggests that northwestern India, not Central Asia, is the Indo-European homeland and that Indo-European language and culture spread from India to Ireland (the extreme eastern and western ends of the Indo-European cultural sphere), rather than out of Central Asia in both directions.[7]

Mainstream scholarship tends to reject this view, based on such factors as the non-Indo-European substrate elements in Vedic Sanskrit—the most ancient Indo-European language found in India—and various discontinuities between the culture of the Indus Valley and that described in the *Vedas*—such as the nearly total absence of the horse in the Indus Valley culture and its ubiquity in Vedic writings. The Indo-European homeland would show evidence of a "pure" Indo-European language, not an Indo-European language that has been transposed onto an older set of indigenous languages, as Vedic Sanskrit is. And if the Indus Valley culture is in direct continuity with Vedic culture—rather than being one element among many that constitute it—one would expect stronger continuities than those that have been discovered.

At the same time, it is fair to say that there remain a good many unknown factors at play in this issue—not the least of which are the language and the meaning of the small pieces of text that are available in the Indus Valley script. Therefore a full, comprehensive, and uncontested picture of the ancient history—or prehistory—of Hinduism remains elusive.[8]

THE LATER VEDIC PERIOD: THE EMERGENCE OF THE FOUR YOGAS

Our picture of Hinduism becomes much clearer, and less contested, as we move beyond the early Vedic collections and into the later Vedic texts of the first millennium BCE—like the *Brāhmaṇas* ("Priestly Texts"), *Āraṇyakas* ("Forest Texts"), and *Upaniṣads* ("Esoteric Teachings"). Through these successive "layers" of text, one can trace the development of Vedic thought from a series of reflections on the nature of ritual to a grand cosmological vision of the oneness of existence.

Later Hindu tradition conceives of spiritual practice as consisting of three, and sometimes four, distinct disciplines (*yogas*) or paths: the *karma yoga*, or the way of action; the *jñāna yoga*, or the way of wisdom; and the *bhakti yoga*, or way of devotion. *Dhyāna yoga*, or meditation, (also known as *rāja yoga*, the royal path) is sometimes added to these as a fourth.[9] Each of these four types of Hindu practice can be seen as representing a distinct historical trend, or movement, within the history of the tradition.

Karma yoga, the way of action, originated as the practice of Vedic ritual as outlined in the early Vedic collections of hymns and the *Brāhmaṇas*, or "Priestly Texts," which date from roughly 800 to 600 BCE. The main emphasis of early Vedic religion was correct performance of the ritual of sacrifice, or *yajña*, which was seen as essential to upholding and maintaining the world. The oldest Vedic sacrifices were modeled on and conceived as repetitions of the original sacrifice by which the gods (or *devas*) created the world from the body of a primordial being—the Cosmic Man, or *puruṣa*. These sacrificial rituals tapped into the power of creation itself—an energy field known as Brahman (literally, "that which is expansive"). The Vedic priest, or Brahmin, was one who had the knowledge of the correct performance of the sacrifice and was thus able to tap into and deploy this creative power for ends such as ensuring the health and prosperity of the community.

In the *Āraṇyakas*, or "Forest Texts" (composed from around 600 to 500 BCE) and even more fully in the *Upaniṣads* (secret or esoteric doctrine—composed from around 500 BCE up to the first century of the Common Era), the emphasis shifted from the performance of ritual action to the transformative power of the knowledge that made such ritual action effective. This knowledge came to be seen as the true and final purpose, or "end," of the Veda (*Vedānta*), of which the ritual was merely an outward expression or manifestation. It was a knowledge that consisted of the realization that

Brahman, the ground of being, and one's innermost self, or *ātman*, were one and the same.

With this emphasis on the way of wisdom—what later came to be known as jñāna yoga—there emerged a distinctive worldview in which the ritual of the sacrifice was extended to encompass all of life. A ritual act, or *karma*, which in the early Vedic literature was said to lead to a desired effect if performed well and to its opposite if performed poorly, came to refer to all action. Karma began to take on a distinctly ethical tone, as referring to any morally good or evil action, along with the inevitable effects of such actions—an effect of the unity of existence as constituting a single, internally connected cosmic ritual arena.

Because one did not experience all the good and bad effects of one's actions in a single lifetime, it was deduced that one would eventually be reborn to experience these effects in a future lifetime. Similarly, the unequal circumstances of the births of all living beings came to be explained as being the result of actions performed in previous lives. The goal of the way of wisdom is to become free from this cycle of action and reaction: to achieve a true and lasting peace rather than the merely temporary goods and to escape from the inevitable loss and suffering that characterize life in the rebirth cycle.

The way of wisdom was seen as difficult, requiring one to separate oneself from the day-to-day activities and ritual responsibilities characterizing the way of action—actions that could draw one back into the cycle of rebirth. Renunciation—or *sannyāsa*—is the way of life of the Upaniṣadic sage who has withdrawn from society to seek spiritual wisdom, a way of life still pursued by Hindu ascetics today.

In the later *Upaniṣads*, such as the *Śvetāśvatāra Upaniṣad* (composed between about 400 and 300 BCE), but even more so in the post-Vedic *smṛti* literature of the first millennium of the Common Era, another path emerged that made the goal of liberation from rebirth available to a wider cross section of society—one that did not rely on Brahmanic priestly ritual or the wisdom of ascetic renouncers. This was the way of devotion, or bhakti yoga, the basic premise of which is that the supreme Brahman that is the ultimate object of all spiritual aspiration is not merely an impersonal energy or a pure state of consciousness but is also a loving personal deity who desires the salvation of all beings. One opens oneself to the saving power of the divine by cultivating a personal relationship with this supreme reality—a relationship of loving devotion, or bhakti.

The precise form that this devotion takes varies within distinct Hindu traditions, which orient themselves toward Viṣṇu, Śiva, the Mother Goddess or universal energy (Śakti), or any of a number of other personae of the supreme reality. These distinct theistic Hindu traditions—Vaiṣṇavism, Śaivism, Śāktism, and other theistic traditions centered on other forms of the divine—

have been the dominant forms of Hinduism from the first millennium of the Common Era to the present.

The fourth yoga—dhyāna or rāja yoga, the discipline of meditation—is another current of Hindu practice that has coexisted and interacted with the other disciplines—Vedic ritual, Vedāntic contemplation, and theistic devotion—for millennia. It is a practice that could be an inheritance of the Indus Valley Civilization. It was cultivated primarily by renouncer traditions, both Vedic and non-Vedic (like the Jain and Buddhist traditions), in the first millennium before the Common Era—and is also a prominent theme of the *Upaniṣads*. It finds its classic form of expression in the *Yoga Sūtra* of Patañjali (which may have been composed, in its current form, anywhere from 100 BCE to 500 CE). Its goal is the direct realization of Brahman not as an object of knowledge or devotion, but experientially, through the absorption of consciousness in Brahman to such a degree that the distinction between subject and object that characterizes most experience disappears—an experience known as *samādhi*.

THE CLASSICAL PERIOD: FROM ELITE BRAHMANISM TO POPULAR HINDUISM

The distinct cultural threads represented by the four yogas have rarely been practiced in isolation from one another throughout the history of Hinduism. Rather, these threads are like the threads of a tapestry, interweaving and interconnecting to make up the total way of life and the civilizational ethos that is Hinduism.

The path of action—which originated in the ritual practices enjoined in the *Vedas*—came to encompass all of society and all of life in the form of *dharma*, or duty. The *Dharma Śāstras*, or legal texts, which were composed from approximately 300 BCE to 100 CE, set out a comprehensive vision of both society and the life of the individual—the former being encompassed by the system of castes, or *varṇas*, the latter being encompassed by a series of four *āśramas*, or stages of life. The path of wisdom found its expression in the *sūtra* literature of the six systems of philosophy, or *darśanas* ("views"). Both of these are elite literatures, composed in Sanskrit by Brahmins, and tend to orient themselves in terms of the authority of the *Vedas*, with the Vedic systems being regarded as "orthodox" (*āstika*) and the non-Vedic systems (Jainism, Buddhism, and materialism) being regarded as "unorthodox" (*nāstika*).

The path of devotion, however, found expression not only in elite literatures, such as the *Purāṇas* of the various theistic schools of thought, but also in the ecstatic poetry of devotees hailing from all the stations of society—including many women—composed in vernacular languages, such as

Tamil, Bengali, and Hindi. The bhakti movement, starting early in the first millennium of the Common Era and gaining momentum in the second, did not so much overturn the Brahmanical social order as render it irrelevant to the spiritual path, offering liberation from the rebirth cycle to all sincere devotees, regardless of caste or gender. This movement was so popular that it had a significant impact upon the formal religion of the Brahmins, which itself came to emphasize theistic devotion, while at the same time maintaining its earlier emphasis on ritual purity. The tension between these two continues to characterize Hinduism today, with "orthodox" Brahmins emphasizing formal ritual—denying entry into temples, for example, to persons regarded as impure—and others, both Brahmin and non-Brahmin (and even non-Indian), emphasizing sincerity of devotion as evidenced in one's character and personal qualities as being a more important measure of spiritual attainment than caste or social status.

The tension between popular spiritual aspiration and formal Brahmanical injunctions can be traced back to the first millennium BCE, when the sages of the *Upaniṣads* downplayed the performance of Vedic ritual and emphasized ascetic practice and moral qualities such as honesty, which were seen as a barometer of spiritual realization. Even more radical than the sages of the *Upaniṣads* were the ascetics of the *śramaṇa*, or "striver" movement, who did not merely de-emphasize but actively rejected the Vedic ritual of sacrifice—especially the practice of animal sacrifice, which came to be seen as an inherently violent karma that could only lead to a bad rebirth, rather than as an offering that pleasing to the gods.

Due to their rejection of Vedic authority, the śramaṇa traditions are seen by most scholars as distinct traditions from Hinduism—which, the reader will recall, has come to be defined as the family of Vedic traditions. The two surviving śramaṇa traditions that are practiced today are Buddhism and Jainism. But though seen as different religions according to the current scholarly conventions, these traditions had an enormous impact on the practice of what has come to be regarded as Hinduism, with the practice of animal sacrifice being largely abandoned by even the most orthodox of Brahmins and replaced, in most parts of India, by vegetarian substitutes. The bhakti movement takes the śramaṇic critique of the Brahmanical tradition, in one sense, even further. Though maintaining at least a nominal reverence for the *Vedas*, it makes liberation available to all—even the householder.

At the furthest remove from Brahmanical orthodoxy—or, more accurately, "orthopraxy," given that the conservative Brahmanical emphasis is on right behavior and allows for a good deal of variety in the area of belief (such as six systems of philosophy)—is Tantra. A system of yoga, or spiritual practice, that inverts the traditional yogic emphasis on turning away from the senses and bodily impulses, such as sexuality, Tantra, like bhakti, is in its origins a popular movement that makes advanced spiritual attainment available to anyone regardless of caste, gender, or social status. Tantric practice is based on the premise that one can utilize the senses in order to transcend the senses. At its most extreme, the "Left-Handed" or *Vāmācāra* practice of Tantra deliberately transgresses Brahmanical norms of purity, the aim being to demonstrate the nondualistic realization that all is Brahman. If all is Brahman, then purity and impurity are effects of a false, dualistic consciousness that seeks to divide the fundamental unity of existence. Practitioners meditate in cremation grounds—traditionally regarded as a highly impure, not to mention frightening, space—and utilize human skulls as begging bowls. Other rituals are of an overtly sexual nature. Less extreme, but based on the same fundamental philosophy of using the senses in order to transcend the senses, are practices such as the chanting of mantras and the use of very beautiful visual images such as *mūrtis* (images of deities), *yantras* (abstract geometric forms of a deity), and *maṇḍalas* (diagrams of the universe) as objects of contemplation.

As with bhakti, the Brahmanical tradition has been open to assimilating and appropriating these popular forms of worship. Though few Hindus today would describe themselves as practitioners of Tantra, the entire structure of Hindu temple ritual is based upon Tantric principles, and the use of mantras and yantras is part of the training of even conservative Brahmins. Like bhakti, Tantric practice emerged in the latter half of the first millennium of the Common Era. Both bhakti and Tantra may be much older than these dates suggest, but it is to this period that the texts that articulate the principles of these traditions can be traced, with bhakti texts emerging somewhat earlier than Tantric writings.

HINDUISM AND ISLAM

As the first millennium ended and the second began, India began to experience incursions from outside powers, such as the Arabs, the Turks, and the Mughals. With the coming of Islam—at first brought peacefully, through trade, and then through successive waves of Arab, Turkish, and Mughal military incursion—Hinduism entered a period characterized, on the one hand, by great insecurity, and on the other, by equally great creativity. There is some evidence that the caste system, at this point, became more rigid in practice than ancient texts suggest had been the case in earlier periods—a process that intensified later, under the British Rāj.[10] Brahmanical texts of this period indicate a sharply pronounced preoccupation with the preservation of society coupled with an almost apocalyptic sense of impending doom. Due to the foreign invasions, many temples and monastic institutions were destroyed at this time, and major blows dealt to the Indic traditions. Buddhism died out almost completely in India during this period, surviving as a tradition only because it had already spread across Asia. It had effectively ceased to exist in India by the year 1300. Hindu traditions survived this period because the practices, stories, and beliefs that make up the Hindu civilizational ethos pervaded the lives of the common people and were not dependent on vulnerable monastic institutions, making them difficult to uproot. The decentralized nature of Hinduism essentially spared it the fate of Buddhism, as did the peripatetic nature of most of Hindu monasticism. Powerful Hindu dynasties, such as the sizeable empire of Vijayanāgara, thrived in the southern half of the subcontinent until the 16th century but eventually succumbed to repeated invasion and attack.

As the initial shock of invasion subsided, however, and Islam became a part of the Indic religious landscape, Hindus and Muslims began to respond in very creative ways to one another. Adherents of Hindu bhakti movements and the Sufis of Islam, especially, began to see one another's traditions as potential repositories of deep spiritual wisdom and of practices that each could appropriate for the attainment of greater nearness to the divine. Hindus began to adopt Sufi spiritual guides, or *pīrs*, as *gurus*, or teachers, and Muslims were similarly drawn toward Hindu spiritual figures. Kabīr, for example, who lived from 1440 to 1518, is even today claimed by both Hindus and Muslims as a revered teacher of sacred wisdom.

This interreligious cooperation and cross-fertilization is remarkable given the fact that it is hard to conceive of two religions more different from one another than Hinduism and Islam. Islam is emphatically monotheistic, regarding even the Christian trinity as a pagan remnant and a corruption of the original monotheism taught by the Prophet Jesus (as he is seen by Muslims). It is equally emphatically aniconic, associating images of the divine with the corrupt social order of pre-Islamic Arabia, in which a wealthy priesthood could determine who got to see the gods and who did not, charging exorbitant rates to devotees for a glimpse of their deities. The diversity of the forms of the divine in Hinduism and its celebration of imagery are seen even today by many Muslims as blasphemous—a holdover from a pagan era.

Similarly, Islam is generally insistent that there is one way to salvation: through obeying the injunctions of God as conveyed by God's messenger, the Prophet Muhammad. This is a stark contrast with the pluralism of yogas and forms of the divine available as objects of devotion in Hinduism (though there are Hindu traditions that are equally insistent upon the unique efficacy of particular practices and the unique divinity of specific figures, such as the Vaiṣṇava Dvaita Vedānta of Madhva, which sees devotion to Kṛṣṇa alone as being efficacious for salvation, though such exclusivism is more the exception than the rule for Hindu traditions). Islam, consequently, is an actively proselytizing tradition, while most Hindu traditions are not.

In the popular piety of medieval India, however, one sees members of both communities—Hindus and Muslims—shaking off the formal distinctions that their respective religious leaders would prefer to maintain between the two traditions. Rather than focusing upon their differences, however, Hindu and Muslim figures of this time emphasized a shared sense of the ubiquity of the divine presence and its availability to all who approach it with true devotion and a sincere and humble heart. Sufi saints began to incorporate the names of Hindu deities into their litanies of the many names of Āllāh, and Hindu devotees began to chant verses from the Qur'an and to make pilgrimages to the tombs of Sufi saints. The sharing of one another's holy days and holy places remains a characteristic of Hindu and Islamic practice in many parts of South Asia even today.[11]

This mutual accommodation was made possible by the strong presence in both traditions of movements that were generally uncomfortable with—and often rejected in the strongest terms—any emphasis on rigid formality, which was seen as interfering with the sincere and spontaneous quest of the individual devotee for the experience of the divine presence. Sufism—viewed in some quarters of the Islamic world with suspicion as a movement of dubious orthodoxy—found a highly receptive welcome in South Asia. And in Hinduism, the bhakti movement, with its rejection of Brahmanical formality and caste distinctions, was open to sincere devotion in any form—even forms that at first appeared foreign. Sufi and bhakti leaders clearly saw in one another kindred spirits in the search for authentic experience as opposed to the dry formality of the "official" exponents of their respective traditions.

This process of popular mutual assimilation was eventually facilitated at the level of the state. The Mughal emperor Akbar, who reigned from 1556 to 1605, formally adopted a policy of toleration toward all religions—including the Christianity taught by the European missionaries arriving with Portuguese merchant ships on the southwest coast of India in his time. Allowing his Hindu wife to build a temple to her deity, Kṛṣṇa, in his palace and even developing his own religion, a synthesis of all of the religions of India of which he knew, Akbar consistently ran afoul of the exponents of Islamic orthodoxy in his imperial court. His policy of toleration both mirrored and accelerated what was already happening at the popular, village level between Hindus and Muslims in his realm.

The *Sant*—or "saint"—movement of this period consisted of figures of Hindu and Islamic origins, such as the aforementioned Kabīr, who claimed and were claimed by both religions, seeing sincere devotion as having far greater importance than formal sectarian affiliation or religious identity. This movement culminated in the figure of Guru Nānak, who lived from 1469 to 1539. In his famous teaching that "there is no Hindu, there is no Muslim," Nānak captured the spirit of this era. Rather than leading to a unification of the two traditions, however, Nānak's teaching led to the emergence of a third, new tradition—Sikhism—a religion distinct from both Hinduism and Islam, while yet containing elements of both in its practices and doctrines.

At the same time, however, there were reactions against this widespread spirit of mutual synthesis and accommodation. The Mughal emperor Aurangzeb, who reigned from 1658 to 1707, aggressively sought the forcible conversion of both Hindus and Sikhs to Islam, returning to the earlier policy of destroying temples and torturing and slaughtering any intransigent religious leaders who refused to convert. The memory of the wounds of this period still runs sufficiently deep to lead to a situation in which later leaders—including the British and the political parties of independent India and Pakistan—have been able to exploit the fears of both communities for the sake of political gain. And yet such division and mutual suspicion occurs against a wider backdrop of toleration, mutual respect, and assimilation established in the period of the more enlightened interreligious relations that characterized the Sant movement and the rise of Sikhism. But this larger environment of tolerance and pluralism is endangered by militancy and a hardening of negative attitudes on both sides—a militancy driven at least as much by the aspirations of Hindu and Islamic political organizations as by what one might call authentically religious concerns.

HINDUISM AND THE WEST

The European—and especially the British—colonization of India, which began in earnest in the 18th century, marks another occasion for great insecurity and also great creativity for the Hindu traditions. The twin challenges of Western science and Christianity led to a crisis for many Hindus, especially in Bengal, in eastern India, in the late 18th and early 19th centuries, due to the fact that Bengal was the first region to experience a large-scale British presence, Calcutta being the main administrative center of the British East India Company. Hindu responses to British culture ranged from, on the one hand, complete indifference—particularly from those orthodox Brahmins who saw the foreigners as mere barbarians, with nothing of great interest to say religiously or philosophically—to a total capitulation on the part of those Hindus who found European civilization superior to their own. The most creative response, however, came from those Hindus who found much to admire in British culture—accepting the validity of many criticisms of Hinduism launched by Christian missionaries—but who were also critical of what they perceived as Western materialism and a lack of spiritual depth that they found in their ancient texts and systems of thought.

The first of the Hindu reformers, often called the "father of modern Hinduism," was Rām Mohan Roy, who lived from 1772 to 1833 and founded a reform organization called the Brahmo Samāj, or "Community of Brahman." Translating the *Upaniṣads* into vernacular languages and successfully lobbying the British administration to ban the practice of *satī*, or widow immolation, Roy interpreted Hinduism in monotheistic and Unitarian terms, as a wisdom tradition centered on the worship of a formless divinity. He was critical of all aspects of both Hinduism and Christianity that he regarded as nonrational.

Similarly critical of the *Purāṇa*-based Hinduism of this period was Swāmī Dayānanda Sarasvatī, who lived from 1824 to 1883 and established the Ārya Samāj—northern India's answer to the Brahmo Samāj. Rather than the *Upaniṣads*, Dayānanda focused upon the early Vedic *Saṃhitās* as the wellspring of authentic Hindu practice. He both revived and popularized the practice of worship centered on the sacred fire, as opposed to the use of images, which he viewed as a later accretion upon "pure" Vedic worship.

These movements, however, failed to capture the imagination of the Hindu community as a whole, primarily due to their rejection of the use of images in worship, or *mūrtipūjā*, a practice that had been central to Hindu religious expression for centuries. True success in the area of Hindu reform came with the Vedānta movement inspired by Sri Ramakrishna (1836–1886) and led by his chief disciple, Swāmī Vivekānanda (1863–1902).

Ramakrishna himself was not a Hindu reformer but a highly traditional Hindu spiritual figure in the mold of the great bhakti saints of the classical and medieval periods. Known for his powerful ecstatic visions, he claimed to have experienced *samādhi*, or absorption in the divine, by practicing all of the major Hindu spiritual paths, as well as Christianity and Islam. He concluded, on this basis, that all religions are paths to the divine. Though barely literate, he could discuss the finer points of Hindu philosophy with highly learned scholars on the basis of his direct experience of spiritual realities. The Western-educated elites of Bengali society—including many members of the Brahmo Samāj—were captivated by his teaching and personality. Because he based his teaching on direct experience and not on the interpretation of scripture, Ramakrishna's path was seen as open to scientific verification, and so more in keeping with a modern sensibility than traditions based upon ancient texts alone. And yet his path involved a wholehearted embrace of many practices and a sensibility that the reformers had rejected—such as the use of images and a highly emotionally charged spirituality of devotion. It was a heady mix for those Hindus who wanted to embrace the social reforms and rationalistic approach of the reformers but who also felt nostalgic for the traditions of their upbringing. Under the leadership of Swāmī Vivekānanda, the Ramakrishna Mission and the wider movement it inspired had a broader impact than the Brahmo and Ārya Samāj.

GLOBAL HINDUISM

Vivekānanda had the further effect of transforming Hinduism from a family of traditions confined largely to the Indian subcontinent and almost exclusively to persons of South Asian ethnic origin to a world religion, open to non-Indian as well as Indian adherents. It was already the case in Vivekānanda's time that many Westerners were drawn to Hindu traditions, such as the Transcendentalists of New England and the Theosophists, who had come to South Asia as "reverse missionaries" to instill pride among both Hindus in India and Buddhists in Sri Lanka in their religious heritage. But Vivekānanda took the step of initiating Westerners into a Hindu monastic order for the very first time, beginning with Margaret E. Noble (better known to Hindus by her monastic name, Sister Nivedita). His celebrated speech to the Parliament of the World's Religions in Chicago in 1893 is seen by many Hindus as marking the arrival of Hinduism on the world stage.

By initiating Westerners into Vedānta, Vivekānanda opened the proverbial floodgates to a range of Hindu spiritual masters who visited the West—many settling permanently—and taught their paths and practices to audiences eager for an alternative to what many saw, and continue to see, as the narrow, dogmatic provincialism of Christianity and the equally narrow—and spiritually stultifying—worldview of scientistic materialism. The first master to follow in Vivekānanda's footsteps was another Bengali, Paramahāṃsā Yogānanda (1893–1952), whose Self-Realization Fellowship, established in California in 1920, was designed to promote the practice of Kriya Yoga, the form of meditation that was taught to Yogānanda by his guru, Sri Yukteśwar Giri. The acceptance of Yogānanda's teachings by Westerners was facilitated by his emphasis on Jesus as an enlightened master and an exemplar of yogic wisdom. Jiddu Krishnamurti (1895–1986), emerging from the shadow of the Theosophical movement, which had groomed and hailed him as the next "World Teacher," a messianic figure known as Maitreya, broke away from the Theosophists and taught a path of radical self-inquiry, finding a ready audience in the counterculture of the 1960s. Maharishi Mahesh Yogi (1918–2008) similarly appealed to the counterculture via its heroes, the Beatles, who aided him in his promotion of Transcendental Meditation by very publicly attending his seminars in England and Wales, and following him to India in the summer of 1968 for a retreat at his Rishikesh ashram in India, in the foothills of the Himālayas.

A. C. Bhaktivedānta Swāmī Prabhupāda (1896–1977), in a dramatic contrast with his contemporaries, who carefully tailored their traditions to the tastes and concerns of their Western audiences, brought a very traditional form of Vaiṣṇava devotionalism to North America in 1966, establishing the Hare Krishna movement. However, like the Maharishi, Bhaktivedānta also found endorsement from the royalty of the counterculture, with the

Mahāmantra of Gauḍīya Vaiṣṇavism being included as the refrain of George Harrison's 1970 hit song, "My Sweet Lord."

In addition to the jñāna and dhyāna yogas taught by Vivekānanda, Krishnamurti, and the Maharishi and Yogānanda, respectively, and the bhakti emphasis of Bhaktivedānta, the Tantric traditions of Hinduism also found representatives among the Hindu teachers who came to the West in the 20th century. Swāmī Muktānanda (1908–1982) brought the Siddha Yoga tradition of his master, Swāmī Nityānanda. He was also succeeded by a prominent female guru, Swāmī Chidvilāsānanda, or Gurumayī, who presides over this tradition to the present day. And most controversial of all was Bhagwan Rajneesh, later known as Osho (1931–1990), whose endorsement of left-handed Tantric practice, with its accompanying emphasis on sexual freedom, dovetailed better with the sexual revolution of this period than with the traditionally conservative sexual morality of Indian Hindus.

Meanwhile, as these and other Hindu teachers brought their varied teachings and forms of practice to the West, Vivekānanda's original Vedānta Society continued to be active. A steady stream of monks of the Ramakrishna Order came to North America, establishing and nurturing Vedānta centers in cities such as New York, Boston, Washington, D.C., Los Angeles, and San Francisco. California, especially—both prior to and during the period of the counterculture—was a major center for Hindu activities that appealed primarily to a Western audience. Swāmī Prabhavānanda (1893–1976), a highly active monk of the Ramakrishna Order and founder of the Vedānta Society of Southern California in 1930, initiated literary luminaries such as Aldous Huxley and Christopher Isherwood, who in turn did much to promote the Vedānta tradition among their readers.

A skeptic could of course question the extent to which any of the movements based on the teachings of spiritual teachers from India have become—or will become—deep-rooted and authentically "Western" forms of religiosity. Like Western Buddhism, however, the Western Hindu traditions have begun to produce their own leaders, raised with a Western cultural ethos, and are not simply depending upon Indian teachers for their spiritual and organizational sustenance. With Satguru Śivāya Subramuniyaswāmī (1927–2001), who was born Robert Hansen and inherited the mantle of a Śaiva Siddhānta saṃpradāya, or teaching lineage, from his master, Yogaswāmī, Western Hinduism produced a spiritual master who was acknowledged as such not only by his devotees but also by Hindus globally—including quite conservative Hindus, such as the founders of the Hindu Ācārya Sabhā, of which Subramuniyaswāmī was a member. The journal that Subramuniyaswāmī founded, *Hinduism Today*, presents itself as "the voice of the global Hindu community"—a claim that the community on the whole appears to endorse. The phenomenon of high-profile, celebrity adherents endorsing Hinduism or specific Hindu practices—such as the Beatles' endorsement of Transcendental Meditation and former Beatle George Harrison's close and lifelong affiliation with the Hare Krishna movement—continues, with the most recent example being the actress Julia Roberts, whose film version of Elizabeth Gilbert's autobiographical memoir, *Eat, Pray, Love*, includes a representation of life in the Siddha Yoga ashram in Ganeshpuri, India.[12] Though it is far from being a mass movement, Hinduism does seem to have found a home in the West.[13]

TWO CONTRARY IMPULSES: UNIVERSALISM AND NATIONALISM

If Vivekānanda articulated a vision for Hinduism as a tradition of rationality, tolerance, and a world-embracing spirituality, Mohandas K. Gāndhī (1869–1948) translated this vision into an ambitious program for comprehensive political and social reform. Tapping into ancient Hindu ideals such as *ahiṃsā* (nonviolence), the inherent power of truth (*satyāgraha*), and the divinity of all beings, Gāndhī—known to his admirers by the ancient title of *mahātma*, or "great soul"—led a movement of nonviolent resistance to British rule that has inspired movements for social justice around the world, including the movement for African American civil rights led by Martin Luther King Jr. and the South African antiapartheid movement of Nelson Mandela.

At the same time, Gāndhī's successes—particularly in the areas of the reform of the caste system and Hindu–Muslim relations—unleashed reactionary forces that ultimately resulted in his assassination. His attempts to abolish the practice of untouchability met with both the resistance of conservative Hindus and the scorn of leaders within the Dalit, or lower caste, community, such as B. R. Ambedkar, who believed that he did not go far enough. His attempts to effect a reconciliation of the divisions between Hindus and Muslims were unable to prevent the partition of India and Pakistan when independence was achieved on 15 August 1947. Many Hindus blamed—and continue to blame—Gāndhī for the deaths that resulted from the partition, when riots broke out across the subcontinent as Hindus fled Pakistan and Muslims fled India out of fear of being persecuted in a place where they would constitute a religious minority. Gāndhī was assassinated by Nathuram Godse, an adherent of Hindu Nationalism, on 30 January 1948.

The subsequent history of Hinduism is characterized by the tension between the forces of Hindu Nationalism, which see Hinduism and India as under constant attack by opposing movements, such as Islam, Christianity, and secularism, and the visionary Hinduism of Gāndhī and Ramakrishna, which sees all religions as part of a greater harmony that India can embody as an inspiration for the rest of the world to follow. It is a history that has been punctuated by outbursts of dramatic violence—such as the Hindu–Sikh riots of 1984 and the Hindu–Muslim riots of 1992 and 2002—standing out against a routine background of relative peace and harmony, in which the members of different religious communities celebrate each other's holidays, make pilgrimages to one another's places of worship, and elect members of minority communities to high public office, including the presidency and the prime ministership of India. It is also a history of expansion, as more non-Indians adopt Hindu practices—even to the point of formal conversion—and as Indian Hindus also continue to immigrate across the globe to Europe, North America, Africa, Australia, and other parts of the world as well.

WHAT HOLDS HINDUISM TOGETHER?

As mentioned previously, there are those scholars who will argue that "Hinduism does not exist." I have also described Hinduism on a number of occasions, and only half-jokingly, as "the world's least organized religion." What gives this tradition, or family of traditions, cohesion? It has no founder and no central administrative institution—no pope or Vatican. There is no test of orthodoxy or creed upon which all Hindus must agree to adhere in order to be regarded as Hindu. There is even some disagreement about who is a Hindu. Must one be born as a Hindu, or are non-Indian practitioners of Hindu-inspired paths such as those described earlier—Vedānta, Transcendental Meditation, Siddha Yoga, the Hare Krishna movement, and so on—authentic Hindus? Are the Jains, the Buddhists, and the Sikhs—practitioners of originally Indian, and therefore, in the sense of *Hindu* as *Indian*, "Hindu" traditions—to be regarded as Hindus? Why has Hinduism not fragmented into nonexistence? Why does it seem, on the contrary, to be in a period of resurgence and renaissance?

It is tempting to say that Hinduism survives and perseveres because of the inherent appeal of its teachings and practices—that it survives because it is true, because it holds insight and wisdom that are highly relevant to the lives of its adherents. But satisfying though it may be to Hindus, such an answer is not what an outside observer—still less a historian—has in mind when asking the question, "What holds Hinduism together?" What is it that gives whatever cohesion it has to this vast collection of varied beliefs and practices?

The answer, as with the answers to most questions about Hinduism, is complex and is not capable of being boiled down to one single factor that constitutes *the* answer. Two primary factors, however, spring to mind.

First, regarding founding figures and organizational structures—it is not that such figures and structures are absent. It is that there is no *single* figure or structure upon which all Hindus agree or to which all Hindu belief and practice can be traced or on which it can be said to be centered. On the contrary, there are many founding figures who have started organizational structures that have thrived and persisted for many centuries. This book documents a host of such figures, structures, and movements: enlightened sages, monks, inspired poets, and the communities that emerged around them—sometimes spontaneously but sometimes cultivated in a highly organized and systematic manner. None of these is, however, identical to Hinduism as a whole. At least some part of what holds Hinduism together is the fact that Hindu adherence to particular traditions and organizations has a certain fluidity that allows for the phenomenon of multiple religious belonging. It is rare for a specific Hindu tradition to demand exclusive allegiance of its followers. If one were to add up the total number of Hindus engaged in some degree of some participation in all of the world's Hindu organizations, this number would be considerably larger than the total number of Hindus. This fluidity and ease of multiple membership is, in turn, made possible by the fact that the many Hindu traditions, despite their various differences in the areas of doctrine and practice, also share a good deal in these areas as well. Belief in karma and rebirth, a soteriological aspiration for liberation from the rebirth cycle, as well as a concern with more immediate goods, such as prosperity and good fortune both in this life and the next, cut a wide swath across most Hindu schools of thought and systems of practice. Similarly, a core of ethical practice, enshrined in ideals such as nonviolence, honesty, sexual restraint, and nonpossessiveness, is widely shared. These core ideas and practices are "portable," in the sense that one can move fairly easily among Hindu groups without finding them sharply questioned or turned into points of contention.

Secondly, and pertaining especially to the realm of practice, there is the caste system. In many ways controversial, particularly in the modern period, due to the inequities that it enshrines, this hereditary system of occupations has also served as a major acculturating force, for it is not only occupations that are passed on to one through one's family. It is also narratives and practices related to correct ritual conduct that become second nature even to Hindus who, later in life, completely reject, at a cognitive level, the specifically religious dimensions of their traditions. Much as there are people who are "culturally Jewish," scrupulously observing the high holy days, for example, but perhaps professing atheism, in terms of their personal beliefs about the nature of reality, there are, similarly, "cultural Hindus," who may or may not hold "Hindu" views but who have thoroughly absorbed the civilizational ethos of Hinduism. It has been noted that caste has become more rigid during periods of colonial domination than at other times in Hindu history, when the more fluid and easygoing attitude toward boundaries that characterizes Hindu religious organizations can also be found in regard to caste boundaries and restrictions. This is evidence that, for most Hindus, Hinduism has at least as much to do with family loyalty and the preservation of tradition as with specifically religious preoccupations such as salvation and contemplating the nature of existence. To the degree that the Hinduism of non-Indian practitioners is called into question, it is to the same extent that the practice of these adherents is rooted in voluntary religious considerations alone and has not been absorbed from childhood as part of a cultural ethos. But one must bear in mind that, as was stated at the outset of this introduction, the authenticity or inauthenticity of any given expression of Hinduism—whether a given person, practice, movement, or philosophy is "really" Hindu—is really a question about how these terms—*Hindu* and *Hinduism*—are to be defined and deployed, rather than a question of how well these phenomena correlate with some eternal or unchanging essence. Hinduism, like all *isms*, is a construct.

CONCLUSION

The future of Hinduism, as of all religions, is impossible to forecast with any reliability. Challenges to the tradition include the aforementioned Hindu Nationalism and casteism—or caste prejudice—and issues relating to patriarchy and the full participation of women as equal members of the Hindu community.

If the past can be used to predict the future, one can expect Hindus to address these issues much as they have previous challenges—with creativity and flexibility tempered by a deep commitment to the principle that the wisdom of the ancient past always has a continuing relevance to the present.

NOTES

1. Lisa Miller, "We're All Hindus Now," *Newsweek*, 15 August 2009.
2. The question of the ancientness of Hinduism versus its status as a relatively recent construct of colonial scholarship is explored in D. N. Jha's *Rethinking Hindu Identity* (London: Equinox, 2009) and by a variety of authors in J. E. Llewellyn's edited volume *Defining Hinduism: A Reader* (New York: Routledge, 2005).
3. Wendy Doniger, *The Hindus: An Alternative History* (New York: Penguin, 2009), 65–66.
4. Klaus K. Klostermaier, *A Survey of Hinduism*, 3rd ed. (Albany: State University of New York Press, 2007), 25.
5. See Jonathan Mark Kenoyer, *Ancient Cities of the Indus Valley Civilization* (Oxford: Oxford University Press, 1998), Dilip K. Chakrabarti, *India: An Archaeological History* (New Delhi: Oxford University Press, 1999), Gregory L. Possehl, *The Indus Civilization: A Contemporary Perspective* (Walnut Creek, Calif.: Altamira Press, 2002), and Jane R. McIntosh, *A Peaceful Realm: The Rise and Fall of the Indus Civilization* (Boulder, Colo.: Westview Press, 2002).

6. Such claims are common in modern Hindu reform movements, such as the Ārya Samāj, which condemn the hierarchical and hereditary nature of caste but do not reject the basic concept.

7. For a defense of this revisionist version of the standard model, see Klostermaier, *A Survey of Hinduism*, 18–29.

8. The most authoritative and even-handed study of the scholarly debate over ancient India—acknowledged as such by persons on both sides of the conversation—is Edwin Bryant's *The Quest for the Origins of Vedic Culture: The Indo-Aryan Migration Debate* (New York: Oxford University Press, 2004).

9. A formal and systematic understanding of Hindu practice as consisting of four yogas, as described here, is a very recent one indeed—first articulated in this precise way by Swāmī Vivekānanda during the modern period. But the systems of practice and the accompanying soteriological paradigms that these four yogas represent are ancient and do date back to at least the later Vedic period. I find them a useful heuristic tool for presenting the historical phases of Hindu practice. But this should not be confused with the claim that a *system* of four yogas, as this is understood today, was present during the later Vedic period. I am certainly *not* making this claim.

10. See Nicholas Dirks, *Castes of Mind: Colonialism and the Making of Modern India* (Princeton, N.J.: Princeton University Press, 2001) and Bernard S. Cohn, *India: The Social Anthropology of a Civilization* (Englewood Cliffs, N.Y.: Prentice Hall, 1971).

11. See Peter Gottschalk, *Beyond Hindu and Muslim: Multiple Identity in Narratives from Village India* (New York: Oxford University Press, 2005).

12. Hindu Press International, 8 August 2010, http://www.hinduismtoday.com/modules/xpress/category/hindu-press-international.

13. See Phil Goldberg, *American Veda: From Emerson and the Beatles to Yoga and Meditation—How Indian Spirituality Changed the West* (Bourgon, Ind.: Harmony, 2010) and Lola Williamson, *Transcendent in America: Hindu-Inspired Meditation Movements as New Religion* (New York: New York University Press, 2010).

A

ABHAYA-MUDRĀ. Mudrā, or hand gesture, which means, "Do not be afraid." Hindu deities are frequently depicted with this gesture, which consists of the right hand (or one of the right hands, given that Hindu deities are frequently depicted with more than one pair of arms and hands) in an upright and slightly bent back position, with an empty palm facing outward, toward the viewer of the image. *See also* MŪRTI.

ABHIMANYU. Character in the ***Mahābhārata***; son of **Arjuna**, tragically slain in the battle of **Kurukṣetra**, but not before fathering **Parikṣit**, the heir who would inherit the **Pāṇḍavas**' kingdom.

ABHINAVAGUPTA (950–1020). Philosopher known for systematizing the teachings of the **Kaula Tantra** sect of **Kaśmīr Śaivism**. A remarkably learned scholar with a wide-ranging intellect, Abhinavagupta studied under an unusual variety of teachers, mastering **music**, **poetry**, and drama, as well as **philosophy** and logic. His writings encompass such diverse topics as aesthetic experience, levels of consciousness, and the ultimate nature of reality. He synthesized traditional **Brahmanism** and Tantric thought, which before this time had been perceived as being in conflict. In keeping with a Tantric understanding of the role of the senses in the path to **liberation**, Abhinavagupta emphasized not so much the suppression of the senses as the cultivation of aesthetic enjoyment in an anticipation of the bliss of ultimate union with **Śiva**. Abhinavagupta did not reject rival systems of thought as false but viewed them in an inclusive fashion as steps toward his position. His spiritual journey was sparked by an early childhood tragedy—the death of his mother, Vimalā. His system of philosophy has affinities to both **Advaita Vedānta** and **Tantra**, inasmuch as it is monistic (like Advaita) and affirms sensory experience (like Tantra). A prolific writer, his best-known works are the encyclopedic *Tāntraloka* and his **bhāṣya**, or commentary, on the *Nāṭya Śāstra*. *See also* ŚAIVISM.

ABHIṢEKA. Anointing, consecration, ritual bathing; ceremony of bathing an image of a deity (**mūrti**) with sacred substances such as water, milk, **ghee**, yogurt, saffron, etc.

ĀCĀRYA. Sanskrit term meaning *teacher*, but most commonly referring to a teacher of particularly high rank, such as the leader of a teaching lineage or sect (**saṃpradāya**), or the head of a monastic institution (**maṭha**). The term is sometimes used as a synonym for **guru**, but the term *guru* more often refers to a teacher with whom one has developed a personal relationship as a student or disciple (**śiṣya**), whereas an ācārya is a more public figure—the teacher of an entire community. The title of ācārya is usually given through **dīkṣā**, or initiation, and ordination as the successor to the leadership of a spiritual lineage. A **Christian** equivalent to *ācārya* might be either "abbot" or "bishop," the former being the head of a monastery and the latter implying religious authority over a specific geographic region, both of which can characterize the duties of an ācārya.

ACTION. Action, or **karma**, is an issue of central concern to Hindu traditions. There is the regulation of action—the enjoining of right action, or **dharma**, and the avoidance of its opposite, which is a characteristic of most religious traditions—and then there is the effort to transcend action and its effects, a concern more distinctive of the Indic religions, such as Hinduism, **Buddhism, Jainism**, and **Sikhism**. Action is widely understood to follow a principle of cause and effect, also widely termed *karma*, according to which all actions produce results of the same moral character as themselves—good actions leading to good results (**puṇya** karma), and evil actions to evil results (**pāpa** karma).

The reciprocal process of intentional moral actions producing like effects fuels the perpetual cycle of **rebirth** (**saṃsāra**), release from which (**mokṣa**) requires one to in some way negate or transcend the principle of cause and effect. The various Indic traditions often present themselves as strategies for achieving this negation or transcendence. The ***Bhagavad Gītā***, for example, presents a **yoga** of action (**karma yoga**) that aims at mokṣa through engaging in action without attachment to the results. On this understanding, it is not action itself but the **desire** that motivates it that brings about karmic effects.

ADHARMA. Lack or opposite of **dharma**, not dharma, evil, lack of virtue. Adharma also refers to chaos or anything that goes against the order of nature. Adharma is often embodied in Hindu **literature** by demonic beings, such as **asuras** and **rākṣasas**, who are defeated in battle by a **god** or **goddess**, usually either an **avatāra** of **Viṣṇu** or a form of the **Mother Goddess**. In the ***Bhagavad Gītā***, **Kṛṣṇa** cites the destruction of adharma and the protection of dharma as the chief reason for his repeated incarnations or avatāras (*Bhagavad Gītā* 4.7). Adharmic behavior results in misfortune, both for its immediate victims and for its perpetrators. This misfortune can occur quickly or it can be deferred, being experienced in this lifetime or in a future **rebirth**. *See also* KARMA; PĀPA.

ADHIKĀRA. Authority; the right to acquire higher spiritual knowledge. According to **Brahmanism**, only a male **Brahmin** is eligible to study the ***Vedas***, which are the source of spiritual knowledge. This concept is challenged, however, by many Hindu traditions, as well as by modern Hindu reformers such as **Swāmī Vivekānanda**.

ADHVARYU. Brahmin priest whose role in the **Vedic** sacrifice, or **yajña**, is to oversee the physical details of the ritual, such as measuring out the sacred space, building the fire altar, lighting the fire, and so forth. While performing these **actions**, the Adhvaryu recites relevant portions of the ***Yajur Veda*** that describe what is to be done. In ancient times, when **animal sacrifices** were more widely performed, the task of the Adhvaryu included the slaughter, cooking, and offering of the bodies of sacrificial victims.

ADITI. Goddess whose name means *infinity*. Wife of the sage **Kaśyapa** and mother of 12 **devas**, or deities, called the **Ādityas**: **Indra**, **Dhātṛ**, **Aryaman**, **Mitra**, **Varuṇa**, **Aṃśa**, **Bhaga**, **Vivasvat**, **Pūṣan**, **Savitṛ**, **Tvaṣṭṛ**, and **Viṣṇu**. Aditi is also the mother of the eight **Vasus** and the 11 **Rudras**.

ĀDITYAS. The 12 major **Vedic** deities, or **devas**. They are the sons of the goddess **Aditi** and the sage **Kaśyapa**. Their names are **Indra**, **Dhātṛ**, **Aryaman**, **Mitra**, **Varuṇa**, **Aṃśa**, **Bhaga**, **Vivasvat**, **Pūṣan**, **Savitṛ**, **Tvaṣṭṛ**, and **Viṣṇu**.

ĀDIVĀSĪS. First dwellers; aboriginal tribal peoples of the Indian subcontinent, many of whose religious traditions have become part of Hinduism over the centuries. Tribal peoples have tended to live on the margins of Hindu society.

ADVAITA VEDĀNTA. The **nondualistic** system of **Vedānta philosophy**, prominently associated with its chief exponent and systematizer of the classical period, **Śaṅkara** (788–820), though having roots in more ancient texts like the ***Upaniṣads***, the ***Brahma Sūtras***, and the ***Bhagavad Gītā***. According to Advaita Vedānta, these ancient texts (collectively called the **prasthāna traya**) all teach the view of Advaita, although this interpretation of these texts is of course not shared by other systems of Vedānta.

Advaita Vedānta is a deeply monistic system and teaches that **Brahman** is the sole reality. The existence of multiple entities, such as those that make up the world—and even the distinction between the world, the self, and **God**—is a mere appearance, or **māyā**. Māyā, in turn, is an effect of **avidyā**, or primordial ignorance of the true nature of reality.

According to Advaita Vedānta, Brahman as such has no limiting qualities. It is **nirguṇa**. Brahman does not possess, but rather, it *is* infinite being (**sat**), consciousness (**cit**), and bliss (**ānanda**). As the only truly real entity,

Brahman is identical to the self (**ātman**), the self–other distinction being an effect of māyā. Realization of the identity of Brahman and ātman gives rise to **mokṣa**, or **liberation** from the **rebirth** process. The basis of this realization, according to Śaṅkara, is the **Vedic** scriptures—primarily the *Upaniṣads*. Good works, **devotion**, and **meditation** can only prepare one for this **knowledge**. Hearing the **truth** that Brahman and ātman are one (**śravaṇa**), reflecting upon it (**manasā**), and contemplatively realizing it (nidhidhyāsana) are the three necessary steps that produce the awakening required for liberation. This classical understanding of Advaita is distinct from **Neo-Vedānta**, which emphasizes direct experience (**anubhāva**) over **scripture**.

It is possible to achieve liberation while still alive, an attainment that is known in the Advaita system as **jīvanmukti**. After death, one who has attained liberation while alive—a jīvanmukta—is no longer subject to rebirth, being absorbed in Brahman (though it is more correct to say that this "absorption" is apparent, the reality being that one has never actually been separate from Brahman).

Advaita Vedānta has traditionally been most influential in southern India, but it has also exerted a strong influence on Neo-Vedānta, particularly as expressed by modern exponents such as **Swāmī Vivekānanda** and **Sarvepalli Radhakrishnan**.

ĀGAMA. Tradition, that which comes down or is handed down from past generations. A set of **scriptures** associated preeminently with one of the three major theistic Hindu sects—the **Vaiṣṇava**, **Śaiva**, and **Śākta** traditions. Largely "how to" manuals, these texts are mainly concerned with the correct performance of ritual, particularly **pūjā** devoted to the respective deities of these three traditions (**Viṣṇu**, **Śiva**, and the **Mother Goddess**), and with yogic practice and **temple** construction and consecration. Vaiṣṇava Āgamas are often called **Saṃhitās**, and Śākta Āgamas are usually referred to as **Tantras**. The Śaiva Āgamas, however, are generally called Āgamas. The **Jain** scriptures are also known as Āgamas.

AGASTYA. **Vedic** sage attributed with transmitting the *Vedas* to southern India and inventing the **Tamil** language. One of the hymns of the *Ṛg Veda* is attributed to him. He is said to have forced the Vindhya Mountains, in central India, to submit to him. **Rāma** visited the sage Agastya during the period of his exile in the ***Rāmāyaṇa***.

AGEHĀNANDA BHĀRATĪ, SWĀMĪ (1923–1991). Born **Leopold Fischer**, Swāmī Agehānanda Bhāratī was one of the first scholar-practitioners to teach Hindu traditions in a Western academic context, teaching at Syracuse University for more than 30 years.

AGHORĪ. Free from terror; member of a **Śaiva** tradition that split from the **Kāpālikas**, another Śaiva sect, in the 14th century. A **Tantric** sect, Aghorī practice is designed both to express and cultivate a state beyond fear. Condemned by many Hindus for being too extreme, Aghorīs **meditate** in cremation grounds and even eat the corpses of the dead. The begging bowl of an Aghorī monk is a human skull.

AGNI. Fire. Agni is the **Vedic** deity, or **deva**, who personifies fire, particularly the fire of the Vedic **yajña**, or sacrifice. Because all Vedic sacrifices are offered into the fire, Agni is seen as the intermediary between human beings and all of the Vedic deities. As such, he is also viewed as the prototypical Vedic priest and is proclaimed as such in ***Ṛg Veda*** 1.1. The first offering in any sacrifice is made to Agni, who would otherwise consume the offerings intended for the other deities. As the intermediary between the divine and the human worlds, Agni is of great importance in Vedic religion. The number of hymns of the *Ṛg Veda* devoted to Agni is second only to those devoted to **Indra**, lord of the Vedic deities. Eight of the 10 books, or **maṇḍalas**, of the *Ṛg Veda* begin with hymns to Agni (the exceptions being the eighth and ninth books).

Unlike other Vedic deities, whose realms are confined to one of the three regions of Earth, the upper atmosphere, and the heavens, Agni operates in all three realms (in the forms, respectively, of fire, lighting, and the sun).

AGNIHOTRA. A relatively brief and simple sacrifice or **yajña** that is offered to **Agni**. Orthodox **Brahmins** perform this ritual daily. The Agnihotra, although an ancient ritual mentioned in both the ***Atharva Veda*** and the ***Gṛhya Sūtras***, has been revived and promoted for wider use in the modern period, primarily by the **Ārya Samāj**, as a rite of purification. *See also* HAVAN; HOMA; *VEDAS*.

AGNIṢṬOMA. A five-day sacrifice or **yajña** offered to **Agni**, **Indra**, and other **Vedic** deities. A fairly elaborate ritual, the Agniṣṭoma involves 15 priests. Traditionally offered by a **Brahmin householder**, its goal is **rebirth** in heaven (**svarga**).

AGNIVEŚA, SWĀMĪ (1939–). Founder and president of the **World Council of the Ārya Samāj**, an organization distinct from the **Ārya Samāj**, a Hindu reform organization established in 1875 by **Swāmī Dayānanda Sarasvatī (1824–1883)**. Swāmī Agniveśa is best known for his social and political activism, taking up such issues as alcohol abuse, **women**'s rights, peace, interreligious dialogue, female infanticide, and **casteism**.

Agniveśa became a monk, or **sannyāsin**, in 1970, under the auspices of the Ārya Samāj. In 1987, he led a large protest against a **sati** that occurred in Deorala, Rajasthan. Due to a variety of internal controversies, Swāmī Agniveśa was expelled from the Ārya Samāj in 1992, but he continues to claim fidelity to the original ideals of the organization and its founder.

AGRAHAYAṆA. Month of the **Hindu calendar** that corresponds roughly to the period from mid-November to mid-December.

AHAṂKĀRA. Ego; literally the "I-maker"; one of the basic elements that constitute existence, or **tanmātras**, of the **Sāṃkhya** system of **philosophy**. In the **Yoga** system of **Patañjali**, ahaṃkara, in combination with **buddhi** (intellect) and the **indriyas** (senses), constitutes **citta** (the **mind**).

ĀHAVANĪYA. One of the three types of fire altar used in **Vedic** rituals of sacrifice, or **yajñas**. The āhavanīya altar has a square shape. The four sides of this square represent the four major directions of space: north, south, east, and west. The āhavanīya altar is located in the eastern portion of the larger Vedic sacrificial arena. Specifications for the construction, location, and use of the āhavanīya are found in the ***Yajur Veda***.

AHIṂSĀ. Nonviolence in thought, word, and deed; absence of even the desire to do harm to any living being. Ahiṃsā is the first of the five **yamas** or moral restraints taught in the ***Yoga Sūtras*** of **Patañjali** (composed between 100 BCE and 500 CE), and making up the first of the eight "limbs" of the eight-limbed (**aṣṭāṅga**) system of **yoga**. Though it is phrased in negative terms, as the absence of violent impulses, ahiṃsā is understood in those traditions that practice it as entailing positive compassion toward all beings. In the modern **Vedānta** of **Swāmī Vivekānanda**, nonviolence is seen as being entailed by the oneness of all beings as manifestations of **God**, or **Brahman**.

The virtue of nonviolence gradually increases in both prominence and importance in Brahmanical texts from the period of the principal ***Upaniṣads*** (c. 500–100 BCE) to the Common Era. The ***Mahābhārata*** contains the statement "Ahiṃsā is the highest virtue" (13.125.25), and in the ***Bhagavad Gītā*** (16.2), ahiṃsā is listed as one characteristic of an **enlightened** person (despite the setting of this text on a battlefield and its endorsement, in an earlier chapter, of violence for a **kṣatriya** fighting in a just war).

Ahiṃsā is a central virtue of **śramaṇa** traditions such as **Jainism** and **Buddhism**, which include it in their respective sets of five moral precepts, and which are both close in content to Patañjali's **yamas** (the Jain set, in fact, being identical to Patañjali's). The gradually increasing emphasis on ahiṃsā in Hindu texts from shortly before and in the early centuries of the Common Era is sometimes attributed to the influence of these two śramaṇa traditions, though grounds for ahiṃsā can certainly be found in the *Upaniṣads*.

The practice of **vegetarianism** in all three traditions—Jain, Buddhist, and Hindu—is a result of their emphasis on the practice of ahiṃsā toward all living beings. Indeed, it is in the area of dietary practice that the increased emphasis on ahiṃsā in Hinduism is most prominent, with the **Brahmins**, who in ancient times offered **animal sacrifices**, being generally expected in later centuries to practice vegetarianism.

In the 20th century, **Mohandās K. Gāndhī** made ahiṃsā—originally conceived as a purely personal virtue developed in the pursuit of individual spiritual realization—into a cornerstone of his strategy for attaining Indian independence from the British Empire, insisting—in keeping with the idea of **karma**—that only pure means could bring about a pure end. *See also* COW, SACRED.

AHURA MAZDA. The Wise Lord; the supreme **God** of **Zoroastrianism**, a religion of ancient Iran that today claims a small but devout following in India. Zoroastrianism is, in its origins, closely related to **Vedic** religion. The word *ahura* is the Iranian equivalent of the Sanskrit **asura**. In early Vedic texts, the term *asura* simply means *powerful* and is used to describe several Vedic deities, particularly **Varuṇa**. It is only in later Vedic texts that asuras become the demonic enemies of the **devas**.

In Zoroastrianism, Ahura Mazda is not one god among many, but God—the one, supreme deity in a monotheistic sense—and the creator of the world. Through the cultural influence of the Persian Empire, Zoroastrian **monotheism** helped to shape the Abrahamic religions. Via Judaism, it was the source of such **Christian** and **Islamic** concepts as the existence of an evil adversary of God (the devil), one lifetime (as opposed to **rebirth**), and a final judgment, as well as the idea of a recurring series of divine messengers, which may also have shaped the Hindu **avatāra** concept. *See also* ZARATHUSTRA.

AIHOLE. Pronounced "Eye-ho-lé"; village in northern **Karnataka** that, from the fourth to the sixth centuries CE, was a major city: the capital of the **Cālukya** dynasty. The site is noteworthy for the numerous Hindu **temples**, in a variety of architectural styles, which the Cālukyas built there.

AIRĀVATA. Celestial elephant; vehicle of **Indra**. Airāvata was one of the treasured items to emerge from the cosmic ocean when it was churned by the **devas** and **asuras**. In one account of the life of **Gaṇeśa**, Gaṇeśa's father, **Śiva**, after unknowingly decapitating his son, seeks to atone for this misdeed by replacing Gaṇeśa's head with that of Airāvata, thus explaining why Gaṇeśa has the head of an elephant.

AIŚVĀRYA. Blessing; in some contexts, a superhuman power; to be blessed by **God**; derived from **Īśvara**.

AIYANAR. Deity who protects villages in southern India from evil spirits.

AJANTA. Site in central India with numerous Hindu, **Buddhist**, and **Jain temples** and monasteries. Numerous caves dot the region, many of which have been used as sites for **meditation** through the centuries, being at various times extended and connected for the use of whole communities of monks. The site is particularly famous for bright frescoes depicting the life story of the **Buddha**.

ĀJĪVIKAS. Extinct **śramaṇa** sect attributed with a strong doctrine of **nīyati**, or fate, according to which no **action** can facilitate one's attainment of **mokṣa**, or **liberation** from **rebirth**. Mokṣa will simply occur when it is destined to occur. This, at least, is how the doctrine of the Ājīvikas is presented in the **scriptures** of the two surviving śramaṇa sects, **Jainism** and **Buddhism**. The sect's founder, **Makkhali Gosāla**, was a contemporary of both **Mahāvīra** and the **Buddha**, who represent his teaching as inimical to the practice of **asceticism**. Yet the Ājīvikas are also represented as strict ascetics.

Recent scholarship suggests that Jain and Buddhist representations of the Ājīvika doctrine likely involve polemically motivated distortion. The actual Ājīvika doctrine was probably that one can do nothing about one's already actualizing **karma**—called in later Hindu texts **prarabdha karma**—but that one can avoid the taking on of additional karma through adherence to ascetic practice (tapasya).

ĀJÑĀ CAKRA. Cakra, or energy center, located in the subtle body (**sukṣma śarīra**) in the space corresponding to the center of the forehead, just above the eyebrows. It is sometimes called the "third eye." The practice of locating a **tilak** or bindi in the center of the forehead may be related to this concept. *See also* TANTRA.

ĀKĀŚA. Space, the medium of sound, one of the five **elements** or states of being that constitute the physical world (**mahābhūtas**). The five elements are earth (**pṛthvi**), air (**vāyu**), fire (**agni**), water (**ap**), and space (ākāśa). In esoteric Hindu thought, the ākāśa also refers to a mental or spiritual space, a kind of collective **mind** in which all events are stored in a universal memory that can be read by persons who have developed the **siddhi**, or paranormal ability, of doing so.

AKBAR (1542–1605). Mughal emperor who reigned from 1556 to 1605; known for his policy of religious tolerance and appreciation for India's religious diversity. Beginning his rule at the young age of 13, the early years of Akbar's reign were preoccupied with the conquest and consolidation of his empire. His opponents during this period included both Hindu and Muslim kings. He formed alliances with the Hindu **Rajputs** and married Rajput princesses. It was during this period that his interest in and tolerant views about religion emerged. He included Hindus in his administration and sponsored debates in which intellectuals from varied religious communities—including Muslims, Hindus, **Jains**, Sikhs, skeptics, Jews, and Jesuit missionaries—would discuss various issues for Akbar's edification. He tried to start his own religion, *Din-i-Ilahi* or "the Divine Faith," made up of teachings from all the traditions of which he was aware. But this new tradition did not survive his **death**. Under Akbar's reign, a hybrid Hindu–**Islamic** culture began to emerge in India, leading to a good deal of creative activity in the visual **arts**, **music**, architecture, and religion itself. *See also* KABĪR; NĀNAK, GURU; SANT; SIKHISM.

AKKA MAHĀDEVĪ. *See* MAHĀDEVIYAKKA.

AKṢAMĀLĀ. Garland of beads, often worn by Hindu deities. Typically, the garland is usually made up of 50 beads, symbolizing the sounds of the **Sanskrit** alphabet. One also finds garlands of 81 or 108 beads, the latter type often being used in the practice of **japa** (**meditation** on a **mantra**), in which case it is also referred to as a **japamālā**.

AL-BĪRŪNĪ (973–1048). *See* BĪRŪNĪ, AL-.

ALLAHABAD. Modern name of the city at the sacred confluence of the **Gaṅgā** (or Ganges) and Yamuna Rivers, traditionally called **Prayāga**; one of the traditional locations of the **Kumbha Melā**.

ĀḶVĀRS. Literally, "those who are immersed deeply in **God**." The Āḷvārs were 12 early medieval devotees of **Viṣṇu**, and exponents of **bhakti**, or devotion, as the supreme path to **mokṣa**. The teachings of the Āḷvārs are expressed in the form of **Tamil poetry**.

According to the **philosophy** of bhakti, **caste** and gender are irrelevant to the level of devotion of which one is capable—and thus to the attainment of mokṣa. This is in clear contrast with more conservative Brahmanical traditions, according to which **rebirth** as a male **Brahmin** is a prerequisite for the practices needed for the attainment of mokṣa. The Āḷvārs illustrate this spiritual egalitarianism, coming from a wide range of backgrounds. They include a woman (**Āṇḍāl**) and members of the humblest strata of Indian society.

The collected poetry of the Āḷvārs, called the *Nālāyirap Pirapantam* (or *Nālāyira Prabandham* in Sanskrit) is held in such high regard that it is sometimes referred to as the Tamil **Veda**. The **Vedānta** teacher **Rāmānuja**, founder of the **Viśiṣṭādvaita** system of Vedānta, regarded it as the fifth Veda. The Āḷvārs are therefore particularly revered in the **Śrīvaiṣṇava** tradition that Rāmānuja also established, and their poems are frequently recited in Śrīvaiṣṇava **temples** and homes.

The Āḷvārs composed roughly 4,000 poems in all, most of which are attributed to **Nammāḷvār** and **Tirumankai**. The Āḷvārs flourished from approximately 600 to 900 CE.

AMAVASYA. New moon; day marking the end of the **Kṛṣṇa Pakṣa**, or "dark half" of a month, in which the **moon** is waning, and the beginning of the **Śukla Pakṣa**, or "bright half," in which the moon is waxing. In the **Śākta** traditions of **Bengal**, it is customary to perform a **pūjā** to **Kālī** on this day. Amavasya is the last day of the Hindu month, the following day being the first day of the bright half of the next month.

AMBĀ. Literally "mother" or "good woman"; epithet of the **goddess Durgā**. In Hindu iconography, Durgā in her form as Ambā is depicted riding a tiger and having eight arms, whereas Durgā proper is depicted riding a lion and having 10 arms. Ambā is also known as Ambikā, Ambālikā, and Jagaddhātrī. She is one of several forms—along with **Pārvatī** and **Kālī**—of the **Mother Goddess** worshiped in the **Śākta** tradition. Ambā, Ambikā, and Ambālikā, respectively, symbolize the characters A, U, and Ṃ, that make up the syllable **Oṃ**.

Ambā is also the name of a character in the ***Mahābhārata***, the daughter of a king of **Kāśī** (with sisters named Ambikā and Ambālikā). Ambā and her sisters were captured by **Bhīṣma**. Ambā's sisters were married to Bhīṣma's brothers, but Ambā was betrothed to another warrior who refused to marry her after her capture by Bhīṣma. Bhīṣma also would not marry her, due to his vow of celibacy. Abandoned, shamed, and homeless, Ambā vowed to destroy Bhīṣma, whom she blamed for her misfortunes. By the power of her **asceticism** she was reborn as the male warrior Śikhandin, who slew Bhīṣma in battle.

AMBEDKAR, BHĪMRAO (1891–1956). Dalit leader and primary author of the Indian constitution. Born in a village in Mahārāṣṭra, Ambedkar received financial support from the Mahārāja of Baroda to pursue his higher education. In 1912, he became the first Dalit to receive a bachelor's degree at Elphinstone College in Bombay. He earned his doctoral degree at Columbia University in New York in 1927. He also studied at the London School of Economics and, like his contemporary **Mohandās K. Gāndhī**, earned his law degree in London as well.

Ambedkar made the upliftment and empowerment of the lower **castes** the central cause of his life. Advocating the complete abolition of the caste system, Ambedkar was highly critical of reformist Hindus, such as Gāndhī, who believed that this system could be rehabilitated if the practice of **Untouchability** were to be eradicated.

Convinced, by 1951, that caste prejudice, or **casteism**, was inherent to Hinduism, Ambedkar led a mass conversion of thousands of Dalits to **Buddhism**. In addition to its implied critique of Hinduism, this move also led to a reinvigoration of Indian Buddhism, which had largely vanished by the 14th century of the Common Era.

Ambedkarite Buddhism, as this movement is called, has many continuities with traditional Buddhism and has led to a reinvigoration of interest in Buddhism in India. But it is distinguished by its strong political dimension as a critique of the caste system. Ambedkarite Buddhists usually have a home shrine that includes an image of Ambedkar, who is regarded as a *bodhisattva*, or **enlightened** being. *See also* HARIJAN.

AMBEDKARITE BUDDHISM. Movement established by Dr. **Bhīmrao Ambedkar** in 1951. Ambedkar led a mass conversion of thousands of his fellow **Dalits** to **Buddhism** as a protest against the **caste** system of Hinduism. Ambedkar had come to see **casteism** as inherent to Hinduism, thus requiring not reform but a break with the entire tradition.

Though having many continuities with traditional Buddhism—the study of which this movement has reinvigorated in India—this movement is distinguished by its strongly political dimension as a critique of **casteism** and the caste system more generally. Many Indian Buddhists today worship Ambedkar as a *bodhisattva*, or **enlightened** being, a ritual practice unique to this form of Buddhism.

AMMA (1953–). Literally "mother"; an epithet of the contemporary female **guru Mātā Amritānandamayī**, also called the "Hugging Saint."

AMRITĀNANDAMAYĪ, MĀTĀ (1953–). "Mother who is permeated with the bliss of **immortality**," also widely known as **Amma**, Ammachi, and the "Hugging Saint." Born Sudhamani Idamannel in a poor village in **Kerala**, in her childhood she began to show generosity to those who were even less fortunate than herself, and also began the practice of spontaneously embracing those in sorrow. Spiritual seekers began to gravitate to her and in 1981 her organization, the Mātā Amritānandamayī Maṭha, was founded.

AMṚTA. "**Immortality**." Elixir of life churned from the cosmic ocean by the **devas** and **asuras**. This event, depicted frequently in Hindu **art** and **literature**, involved the devas and asuras in a rare act of cooperation, since neither group alone had the strength to churn the ocean of milk. This venture was the occasion for the appearance of **Kūrma**, the second **avatāra** of **Viṣṇu**, which had the form of a giant tortoise. Kūrma permitted the devas and asuras to place **Mount Mandara** on his back to use as the axis of a great churn, the rope of which was formed by the giant serpent **Vāsukī**, king of the **Nāgas**.

When the elixir emerged from the ocean, the asuras stole it from the devas, who in turn recovered it from the asuras through trickery. From drinking the amṛta, the devas became immortal. In Hindu thought, however, the concept of immortality does not imply that one never dies, but only that one has a full and lengthy life span; even the devas die at the end of a **kalpa**, or a cosmic cycle. In some **Vedic** texts in which amṛta is an object of human aspiration, it is described as a life span of a hundred years.

It is said that at the time of the churning of the cosmic ocean of milk, four drops of amṛta fell to the Earth at the locations of the holy cities **Haridwar**, **Nāsik**, **Ujjain**, and **Prayāga**. A great festival of pilgrimage, or **Kumbha Melā**, is therefore held at each of these cities on a rotating basis every three years.

In esoteric Hindu thought, amṛta refers to a vital energy within the body that one can control through **yoga** in order to promote physical health and well-being. The earliest references in Hindu texts to an elixir of immortality are to the **soma** of the ***Vedas***. In the Vedic literature, the devas and asuras fight over the soma, a possible precursor to the story of the amṛta being churned from the cosmic ocean.

AṂŚA. Early **Vedic** deity, one of the 12 **Ādityas**—sons of the **goddess Aditi** and the sage **Kaśyapa**. The term also refers to the portion of the Vedic sacrifice that goes to the **gods**—the invisible portion of the food offered to the gods that they receive before this food is consumed by human beings.

The word *aṃśa* literally means *portion* and is a technical **Vaiṣṇava** term referring to an **avatāra** of **Viṣṇu**, the concept being that an avatāra is a manifestation of a portion of Viṣṇu's total existence, with some avatāras manifesting a relatively small portion of the divine, and others, such as **Kṛṣṇa**, being full manifestations, with others in between.

ANĀHATA CAKRA. Cakra, or energy center, which is located in the subtle body (or **sukṣma śarīra**) in the space corresponding to the heart. *See also* TANTRA.

ĀNANDA. Bliss, joy, having no limitations. Along with infinite being (**sat**) and pure consciousness (**cit**), one of three inherent attributes of **Brahman** according to **Vedānta**. Etymologically related to the **Sanskrit** word *ananta*, meaning infinite, or without limits. The names of many Hindu monks contain the word *ānanda* as a suffix, meaning "one whose bliss is" whatever quality is signified by the word to which ānanda is added. As an attribute of Brahman, ānanda is sometimes used as a synonym for **mokṣa**.

ĀNANDA MĀRGA. "Way of Bliss." Modern Hindu religious movement established in 1955 in **West Bengal** by Prabhat Ranjan Sarkar, better known as **Ānandamūrti**. The movement spread to the United States in 1969. In the early 1970s it was a center of controversy due to the political activism of its members on behalf of Sarkar, who was imprisoned by the government of India. Some of his followers immolated themselves in protest. Sarkar was eventually released and spent the rest of his life pursuing his mission of "self-realization and service to all."

ĀNANDA-MAYA-KOŚA. Layer made up of bliss. One of the five layers or "sheaths" (**kośas**) surrounding the self (**ātman**). The ānanda-maya-kośa is the inmost layer, closest to the self. *See also* ĀNANDA.

ĀNANDAMĀYĪ MĀ (1896–1982). "Mother who is permeated with bliss." Spiritual teacher from **Bengal**. Born into a devout **Vaiṣṇava** family, her given name was Nirmala Sundarī Devī. Her title of Ānandamāyī Mā was conferred upon her by her disciples in the 1920s due to her blissful, God-absorbed nature. From an early age, she would often go into a very deep **meditative** state. In 1922, at the age of 26, she gave herself spiritual initiation, or **dīkṣa**. Breaking with the tradition of going to a **guru** for such initiation, she acted as her own guru. Five months later, she initiated her husband as well. She began to develop a large following of disciples. In 1932, she moved from Bengal to Dehradun, in the foothills of the **Himālayas**, but traveled frequently throughout India for the rest of her life, teaching and establishing **āśramas** and hospitals. Her disciples, most of whom were **women**, included Kamala Nehru, the wife of the first prime minister of India, **Jawaharlal Nehru**. She also met both **Mohandās K. Gāndhī** and **Paramahāṃsa Yogānanda**—the latter meeting being recounted in a chapter of Yogānanda's famous *Autobiography of a Yogi*. Ānandamāyī Mā taught that "The supreme calling of every human being is to aspire to self-realization. All other obligations are secondary." Though having followers from all over India, her following is particularly large in her native Bengal.

ĀNANDAMŪRTI (1921–1990). Prabhat Ranjan Sarkar; founder in 1955 of the **Ānanda Mārga**, a modern Hindu religious movement.

ANAṄGA. Having no limbs, or no body; epithet of **Kāmadeva**, the Cupid-like **god** of love. Kāmadeva is called Anaṅga because **Śiva** destroyed his body with a blast of energy from his **third eye** when Kāmadeva once tried to distract Śiva during his **meditation** by shooting one of his arrows into Śiva's heart.

ANANTA. "Infinite, unlimited"; one of the attributes of **Brahman**. Also the name of the giant serpent with a thousand heads on whom **Viṣṇu** reclines on the cosmic ocean, dreaming the cosmos into existence. Ananta is also called **Śeṣa**, or remainder, because he is all that remains after the universe has been absorbed back into Viṣṇu at the time of the **mahāpralaya**, or great dissolution at the end of a **kalpa**, or cosmic cycle. Śeṣa is said to have incarnated as **Lakṣmaṇa** and **Bālarāma**, the brothers, respectively, of **Rāma** and **Kṛṣṇa**, the two most prominent **avatāras** or incarnations of Viṣṇu.

ANCESTRAL RITES. Two Hindu rituals dedicated to honoring one's ancestors are the funeral, or **antyeṣṭi**, which occurs as soon as possible after **death**, and the **śrāddha**, which occurs periodically and consists of offering food and water. If one does not offer śrāddha to one's ancestors—typically in the form of balls of rice called **piṇḍa**—one may run the risk that they will wander through the world as **pretas**, or hungry ghosts. The food offered in the śrāddha is also said to become the food of one's ancestors in their next **rebirth**.

ĀṆḌĀL (fl. 9th century CE). One of the **Āḻvārs**, or 12 **Vaiṣṇava poets** of south India. She composed approximately 107 of the roughly 4,000 **Tamil** poems that make up the *Nālāyirap Pirapantam*, the collected works of the Āḻvārs, which **Śrivaiṣṇavas** regard as inspired **scriptures** on the same level of authority as the ***Vedas***. Āṇḍāl's revered position as a woman in this tradition is significant, being illustrative of the **philosophy** of **bhakti**, or devotion, according to which social categories such as gender and **caste** are irrelevant to one's spiritual status or proximity to salvation. *See also* WOMEN.

AṄGIRASA. According to some lists, one of the Seven Sages (**Saptarṣi**) presiding over the cosmos. The term is also sometimes used to refer to the ancestors of humanity, who are descendants of the sage Aṅgirasa. Portions of the ***Atharva Veda*** are attributed to the authorship of Aṅgirasa.

ANGKOR WAT. Magnificent **temple** complex built in Cambodia in the 12th century CE by the Khmer king Sūryavarman II. A striking example of Hindu influence on the culture of **Southeast Asia**, Angkor Wat is one of the largest temples in the world. It is modeled on the Hindu cosmos, centered on **Mount Meru**, and includes representations of numerous events from Hindu sacred **literature** and from the past lives of the **Buddha**. This complex includes temples dedicated to the Buddha, **Viṣṇu**, and **Śiva**. It can thus be seen as an architectural embodiment of the **syncretism** frequently encountered among the South Asian religions.

ANIMAL SACRIFICE. The ritual offering of the life of an animal as a way to seek the favor of a deity or deities. The practice is controversial in Hinduism, being a part of the ancient **Vedic** rite of **yajña**, and even today practiced in some corners of the Hindu world such as the **Kālīghāt**, a **temple** to the **Mother Goddess** in her fierce form as **Kālī**, in the city of **Calcutta** (Kolkata), as well as in **Nepal**. But the mainstream Hindu tradition has abandoned animal sacrifice, adopting the view of the **śramaṇa** traditions that the killing of animals is a source of bad **karma**, and not at all meritorious.

When animal sacrifices were more widely performed, in the early Vedic period, the task of the **Adhvaryu** priest—a type of **Brahmin**—included the slaughter, cooking, and offering of the bodies of sacrificial victims. But starting in the period of the ***Upaniṣads***, a growing number of Brahmins de-emphasized—and the śramaṇa movement even actively rejected—the Vedic ritual of sacrifice, especially the practice of animal sacrifice, which came to be seen as an inherently violent karma that could only lead to a bad **rebirth**, rather than as an offering that was pleasing to the gods. By the middle of the first millennium of the Common Era, the practice of animal sacrifice had been largely abandoned by even orthodox Brahmins and replaced, in most parts of India, by vegetable substitutes. The embrace of the ideal of **ahiṃsā**, or nonviolence, on the part of the Brahmins led to this development, as well as to the expectation that Brahmins should practice **vegetarianism**.

Evidence that the abandonment by most Hindus of the practice of animal sacrifice was due at least in part to the influence of śramaṇa traditions, such as **Buddhism** and **Jainism**, exists in the form of the story of the **Buddha avatāra**, who is presented in some accounts as a Vedic reformer who ended the practice of animal sacrifice to promote the ideal of compassion.

Animals offered in ancient Vedic animal sacrifices included bulls and goats. The sacrifices still carried out at the Kālīghāt and in Nepal are primarily of goats. *See also* COW, SACRED; GĀNDHĪ, MOHANDĀS K.

AÑJALI. Gesture of reverence and respect consisting of the placing of the palms of the hands together. The añjali is typically offered during **darśana**, when one encounters an image, or **mūrti**, of a deity, as well as when wants to offer respect to another person. In the latter case, the añjali is often accompanied by the utterance "**Namaste**," which means "I offer reverence to the divinity within you."

AÑJANEYA. Son of Añjanī, epithet of **Hanuman**, whose mother is named **Añjanī** and whose father is **Vāyu**, the **Vedic** deity of the wind.

AÑJANĪ. Mother of **Hanuman**, who for this reason is also known as Añjaneya.

ANNA-MAYA-KOŚA. Food layer; layer made of food; outermost of the five **kośas**, or layers, surrounding the self (**ātman**) according to **Vedānta**; the physical body (**sthūla śarīra**).

ANTYEṢṬI. The **Vedic** funeral ritual of Hinduism; one of the major Hindu **saṃskāras** or sacraments. This ceremony is conducted as soon as possible after **death** and includes the **cremation** of the deceased. The particulars of the funeral ritual vary a great deal, depending upon region and **caste**, but often extend over the course of several days.

Traditionally, the son of the deceased plays a major role in this ritual, which is often seen as essential to the transition of the **soul** of the deceased peacefully to its next life. This is one of the reasons that sons are highly prized in traditional Hindu families. *See also* ANCESTRAL RITES; ŚRĀDDHA.

ANUBHĀVA. Experience; the direct experience of reality; the most authoritative source of **knowledge** according to **Neo-Vedānta**.

ANUGĪTĀ. "Little *Gītā*," part of the ***Mahābhārata***, a brief summary and restatement by **Kṛṣṇa** to **Arjuna**, after the *Mahābhārata* war, of the teachings contained in the ***Bhagavad Gītā***. It is in the 14th book of the *Mahābhārata*.

ANUMĀNA. Inference; a **pramāṇa**, or valid source of **knowledge** in Indian **philosophy**; reasoning from a set of premises and/or observations to a conclusion.

AP. Water; the medium of taste (**rasa**); one of the five elements or states of being that constitute the physical world (**mahābhūtas**). The five elements are earth (**pṛthvī**), air (**vāyu**), fire (**agni**), water (ap), and space (**ākāśa**).

APARIGRAHA. Nonattachment; nonpossessiveness; the fifth **yama** or restraint that is enjoined in the ***Yoga Sūtra***; also included among the moral precepts of **Jainism**.

APSARAS. Nymph; celestial maiden. *See also* URVAŚĪ.

ĀRAṆYAKAS. "Forest texts." The third of the four sections contained within each of the four ***Vedas***. This collection of Vedic writings was composed during the period roughly between the composition of the ***Brāhmaṇas*** and the ***Upaniṣads***, approximately 600 to 500 BCE according to most contemporary scholarship. They are called "forest texts" because the teaching within them is considered sufficiently esoteric that it should be conveyed in the forest, away from society, where it might be overheard. The term also evokes the forest academies, or ***āśramas***, in which **Vedic** sages pursued contemplative activities away from society and taught their wisdom to their students.

The *Āraṇyakas* are known as the **Upāsana Kanda**, or "contemplative portion" of the *Vedas*, in contrast with the earlier **Karma Kanda**, or **action** portion, consisting of the more ritualistic Vedic hymns and the *Brāhmaṇas*, and the **Jñāna Kanda**, or "wisdom portion," consisting of the *Upaniṣads*.

In terms of their style and content, the *Āraṇyakas* can be seen as transitional texts, marking a shift from the more ritualistic concerns of the earlier portions of the Vedic **literature** to the more philosophical and speculative interests reflected in the *Upaniṣads*.

The boundaries between the genres of *Brāhmaṇa*, *Āraṇyaka*, and *Upaniṣad* being somewhat fluid, one of the later *Āraṇyakas*, the ***Bṛhadāranyaka***, is also known as one of the oldest *Upaniṣads*. The content of the *Āraṇyakas* is chiefly concerned with the inner meaning of the Vedic rituals.

ĀRATĪ. Brief ceremony, typically performed daily in **temples**, as well as at home by individual devotees. Āratī involves the waving of a flame—either

Priest performing āratī during Durgā Pūjā.

a lit oil lamp (**dīyā**) fed by **ghee**, **camphor**, or oil, or a lit candle or set of lit candles placed on a plate—in front of an image (**mūrti**) of a deity or in front of a living, revered person, such as a **guru**. The flame is typically waved in a clockwise circular motion or the devotee might also trace out the syllable **Oṃ** in the air with the flame. The āratī is accompanied by the ringing of a bell, and usually with either the chanting of **mantras** or singing. A particularly popular song that is sung to accompany āratī in the modern period is **Oṃ jaya Jagadiśa Hare**, as recorded by the popular **Hindi** singer Lata Mangeshkar.

ARDHANARĪŚVARA. Half-female lord; a representation of the divine couple, **Śiva** and **Śakti** as one being. Typically, the right half of the image has the form of the male deity, Śiva, and the left half of the image has the form of his wife, the **Mother Goddess**, Śakti. Symbolically, this image communicates the idea that the divine includes attributes that are both masculine and feminine, ultimately transcending both. It also represents the inclusion of all opposites within the divine, the fact that the divine reality incorporates and transcends all limiting qualities. This image is especially popular in **Tantric** forms of Hinduism, and the **philosophy** that underlies it reflects a Tantric sensibility. *See also* WOMEN.

ARDHAPADMĀSANA. The half-lotus posture of **Haṭha Yoga**, formed by placing the right foot on the left thigh. *See also* ĀSANA; YOGA.

ARJUNA. One of the **Pāṇḍava** brothers, hero of the ***Mahābhārata***, and interlocutor of **Kṛṣṇa** in the ***Bhagavad Gītā***. Among the Pāṇḍavas, Arjuna is regarded as the greatest warrior, his favored weapon being the bow and arrow. It was Arjuna who won the hand of **Draupadī** in marriage by winning the contest of arms at her **svayaṃvara**. Though his legal father was **Paṇḍu**, Arjuna also had a divine father, **Indra**, who was invoked by his mother, **Kuntī**, when Paṇḍu became unable to conceive heirs due to a curse. When the Pāṇḍavas were required to live incognito for a year, Arjuna disguised himself as a female dance instructor.

Arjuna was the father of the boy warrior Abhimanyu, who was tragically slain in the *Mahābhārata* war. Arjuna's greatest rival was **Karṇa**, whom he slew in the battle of **Kurukṣetra**, along with his teacher, **Droṇa**.

ĀROGYA. Freedom from disease; one of the main goals of traditional Hindu medical science, or **Āyur Veda**.

ARṢA VIDYĀ GURUKULAM. Āśrama and Hindu educational center built by **Swāmī Dayānanda Sarasvatī** in 1986 and located in Saylorsburg, Pennsylvania. Its purpose is to promote Hindu thought and practice in the

United States. The āśrama offers courses in Sanskrit and Indian **philosophy**, with a strong emphasis on **Advaita Vedānta** philosophy.

ART. Art, in all its varied forms—the visual arts, **dance**, **literature**, **music**, and **poetry**—plays a major role in Hindu practice. Two particular currents of Hindu thought—the **philosophy** of **bhakti**, or devotion, and the movement known as **Tantra**—endorse the idea that sense experience can point beyond itself to the realm of the transcendent, and that the aesthetic impulse toward beauty, rather than being a distraction from spiritual pursuits, is a force that can be channeled toward the divine, which is its ultimate proper object. Hindu art is not, therefore, traditionally seen as "art for art's sake" but as a form of what scholar of religion Huston Smith calls "spiritual technology"—a way of inspiring the aesthetic sense and directing it toward spiritual ends.

The aesthetic sense—**rasa**, or "taste" in **Sanskrit**—has been theorized extensively by Hindu thinkers, particularly in the ***Nāṭya Śāstra*** of **Bharata**, a text of the early first millennium of the Common Era, by the 10th–11th century **Kaśmīr Śaiva** philosopher **Abhinavagupta** and by the **Gosvāmins**, or **Vaiṣṇava** theologians of the late medieval period. Abhinavagupta saw rasa, or aesthetic experience, as being akin to the experience of **mokṣa**, and as itself a potentially liberating phenomenon. The Gosvāmins applied this Tantric insight to their devotional practice, arguing that listening to and visualizing oneself as a participant in the stories of the deity **Kṛṣṇa** and his earthly activities can evoke an aesthetic experience that, by Kṛṣṇa's grace, can lead to the state of **liberation**.

In terms of visual art, one of the most striking features of Hindu ritual practice is its deployment of **mūrtis**, or sculptured images of deities in worship. The basic worship ritual, or **pūjā**, involves evoking the presence of the divine within the image—which, in effect, and for the duration of the ritual, "becomes" the deity, who is then treated just as an honored human guest would be treated when visiting a home. Pūjā is one of the most common expressions of bhakti and is carried out both in the home and in the **temple**. A temple is also, itself, a work of art and is designed both to express and evoke devotion.

On the more Tantric side, other works of visual art used to cultivation experience of the divine are the **yantra** and the **maṇḍala**—abstract diagrams that are used as objects of **meditation**.

Both pūjā and meditation are accompanied and aided by music. Sacred chanting is one of the most ancient of Hindu practices. The correct practice of chanting the ***Vedas*** is laid out in the ***Sāma Veda***, a text dating from roughly 1200 to 1000 BCE that forms the basis for later Indian classical music. A wide range of musical genres have emerged in subsequent periods, designed to evoke either a meditative state or devotional feelings.

Dance, too, which combines the visual sense with music, has been developed to a high degree of sophistication, with a variety of styles emerging in different periods and in different parts of the Indian subcontinent—a process that continues today, in the era of global Hinduism. In classical Indian dance, every move—even the facial expressions—of a dancer carry a meaning and form a vocabulary through which a story is told or a lesson is taught.

Finally, literature, including poetry, plays a foundational role in Hindu practice. The preferred medium for communicating philosophical concepts is storytelling. Ancient Hindu bards, known as **sutas**, memorized vast narratives, such as the epic ***Mahābhārata*** and ***Rāmāyaṇa***, and the **Brahmins**, or priestly community, committed vast portions of the Vedic literature to memory as well. In the first millennium of the Common Era, the practice of writing became more widespread—though the earlier tradition of memorization also persisted—and a profusion of texts resulted, with genres spanning a range including drama, poetry, legal writing, and philosophical speculation. Poetry, in particular, was the preferred medium by which the saints of the bhakti movement expressed their devotional feelings—often in vernacular languages, rather than the more formal Sanskrit of the Vedic tradition. These poems, set to music, became the popular hymns or **bhajanas** sung in the setting of Hindu temples and religious gatherings even today.

ARTHA. Wealth, power, worldly success, the ability to fulfill one's desires. Along with sensory pleasure (**kāma**), virtue (**dharma**), and **liberation** (**mokṣa**), one of the four goals of humanity (**puruṣārthas**). This term also refers to goals in general, as well as to the meaning of a word—the "object" or purpose to which a word points beyond itself.

ARTHA ŚĀSTRA. Sanskrit text of political science traditionally attributed to **Kauṭilya** (350–283 BCE, also known as Canakya), a **Brahmin** and the chief political advisor to Candragupta **Maurya**. The oldest parts of the text were likely composed around 300 BCE, with additions made by various authors over the course of the next few centuries.

The **philosophy** of kingly rule outlined in the text was widely followed by Hindu kings for centuries, particularly its **maṇḍala** theory of interstate relations, according to which a king should see himself as being in the middle of a series of concentric circles of alternating enemies and allies. The text covers such topics as diplomacy, administrative structures, military organization, **laws**, and punishments for specific crimes.

The *Artha Śāstra* is frequently compared to the later work of Niccolò Machiavelli, with its sometimes shockingly frank approach to topics such as the deployment of espionage and subterfuge as legitimate tools for the advancement of state interests. At the same time, the text does contain ethical reflections and sets forth the criteria by which an ideal king should strive to live. But its approach to the issues a king might face is best characterized as *realpolitik*.

ĀRYA SAMĀJ. Hindu reform organization that was established by **Swāmī Dayānanda Sarasvatī** (1824–1883) in 1875 and devoted to the practice and promulgation of what it regards as a pure, **Vedic** Hinduism. The Ārya Samāj does not utilize **mūrtis**, or images of deities. It regards the ***Pūrāṇas*** and the customs associated with Pūrāṇic Hinduism as later additions to the original Vedic tradition. Ārya Samāj rituals consist of adaptations of Vedic rituals centered on a sacred fire, such as the **havan**, or fire offering accompanied by Vedic prayers.

In the late 19th century, the Ārya Samāj initiated a ritual enabling non-Hindus to convert to Hinduism. Although this ritual is available to non-Indians, its main historical emphasis has been upon "reconversion"—or rather, conversion of non-Hindus of Indian descent whose ancestors had converted to non-Indic traditions such as **Christianity** and **Islam**.

The Ārya Samāj does not completely reject the concept of **caste**, because the four **varṇas** are mentioned in the ***Ṛg Veda*** and therefore have Vedic sanction. But it does reject the idea of **jāti**, or birth caste, maintaining that one's caste should be a matter of individual merit. Its conversion ceremony has sometimes been utilized to ritually raise the caste status of low-caste persons, a version of the process of acculturation to Vedic norms known as **Sanskritization**. In 1893, a division arose between those within the Ārya Samāj who advocated **vegetarianism**, long an upper-caste custom, and those who opposed dietary restrictions as a later, non-Vedic development due to **śramaṇa** influence.

The Ārya Samāj has been actively involved in political and social issues since its inception, particularly the Indian independence movement. Since independence and the partition of India and Pakistan, it has also been associated with the **Hindu Nationalist** movement, promoting the growth of such Hindu nationalist organizations as the **Hindu Mahāsabhā** and **Bhāratīya Janata Party**.

In 1992, **Swāmī Agniveśa** was expelled from the Ārya Samāj, forming the **World Council of the Ārya Samāj**, a distinct organization from the original Ārya Samāj, that sees itself as maintaining fidelity to the original ideals of Swāmī Dayānanda Sarasvatī.

ARYAMAN. Literally "companion." Early Vedic **deva**, or deity; one of the 12 **Ādityas**, sons of the **goddess Aditi** and the sage **Kaśyapa**. Aryaman is closely associated with the sun and the Milky Way, and is said to be the eye of the **Puruṣa**, or "cosmic man," from whose sacrificed body the universe was fashioned according to the ***Puruṣa Sūkta*** of the ***Ṛg Veda***. He is in charge of honor, chivalry, and nobility—the qualities of an **āryan**—and the rules of society.

ĀRYAN. Noble, cultured, "gentleman," a term by which ancient **Vedic** peoples referred to themselves and to their cultural and religious practices (in contrast with a **mleccha**, or "barbarian"). The term *ārya* had no ethnic or racial connotations until 19th-century European scholarship thus interpreted it, on the false assumption of a correlation between culture and ethnicity. The term refers not to ethnic characteristics but to cultural and spiritual ones. It is pervasive in Indic traditions, including **Buddhism**, where it is used in such contexts as the "Four Noble **Truths**" and the "Noble Eightfold Path" to refer to that which confers the dignity of spiritual realization. Its range of connotations is comparable to the English word "civilized." Based on the assumption that the practitioners of ancient Vedic cultures formed a single ethnic group, the term *Aryan* was coined in the 19th century to refer to a primordial "white" European race, a concept foundational to racist political ideologies such as Nazism. *See also* ĀRYAN INVASION THEORY; INDO-ĀRYAN; INDO-EUROPEAN.

ĀRYAN INVASION THEORY. Indological theory developed by 19th-century scholars, and most prominently associated with **Friedrich Max Müller** (1823–1900), to account for the many strong resemblances between **Vedic** language and culture and the other languages and cultures of the **Indo-European** linguistic family. The theory is controversial. Having subsequently been modified into the **Āryan Migration Theory** in order to better account for the available data, it is still contested by some scholars who prefer a model that locates the Indo-European homeland in India.

According to the Āryan Invasion Theory, Indo-European languages and cultures were brought into India shortly before 1500 BCE through a massive invasion of light-skinned, **chariot**-riding, Indo-European warriors who then conquered the darker-skinned indigenous population. These invaders, according to this theory, then settled in India and imposed their language and culture, including the **caste** system, upon the native Indians. The discovery of the **Indus Valley civilization** was initially thought to lend credence to this theory, being thought to consist of the remains of the civilization destroyed by the Āryans. But it has since been confirmed that this civilization never suffered an invasion.

The Āryan Invasion Theory has proven controversial for a variety of reasons, both scholarly and ideological. As knowledge of ancient India has improved, the theory has been gradually modified over time, and its contemporary form is more accurately known as the Āryan Migration Theory, which postulates not a massive, violent invasion but a gradual acculturation process that very likely involved a relatively small number of actual migrants from Central Asia.

Partly in reaction to the implication of this theory in racist ideologies, and partly on the basis of **Hindu Nationalist** assumptions, some Hindu scholars have proposed the **Out of India Theory** as an alternative model of Vedic origins.

ĀRYAN MIGRATION THEORY. Indological theory that has superseded the **Āryan Invasion Theory** as the mainstream scholarly model of ancient Indian history—and in particular, of **Vedic** origins. The Āryan Migration Theory could be regarded either as a new theory or as a revised form of the old invasion theory. It preserves, from the earlier theory, the postulate that **Indo-European** linguistic and cultural forms were brought to India by migrants from Central Asia. Unlike the earlier invasion theory, however, the newer migration theory suggests that this process was gradual, at least largely peaceful, and that it involved a relatively small number of actual human migrants.

Importantly, this theory also rejects the earlier theory's conflation of culture and ethnicity that helped to fuel racist ideologies in the first half of the 20th century. It essentially seeks to balance the linguistic evidence, which strongly suggests that Indo-European language and culture had a point of origin outside of India, with the lack of any evidence for a massive invasion of the kind postulated in the original invasion theory: no devastated cities, no large influx of genetic material significantly different from the types already found in India, and no clear or unambiguous record of an invasion having ever occurred (though sections of the ***Ṛg Veda*** had long been interpreted by European scholars as providing such an account).

The Āryan Migration Theory is contested by the proponents of the **Out of India Theory**. This theory postulates India as the homeland of Indo-European culture, which then spread to Central Asia and Europe, and (usually) Vedic **Sanskrit** as the Proto-Indo-European language. This model is largely rejected by mainstream scholars due to the presence of non-Indo-European substrate elements in Vedic Sanskrit, indicating that this language cannot be identical to Proto-Indo-European (as proponents of this theory often claim), as well as deep discomfort with the **Hindu Nationalist** ideological bias perceived to motivate at least some versions of this model, which leads to a selective reading of the evidence driven by the foregone conclusion that India *must* be the Indo-European point of origin. The academic conversation surrounding the issue of Vedic origins remains very highly politically charged.

ĀṢĀḌHA. Month of the **Hindu calendar** that corresponds roughly to the period from mid-June to mid-July.

ĀSANA. Yogic posture, literally "seat." In **Haṭha Yoga**, the branch of yoga concerned with the physical postures most conducive to **meditative** practice **(dhyāna)**, a complex system of postures and exercises has been developed. A couple of the most well known are the lotus posture (**padmāsana**) and the half-lotus posture (**ardhapadmāsana**), but there are a great many others as well. Indeed, new āsanas continue to be developed even today.

Most āsanas share the characteristic of keeping the back straight and the head and neck in alignment in order to facilitate deep breathing exercises (**prāṇayāma**). Āsana is one of the limbs of the **aṣṭāṅga** or "eight-limbed" system of **yoga** set forth in the ***Yoga Sūtras*** of **Patañjali**. But, contrary to popular belief, the elaborate system of postures that is associated with Haṭha Yoga cannot be found in this text, which simply states that one's yogic posture should be "stable" and "comfortable."

ASCETICISM. The sacrifice of specific comforts or pleasures or the taking on of extra discomfort in order to discipline oneself and to attain spiritual goals. Derived from the Greek *askesis*, a term that originally refers to athletic and military training, "asceticism" is the most common translation of the **Sanskrit** term *tapasya*. An ethos of asceticism is a strong element of many Hindu traditions, which teach renunciation as a means to **mokṣa**.

In ancient Hindu literary works, such as the ***Mahābhārata***, the ***Rāmāyaṇa***, and the ***Pūrāṇas***, one finds a widespread view that the rigorous practice of asceticism can lead to paranormal powers for the practitioner. Ascetics are frequently depicted as receiving special boons from the **gods** as a reward for their practices. In later **Vedic literature**, ascetic practice takes on a role similar to that of Vedic sacrifice in its ability to evoke divine favors. Ascetics are widely viewed as powerful, and sometimes dangerous, figures. *See also* BRAHMACARYA; SANNYĀSA.

ĀŚĪRVĀDA. Blessing; benediction.

ĀŚRAMA. One of the stages of life. Also a hermitage or place of spiritual retreat where one resides for a period of time, usually with one's **guru**.

The stages of life are the student stage (**brahmacarya**), the householder stage (**gārhasthya**), the retirement—or literally, the "forest dweller"—stage (**vanaprastha**), and renunciation (**sannyāsa**). The brahmacārya stage traditionally lasts from roughly the age of 12 to 24, gārhasthya from 24 to 48, and vanaprastha from 48 to 72 (until either **death** or renunciation). Sannyāsa can be undertaken at any point along the process, but it is a drastic step, being permanent and involving the complete renunciation of one's previous social identity and family connections. The ***Dharma Śāstras*** recommend that one should undertake sannyāsa only after going through the other three stages, so only around the age of 72 or later. The first two stages, those of the student and householder, make up the ***pravṛtti mārga***, the path of engagement with the world, in which one pursues the first three of the four goals of life (**puruṣārthas**): pleasure (**kāma**), wealth (**artha**), and virtue (**dharma**). The latter two stages, retirement and renunciation, make up the ***nivṛtti mārga***, the path of **asceticism** and disengagement from the world in the pursuit of **mokṣa**, or **liberation** from the cycle of **rebirth**, the fourth goal of life.

Some scholars have speculated that the inclusion of sannyāsa as the fourth stage of life is a late development—a reaction to ascetic traditions like **Jainism** and **Buddhism**.

The āśramas can be seen as defining the horizontal axis of a grid on which the traditional Hindu way of life, or dharma, could be comprehensively mapped out, with **varṇa** or **caste** making up the vertical axis. At any given time, a human being is located somewhere on this grid, though sannyāsa could be seen as stepping off of it for the sake of liberation.

AṢṬĀṄGA YOGA. The eight-step, or literally "eight-limbed" **yoga** system presented in the ***Yoga Sūtras*** of **Patañjali**. The eight steps consist, first, of five moral precepts or "restraints" (**yama**), five observances or good habits (**niyama**), the mastery of a posture (**āsana**), control of the breath (**prāṇāyāma**), the control of reactions to sensory stimuli (**pratyāhāra**), concentration on a single object (**dhāraṇā**), **meditative** absorption into that object (**dhyāna**), and contemplative union with that object (**samādhi**).

Later traditions that utilize the *Yoga Sūtras* distinguish between samādhi in which there remains a sense of subjectivity (**savikalpa samādhi**) and samādhi without subject–object duality (**nirvikalpa samādhi**). This distinction is most prominent in **Buddhism**, **Kaśmīr Śaivism**, and the **Neo-Vedānta** tradition of **Ramakrishna**.

The moral precepts of Patañjali's system are identical to the vows or **vratas** of **Jainism** and four of them are identical to four of the Five Precepts of Buddhism. This suggests a shared origin of Patañjali's system in the **śramaṇa philosophy** that gave rise to both the Buddhist and Jain traditions. In the *Yoga Sūtras*, the complex system of āsanas associated with **Haṭha Yoga** is not present. It is simply said that one's posture must be "firm and comfortable."

AṢṬĀVAKRA GĪTĀ. **Advaita Vedānta** text composed in the first millennium CE, very likely before **Śaṅkara** (788–820), but after the composition of the ***Brahma Sūtras*** (first or second century CE). It recounts a dialogue between the sage Aṣṭāvakra, for whom the text is named, and the enlightened king, **Janaka** (who is also mentioned in the ***Upaniṣads*** and represented as the father of **Sītā** in the ***Rāmāyaṇa***).

ASTEYA. Nonstealing. The third of the five **yamas** or moral restraints enjoined in the ***Yoga Sūtras*** of **Patañjali**. Also included among the moral precepts of both **Jainism** and **Buddhism**.

ĀSTIKA. Literally "one who says 'it is'"; orthodox. In classical Hinduism, the test of orthodoxy is acknowledgment of the authority of the ***Vedas***. Systems of philosophy (**darśanas**) that affirm **Vedic** authority (**Nyāya**, **Vaiśeṣika**,

Mīmāṃsā, and **Vedānta**) or that do not reject it outright (**Sāṃkhya** and **Yoga**) are āstika, or orthodox, and those that reject Vedic authority (**Cārvāka**, **Jainism**, and **Buddhism**) are heterodox, or **nāstika**. In contemporary Hinduism, the terms *āstika* and *nāstika* sometimes refer to theism and atheism, respectively, but this is not their original sense.

ASTROLOGY. There is a strong emphasis in Hinduism on determining the most auspicious time to undertake any important venture. Astrology—the determination of auspicious occasions through the observation of the relative motions of the stars and planets—is an ancient and mathematically sophisticated system in Hinduism. The moment of a child's birth will often be used to choose a name for the child, and the astrological charts of a prospective bride and groom will be used to determine if they are a suitable match, and also to determine the most auspicious date and time for their wedding. *See also* CALENDAR, HINDU; NAVAGRAHAS.

ASURA. Powerful one, titan, anti-god, demonic, a demonic being. A species of being usually depicted as in perpetual conflict with the **devas**. Interestingly, not all Hindu texts that depict the conflict of the asuras and the devas present the asuras as uniformly evil or the devas as uniformly good, though over time these two classes of being did come to be viewed in this way.

In its original meaning, the word *asura* simply means a powerful being. In fact, it is a frequently used title for the deva **Varuṇa** in the ***Ṛg Veda***, who might have been the supreme deity early in the development of the Vedic religion. Over time, an etymology developed that defined these beings as "not sura," that is, non-devas, or anti-**gods**.

Prominent asuras in later Hindu sacred **literature**—the ***Purāṇas***—are **Hiraṇyakṣa**, who is slain by the **Varāha** (boar) **avatāra** of Viṣṇu; **Hiraṇyakaśipu**, who is slain by the **Narasiṃha** (man-lion) **avatāra** of **Viṣṇu**; and the **Mahiṣāsura**, or Buffalo Demon, who is slain by the **goddess Durgā**. Symbolically, the slaying of asuras by Viṣṇu or Durgā is said to represent the lower impulses—greed, selfishness, hatred—being overcome by one's divine inner self. In **Tantric** thought, it is said that all the devas and asuras are contained within oneself and that the conflict between them represents an inner struggle among the various aspects of **self**. In the ***Mahābhārata***, the fabulous palace of the **Paṇḍavas** in **Indraprastha** is designed by an asura architect named **Māya**. In both the *Mahābhārata* and the *Purāṇas*, it is said that the devas and asuras once cooperated in order to churn the elixir of **immortality, amṛta**, from the cosmic ocean.

In chapter 16 of the ***Bhagavad Gītā***, divine and demonic, or devic and asuric, qualities are contrasted. The asuric personality is described as egotistical, atheistic, and selfish, whereas the devic personality is benevolent, devout, and generous.

It is possible that the opposition between the devas and asuras reflects an ancient ideological conflict among the ancient **Indo-Europeans**. It is noteworthy in this regard that these two terms take opposite meanings in the Indo-European culture of Iran, where **Ahura Mazda**—the Great Asura—becomes the supreme deity of **Zoroastrianism**, whereas the devas come to be depicted as demonic beings, and later influence the etymology of the English word "devil" (as well as the Latin "deus," the Greek "theos," and the English "divine," which comport better with the Indic valuation of a deva as a deity). Similarly, the *Aesir* of ancient Norse religion seem to be related to the asuras.

AŚVAMEDHA. Horse sacrifice. **Vedic** ritual intended to ensure the success of a king. *See also* ANIMAL SACRIFICE; YAJÑA.

AŚVATTHĀMA. Character in the ***Mahābhārata***; son of **Droṇa**. Aśvatthāma avenged his father's **death** by cutting the throats of many **Pāṇḍava** warriors in their sleep. Droṇa had been killed through deception, laying down his arms when hearing that Aśvatthāma, who was still alive, had been slain.

AŚVINA. Month of the **Hindu calendar** that corresponds roughly to the period from mid-September to mid-October.

AŚVINS. "Horsemen"; twin **Vedic** deities, sometimes said to have the heads of horses. Their father is **Vivasvat**, the solar deity, and one of the 12 **Ādityas**. The Aśvins have healing powers, due to their great **knowledge** of plants and herbs, and are associated with the offering of **soma**. As well as being divine physicians, they are also associated with agriculture. In the ***Mahābhārata***, they are the fathers of the twin **Paṇḍava** brothers, **Nakula** and Sahadeva.

ATHARVA VEDA**.** The fourth of the original four ***Vedas*** to be written. It consists of prayers and brief rituals (in contrast with the more elaborate rituals of the ***Yajur Veda***), as well as philosophical reflections that anticipate those of the ***Upaniṣads***. Due to the many differences in style and content between the *Atharva Veda* and the other three *Vedas*, as well as early references to "the three *Vedas*," scholars have concluded that this text was compiled at least a century or two later than the other *Vedas*.

ĀTMAN. Self, soul, or principle of identity. In its earliest uses, this term refers to the physical body, or to the breath. But fairly early, in the ***Upaniṣads***, it comes to refer both to a universal Self that is ultimately identical with **Brahman**, the ultimate reality, and to the individual self or soul that undergoes **rebirth**, or reincarnation, remaining essentially the same through the various changes of form in which it is embodied. In the *Upaniṣads*, it is stated that the individual, reincarnating ātman is ultimately identical to the universal Self. According to the **Advaita Vedānta** interpretation of the *Upaniṣads*, the realization of the fundamental identity of the individual self and the universal Self is constitutive of **mokṣa**, or **liberation** from the cycle of rebirth.

In later forms of **Vedānta**, a distinction is made between individual reincarnating souls, or **jīvātman**, and **God**, the Supreme Soul that resides in all souls: the "oversoul" or **paramātman**. Advaita Vedānta teaches that the ātman is the basis of all experience, the transcendental condition for any experience whatsoever. Though its existence cannot be proven, it can be experienced directly as awareness and as one's very self.

Advaita Vedānta, as well as **Sāṃkhya** and **Yoga philosophy**, identify the ātman with consciousness and view it as all pervasive. But Advaita sees the ātman as ultimately singular, with the differences among **jīvas** being an illusion. Sāṃkhya, Yoga, **Jainism, Nyāya, Vaiśeṣika**, and the other forms of Vedānta, on the other hand, affirm the plurality and the numerical distinctness of souls and do not affirm a singular ātman.

Nyāya, Vaiśeṣika, and **Dvaita** and **Viśiṣṭādvaita Vedānta** say that the ātman is atomic in size. These two traditions also maintain that the ātman is ontologically distinct from **God**, the supreme ātman. The ***Bhagavad Gītā*** emphasizes its imperishability and its self-identity through many births. A central teaching of most forms of Hinduism is that we are all, in reality, the ātman, not the physical body. The physical body is merely the temporary vehicle of the ātman.

Although the term *ātman* can be, and often is, loosely translated as soul, as pure consciousness, it is distinct from the **mind**, and so different from the soul as traditionally conceived in the Abrahamic traditions, where the soul is often seen as a rational principle. Mind, on a Hindu understanding (such as in Advaita Vedānta, Sāṃkhya, and Yoga), is a part of the material continuum—**māyā** or **prakṛti**—and so distinct from the ātman. In the *Upaniṣads*, it is taught that the ātman is surrounded by a series of progressively more material sheaths or **kośas**. The innermost, and closest to the ātman, is the sheath of bliss (**ānanda-maya-kośa**), followed by the sheath of intellect (**vijñāna-maya-kośa**), the sheath of mind (**mano-maya-kośa**), the sheath of life force or breath (**prāṇa-maya-kośa**), and the gross, physical sheath (**anna-maya-kośa**).

ATRI. According to some lists, one of the Seven Sages (**Saptarṣi**) presiding over the cosmos; father of the sage **Durvāsa**.

AUM. *See* OṂ.

AUROBINDO, SRI (1872–1950). *See* GHOSE, AUROBINDO.

AVATĀRA. Divine incarnation, manifestation of a deity, usually **Viṣṇu**, in a physical, sometimes human, form. Several lists of avatāras exist, but the most common lists name 10 such incarnations of Viṣṇu: **Matsya** the fish avatāra, **Kūrma** the tortoise avatāra, **Varāha** the boar avatāra, **Narasiṃha** the man-lion avatāra, **Vamana** the dwarf avatāra, **Paraśurāma**, **Rāma**, **Kṛṣṇa**, **Balarāma** (who is replaced in later versions of this list by **Buddha**), and **Kālkin** the future **avatāra**. **Aurobindo Ghose** interprets this list in light of modern theories regarding evolution. Other lists of avatāras include as many as 22, or even 108, incarnations, including such figures as the sage **Kāpila**, the founder of **Sāṃkhya philosophy**, and **Ṛṣabha**, the first **Tīrthaṅkara** of **Jainism**.

According to some **Vaiṣṇava** traditions, the ape deity **Hanuman** is an avatāra of **Śiva** who came to Earth to assist Rāma in his mission to destroy **Rāvaṇa**. There is also a **Smārta** tradition according to which **Śaṅkara**, the chief exponent of **Advaita Vedānta**, is an incarnation of Śiva. But most **Śaiva** traditions do not accept the avatāra doctrine, holding that Śiva, as pure consciousness, does not take on a physical form.

Over the centuries, a number of teachers and spiritual figures have been regarded as avatāras, including in the modern period. The 15th-century **ācārya** and Vaiṣṇava saint **Caitanya** is sometimes called the **Golden Avatāra**. It is also held by some in the Vedānta tradition of **Ramakrishna** that Ramakrishna is a divine incarnation. In both **Bengal** and **Nepal**, it is not uncommon for a young girl to be viewed as a divine incarnation of the **Mother Goddess**. On some interpretations of **Vedānta**, all beings are, in a sense, avatāras, because all beings are in fact **Brahman**.

AVIDYĀ. Primordial ignorance. Avidyā is ignorance, not merely in a cognitive sense but a profound lack of awareness of one's true nature as **Brahman**—infinite and unlimited being (**sat**), consciousness (**cit**), and bliss (**ānanda**). According to **Advaita Vedānta**, avidyā is the root cause of one's bondage to **saṃsāra**, the beginningless cycle of birth, **death**, and **rebirth**. Avidyā can only be removed by awakening to one's true nature. An awakening of this kind requires one to learn the **truth** that the self (**ātman**) is identical to Brahman—**knowledge** found only in the **Vedic** scriptures (specifically, in the ***Upaniṣads***). Hearing this truth (**śravaṇa**), reflecting upon it (**manasā**), and contemplative realizing of it (nidhidhyāsana) produces the required awakening.

AYODHYĀ. Town in northern India, located in what is now the state of Uttar Pradesh, believed to be the birthplace of **Rāma** and the capital city of his ancient kingdom. In the ***Rāmāyaṇa***, Ayodhyā is ruled by Rāma's father, **Daśaratha**, who wishes to pass its reign on to Rāma. Before Rāma can be made king, however, Daśaratha is forced by his wife, Kaikeyī, to send Rāma into exile. Rāma returns from exile and rules Ayodhyā only after slaying the demonic **Rāvaṇa**. Rāma's rule is said to be highly just and becomes the ideal of Hindu kingship (*Rāma rājya*). In the modern period, the concept of *Rāma rājya* has become central to the ideology of **Hindu Nationalism**, in which this concept of an ideal Hindu society ruled by **dharma** is contrasted with contemporary political corruption.

In December 1992, Ayodhyā became a center of controversy when a group of Hindu Nationalists demolished a mosque called the **Babrī Masjīd** (Babur's Mosque), which they believed had been built from the remains of a **temple** on the same location marking the exact spot of Rāma's birth (*Rāma-janma-bhūmī*). This demolition sparked riots in India, Pakistan, and Bangladesh between Hindus and Muslims, in which many members of both communities were killed, and a number of Hindu temples destroyed in retaliation. In September 2010, an Indian high court ruled that the property should be divided among Hindu and Muslim organizations, a compromise that appears to have defused the issue, at least for the time being.

ĀYU. A long life; one of the central goals of **Āyur Veda**.

ĀYUR VEDA. Science of long life, traditional system of Hindu medicine. Among the figures who were responsible for developing this ancient system were **Caraka**, Suśruta, and Vāgbhata. It is a holistic system of medicine, focused on balancing bodily energies, or humors (dośas). Its chief aims are long life (**āyu**) and freedom from disease (**ārogya**). It utilizes herbs and minerals to treat disease and maintain good health.

AYYAPPAN. Deity believed to reside at the top of **Sabarimalai**, a hill in **Kerala** that is sacred to Ayyappan's sect. Ayyappan is regarded as the son of **Viṣṇu** and **Śiva**, from a time when Viṣṇu appeared to Śiva as a beautiful **woman** called **Mohinī**. According to one version of the story of Ayyappan, Viṣṇu took the form of Mohinī so a deity could be born from the union of Viṣṇu and Śiva that would have their combined power in order to defeat the **asura** Princess Mahiṣī, sister of the **Mahiṣāsura** or Buffalo Demon.

Devotion to Ayyappan is a relatively recent development in Hinduism and is most popular in southern India.

B

BABRĪ MASJĪD. Babur's mosque; mosque demolished in 1992 by **Hindu Nationalists** who believed it to have been built from the remains of a **temple** on the location marking the exact spot of Rāma's birth, in the town of **Ayodhyā**. This demolition sparked riots in India, Pakistan, and Bangladesh between Hindus and Muslims, in which many members of both communities were killed, and a number of Hindu temples destroyed in retaliation. In September 2010, an Indian high court ruled that the property should be divided among Hindu and Muslim organizations, a compromise that appears to have defused the issue, at least for the time being.

BACK TO GODHEAD. Magazine published by the **International Society for Krishna Consciousness** (ISKCON). First published in India in 1944 by **Abhay Charan De**, who is better known by his monastic name of **Bhaktivedānta Swāmī Prabhupāda**.

Publication of the magazine was interrupted in 1965 when Prabhupāda traveled to the United States to spread the **Gauḍiya Vaiṣṇava** tradition. After founding ISKCON, Prabhupāda resumed publication of *Back to Godhead* in the United States, where it has remained in print continuously since 1967.

BĀDĀMĪ. Site located in northern **Karnataka**, capital of the **Cālukya** dynasty from the sixth to the eighth centuries CE. Bādāmī is the site of numerous royal inscriptions and a variety of **temples**—**Vaiṣṇava**, **Śaiva**, **Buddhist**, and **Jain**—all of which received Cālukya patronage.

BĀDARĀYAṆA. Author of the ***Brahmā Sūtras***. Bādarāyaṇa is sometimes identified with **Vyāsa**, traditional author of the ***Mahābhārata*** and compiler of the ***Vedas***. Along with the ***Upaniṣads*** and ***Bhagavad Gītā***, the *Brahma Sūtras* (or ***Vedānta Sūtras***) form the ***Prasthāna Traya***, or threefold foundation of **Vedānta**, on which all Vedāntic **ācāryas** are expected to write commentaries (**bhāṣyas**).

BADRĪNĀTH. Popular site for **pilgrimage** located in the **Himālayas**. It is home to one of the four monasteries or **maṭhas** of the **Daśanāmi Order** of Hindu monks founded by **Śaṅkara**.

BALARĀMA. Brother of **Kṛṣṇa**, the ninth in the traditional list of 10 **avatāras** of **Viṣṇu**, according to earlier versions of this list. In later versions, Balarāma is replaced by the **Buddha**, with Balarāma becoming seen as an incarnation of **Śeṣa**, the cosmic serpent upon whose belly Viṣṇu reclines. Balarāma's original presence on the list of the avatāras of Viṣṇu, alongside Kṛṣṇa, shows that, according to the **Vaiṣṇava** avatāra concept, it is possible for Viṣṇu to assume more than one form at the same time (given that Balarāma and Kṛṣṇa were contemporaries).

BALI. Island in Indonesia where a Hindu culture is predominant. Also an **asura** that was defeated by **Vāmana**, dwarf **avatāra** of **Viṣṇu**. *See also* SOUTHEAST ASIA.

BANARAS. Holy city along the river **Gāṅgā**, or Ganges, revered as sacred to **Śiva**, and the location of the **Viśvanātha Mandir**, a **Śaiva temple** that is a popular pilgrimage site, as are the bathing **ghats** along the edge of the river. In ancient times, the city was called **Kāśī** and was the center of the one of the 16 city-states or Mahājanapadas of the first millennium BCE. The **Buddha** is believed to have preached his first sermon here.

BANARAS HINDU UNIVERSITY. University established in 1915 by Pandit Madan Mohan Malaviya with the assistance of **Annie Besant**, and one of the most prominent research universities in India. Though it is called a "Hindu University" and was founded, in part, with the mission of promoting **knowledge** of Hinduism, students of all religious communities are accepted, and Banaras Hindu University offers degrees in a wide array of secular disciplines, such as agriculture, medicine, business, and **law**.

BASAVA (1134–1196). Śaiva bhakti poet and founder of the **Liṅgāyat** or **Vīraśaiva** sect. Though born a **Brahmin**, Basava was opposed to **casteism** and taught the equality of all human beings. He was also opposed to sacrifice, pilgrimage, and the use of images in worship. The only image used in the Vīraśaiva tradition is the abstract form of **Śiva**, the **liṅga** (hence the alternative name, Liṅgāyat, for this tradition). Śiva is regarded in the tradition of Basava as **God** in a **monotheistic** sense—the one supreme deity. Basava was from **Karnataka**, where his Liṅgāyat movement has continued to be most prominent since his time. He held high government office as a minister in the court of the **Cālukya** King Bijjala and used this position to advance his progressive social and religious ideals.

BASHAM, ARTHUR LEWELLYN (1914–1986). Renowned **Indologist** and historian. He completed all of his degrees at the School of Oriental and

African Studies in London and taught there as well. In 1965, he accepted a professorship at the Australian National University in Canberra. His most famous book, *The Wonder That Was India*, has been reprinted numerous times and is a popular as well as a scholarly work, which has been responsible for sparking the interest of numerous scholars in India and Hinduism. He had a particular appreciation for **Swāmī Vivekānanda**, whom he regarded as a major figure of the modern world. Basham's students included **Romila Thapar**.

BAULS. **Bengali** traveling singers and mystical **poets**. Known for intense devotion and unconventional behavior, the Bauls have a generally Tantric orientation and can be identified with the **Sahajiyā** form of **Tantra**, a style of religiosity known for its emphasis on spontaneity and general rejection of concern for worldly conventions. The religious orientation of the Bauls can be described as a mix of **bhakti** and Tantra. The **music** of the Bauls was tremendously influential upon the music and poetry of the modern Bengali **artist Rabindranāth Tagore**.

BELUR. Site located in southern **Karnataka**; home to a variety of **temples** dating to the 11th and 12th centuries CE. The temples, built by the Hoysala dynasty, are among the most elaborately carved Hindu temples in India, with walls and pillars that appear to be almost alive with motion, due to practically every space upon them being carved with realistic figures of deities enacting scenes from the Hindu **scriptures**.

BELUR MAṬH. Home monastery and main administrative center of the **Ramakrishna Order**, located in **Calcutta**.

BENARES. Alternative spelling of **Banaras**.

BENGAL. Region in northeastern India, home of a number of prominent Hindu reform figures of the early modern period, such as **Rām Mohan Roy**, **Ramakrishna**, **Swāmī Vivekānanda**, and **Aurobindo Ghose**, and literary figures such as **Bankim Chandra Chatterjee** and **Rabindranāth Tagore**. Bengal was the first part of India to experience extensive interaction with the British, being home to **Calcutta** (Kolkata), the location of the headquarters of the **British East India Company**. This interaction was among the main catalysts for the Hindu reform movement, often called the "Bengal Renaissance."

Buddhism was prominent in Bengal in the first millennium CE, as were Buddhist and Hindu forms of **Tantra**, and Tantric practices associated with the **Goddess**-oriented **Śākta** traditions continue to be relatively popular in contemporary Bengal. **Durgā Pūjā** is the largest holiday in Bengal, and Bengalis traditionally perform **Kālī** Pūjā on the night celebrated by most other

Hindus as **Dīwali**. Bengal is also home to the **Bauls**, wandering minstrels whose spirituality and famous folk songs reflect currents of both **Tantra** and **bhakti**.

In the late first and early second millennia of the Common Era, highly devotional **Vaiṣṇava** traditions, such as **Gauḍīya Vaiṣṇavism**, became a major element of Bengali Hinduism, with Bengal being the home, in the medieval period, to **Caitanya**, and in the modern period, to **Bhaktivedānta Swāmī Prabhupāda**.

BESANT, ANNIE (1847–1933). Social and political reformer and prominent member of both the **Theosophical Society** and the Indian National Congress. Besant was an early advocate of freedom of thought, secularism, and socialism. Of Irish origin, she supported independence for both Ireland and India.

In her youth, Besant was committed largely to political activism and had a strong leaning toward Marxism. But after reading **Helena Petrovna Blavatsky**'s *The Secret Doctrine* in 1889, she joined the **Theosophical Society**, of which she became president in 1908. Though never rejecting her progressive political commitments, for the rest of her life she would contextualize these within a Theosophical worldview.

A prolific author, Besant wrote numerous books and tracts on various aspects of theosophical thought, as well as a translation of the ***Bhagavad Gītā***. Wanting to promote Hindu ideals and culture through education, in 1915 she assisted Pandit Madan Mohan Malaviya in establishing **Banaras Hindu University**. She also served as the president of the Indian National Congress in 1917. She was arrested by the British government for her political activities during that same year. Her commitment to Indian independence was profound, and she corresponded with **Mohandās K. Gāndhī**.

The latter part of Besant's career was devoted to promoting the idea that **Jiddu Krishnamurti** was the "World Teacher"—the next **Buddha**, Maitreya—a messianic being whose coming is predicted in the **scriptures** of **Buddhism**. Krishnamurti himself did not endorse this idea, and famously left the Theosophical Society to teach a path of radical questioning of all forms of authority. Besant and Krishnamurti, however, remained on good terms until Besant's death in 1933.

BHADRA. Month of the **Hindu calendar** that corresponds roughly to the period from mid-August to mid-September.

BHAGA. Literally "fortunate," or "dispenser of wealth." Early Vedic deity, one of the 12 **Ādityas**, sons of the **goddess Aditi** and the sage **Kaśyapa**. Bhaga is sometimes pared with **Aṃśa**, the **gods**' share of the sacrifice. Bhaga is the human beings' share.

When suffixed with the syllable "-vant," meaning "possessed of," the term *bhaga* becomes the basis of the word **Bhagavān**, or "blessed," often used as an epithet of such figures as **Kṛṣṇa** and the **Buddha**, and, in contemporary Hinduism, a term for **God**.

BHAGAVAD GĪTĀ. Song of the Blessed One, Song of the Lord, Song of **God**; likely composed between 100 BCE and 100 CE. This 18-chapter segment of the sixth book of the ***Mahābhārata*** has come to be viewed as an authoritative **scripture** in its own right, particularly in the modern period, though numerous premodern commentaries (**bhāṣyas**) were written upon it as well. Many Hindus see this text as a comprehensive summary of Hindu **philosophy**. As a scripture, it serves a function in contemporary Hinduism closer to that of the Bible in **Christianity** than do the venerable, but less popular, ***Vedas***.

Occurring at the point in the *Mahābhārata*'s narrative when the climactic battle of **Kurukṣetra** is about to take place, the *Bhagavad Gītā* consists of a dialogue between the **Paṇḍava** hero **Arjuna** and his best friend and cousin, **Kṛṣṇa**, who has agreed to act as Arjuna's charioteer in the battle and who is also an **avatāra** of **Viṣṇu**. Deeply troubled by the moral dilemma that he faces, having to fight in a just war that will require him to slay such revered persons as his grandsire **Bhiṣma** and his teacher **Droṇa**, Arjuna falls into despair. Kṛṣṇa's counsel to Arjuna at this point takes the form of a conversation that ranges over a great variety of topics and views current in Indian philosophy at the time of the text's composition (c. 100 BCE–100 CE by most scholarly estimates). Currents of thought that can be discerned in the *Bhagavad Gītā* include **Sāṃkhya**, **Yoga**, **Vedānta**, **Buddhism**, and **Jainism**, as well as an early articulation of the theistic philosophy of the **bhakti** movement, which became highly popular in the centuries to follow.

Later Hindu tradition gives the text an increasingly privileged status as a summary of all Hindu thought. It is often called simply "the *Gītā*," despite there being many texts in the gītā genre. Along with the ***Upaniṣads*** and the ***Brahmā Sūtras***, the *Bhagavad Gītā* forms part of the ***Prasthāna Traya***, or threefold foundation of Vedānta philosophy, upon which all the major Vedāntic **ācāryas**, such as **Śaṅkara**, **Rāmāṇuja**, and **Madhva**, have commented. **Mohandās K. Gāndhī** referred to this text as his "dictionary of daily reference" and cited it as a major influence on his philosophy of active engagement with the world as an important part of the spiritual path. **Aurobindo Ghose** also commented upon it in a work entitled *Essays on the Gītā*, which focuses on the text's philosophy of yoga.

The most controversial aspect of the text is its location on a battlefield, coupled with the fact that Kṛṣṇa encourages Arjuna to fight in battle, rather than taking a path of nonviolence—although Kṛṣṇa, somewhat paradoxically, does commend **ahiṃsā** to Arjuna as one of the virtues of an **enlightened** person (16.2).

Commentators have responded to the question of violence and nonviolence in the *Bhagavad Gītā* in a variety of ways: ignoring it, frankly accepting the violence entailed as a part of life in ancient India or of life in general, viewing the entire episode in terms of the symbolism that the text itself suggests (13.1)—with the body as the field of battle and the real enemies being negative qualities such as ignorance, desire, and egotism—or, in the case of Gāndhī, seeing the violence of the epic context as irrelevant to and even incompatible with the deeper spiritual message of the text, which becomes abstracted from its literary context. A related issue on which scholars disagree is whether the *Gītā* is a later interpolation, inserted into the *Mahābhārata* at a later date—and in disagreement with it on the issue of violence—versus whether it should be seen as integral to the epic.

The Vedāntic ācāryas do not agree amongst themselves on the relative roles of **jñāna**, or wisdom, and bhakti, or devotion, as paths to **mokṣa** in Kṛṣṇa's teaching. The **Advaita** tradition, following Śaṅkara, sees this text as commending jñāna yoga, whereas the **Vaiṣṇava** ācāryas, such as Rāmāṇuja, Madhva, and **Caitanya**, see it as primarily a text of bhakti. **Swāmī Vivekānanda** sees the text as commending **four yogas**—the paths of **action**, wisdom, devotion, and **meditation**—as being equally efficacious. Gāndhī also follows Vivekānanda in this regard, though giving primary attention to the way of action.

BHAGAVĀN (BHAGAVAT). Lord, Blessed One, **God**. Usually an epithet associated with **Kṛṣṇa**, though also used in the literary works of various traditions to refer to a deity or founding figure. The **Buddha**, for example, is called Bhagavān in many **Buddhist** texts. In contemporary Hinduism it is not uncommon to hear this term being used as an exclamation with essentially the same semantic range as the English, "Oh my God!"

BHĀGAVATA PURĀṆA. One of the 18 major ***Purāṇas***, or texts of ancient lore focused on the lives and deeds of the Hindu deities. The *Bhāgavata Purāṇa* is concerned chiefly with the life of **Kṛṣṇa**. It is a text particularly revered by **Vaiṣṇavas**, most especially those whose devotion is centered chiefly upon Kṛṣṇa. This text is a major locus for the development of the **philosophy** of **bhakti**, or devotion as the preeminent means for the attainment of **mokṣa**.

The main focus of the narrative is the early life of Kṛṣṇa, prior to the events of the ***Mahābhārata***. Shortly after his birth, Kṛṣṇa's parents need to hide him from his wicked uncle, a king named **Kāṃsa**, who wants to slay him because of a prediction that Kṛṣṇa would one day slay him and take control of his kingdom. On a number of occasions in his infancy and childhood, Kṛṣṇa displays paranormal powers.

A major theme of the text is the relationship between Kṛṣṇa and the **gopīs**, or milkmaids of **Vṛndāvana**, who are represented as his ideal devotees. Foremost among the gopīs is **Rādhā**, whose loving relationship with Kṛṣṇa is the ultimate model of devotion. This relationship is further explored in the ***Gītāgovinda*** of **Jayadeva**. The *Bhāgavata Purāṇa* was composed from roughly 800 to 950 CE.

BHĀGAVATA SECT. Very early **Vaiṣṇava** sect focused on **bhakti** toward **Kṛṣṇa** as the best path to **mokṣa**. The name of the sect arises from their use of the title **Bhagavān** to refer to Kṛṣṇa. The earliest textual evidence for the existence of this sect can be found in the ***Mahābhārata***, including the ***Bhagavad Gītā***, which advocates devotion to Kṛṣṇa.

BHAJANA. Devotional song. Bhajanas are often sung during group worship in a call-and-response fashion, in which the lead singer sings the refrain—typically a **mantra**—that is then repeated by the congregation. The tempo of a bhajana usually starts out slow, and then picks up speed as the bhajana is sung, usually becoming quite fast near the end. But on the final call-and-response, the tempo returns to its original pace. *See also* BHAKTI.

BHAKTI. Devotion, one of the **four yogas** or spiritual disciplines that Hindu traditions present as a path to **liberation**—or **mokṣa**—from the cycle of **rebirth**, along with **karma yoga**, **jñāna yoga**, and **dhyāna** or rāja yoga.

Bhakti as a path to liberation is first developed in later **Vedic** texts such as the ***Śvetāśvatāra Upaniṣad***, as well as the ***Bhagavad Gītā***. It is also mentioned in the ***Yoga Sūtras*** of **Patañjali** under the name of **Īśvara-praṇidhāna**, or "surrender to the Lord." Bhakti is typically focused upon a specific, personal form of the divine—such as **Viṣṇu**, **Śiva**, or **Devī**—in contrast with jñāna, which is a more abstract, impersonal realization.

Bhakti is emphasized most prominently in the **Vaiṣṇava** traditions of Hinduism, although it is an important component of most forms of Hinduism. It is a major theme of such texts as the ***Bhāgavata Purāṇa***, as well as the Vaiṣṇava-oriented **Vedānta** systems of **Rāmāṇuja**, **Madhva**, and **Caitanya**, all of whom see bhakti as the preeminent path to mokṣa, for which the other three yogas are preparatory (unlike **Advaita Vedānta**, where jñāna, or knowledge, is primary). Bhakti is not merely an emotion but involves a real metaphysical connection and mutual participation between the devotee and the divine.

The deep, intense spiritual longing associated with bhakti is famously expressed in the poems and songs of devotees of the bhakti movement, such as the **Āḷvārs**, **Basava**, **Mīra Bai**, and **Tulsīdās**, to name only a few. An important characteristic of bhakti in the works of these **poet**-saints—who came from all walks of life and included many **women**—is its spiritual egalitarianism.

Bhakti can be cultivated by any person, regardless of **caste** or gender, thus making liberation available to all.

Bhakti is usually cultivated and expressed through the practice of worship or **pūjā** directed to a personal form of the divine and the singing of **bhajanas**. **Ramakrishna** was intensely devoted to **Kālī**. His chief disciple, **Swāmī Vivekānanda**, places bhakti on the same level as all the other yogas, the equality of which is a distinctive teaching of the modern or **Neo-Vedānta** tradition that Ramakrishna and Vivekānanda initiated.

BHAKTIVEDĀNTA SWĀMĪ PRABHUPĀDA (1896–1977). Founder and **ācārya** of the **International Society for Krishna Consciousness** (ISKCON). Bhaktivedānta (born **Abhay Charan De**) brought the **Gauḍīya Vaiṣṇava** tradition to North America in 1965, establishing ISKCON and beginning the **Hare Krishna movement**. Bhaktivedānta first arrived in New York and found a home with a group of young people who were part of the countercultural movement of that period. It was largely from this movement that the following of ISKCON was first drawn, though it has since become somewhat more of a mainstream group.

BHARADVĀJA. According to some lists, one of the Seven Sages (**Saptarṣi**) presiding over the cosmos.

BHARATA. Legendary king of ancient India and founder of the **Bhārata** dynasty. The major characters of the ***Mahābhārata*** are members of this dynasty, and the *Mahābhārata* itself is the tale of Bharata's descendants. In **Jainism**, Bharata is represented as the son of **Ṛṣabha**, the first **Tīrthaṅkara** of the Jain tradition. Bharata is also one of the brothers of **Rāma** in the ***Rāmāyaṇa*** (not to be confused with the first Bharata).

A later, historical figure from the first millennium CE named Bharata is the author of the ***Nāṭya Śāstra***, the authoritative guide to Indian classical theater and **dance**.

BHĀRATA. The ancient royal dynasty descended from King **Bharata** and whose adventures are depicted in the ***Mahābhārata***. Also a name for India, Bharata's kingdom, which is also used in official documents of the contemporary Republic of India.

BHARATA-NĀṬYAM. Popular form of Indian classical **dance** originating in southern India and inspired by the depictions of **Śiva Nāṭarāja** (Lord of the Cosmic Dance) at the famous **Śaiva temple** at **Cidambaram**. Its complex gestures convey symbolic meaning, allowing the dancer to tell stories from Hindu **literature** in dance form. It is one of the four traditional schools of Indian classical dance.

BHĀRATI. One of the ten subsets of the **Daśanāmī Order** of monks established by **Śaṅkara**. *See also* BHĀSKARARĀYA MAKHIN.

BHĀRATĪYA JANATĀ PARTY (BJP). "Indian People's Party," popular **Hindu Nationalist** political party established in 1980. Within the Indian political spectrum, this party is seen as right wing, perhaps analogous to the Republican Party in the United States, with a strong advocacy of traditional values with clear religious—in this case, Hindu—overtones.

More widely known as the BJP, this political party governed India from 1998 to 2004. With close ties to organizations like the **Rāṣṭrīya Svayamsevak Saṅgh** and the **Viśva Hindu Pariṣad**, its Hindu nationalist leanings have been a source of controversy for this party, as was its decision to test nuclear weapons in 1998 in response to similar nuclear tests undertaken by the government of Pakistan. The BJP has also advocated the building of a **temple** to **Rāma** at the disputed site of the **Babrī Masjīd** in **Ayodhyā** and the implementation of a uniform civil code, doing away with the different systems of personal **law** for various religious communities currently in place. It has also expressed concern about the proselytizing activities of **Christian** missionaries and, in some states, has sought to curb these through "conversion **laws**," which have been controversial due to concerns regarding religious freedom.

The party characterizes its ideology as "integral humanism" and describes its aim as making India a progressive, modern state in a way that draws upon and is in keeping with its ancient heritage. Its opponents, however, see it as advancing the ideal of a Hindu state or *Rāma rājya* in opposition to the secular ideals on which the Indian constitution is based. For its part, the BJP criticizes what some of its members refer to as the "pseudo secularism" of other Indian political parties, advocating an American model of separation of religion and government as opposed to what Hindu Nationalists regard as preferential treatment for religious minority communities.

BHĀRATĪYA VIDYĀ BHAVAN. "Palace of Indian Wisdom"; Indian educational trust established in 1938 by K. M. Munshi. The Bhāratīya Vidyā Bhavan has a large number of affiliated Indian educational institutions, as well as a handful of institutions outside India. Its chief purpose is to promote the study of **Sanskrit** and Hindu culture and has engaged in a good deal of publishing, since its inception, on topics related to traditional Indian and Hindu culture.

BHĀRGAVA. Descendant of **Bhṛgu**, one of the Seven Sages (**Saptarṣi**) presiding over the cosmos; a group of **Brahmins** claiming descent from the sage Bhṛgu and involved in the oral transmission of the ***Mahābhārata***.

BHARTṚHARI (fl. 6th–7th centuries CE). Sanskrit grammarian and **poet** who developed the **sphoṭa** theory of Sanskrit grammar, according to which the letters or sounds that make up a word have a special power to manifest the meaning of that word. This power to make meaning is the true essence of a word. The letters and sounds that make up the word are merely the means by which this true essence is revealed.

BHĀSKARARĀYA MAKHIN (1690–1785). Tantric theologian who systematized the **Śrīvidyā** system of **Tantra**, which is focused upon the **Mother Goddess** as the supreme form of divinity. Bhāskararāya Makhin was born in Maharashtra, coming from a very scholarly family, and was highly skilled in philosophical debate. His major works are the *Setubandha* (a detailed technical guide to Tantric practice), the *Varivasya Rahasya*, and a commentary, or **bhāṣya**, on the *Lalitāsahasranāma*, a text dedicated to the worship of the **Divine Mother**. Contemporary worship of the Mother Goddess largely follows the system outlined in Bhāskararāya Makhin's texts. As a systematizer of a Tantric practice, he has played a role similar to that played by **Abhinavagupta** in relation to the **Kaula Tantra** system of **Kaśmīr Śaivism**.

BHĀṢYA. Commentary; interpretation of an earlier text that is regarded as authoritative. This is the primary literary genre through which a philosophical system is developed in classical Hindu thought. Rather than valuing novelty, Hindu traditions have tended to see all important **truth** as having been revealed in the distant past. The task of the thinker is therefore not to develop new ideas but to unpack, unfold, and re-present the deep truths embedded in the words of the ancients as appropriate to new historical situations. *See also* DARŚANA.

BHAVĀNĪ. Epithet of **Pārvatī**, the **Mother Goddess** in her peaceful, benevolent form, as the wife of **Śiva**.

BHAVE, VINOBHA (1885–1982). Close associate and disciple of **Mohandās K. Gāndhī**, freedom fighter, and postindependence Indian political and social activist. His thought closely followed that of Gāndhī, with a strong emphasis on **ahiṃsā** (nonviolence) and the inseparability of political and social activism from spirituality. He is best known for his **Sarvodāya** ("Uplifting of All") movement, as well as his Bhūdān, or "Gift of the Earth" campaign, which was aimed at the redistribution of land to the poor. Bhave's **death** was somewhat controversial, as he undertook *sallekhanā*, the traditional **Jain** fast to the death.

BHĪMA. Character in the ***Mahābhārata***, second of the **Pāṇḍava** brothers, fathered by **Vāyu**, the **Vedic god** of the wind. Bhīma, like his divine father, is known for his great strength and quick temper. He frequently engages in physical combat with **asuras** and other enemies. It is Bhīma who delivers the final killing blow to **Duryodhana**, the main villain of the epic. This blow is controversial, because Bhīma violates the rules of battle and strikes Duryodhana on the thigh with his club.

BHĪṢMA. Character in the ***Mahābhārata***, son of King Śantanu and the goddess **Gaṅgā**. The name "Bhīṣma" is actually an epithet meaning "terrible," the character's birth name being Devavrata. Bhīṣma received this epithet due to the terrible, unnatural vow that he took to remain celibate and renounce his claim to his father's throne in order to allow his father to remarry after the departure of Gaṅgā back to the heavens. This would enable his father's descendants through his new wife, Satyavatī, to inherit the kingdom—a condition imposed by Satyavatī's father before he would permit his daughter to marry Śantanu.

Bhīṣma became a mighty warrior and lived to a great age. He was slain in battle at **Kurukṣetra** by Śikhandin, a reincarnation of **Ambā**, a woman who had vowed to take revenge on Bhiṣma many years previously, after having been abandoned by him. Bhīṣma had the ability to choose the time of his own **death**, however, and lay on the battlefield for many days, passing on his wisdom to the **Pāṇḍavas**, who had gathered around him. The words of Bhīṣma on his deathbed are contained in a book of the *Mahābhārata* known as the *Bhīṣma Parvan*, a collections of aphorisms on Hindu **philosophy**, politics, and ethics.

BHṚGU. According to some lists, one of the Seven Sages (**Saptarṣi**) presiding over the cosmos; ancestor of a group of **Brahmins** called the **Bhārgavas**. A work on **astrology**, the *Bhṛgu Saṃhitā*, is attributed to him.

BHŪ. The Earth. One of the "three worlds" of **Vedic** thought, including the Earth, the upper atmosphere, and the heavens, and invoked in the first line of the **Gāyatrī mantra**: ***Oṃ*** *bhūr bhuvaḥ svaḥ*. *See also* BHŪDEVĪ; TRILOKA.

BHŪDEVĪ. Goddess of the Earth; "Mother Nature"; a personification of the Earth in the form of a **divine mother**. In his incarnation as a boar (**Varāha**), **Viṣṇu** rescues Bhūdevī from the demonic **Hiranyakṣa**. In the ***Mahābhārata***, Bhūdevī again calls out to Viṣṇu to relieve the weight of proliferating humanity on her surface. He accedes to this request, taking on the form of **Kṛṣṇa** and overseeing the events of the *Mahābhārata* war.

BHŪTA. Literally "being," entity. Element; fundamental component of existence. Five such elements are delineated in most Hindu systems of **philosophy**: earth, air, water, fire, and space (**ākāśa**).

Also, a ghost or unquiet spirit that has not yet moved on to its next **rebirth**, usually due either to tragic circumstances surrounding its **death** in its previous incarnation or to unfinished business from that lifetime. *See also* MAHĀBHŪTAS; PRETA.

BHUVANEŚVARA (BHUBANESHWAR). Capital of the Indian state of **Orissa**, site of many **temples** constructed during the classical and early medieval periods. Prominent among these are Liṅgarāja, which is dedicated to **Śiva** (Tribhuvaneśvara, or "Lord of the Three Worlds") and was constructed in the 12th century CE; Vaital **Mandira**, dedicated to **Kālī** (**Cāmuṇḍā**) and constructed in the eighth century CE; and Brahmeśvara, dedicated to Śiva and constructed in the ninth century CE.

BĪJA MANTRA. Seed **mantra**; monosyllabic mantra held to contain the essence of the deity that it evokes, particularly prominent in the practice of **Tantra**. Bīja mantras are seen as being especially powerful. They are often embedded in longer mantras. The best known and most frequently used bīja mantra is **Oṃ**, seen as containing the essence of all mantras, and indeed of all sound and the cosmos itself. Other commonly found examples include *huṃ*, *hrīṃ*, *śrīṃ*, *gaṃ*, *klīṃ*, and *aiṃ*. Bīja mantras do not have a literal meaning, in the sense of a specific denotation by which they can translated. Their power is more evocative than denotative. They make present, in auditory form, the deity or power that they symbolize.

BĪRŪNĪ, AL- (973–1048). Arab Muslim scholar who traveled in India and wrote about Indian customs, particularly religious practices. His *Kitab al-Hind* ("Book of India") and his Arabic translation of the ***Yoga Sūtras*** of **Patañjali** presented a relatively accurate and sympathetic portrayal of Hinduism to the **Islamic** world.

BISHNOIS. Small **Vaiṣṇava** community based primarily in Rājasthān, known for their commitment to the protection of the environment. They have been a central inspiration to the **Chipko movement**. The founder of the Bishnois, a 15th-century figure, Guru Mahārāj Jambajī, established 29 rules for his community, including a ban on the cutting of green trees and the killing of animals. In the region of the largely arid state of Rājasthān where the Bishnois resided, the Bishnoi practice of not cutting green trees is said to have led to the growth of a lush forest, which was targeted by the Mahārāja of Jhodpur, who wished to use the wood from the trees to build a palace for himself. The Bishnois sought to protect the trees by encircling them and chaining themselves to the tree trunks. The Mahārāja was moved by this act and ordered his servants not to harass the Bishnois. In 1973, the founders of the Chipko movement, based in what is now the state of Uttarakhand, followed the lead of the Bishnois, protecting forests from being cut down by loggers by forming a human chain encircling the trees and by hugging the trees—a practice which led to the name "Chipko" and, beyond India, to the term "tree hugger" for anyone concerned about the protection of the environment.

BLAVATSKY, HELENA PETROVNA (1831–1891). Cofounder of the **Theosophical Society**; Russian heiress. In her youth she traveled widely, claiming to have visited Tibet and studied under **enlightened** masters. Having a profound interest in spiritualism and the occult, Blavatsky arrived in the United States in 1873. Along with **Henry Steele Olcott**, she established the Theosophical Society in 1875. The objectives of the society were "to form a nucleus of the universal brotherhood of humanity without distinction of race, creed, sex, **caste**, or color," "to encourage the study of comparative religion, **philosophy**, and science," and "to investigate the unexplained **laws** of nature and the powers latent in man."

A prolific author, Blavatsky's two major works are *Isis Unveiled*, published in 1877, and *The Secret Doctrine*, published in 1888. The latter book reflects the gradually increasing influence of Hinduism and **Buddhism** on Blavatsky's thought. Much of the conceptual content of theosophy is drawn from these two religious traditions, as well as from Western esoteric traditions.

No stranger to controversy, Blavatsky faced numerous accusations throughout her career of engaging in fraudulent displays of spiritual powers. After she and Olcott moved to India in 1879, the British government suspected her of being a Russian spy. Members of the Theosophical Society played prominent roles in the movement for Indian political independence. Theosophists promoted pride and interest among Hindus and Buddhists in their religious and cultural heritage, acting as "reverse missionaries," articulating the idea that Hinduism and Buddhism preserve an ancient global wisdom tradition, or **perennial philosophy**. At one point a strategic alliance began to form between the Theosophical Society and the **Ārya Samāj**. But **Swāmī Dayānanda Sarasvatī** fell out with Blavatsky and Olcott in 1880, when they announced their conversions to Buddhism in **Sri Lanka**. Blavatsky later returned to Europe and died in London in 1891.

BOAR AVATĀRA. *See* VARĀHA.

BOCĀSANVĀSĪ AKṢAR PURUṢOTTAM SWĀMĪNĀRĀYAṆ SANSTHĀ (BAPS). *See* SWĀMĪNĀRĀYAṆ MOVEMENT.

BRAHMĀ. Creator deity; member, along with **Viṣṇu** and **Śiva**, of the **Trimūrti**. When a new cosmic cycle begins, it is Brahmā who brings about the **creation** of the world. He is therefore not a creator *ex nihilo* (from nothing), but the re-creator of the world at the beginning of each cosmic cycle (**kalpa**). The cosmos is then preserved for many eons by Viṣṇu before being destroyed—in order to be renewed and re-created—by Śiva. Brahmā is often identified with the **Vedic** creator deity, **Prajāpati**. He was worshiped as a major deity in ancient India (from roughly 500 BCE to 500 CE) but has not been a prominent object of **devotion** among most Hindus for many centuries, having been overshadowed by Viṣṇu, Śiva, and the **Mother Goddess**. He is usually paired with the **goddess Sarasvatī** as her husband.

BRAHMĀ KUMĀRĪS. Daughters of Brahmā. Hindu-based religious movement that was established in 1937 by **Dāda Lekhrāj** (also known as **Prajāpitar Brahmā**) and is now based at the Brahmā Kumārī Spiritual University on Mount Abu, in the Indian state of **Rajasthan**. Lekhrāj passed the leadership of the organization to his female followers, with whom it has remained. The Brahmā Kumārīs teach a path of **asceticism** with special emphasis on abstention from alcohol. They also hold a belief—unusual for a Hindu sect—in the imminent end of the current world order and the coming of a new Golden Age. *See also* WOMEN.

BRAHMA SŪTRAS. Aphoristic root text of the various **Vedānta** systems of **philosophy** that, along with the ***Upaniṣads*** and the ***Bhagavad Gītā***, forms the ***Prasthāna Traya*** or "threefold foundation" of Vedānta—the three authoritative texts on which every **ācārya**, or founder of a Vedāntic tradition, has written a **bhāṣya**, or commentary.

Estimates of the date of composition of the *Brahma Sūtras* vary. An approximate date of 200 BCE is possible, though it is also very likely that the compilation process was gradual, extending into the Common Era. In terms of relative chronology, the text must have been compiled after the composition of the major *Upaniṣads*, which it summarizes, but prior to the *Bhagavad Gītā*, which mentions it (though this reference may or may not be to this specific text, perhaps referring generically to wisdom **literature** on **Brahman**). The *Brahma Sūtras* are traditionally attributed to **Bādarāyaṇa**, who is identified with **Veda Vyāsa**, the traditional author of the ***Mahābhārata*** and the compiler of the ***Vedas***. As the root text of the Vedānta systems of **philosophy**, its verses are also known as the ***Vedānta Sūtras***.

The *Brahma Sūtras* present an inquiry into the nature of Brahman and collect the major threads of thought on this topic found in the *Upaniṣads*. This text also presents criticisms of other major systems of thought, such as **Sāṃkhya**, **Yoga**, **Jainism**, and both realist and idealist forms of **Buddhism**.

BRAHMACARIN. A person in the state of **brahmacarya**. A celibate student, usually a young Brahmin male.

BRAHMACARYA. The first of the four **āśramas**, or stages of life. It also refers to a state of celibacy or the vow by which one enters such a state. As the first stage of life, the brahmacarya āśrama refers to the "student stage." This typically begins around the age of 12 (sometimes a little earlier, sometimes a little later) when an upper-caste male (usually a Brahmin male) is invested with a **sacred thread** through the **upanayana saṃskāra**.

Traditionally, after the investiture with the sacred thread, the **brahmacarin** leaves home to live with his **guru**, or teacher, where he receives instruction in the ***Vedas*** and in various other relevant forms of **knowledge**, like grammar, mathematics, and **astrology**. In modernity, the brahmacarin typically remains at home, though a ceremonial "departure" is sometimes enacted. Ritually speaking, the brahmacarin is now considered an adult. The upanayana saṃskāra is therefore analogous to such coming-of-age rituals as the Bar Mitzvah of Judaism or the sacrament of Confirmation in **Christianity**. The stage of the brahmacarya ends with the ritual of marriage, which begins the second, **householder (gārhasthya)** āśrama.

The connection of the term "brahmacarya" with celibacy is due to the fact that the student stage is a celibate state, although an adult can also become a brahmacarin in the sense of taking a vow of celibacy, even after having lived the life of a sexually active **householder**. **Mohandās K. Gāndhī**, for example, became a brahmacarin after he and his wife had had four sons. This kind of brahmacarya, undertaken later in life, is a form of **asceticism**, typically practiced for spiritual reasons.

BRĀHMA-MUHŪRTA. Period from roughly 4:30 a.m. to 6 a.m., and regarded as the best time to do one's morning worship and practice **meditation**. A **muhūrta** is approximately an hour and a half in length and each day is divided into 16 muhūrtas.

BRAHMAN. The absolute, ultimate reality, the infinite, literally "the expansive." In the early **Vedic literature**, Brahman is the power that makes the Vedic sacrifice or **yajña** work, the energy of **creation**. In the ***Upaniṣads***, Brahman is understood to be an all-encompassing reality, that from which all things have emerged and to which they will return. Anticipations of this concept can be found as early as the ***Ṛg Veda***, in hymns that describe the universe as emerging from the body of a single cosmic being, often seen as having been offered up in sacrifice in order to create the universe. In the *Upaniṣads*, the concept becomes more abstract: the underlying consciousness that makes any experience possible, or the deep mystery of existence, knowing which all things can be known. To realize the identity of Brahman and **ātman**, the self, is to become liberated from **rebirth**.

In some sections of the *Upaniṣads*, Brahman seems to be an impersonal reality, the substance of consciousness. In other parts of the *Upaniṣads*, Brahman is a personal deity—**God**, or **Īśvara**, the Supreme Being. In **Advaita Vedānta**, Brahman is perceived to have impersonal and personal aspects. The impersonal aspect—**Nirguṇa Brahman**—is Brahman without any limiting qualities. In this aspect, which is preeminent, Brahman is infinite being (**sat**), pure or **non-dual** consciousness (**cit**), and unlimited bliss (**ānanda**). The personal aspect is **Saguṇa Brahman**, or Brahman with qualities, who is identical with God (Īśvara) and the world, acting as both the material and efficient cause of the universe. Theistic systems of **Vedānta** deny that Brahman is the material cause of the universe, identifying Brahman entirely with God (though **Viśiṣṭādvaita Vedānta** sees Brahman as both God and world in a relationship not of identity but of organic unity).

BRAHMÁN. Chief priest in the **Vedic** ritual of sacrifice (**yajña**), whose duty is to know the duties of all the other priests and correct any errors that may occur.

BRĀHMAṆA. Priestly text. The second of the four sections contained within each of the four ***Vedas***. The *Brāhmaṇas* were composed primarily during the period between the composition of the original four *Vedas*, or ***Saṃhitās***, and the *Āraṇyakas*, approximately 800 to 600 BCE according to most contemporary scholarship. They form a commentary on the *Saṃhitās*. Being concerned chiefly with the correct performance of Vedic rituals, they form, along with the original *Saṃhitās*, the **Karma Kanda**, or "**action** portion," of the Vedic **literature**.

BRAHMANISM. The ideology associated with the culture that produced and continued to propagate the ***Vedas***. Brahmanism is not identical to Hinduism, which has assimilated and produced many other ideological and cultural currents through the centuries, some of which have been in explicit tension with Brahmanism. But Brahmanism is the locus of many of the guiding concepts and principles that have become central to Hindu thought and practice. Two central principles of Brahmanism are the sanctity and eternal authority of the *Vedas* and the system of **castes** (or **varṇas**) and stages of life (**āśramas**) by which persons are categorized.

These two principles were strongly rejected by the **śramaṇa** traditions of ancient India (such as **Jainism** and **Buddhism**), and questioned, ignored, or otherwise rendered problematic by subsequent Hindu movements, such as **bhakti** and **Tantra**. Concepts that Brahmanism shares with the other Indic systems of thought include **karma**, **rebirth**, and **mokṣa**, though it may have adopted these fairly late (c. 6th century BCE).

BRAHMIN. Member of the priestly **caste** (or **varṇa**), the highest of the traditional four castes into which Brahmanical society is divided. According to

Brahmanism, birth as a Brahmin is a prerequisite for higher spiritual knowledge, which can only be acquired by studying the ***Vedas***. Some late Vedic and post-Vedic texts, however, challenge this idea, as do the Hindu reformers of the modern period.

BRAHMO SAMĀJ. Hindu reform organization first established in **Calcutta** in 1828, under the name *Brahmo Sabhā*, by **Rām Mohan Roy** (1772–1833). The Brahmo Samāj was most popular among middle-class Bengali intellectuals who had received significant exposure to European culture and education, due to the work of Christian missionaries, but who also had a strong sense of identification with Hinduism and Indian culture. The effort of these intellectuals was to reform Hinduism, opposing practices such as **satī** and the use of images (**mūrtis**) in worship, which they saw as later additions to an originally monotheistic Hinduism taught in the ***Upaniṣads***. Roy, a prolific author and energetic activist, translated some of the *Upaniṣads* into Bengali, and wrote many pamphlets as well, decrying what he saw as the evils of certain Hindu practices, and **Christianity** as well. Brahmo Samāj worship was modeled on Protestant worship services, with hymns and sermons drawing upon the *Upaniṣads*, rather than the Bible.

Theologically, the teachings of the Brahmo Samāj display a strong leaning toward Unitarianism, and a number of Brahmo Samāj members traveled to England in the 19th century to study at the Unitarian seminary at Harris-Manchester College in Oxford. With its emphasis on an original, "pure" **Vedic monotheism** later corrupted into popular Hindu **polytheism**, Brahmo Samāj teaching in many ways anticipates that of the **Ārya Samāj** of **Swāmī Dayānanda Sarasvatī**.

Many prominent Bengali Hindu thinkers of the 19th and 20th centuries were connected with the Brahmo Samāj, including Roy's successors to the leadership of the organization, **Debendranāth Tagore** (1817–1905) and **Keshub Chunder Sen** (1838–1884); Tagore's grandson, the renowned **poet**, playwright, composer, and Nobel laureate **Rabindranāth Tagore** (1861–1941); and **Narendranāth Datta** (1863–1902), who is better known by his monastic name, **Swāmī Vivekānanda**, and who was a member of the Brahmo Samāj until he became a disciple of **Ramakrishna**.

Though highly influential in the 19th century, the Brahmo Samāj maintains a relatively small but devoted following today, largely confined to **Bengal**.

BRAJ. Hindi pronunciation of **Vraja**.

BṚHADĀRAṆYAKA UPANIṢAD. Great Āraṇyaka Upaniṣad; oldest and longest of the *Upaniṣads* (or, alternatively, the latest of the *Āraṇyakas*), it is contained as the conclusion of the *Śatapatha Brāhmaṇa*, which is, in turn, contained within the *Śukla* (White) ***Yajur Veda***. Its length and antiquity have made it a major authoritative source for the **Vedānta** systems of **philosophy**. Probably compiled around 500 BCE (though from oral sources a good deal older), the centerpiece of this text is the teaching of the sage **Yājñavalkya**, the likely originator of the traditions that this *Upaniṣad* preserves. Two different recensions of the text exist—the *Kāṇva* and the *Mādhyandina*—though their philosophical content is not substantially different.

This text contains the first unambiguous Hindu scriptural reference to the process of **rebirth**, the idea that the nature of one's rebirth is determined by one's **actions (karma)**, and the idea that one can attain freedom from rebirth (**mokṣa**) by giving up **desire** and merging with **Brahman** (4.4.5–7).

BṚHAD-DEVATĀ. "Great Text on Deities"; systematic presentation of the attributes and deeds of the **Vedic** deities (**devas**); attributed to **Śaunaka** and likely composed between 500 and 400 BCE. This text has continued to be an authoritative source for a mainstream Hindu understanding of the Vedic deities.

BṚHASPATI. "Great Father"; **Vedic** deity; god of wisdom and teacher, or **guru**, of the **gods**. Bṛhaspati is the presiding deity of the planet Jupiter and the guru referred to in the name **Guruvāra**, the Hindu name for Thursday, the day of the week governed by Jupiter in Hindu **astrology**. He embodies the intellect and the power of speech of the cosmic man (**puruṣa**) from whose body the universe was formed according to Vedic cosmology.

Intriguingly, Bṛhaspati is attributed with developing the **Cārvāka**, or **materialist** system of **philosophy**, which denies the validity of the ***Vedas***. The lost root texts of this system are called the *Bārhaspatya Sūtras*, or "Root Texts Attributed to Bṛhaspati."

BRIGHT HALF. *See* ŚUKLA PAKṢA.

BRITISH EAST INDIA COMPANY. British trade organization established in 1600. It was given a monopoly on British trade with Asia and granted vast resources, including ships, by Queen Elizabeth I for the purpose of expanding the British commercial presence in India and Indonesia. The company established trading posts on the Indian coast that became the basis for large modern cities such as **Calcutta**, Bombay, and **Madras**.

In order to protect company holdings, ever-increasing numbers of British soldiers were sent to India. The company also hired Indian mercenaries (known as *sepoys*) and entered into alliances with local rulers, often becoming embroiled in complex rivalries and conflicts among Indian kings. This ever-expanding military and political presence—combined with the marked disunity among the various Indian polities, which prevented the formation of any serious Indian resistance—eventually led the company to become the dominant force in Indian political and economic life.

Discontent among many Indians with the growing British domination of India and the exploitation and denigration of Indian culture—including Hinduism and **Islam**—that it involved eventually led to an armed revolt by sepoys in 1857. This event continues to be referred to by British historians as the Sepoy Mutiny and by Indian historians as the War of Independence. Alarmed by this rebellion, Queen Victoria dissolved the company in 1858 and put India under the direct rule of the British government.

BROWN, W. NORMAN (1892–1975). Indologist and **Sanskritist** who held the chair in Sanskrit at the University of Pennsylvania from 1926 to 1966 and was curator of Indian **art** at the Philadelphia Museum of Art. He organized the American Oriental Society in 1926 and edited its journal for many years.

BUDDHA (c. 490–410 BCE). The "Awakened One"; Siddhārtha Gautama, founder of **Buddhism** and, in some Hindu accounts, the ninth **avatāra** of **Viṣṇu**. According to the traditional accounts of his life, the Buddha was a prince, the son of the ruler of the Śakya clan, whose territory was located in what is now southern **Nepal**. Becoming a **renouncer** at the age of 30, he attained **nirvāṇa** six years later and began teaching, establishing an order of monks and nuns and lay followers. He died at the age of 80.

A member of the **śramaṇa** movement, the Buddha, like **Mahāvīra** and others, did not accept the claims of **Brahmanism** that one's birth **caste** is a reflection of one's level of spiritual attainment, that a birth in the **Brahmin** caste is a mark of spiritual authority, and that the ***Vedas*** and the ceremonies they enjoin are divinely inspired. He found the sacrifice of animals in the Vedic **yajña** to be particularly objectionable. He shared with Brahmanism—particularly the teaching of the ***Upaniṣads***—the concepts of **karma**, **rebirth**, and **liberation (mokṣa)** from the cycle of rebirth. His teaching on the renunciation of desire as necessary to liberation is quite close to that of the ***Bṛhadāraṇyaka Upaniṣad***.

Buddhism subsequently became a major ideological rival of Brahmanism, both of which shaped what eventually emerged as Hinduism. The concept of the Buddha as an avatāra of Viṣṇu is a Brahmanical attempt to cope with the popularity of Buddhism, and the changes that this concept undergoes reflect the changing relationship of Buddhism to Hindu identity: from fierce rival to assimilated cultural resource. Some early accounts of the Buddha avatāra are of an anti-Buddhist nature, claiming that Viṣṇu took the form of the Buddha for the purpose of deluding demonic persons and persuading them not to perform the sacrifice (or **yajña**) enjoined in the ***Veda***. But later accounts of the Buddha avatāra are more positive, presenting the Buddha as a Vedic reformer who ended the practice of **animal sacrifice** to promote the ideal of compassion. The concept of the Buddha avatāra, both in its critical and in its more appreciative forms, is a Hindu interpretation of the life and teaching of the Buddha, and is generally not accepted by Buddhists.

BUDDHI. Intellect; one of the basic elements that constitute existence, or **tanmātras**, of the **Sāṃkhya** system of **philosophy**. In the **Yoga** of **Patañjali**, buddhi, in combination with **ahaṃkara** (ego) and the **indriyas** (senses) constitutes **citta** (the **mind**).

Also, along with **Siddhi** ("Success"), Buddhi is the name of one of the two wives of **Ganeśa**.

BUDDHISM. **Śramaṇa** tradition established by the **Buddha** (c. 490–410 BCE). By the end of the 13th century CE, this tradition had largely died out in India but had spread beyond India, throughout Southeast and Central Asia and into China, Korea, and Japan to become a major world religion. The major forms of Buddhism are Theravāda (Teaching of the Elders), which is predominant in both **Sri Lanka** and **Southeast Asia**; Mahāyāna (Great Vehicle), which is practiced mainly in China, Korea, and Japan; and Vajrayāna (**Tantric** Buddhism), which has traditionally been prominent in **Nepal**, Tibet, and Mongolia.

Like other śramaṇa traditions, such as **Jainism**, Buddhism shares many core ideas of Hinduism, such as the doctrines of **karma** and **rebirth** and the aspiration for **liberation** (**mokṣa**) from the cycle of rebirth as a central salvific goal. Buddhism shares with other śramaṇa traditions a rejection of the claims of **Brahmanism** with regard to **caste** and the authority of the ***Vedas***. Specifically, it rejects the idea that birth caste is a reflection of one's spiritual attainment (with its implication that the **Brahmins** are the most advanced of human beings) and Vedic injunctions to perform **animal sacrifice**. Buddhism was the main ideological rival of Brahmanism for many centuries. As Hinduism coalesced from many Indic traditions, however, many Buddhist concepts were assimilated into it. For example, although nominal affirmation of the authority of the *Vedas* continues, practices such as animal sacrifice gradually fell by the wayside, being replaced by **vegetarianism**. Though the caste system continues to be practiced, movements that affirm the irrelevance of caste to the spiritual path, such as **bhakti** and **Tantra**, have many Hindu followers.

Buddhism died out in India due to a combination of foreign invasions, resulting in a mass destruction of monasteries and **temples**, and Hindu assimilation. In the 20th century, **Bhīmrao Ambedkar** revived Indian Buddhism, leading a mass conversion of **Dalits** to Buddhism as a protest against the ongoing Hindu practice of caste. An influx of Tibetan Buddhist refugees, led by the Dalai Lama, has also led to a reinfusion of life into Buddhism in India. *See also* AMBEDKARITE BUDDHISM.

BUDDHISM, AMBEDKARITE. *See* AMBEDKARITE BUDDHISM.

BUḌHA. The planet Mercury; son of the deity **Soma** and the **goddess Tāra**. *See also* ASTROLOGY; NAVAGRAHAS.

BUḌHAVĀRA. Wednesday, the day of the week that is governed by Buḍha, the planet Mercury. *See also* CALENDAR, HINDU.

BUFFALO DEMON. *See* MAHIṢĀSURA.

BUITENEN, JOHANNES ADRIANUS BERNARDUS VAN (1928–1979). Dutch-born **Indologist** and **Sanskritist** who founded and chaired the Department of South Asian Languages and Civilizations at the University of Chicago. A prolific scholar, his best-known achievement is the translation of the first five books of the ***Mahābhārata*** and the ***Bhagavad Gītā***.

C

CAITANYA (1486–1533). Bengali Vaiṣṇava saint and devotee of **Kṛṣṇa**; major figure of the **bhakti** movement and founder of the **Gauḍīya Vaiṣṇava** tradition, with which the **International Society for Krishna Consciousness** (ISKCON) is in close continuity. At the age of 22 he met a **sannyāsī** of **Madhva**'s theistic **Dvaita Vedānta** tradition, whose outlook greatly influenced him. He then traveled to and spent most of his life in **Puri**, in what is now the Indian state of **Orissa**, at the **temple** of **Jagannātha**. Much like the **Bauls**, by whom he may also have been influenced, Caitanya promoted ecstatic devotional singing as a way to express and evoke bhakti and give worship to Kṛṣṇa. He made several pilgrimages to **Vraja**, the area of **Mathura** and **Vṛndāvana**, where Kṛṣṇa spent most of his early life according to the ***Bhāgavata Purāṇa***. He reinvigorated Kṛṣṇa devotion in the region, making it a major pilgrimage center. Caitanya also established the **Gosvāmin** theological tradition. According to Caitanya's teaching, Kṛṣṇa is the supreme deity—**God** in a **monotheistic** sense—of whom all other deities are either manifestations or subordinates. Caitanya's followers view him as an **avatāra**.

CAKRA. Literally, a wheel. In **Tantra**, a cakra is an energy center located in the **subtle body (sukṣma śarīra)**. According to Tantric thought, subtle energy bodies exist in the same space as, but on a different vibrational wavelength from, the physical, gross body (**sthūla śarīra**). These subtle bodies are made up of the **kośas**, or sheaths, in which the soul or **ātman** resides (specifically, the four kośas other than the **anna-maya-kośa**, which is identical to the gross body). In the space that corresponds to the base of the spine, a subtle energy, or **śakti**, resides. While it is residing in this space, it is also referred to as the **kuṇḍalini**, or coiled energy, because it is said to resemble a coiled serpent in this state. In Tantric **yoga**, one of the goals of practice is to raise this energy from the base of the spine to the crown of the head, which are linked by a subtle nerve channel called the suṣumna nādī, and which occupies roughly the same space as the spinal cord.

Along the suṣumna nādī are the seven cakras. These energy centers are activated as the śakti or kuṇḍalini rises through the suṣumna nādī. The bottommost of the cakras, the **mūladhāra cakra**, is located at the base of the spine.

The rest of the cakras are the **svādhiṣṭhāna cakra**, which is aligned with the navel; the **maṇipūra cakra**, which is aligned with the solar plexus; the **anāhata cakra**, which is centered in the heart; the **viśuddha cakra**, which is in the throat; the **ājñā cakra** or third eye, which is just above the space between the eyebrows; and, at the crown of the head, the **sahāsrara cakra** or "thousand-petaled lotus," which, when energized by the rising śakti, produces a blissful state that, according to Tantra, advances one quickly toward **enlightenment**.

According to the tradition of **Siddha Yoga**, a contemporary **Śaiva** movement with a strongly Tantric dimension, an enlightened teacher, or **guru**, can raise one's śakti from the base of the spine to the crown of the head—activating all of the cakras in the process—with a thought, word, or touch. This experience is called **śaktipat**.

CALCUTTA. City established by the **British East India Company** in 1696 near the village of Kālīkata and the **Kālīghāṭ temple**. Now known as Kolkata, it is one of the largest cities in India and the capital of the state of **West Bengal**. Calcutta served as the administrative capital of British India until 1911, when the administration shifted to **New Delhi**, which remains the capital of the Republic of India today.

Calcutta has a rich intellectual and cultural history, being the center of much of the Hindu reform that occurred in the 19th and early 20th centuries. Major figures of this period who resided at some point in Calcutta include **Rām Mohan Roy**, **Debendranāth Tagore**, **Keshub Chunder Sen**, **Ramakrishna**, **Swāmī Vivekānanda**, **Aurobindo Ghose**, and **Rabindranāth Tagore**. The city remains the main center of activity for the **Brahmo Samāj**, and it also houses the administrative headquarters of the **Ramakrishna Order**. *See also* BENGAL.

CALENDAR, HINDU. The traditional Hindu calendar is a lunar calendar on the basis of which the dates of Hindu holidays are determined and astrological calculations carried out. The calendar is made up of 12 lunar months, each of which is further divided into a **bright half (śukla pakṣa)**, during which the **moon** is waxing, and a **dark half (kṛṣṇa pakṣa)**, during which it is waning. Distinct from these two halves are **Pūrṇimā** (full-moon day) and **Amavasya** (new-moon day), which mark, respectively, the transition from the bright half to the dark half and from the dark half to the bright half. The Hindu lunar months are called **Chaitra** (March–April), **Vaiśākha** (April–May), **Jyaiṣṭha** (May–June), **Āṣāḍha** (June–July), **Śravaṇa** (July–August), **Bhadra** (August–September), **Aśvina** (September–October), **Kārtika** (October–November), **Agrahayaṇa** (November–December), **Pauṣa** (December–January), **Magha** (January–February), and **Phalguna** (February–March). Each month begins the day after the new-moon day (Amavasya) of the month just before it. Amavasya marks the end of a month, and Pūrṇimā its midpoint. Whenever a **pūjā**, or worship ceremony, is conducted, it is customary near the beginning of the ceremony to announce the date: for example, "the third day of the bright half of the month of Phalguna," or "the fifth day of the dark half of Vaiśākha," and so forth.

The Hindu week consists of seven days: **Ravivāra** (Sunday), **Somavāra** (Monday), **Mañgalvāra** (Tuesday), **Buḍhavāra** (Wednesday), **Guruvāra** (Thursday), **Śukravāra** (Friday), and **Śānivāra** (Saturday). Astrologically, each day of the week is governed by a different planet. The "**planets**" consist of the five planets that are visible to the naked eye (Mercury, Venus, Mars, Jupiter, and Saturn, although not in that order) plus the sun and the moon. There are numerous local variations on this basic calendrical model. *See also* ASTROLOGY.

CĀLUKYA. Hindu dynasty that ruled a large kingdom encompassing much of central and southern India from the sixth to the 12th centuries of the Common Era. At its height, during the seventh and eighth centuries, this kingdom encompassed what are now the states of Maharashtra and **Karnataka**, and much of Andhra Pradesh. The Cālukyas constructed major **temple** complexes at the towns of **Aihole**, **Bādāmī**, and **Paṭṭadakal**.

CAMPHOR. Holy substance used during worship (**pūjā**). A small amount is typically set aflame. The smoke and flame from the camphor are regarded as having a purifying effect. The lit camphor is held in a small lamp or **dīyā** and waved in front of an image (**mūrti**) of a deity—a variation of the ceremony known as **āratī**. *See also* PŪJĀ.

CĀMUṆḌĀ. Destroyer of demons; fierce from of the **Mother Goddess** who emanates from the forehead of the goddess **Durgā** in order to destroy evil. Having a frightening appearance, Cāmuṇḍā has four arms and hands and carries a sword, a noose, and a club. Resembling **Kālī**, she wears a garland of corpses and the hide of an elephant. She is also known as Cāmuṇḍī.

CANAKYA. *See* KAUṬILYA.

CAṆḌĀLA. A member of the lowest **caste**—an **Untouchable** or **Dalit** community. This caste is traditionally responsible for the cremation of corpses, which is regarded as a very polluting activity, given that dead bodies are considered the most impure of substances. Due to their untouchable status, Caṇḍālas are often expected to live far from the rest of the community. **Rabindranāth Tagore** composed a widely acclaimed opera critical of the caste system entitled *Caṇḍālikā*, about a female Caṇḍāla. As a female member of the lowest of the castes, a Caṇḍālikā would be regarded as being at the very bottom of Hindu society. In the opera, the main character, accustomed to being shunned by others, is approached by a **Buddhist** monk who, having no regard for caste restrictions, asks her for a drink of water. This is a transformative moment for the main character, who discovers her human dignity and becomes a Buddhist nun.

CAṆḌĪ (CAṆḌIKĀ). "Wrath," "wrathful"; any fierce form of the **Mother Goddess**, often with either 18 or 20 hands. A wrathful form of this kind is assumed so the goddess can destroy evil. The worship of fierce **goddesses** is especially popular in **Bengal** and is often associated with **Tantra**. The ***Devī Mahātmya***, a text that narrates the deeds of the fierce forms of the goddess, is also known as the *Caṇḍī Paṭh* ("Reading on Caṇḍī"). *See also* DURGĀ; KĀLĪ.

CAṆḌĪDĀS (fl. 15th century CE, born 1408). Vaiṣṇava saint of **Bengal** and member of the **Sahajiya** movement, which emphasized highly spontaneous and ecstatic expressions of devotion and shared the **Tantric** sensibility of using the senses to transcend the senses. The **bhakti poetry** of Caṇḍīdās makes extensive use of the imagery of the love between **Rādhā** and **Kṛṣṇa** to evoke the loving relationship between the devotee and the divine. His songs exerted a strong influence on **Caitanya**. His most famous work is the *Śrikṛṣṇa Kīrtana* ("Glory of Lord Kṛṣṇa"), which narrates the romance of Rādhā and Kṛṣṇa over the course of 412 songs. Altogether, 1,250 songs are attributed to Caṇḍīdās, although it is likely that there was more than one author by this name, perhaps in a shared lineage.

Though he was a devotee of Kṛṣṇa, the name *Caṇḍīdās* means "servant of **Caṇḍī**" (the **Mother Goddess** in her fierce form).

CANDRA. The **moon**; often identified with the **Vedic** deity **Soma**, who also represents the hallucinogenic plant whose juice, mixed with milk, was used by ancient **Brahmins** to evoke an experience of the divine. The phases of the moon represent this substance being consumed by the **devas** (during the dark half of the month, or **Kṛṣṇa Pakṣa**, when the moon is waning) and replenished (during the bright half, or **Śukla Pakṣa**, when the moon is waxing).

CANDRASEKHARA SARASVATĪ, ŚRĪ (1894–1994). The 68th **Śaṅkarācārya** of the Kāñcī Kāmakoti Pīṭa, or **maṭha**, at **Kāñcīpuram** in Tamil Nadu, a role that he held for a record 87 years. He assumed his responsibilities at the unusually young age of 13 when his cousin, the 67th head of the maṭha, died prematurely of a fever.

CARAKA (c. 3rd century BCE). Presumed author of the *Caraka Saṃhitā*, a work of **Āyur Veda**, or traditional Hindu medicine.

CĀRVĀKA (c. 3rd century BCE). Founder of the **materialist** system of Indian philosophy (**darśana**); also a name for the philosophical system itself, which is also known as the **Lokāyata** system. Cārvāka's system is, like **Jainism** and **Buddhism**, a **nāstika** or nonorthodox system of thought that denies the authority of the ***Vedas*** and of the **Brahmin** caste. Unlike all other systems of Indian philosophy, Cārvāka's system denies the reality of **karma** and **rebirth** and sees religion as a fundamentally deluded activity, developed in order to satisfy the greed of those who promulgate it (both Brahmin and **śramaṇa**). This system affirms that sensory perception is the only valid basis for knowledge (**pramāṇa**), thereby denying the validity both of the *Vedas* and of the extrasensory **yogic** knowledge affirmed by Jains and Buddhists. It claims that the sole aim of life is sensory enjoyment.

The original writings of this system survive only in fragmentary form, as quoted in texts of other systems aiming to refute it. The authoritative **sūtras** or root texts of this system are the *Bārhaspatya Sūtras* (that is, texts claiming to derive from the teaching of the sage **Bṛhaspati**), but the full text has not yet been recovered.

CASTE. System of hereditary occupational groups arranged in a hierarchy. The word *caste* is derived from the Portuguese word *casta*, which means "color" and seems to be a translation of the **Sanskrit** term ***varṇa***. Contrary to popular belief, varṇa does not refer to skin color but to a set of colors assigned to the four main subgroups of Hindu society based on the mixture of the three **guṇas**, or essential qualities, that each group is held to possess.

The only reference to the caste system in the earliest **Vedic** texts is in the ***Puruṣa Sukta*** of the ***Ṛg Veda***, where the four main varṇas—**Brahmins** (priests and intellectuals), **Kṣatriyas** (warriors and administrators), **Vaiśyas** (common people, economic producers), and **Śūdras** (servants)—are described as emerging from various parts of the body of the cosmic man from whom the entire universe was formed, according to Vedic cosmology. No reference is made in the Vedic ***Saṃhitās*** to a hereditary system, and indeed the idea of a hereditary system is contradicted by some Vedic hymns in which the speaker and his parents are referred to as practicing different trades.

In later Vedic **literature**, the story of **Satyakāma** in the ***Chāndogya Upaniṣad*** is suggestive of the possibility that one might come by one's caste purely through the possession of the appropriate personal qualities (*guṇas*) rather than through birth, an idea found most prominently in **śramaṇa** traditions, such as **Jainism** and **Buddhism**, and reasserted in the modern period by the founder of the **Ārya Samāj**, **Swāmī Dayānanda Sarasvatī**, as well as by **Mohandās K. Gāndhī**.

But by the period of the ***Dharma Śāstras*** (c. 300 BCE), the idea of castes based on birth (**jāti**) had become predominant in Hindu society. Although the system of four varṇas is the version of caste most commonly mentioned in the Hindu **scriptures**, the effective living unit in actual practice is the jāti, which could be described as a subset or "subcaste" within one of the four main varṇas. Each varṇa contains dozens of jātis, which represent more specialized tasks under the larger rubric of one of the categories of priesthood, political authority, economic production, or servitude.

Though it has typically been the case that caste, seen largely as a matter of birth, has not allowed for social mobility, that has not been a uniform practice. Entire groups have managed to advance in the caste hierarchy through a process of adopting practices associated with higher castes. Scholars have labeled this process **Sanskritization.**

While caste has proved to be highly effective and resilient as a method for both ordering and preserving Indian society, it has also been the target of much internal and external criticism throughout the centuries. So Jains and Buddhists, though continuing to practice caste as a way of organizing society, rejected the notion that one's birth caste was in any way a reflection of one's spiritual advancement, or that caste was a function of one's **karma**—the dominant view of **Brahmanism**. Renunciation came to be seen, even within Brahmanism, as a way of removing oneself from the restrictions of caste, although the most conservative Brahmanical traditions insist that one must be born as a male Brahmin to be eligible for renunciation. **Tantra** and the **bhakti** movements both share the Jain and Buddhist insistence that one's birth caste is irrelevant to one's ability to make progress toward **mokṣa**, or **liberation** from the cycle of **rebirth**. At the same time, though, none of these movements has ever led to a major breakdown of caste in practice. Even Abrahamic traditions such as **Christianity** and **Islam**, which reject the notion of caste and affirm human equality and initially held great appeal for members of the lowest castes—particularly the **Dalits**, or **Untouchables**, whose hereditary professions excluded them from most interaction with the rest of society—did not have a significant impact on the caste system. Many Indian Christians and Muslims are members of castes today, choosing professions and marriage partners accordingly. Caste is deeply rooted in Indian society but is neither limited to nor unambiguously justified by Hinduism.

Only in the modern period have serious efforts begun either to eradicate prejudice based on caste (while preserving the basic concept of the caste system) or to eradicate the caste system altogether. The leading figure in the movement to abolish caste has been Dr. **Bhīmrao Ambedkar**, the primary author of the Indian constitution. **Arvind Sharma** has argued that all Hindus should see themselves as sharing the duties of all four of the varṇas.

It remains debated today whether caste is intrinsic to Hinduism as a religion or is an Indian social system that has been justified on the basis of Hinduism but that may be fundamentally incompatible with some aspects of Hindu **philosophy**, such as its emphasis on the unity of existence and seeing the divine in all beings.

CASTEISM. Prejudice or bigotry based on **caste**, which is illegal under the constitution of India but which nevertheless persists in many parts of India, particularly in rural areas.

CHAITRA. Month of the **Hindu calendar** that corresponds roughly to the period from mid-March to mid-April.

CHĀNDOGYA UPANIṢAD. One of the earliest ***Upaniṣads***, likely composed between 500 and 400 BCE. It is part of the *Chāndogya Brāhmaṇa*, which, in turn, is part of the ***Sāma Veda***. A relatively lengthy Upaniṣad, particularly well-known portions of this text include the sage Uddālaka's teaching to this son, Śvetaketu, on the identity of the self, or **ātman**, and **Brahman**, using the refrain "You are that" (*tat-tvam asi*); early reflections on the esoteric meaning of the **mantra Oṃ**; the story of **Satyakāma**, who is initiated into the study of the ***Vedas*** on the basis of his honesty, despite the fact that his mother is of low caste and the identity of his father is unknown; and the teaching of **Prajāpati** to the **devas** and **asuras**, which establishes **materialism** as the doctrine of the asuras. *See also* VEDĀNTA.

CHARIOT. The image of the chariot is an ancient one in Hindu thought and culture, being found as early as the ***Ṛg Veda***. The technology of chariot making also has great significance for the question of Hindu origins and the issue of the relationship between **Vedic** culture and other **Indo-European** societies. The early Vedic deities, the **devas**, are frequently depicted as riding in chariots, and the image of the sun god riding a chariot daily through the sky is common to many Indo-European belief systems, including Vedic thought. The metaphor of the chariot as a symbol for the physical body, with the **soul** as the rider, the **mind** as the driver, and the senses as the horses, is utilized in the ***Kaṭha Upaniṣad*** (c. 400–300 BCE) and, one could argue, alluded to implicitly as the setting of the ***Bhagavad Gītā***. The same image is utilized by the Greek philosopher Plato in the *Phaedrus*, who was either influenced by Indian thought (perhaps indirectly, through the influence of Pythagoras) or was tapping into the same Indo-European cultural heritage as the authors of the *Upaniṣads*.

In terms of Hindu origins, the appearance of light chariots and chariot technology in India between 1900 and 1700 BCE, but already present in Central Asia between 2300 and 2000 BCE, supports the **Āryan Migration Theory**. Though, as opponents of this theory have pointed out, crossing into India through Afghanistan on such chariots is a practical impossibility, persons with knowledge of this technology crossing into India by other means (such as on foot) is not at all impossible. *See also* JAGANNĀTHA; KONĀRAK; VIMĀNA.

CHATTERJEE, BANKIM CHANDRA (1838–1894). Bengali novelist, **poet**, political activist, and the author of the national song of India, "Vande Mataram." Chatterjee was a major literary figure, pioneering the genre of the novel in Bengali, as well an inspiration to the emerging Indian independence movement. An early **Hindu Nationalist**, the India that Chatterjee envisioned was a Hindu one, independent of both British and **Islamic** rule.

CHATTOPADHYAY, BANKIM CHANDRA. *See* CHATTERJEE, BANKIM CHANDRA.

CHENNAI. Contemporary name for **Madras**.

CHIDVILĀSĀNANDA, SWĀMĪ (1955–). *See* GURUMAYĪ.

CHIPKO MOVEMENT. An Indian environmental movement that emerged in 1973 in opposition to logging in the **Himalayan** foothills of what is now the state of Uttarakhand. Inspired by the **Bishnois** and the nonviolent methods of **Mohandās K. Gāndhī**, the activists of the Chipko movement protected their sacred forest from being cut down by loggers by forming a human chain encircling the trees and by hugging the trees—a practice that led to the name "Chipko" and, beyond India, to the term "tree hugger" for anyone concerned about the protection of the environment.

CHRISTIANITY. The world's largest religion, in terms of numbers of adherents, and a member, along with Judaism and **Islam**, of the Abrahamic family of traditions, sharing a common worldview that includes **monotheism**, divine revelation and divine intervention in human history, a single lifetime, a day of judgment, and an everlasting afterlife either in a heavenly paradise or a hellish state of punishment (though exceptions and variations in regard to this basic worldview can be found across all three of these traditions).

In terms of interactions with Hinduism, Christianity has been present in India for many centuries, the most ancient Indian Christian communities being located in the state of **Kerala**, on the southwest coast of the subcontinent, which is still home to the majority of Indian Christians. According to one Indian Christian tradition, the religion was first brought to India by the Apostle Thomas, and so dates to the first century of the Common Era, and the most ancient group of Christians in India are often referred to as "St. Thomas Christians." Reliable historical data, however, cannot place Christians in India before the fifth century of the Common Era. These early Indian Christians, known as the *Nasranis*, seem largely to have been Jewish converts who fled the Roman Empire after the Second Temple in Jerusalem was destroyed. Their churches are modeled closely on synagogues. Today, these Christians are largely affiliated with the Syrian Orthodox Church.

Religiously significant interaction between these Christians and Hindus seems to have been fairly minimal, though some have argued that Christian influence is discernible in the emergence and popularity of **bhakti** traditions in southern India in the middle of the first millennium of the Common Era. But for all intents and purposes, the Jewish and Christian communities in the southwestern coastal regions of India in ancient times seem to have been largely self-contained, endogamous **castes**.

Extensive Christian proselytizing activity did not occur in India until the 16th century, at the onset of the period of European colonization. The first European Christian missionaries in India were Roman Catholics—mainly Jesuits—operating in southern India, particularly in areas where Portuguese colonies were established, such as Goa. The older indigenous St. Thomas Christians experienced extensive persecution at the hands of the Portuguese government. Protestant missionaries arrived a couple of centuries later, with British colonization. Hindu reactions to Christian missionary activities have ranged from conversion, to indifference, to dialogue and engagement, to hostility.

Conversions have largely been among **Dalits** and tribal peoples (**ādivāsīs**), many of whom have seen the Christian teaching of the equality of all people before **God** as a means to escape the **caste** system (although converts have often continued to engage in caste-based practices even after adopting Christianity).

Indifference has been the predominant reaction of most traditional Hindu religious authorities, such as those **Brahmins** and **sannyāsins** who operate in a largely **Sanskritic** intellectual milieu and who have not seen Christianity as presenting a serious challenge to the worldviews of their particular traditions, or **saṃpradāyas**.

Dialogue and engagement has largely been on the part of those Hindus who have had an extensive exposure to Western education, starting with the Hindu reformers of the 19th century, like **Rām Mohan Roy**, **Debendranāth Tagore**, **Keshub Chunder Sen**, and **Swāmī Vivekānanda**, and continuing into the 20th century with **Mohandās K. Gāndhī**. A significant result of such engagement for Hinduism has been the rise of **Neo-Vedānta**, which accepts the validity of many Christian criticisms of Hinduism—such as missionary criticisms of the injustices of the caste system—but which reformulates Hindu thought and practice rather than abandoning it in favor of Christianity (and often turns a critical eye back upon Christianity itself). The attitudes of Hindus toward Christianity who have engaged with it in this way are complex, often being articulated in terms of a profound appreciation for Christ and his teachings—as found, for example, in the Sermon on the Mount—combined with strong criticisms of institutional Christianity and Christian doctrine. The doctrine that salvation is available only through Christ is considered to be particularly objectionable and is frequently contrasted with Hindu religious pluralism.

Hostility to Christianity has largely been articulated by **Hindu Nationalists**, who connect Christian missionary activity with colonialism and neo-colonialism, seeing it as a form of aggressive and predatory cultural imperialism.

CIDAMBARAM. One of the most important **Śaiva temples**, built in southern India in the 10th century of the Common Era by the **Coḷa** dynasty. It houses 108 images of **Śiva** in his form as Lord of the Cosmic **Dance**, or **Nāṭarāja**, as well as shrines to the members of Śiva's family: his wife, **Pārvatī** (the **Mother Goddess**), and his sons, **Gaṇeśa** and **Skanda** (also called **Kārttikeya**, **Subramaṇya**, **Murugan**, **Kumāra**, and **Ṣaṇmukha**).

CIRCUMAMBULATION. Way of honoring an image, or **mūrti**, of a deity, by walking around the image in a clockwise direction, keeping the image to one's right side. *See also* PRADAKṢINA.

CIT. Consciousness. In **Advaita Vedānta**, cit is distinguished from **vijñāna**, which is our ordinary, dualistic consciousness, which is characterized by the distinction between subject and object and is an effect of **māyā**, or the cosmic illusion produced by **avidyā**, or primordial ignorance of the true nature of reality as **Brahman**. Brahman, according to Advaita Vedānta, is pure consciousness, or cit: that is, consciousness free from the duality of subject and object. It is the simple reality of awareness, without the idea of a subject or object. Cit is all-pervasive and free from limiting factors. In addition to cit, Brahman is also said to be infinite being (**sat**) and unlimited bliss (**ānanda**).

CITTA. Consciousness; **mind**; thought; "mind-stuff," that is, consciousness not in the sense of pure awareness (**cit**), but the medium of consciousness, or that through which consciousness manifests in and as the world of phenomenal experience. In **Patañjali**'s system of **yoga**, citta is made up of intellect (**buddhi**), ego (**ahaṃkāra**), and the senses (**indriyas**) working in concert. It is the fluctuations of citta that yoga is intended to still. In **Kaśmīr Śaivism**, citta is the individual consciousness—that is, universal consciousness (cit) as limited by and manifested in and as an individual mind.

CIVAVĀKKIYAR (fl. 9th century CE). One of the **Nāyanār Śaiva Tamil bhakti poets**. Like many of the poet-saints of the bhakti movement, Civavākkiyar extols the personal encounter with the divine over external worship and ritual. He was particularly critical of **caste** prejudice and the use of **images in worship**.

COCONUT. This fruit is an extremely important and widely used part of Hindu rituals. A coconut placed in a pot and surrounded by leaves is a symbol of both **Lakṣmī, goddess** of wealth, and of fertility. In **pūjā**, or worship, a coconut stands in for the deity. Though a representation of the deity may also be present, it is the coconut that is actually utilized in the ritual. A coconut is often broken before some rituals to ensure divine blessings.

COḶA. Important **Tamil** dynasty that, at its height in the 11th century, ruled all of southern India and **Sri Lanka**, with vassal states in **Southeast Asia** as well. The dynasty rose to ascendancy in the ninth century and was disestablished in the 13th century. This dynasty had a profound impact on Hindu culture in southern India, sponsoring the construction of many prominent **temples**. The bronze sculptures of Hindu deities made in this period are especially prized. Religiously speaking, the Coḷa kings generally favored **Śaivism**, though the construction of **Vaiṣṇava** temples was sometimes sponsored under Coḷa rule. Relations with **Jains** and **Buddhists** tended to be strained.

COMMONER. Translation of the term ***Vaiśya***, which refers to the third of the three **varṇas** or **castes**. In terms of traditional occupation, this caste is made up of trades that involve economically productive activity, such as **arts** and crafts and farming, as well as trade. In the ***Puruṣa Sukta*** of the ***Ṛg Veda*** this caste is said to have been formed from the stomach of the cosmic person. The word *vaiśya*, or "commoner," for this caste also suggests its membership to be relatively large in ancient India.

CONSCIOUSNESS, STATES OF. As enumerated in the ***Upaniṣads***, there are four primary states of consciousness: the waking state, the dream state, the state of dreamless sleep, and the state of transcendence. The ***Māṇḍukya Upaniṣad***, in particular, contains a reflection on these states, connecting them with the various elements that make up **Oṃ**, the most sacred of **bīja mantras**.

The significance of states of consciousness in Hindu thought is considerable. In the *Upaniṣads* and the philosophical **literature** and spiritual practices arising from them, the understanding is that the realization of the identity of the self (**ātman**) and **Brahman** (the highest reality) is essential to one's achieving **liberation** (or **mokṣa**) from the cycle of **rebirth**. This realization is not simply a philosophical doctrine being comprehended in a cognitive sense but a direct awareness arising from reflection on the **scriptures** and from meditative practice that confirms what the scriptures teach: that ātman and Brahman are one. **Meditation**, as outlined in the ***Yoga Sūtras*** of **Patañjali**, involves the stilling of the waking, conscious mind so deeper levels of consciousness can be experienced. Beyond the ordinary waking state, which is characterized by phenomena generated by the senses (**indriyas**) is the dream state, which is characterized by similar phenomena generated by the mind (**manas** or **citta**).

When these dream phenomena are also brought into a state of quiescence, one experiences the state of dreamless sleep, where there is only awareness having no object, and the distinction between subject and object does not exist. But one who is asleep does not remember this blissful (**ānanda**) and limitless (**ananta**) state. Through meditation, one can arrive at this state while awake. Because the distinction between subject and object does not exist in this state, there is no differentiation between Brahman and self. Self (ātman) and Brahman are experienced as being one and the same. This is the fourth state of consciousness (**turīya**)—transcendence. One who experiences this state becomes liberated while still alive (**jīvanmukta**) and need not experience rebirth after death.

CONVERSION. To change one's religious affiliation or identity. Conversion is a topic that generates considerable controversy in contemporary Hinduism, having connotations of the religious exclusivism that many Hindus associate with Abrahamic religions, such as **Christianity** and **Islam**. According to one widespread understanding, Hinduism is not a religion that encourages or requires conversion, either due to the belief that one must be born a Hindu, or because all religions are seen as paths that lead to the ultimate goals of **liberation** and **God-realization**, or a combination of the two. **Mohandās K. Gāndhī**, for example, is known to have actively discouraged conversions both to and from Hinduism, believing the religion to which each person was born was the most appropriate for that person. Because Christians and Muslims do frequently engage in proselytizing, Hindus—particularly **Hindu Nationalist** authors—sometimes express the fear that Hindu traditions will diminish over time as other religions aggressively expand. Proselytizing—the seeking of converts—has been condemned by many contemporary Hindu leaders, such as **Swāmī Dayānanda Sarasvatī**, as a form of cultural violence. (The reference here is to the founder of **Arṣa Vidyā Gurukulam** and the **Hindu Dharma Ācārya Sabhā**, and not the 19th-century founder of the **Ārya Samāj**.)

Historically, however, it is not the case that Hindus have never sought or accepted converts from other traditions. Conversions between what are now regarded as "Hindu" traditions (such as from **Vaiṣṇavism** to **Śaivism**, or vice versa) are attested, though these would today be seen, with the rise and the increasing use of the category of Hinduism, as intra-Hindu conversions. Conversions in both directions involving other Indic religions, however, such as conversions to and from **Jainism** and **Buddhism**, are also attested very widely in ancient sources, as well as active proselytizing—such as that directed by Śaiva enthusiasts at Jains in southern India during the period of the **Coḷa** dynasty.

Contrary to the widely held belief that one must be born Hindu, there was no bar, traditionally, to non-Indians being accepted into Hinduism in ancient times, with entire immigrant communities being incorporated *en masse* into the **caste** system, or to whole kingdoms in **Southeast Asia** systematically adopting Hindu practices and beliefs. And in the modern period, there is the conversion ceremony instituted by the Ārya Samāj by which any person may be inducted into Hindu **dharma**. This last ritual is controversial, however, given how deeply a self-understanding of Hinduism as a nonproselytizing faith has become embedded in the contemporary Hindu consciousness.

COOMARASWAMY, ANANTA KETISH (1877–1947). Born in **Sri Lanka**, A. K. Coomaraswamy was a renowned **art** historian and scholar of South Asian cultures. From 1917 until his death in 1947 he was a research fellow at the Boston Museum of Fine Arts. He advocated the idea of a **perennial philosophy** expressed by traditional Indic culture.

COSMOGONY. Account of the origin and nature of the cosmos. *See also* CREATION.

COW, SACRED. From a non-Hindu perspective, one of the most distinctive of Hindu practices is the veneration of cows. Philosophically, the basis for this veneration is the principle of **ahiṃsā**—harmlessness or nonviolence toward all beings—which, in turn, is based on the idea that divinity is present in all beings: that all beings are manifestations of **Brahman**. From this metaphysical standpoint, there is nothing particularly special about the cow. The gentle reverence displayed toward the cow is simply an example of a universal reverence for life in all its forms.

Historically, however, Hindus have regarded the cow as a special animal since ancient times. Cows and bulls are both frequently depicted in the **art** of the **Indus Valley civilization**, though the specific significance these animals had is unknown. The **Āryans**, whose culture is recorded in the ***Vedas***, prized cattle greatly and used them as a medium of exchange. The cow was utilized not only for providing milk and milk products (such as butter, **ghee**, and yogurt) but also for its dung (which was used as fuel), its urine (which has medicinal uses), its leather, and—controversially in light of the subsequent adoption of **vegetarianism** by many Hindus—its meat. Bulls were offered in sacrifice to the **Vedic** deities and the meat from these sacrifices was, according to some texts, consumed by the **Brahmins** (although this claim is disputed by some Hindus, who argue, on the basis of subsequent practice, that this is a misreading of these texts).

As philosophies that emphasized the virtue of nonviolence increasingly informed Hindu practice around the beginning of the Common Era, **animal sacrifice** began to be practiced less and less, gradually being replaced by vegetarian alternatives, such as **pūjā**. The ancient regard in which the cow was held, however, did not diminish. As a mother, the cow symbolizes and embodies the benevolence and the abundance of the Earth. Cows are, in this sense, a manifestation of the **Mother Goddess**. By the period of the ***Dharma Śāstras***, or legal texts (c. 300 BCE to 100 CE), deliberately killing a cow was regarded as a grave infraction, punishable by **death**.

Cows and bulls play major roles in Hindu religious imagery. **Kāmadhenu**, the wish-fulfilling cow, is venerated, as is **Nandi**, the bull who is **Śiva**'s vehicle.

The veneration of the cow was given new emphasis in the modern period by Hindu reformers such as **Mohandās K. Gāndhī**, who saw the practice of nonviolence toward cows as emblematic of a broader Hindu ethos of nonviolence and respect for all life and for the Earth itself. Simultaneously, cow veneration has emerged as a source of tension between Hindus and beef-eating non-Hindu communities.

CREATION. There is no single doctrine of creation in Hinduism. Many creation stories are presented in the ***Vedas*** and ***Purāṇas***. The predominant worldview is that there is no absolute beginning to existence. There always has been and always will be a universe. It is the case, however, that the universe goes through cycles of emergence, endurance, and dissolution. In Hindu theological discourse, creation stories such as those found in the ***Ṛg Veda*** are typically read through the lens of this understanding, though it is not clear that these stories were composed with this worldview in mind. Such stories can thus be seen as pertaining to the beginning of a cosmic cycle (**kalpa**), or as reflecting an eternal, ongoing process that is occurring at each moment.

Prominent **Vedic** creation stories include **Viṣṇu**'s taking three strides, which form the Earth, the upper atmosphere, and the heavens; the primordial sacrifice of the cosmic man (**puruṣa**), from whose body the universe is formed; the more abstract account of **the One** bringing order (**ṛta**) out of chaos; and the emergence of the cosmos from the Golden Embryo (**Hiraṇyagarbha**).

Some of these accounts have affinities with **Indo-European** creation stories, such as those found in ancient Greek, Celtic, and Norse mythologies.

The *Purāṇas* elaborate on these Vedic themes and integrate them into a complex picture of creation that is centered on the activities of the creator deity, **Brahmā**—though Brahmā is frequently subordinated to Viṣṇu, **Śiva**, or the **Mother Goddess**, depending upon the sectarian affiliation of the Purāṇic text in question (**Vaiṣṇava**, **Śaiva**, or **Śākta**). The vast cycles of cosmic emergence, endurance, and dissolution are conceived in this schema as Brahmā's days and nights. *See also* WORLD AGES.

CREMATION. Traditional Hindu method of disposing of corpses. The body is seen as the temporary vehicle of the soul. Once the body can no longer serve its purpose, it is to be discarded. Traditionally, the body is burned on a wooden pyre. But in the modern period, electric crematoriums have also come into common use. *See also* ANCESTRAL RITES; ANTYEṢṬI; FUNERAL.

D

DAITYA. Children of **Diti** and the sage **Kaśyapa**, and antagonists of their half siblings, the **Ādityas**; a class of demonic beings. *See also* ASURA.

DAKHINI. Demonic female; witch. Dakhinis are powerful beings. They are described as meat-eaters and as attendants of the **Goddess Kālī**.

DAKṢA. Ram-headed deity closely associated with the ritual of sacrifice (**yajña**); one of the sages or **ṛṣis**. He had 50 daughters, including **Aditi**, **Diti**, and **Satī**. Both Aditi and Diti were married to the sage **Kaśyapa**, making Dakṣa the grandfather of the **Ādityas** and the **Daityas**. Satī was married to **Śiva**, whom Dakṣa insulted by failing to invite him to a massive sacrifice to which he had invited all the other sages and deities. Feeling very deeply hurt by this insult to her husband, Satī immolated herself in the sacrificial fire. It was this, and not the previous snub, that enraged Śiva, who destroyed Dakṣa's sacrifice and beheaded him. Later repenting of this act, Śiva resurrected Dakṣa and gave him the head of a ram—an act similar to Śiva's granting of an elephant head to his son **Gaṇeśa** after beheading him, in one version of the story of Gaṇeśa. *See also* PĀRVATĪ.

DAKṢINA. South; also the name of the southern altar in a **Vedic** sacrificial space; also the fee paid to a **Brahmin** for performing a ritual; also the right side, as opposed to the left side. When one practices **circumambulation** or **pradakṣina**, reverently walking in a circle around a sacred image, one keeps the image to one's right. One also gives and receives **prasādam**, the food offered to a deity in **pūjā**, with one's right hand.

DAKṢINAMŪRTI. "South image"; an image of **Śiva** facing to the south, very popular in southern India. The Dakṣinamūrti is an image of Śiva seated and in a teaching posture, often beneath a tree and surrounded by an adoring audience of sages and animals who are listening to his words.

DALITS. "The oppressed"; the name by which many **Untouchables** and other persons of low **caste** prefer to refer to themselves. Another term, coined by **Mohandās K. Gāndhī**, is **Harijan**, or "Children of God." The term *Dalit* emphasizes the suffering that this group has endured as a result of **casteism**. Both of these terms—Dalit and Harijan—have their own political implications, and use of one or the other seems to map onto the attitude of the person employing it toward Hinduism and the degree to which it is seen to be in need of either reform or complete rejection. This, however, is difficult to verify in a scientific fashion, and one does find persons who use the two terms interchangeably. The formal term used by the government of India is **Scheduled Castes**.

DĀNA. "Gift"; can refer either to a specific act of charitable donation or, more broadly, to the virtue of generosity.

DĀNA-MUDRĀ. "Gesture of generosity"; **mudrā**, or hand gesture, which symbolizes divine generosity. Hindu deities are frequently depicted with this gesture, which consists of the left hand (or one of the left hands, given that Hindu deities are frequently depicted with more than one pair of arms and hands) being held out with the palm upward and the fingers pointing downward. It is almost the reverse of the **abhaya-mudrā**, or gesture of fearlessness, which consists of a right hand being held out with the palm downward and the fingers pointing upward. The dāna-mudrā can be seen as representing a deity giving a gift, or reaching out to rescue a drowning devotee from the ocean of misfortune. *See also* MŪRTI.

DĀNAVA. "Children of **Dānu**." Dānu is a daughter of **Diti**. Much like the **Daityas**—the children of Diti—the Dānavas are demonic beings, opposed to the **devas**.

DANCE. Dance is an ancient and highly refined **art** form in India, and a popular way of expressing religious devotion. The authoritative guide to Indian classical theater and dance is the ***Nāṭya Śāstra***, a **Sanskrit** text ascribed to the sage **Bharata** and composed in the first millennium of the Common Era

Four main systems of classical dance arose early in the Common Era, each one of which constitutes a distinct symbolic vocabulary, in the form of postures, gestures, and facial expressions, for communicating stories from Hindu sacred **literature** and concepts from Hindu **philosophy**. Each of the four systems developed in a different part of India: **Bharata Nāṭyam** in **Tamil** Nadu, **Kathak** in Uttar Pradesh, **Kathakali** in **Kerala**, and **Manipuri** in Manipur.

Though dance has traditionally been highly regarded as a skill, the dancers—who have usually been **women**—unfortunately held a very low status in the centuries between the classical and modern periods. They were often employed as **Devadāsīs**. Although the name means "Handmaidens of **God** (or of the **Gods**)," over time, they were forced, in addition to their other duties, to practice prostitution. As an effect of this development, dance gradually ceased to be seen as a respectable occupation.

There has been a revival of Indian classical dance in the modern period, though, largely through the efforts of **E. Krishna Iyer**. It is now very common for young Hindu women and girls to study at least one form of dance and to perform in cultural programs held in **temples** or community centers—a pursuit seen not only as respectable but also a mark of pride in the Hindu community. In addition to the four classical forms, a modern style from **Orissa** called **Odissi** is very popular, as are Westernized forms popularized through the **Hindi** film industry.

Finally, there have always been numerous regional folk dance styles that do not require the degree of technical training demanded by the classical styles and which have traditionally accompanied festivals and other community events, such as weddings. Folk dances, too, such as **Garbha**, are highly popular today and are often part of the mixed repertoire of dance styles that can be seen in contemporary Hindu cultural programs. *See also* GWALIOR; KŪṬIYĀṬṬAM.

DANDEKAR, R. N. (1909–2001). Indologist and Sanskritist. He was educated first at Deccan College in Pune, India, and then at the University of Heidelberg, Germany. He was a professor of **Sanskrit** from 1933 to 1950 at Fergusson College in Pune, and then at Pune University until 1969, after which he became director of the Bhandarkar Oriental Research Institute.

DAṆḌIN (fl. 6th–7th centuries CE). Sanskrit author who lived in **Kāñcīpuram**, in southern India. Daṇḍin is known to have written two major works: a collection of short stories entitled the "Adventures of the Ten Princes" (*Daśakumāracarita*) and a work on **poetics**, or *kāvya*, called "A Look at Poetics" (*Kāvyadarśa*).

DĀNU. Daughter of **Diti** and **Dakṣa**; mother of the **Dānavas**, a group of demonic beings opposed to the **devas**, or **Vedic** deities.

DARBHA. Sacred grass used in **Vedic** rituals and said to have come from the hair of the boar **avatāra** of **Viṣṇu (Varāha)**. Sometimes identified with **kuśa** grass, but sometimes distinguished from it. *See also* YAJÑA.

DARK HALF. *See* KṚṢṆA PAKṢA.

DARŚANA. Literally "view," "vision." As a sacred act, darśana refers to viewing the sacred image **(mūrti)** of a deity, usually in the context of a **tem-**

ple (**mandira**). This act also involves being seen *by* the image, understood to embody the presence of the deity it represents. To receive darśana is therefore to receive a blessing from the deity one sees and by whom one is seen.

Darśana also means "view" in the sense of "worldview," and in this context refers to a system of philosophy. The Indian darśanas are traditionally divided into two basic categories: **āstika**, or "orthodox," and **nāstika**, or "heterodox." The orthodox darśanas are those who affirm (or at least do not explicitly reject) the authority of the ***Vedas*** (and are therefore, by one common definition, "Hindu" systems). The nonorthodox darśanas are those who reject the authority of the *Vedas*.

There are six āstika darśanas, which are often organized into three pairs, due to certain basic affinities that members of each pair have for the other. First, there are the **Sāṃkhya** and **Yoga** darśanas, which share the same basic worldview, with the notable exception being that Sāṃkhya is nontheistic and Yoga is not. But the Sāṃkhya system can be seen as more purely theoretical, whereas Yoga utilizes the main concepts of the Sāṃkhya system to develop a contemplative practice aimed at the attainment of **mokṣa** (**liberation** from the cycle of **rebirth**). Then there are the **Nyāya** and **Vaiśeṣika** systems. Nyāya is concerned primarily with logic and the valid means of **knowledge**. Vaiśeṣika, much like Yoga in relation to Sāṃkhya, applies the logic of Nyāya to the analysis of the phenomenal world. **Pūrva** (or prior) **Mīmāṃsā** and **Uttara** (or later) **Mīmāṃsā**—also known as **Vedānta**—focus upon the interpretation, respectively, of the earlier and later Vedic texts.

The nāstika darśanas are **Jainism**, **Buddhism**, and the **materialist Lokāyata** (or **Cārvāka**) system. Although the term *nāstika* gradually comes to refer to an atheist, this is not its original sense, since some of the āstika darśanas are also nontheistic, or at least not explicitly theistic—namely, Sāṃkhya and Pūrva Mīmāṃsā. All three of the classical nāstika darśanas are also nontheistic, but only the Lokāyata system denies the concepts of **karma** and rebirth.

Each darśana is based on a collection of root texts, or **sūtras**, which summarize the teaching of the sage believed to be the founder of the system in question. According to the traditions of the various darśanas, most of their founding figures lived around the fifth century BCE, though some (such as **Kāpila**, the founder of the **Sāṃkhya** system) lived before that time, while others (such as **Patañjali**, the founder of the **Yoga** system) almost certainly lived later. In most cases, the extant sūtras are likely the result of many generations of compilation, rather than the work of a single author. Philosophical writing in a darśana tradition largely occurs through the genre of the **bhāṣya**, or commentary on the root text, the understanding being that all relevant knowledge is already present in at least an implicit form in the root text. What is required, then, is not innovation, in the sense of discovery of completely new ideas, but an unpacking of the deep **truths** contained in the words of the sages of the past.

DĀSA, DASYU. Barbarian; also slave, servant; terms used for non-**Āryan** tribes in the ***Ṛg Veda*** who are regarded as opponents of the Āryans; sometimes used interchangeably with the term **asura**, or demonic being. **Indra** is described as destroying the forts of the Dasyus. They are described as city-builders and as having magical powers (like the asura **Maya** in the ***Mahābhārata***). During the 19th and 20th centuries, **Indologists** interpreted the Dāsas and Dasyus as indigenous Indians being invaded by the Āryans.

DAŚAHRĀ (DUSSEHRA). Ten-day festival celebrated in the **bright half** of the month of **Āśvina**. In northern India, this festival celebrates **Rāma**'s victory over **Rāvaṇa** and it culminates in **Dīpāvali** (or Dīwali), the festival of lights in honor of the **goddess Lakṣmī**. In **Bengal** and southern India, this festival celebrates **Durgā**'s victory over the Buffalo Demon (**Mahiṣāsura**). In Bengal, it culminates in **Kālī pūjā**.

DAŚANĀMI ORDER. Order of the 10 Names; order of Hindu monks established by **Śaṅkara** (788–820 CE). Śaṅkara established four monasteries. **Śṛṅgerī**, in the south, is the head monastery. **Puri** is in **Orissa**, in the east. **Badrīnāth** is in the foothills of the **Himālayas**, in the north. **Dvārakā** is in Gujarat, in the west. Śaṅkara's monasteries are therefore located in the four corners of India corresponding to each of the four points of the compass. The head of each of these monasteries, or **maṭhas**, is called **Śaṅkarācārya**. Śaṅkara is often called *Ādi Śaṅkarācārya*, or "First Śaṅkarācārya" in order to distinguish him from subsequent holders of this title. Anyone, regardless of **caste** or gender, may join the Daśanāmi Order. The order is generally associated with the **Smārta** tradition of Hinduism and the **Advaita** interpretation of **Vedānta**, though neither of these is rigidly upheld in practice, with members having considerable freedom in regard to theological issues. The ascetics of the **Ramakrishna Order** are members of the Daśanāmi Order.

DAŚARATHA. Character in the ***Rāmāyaṇa***; father of **Rāma**; king of **Ayodhyā**. When hunting in the forest, Daśaratha accidentally slays the son of a **Brahmin** and is cursed to also lose his son. This occurs when Daśaratha is forced to send Rāma into exile, an event that causes Daśaratha to die of sorrow.

DASGUPTA, SURENDRANĀTH (1887–1952). Bengali philosopher and **Indologist**; lecturer in **philosophy** at Cambridge University in 1922 and professor of philosophy at Calcutta University until 1945. He is best known for his five-volume history of Indian philosophy.

DATTA, NARENDRANĀTH (1863–1902). The birth name of **Swāmī Vivekānanda**.

DAYAL, HAR (1884–1939). Founder of the **Ghadṛ movement**, which advocated for the violent overthrow of British rule in India. A **Hindu Nationalist**, Dayal was a scholar who served on the faculty of Stanford University in California from 1911 until 1914, at which time he was arrested by U.S. immigration authorities due to his political activities. While on bail, he fled to Germany, where he resided from 1914 to 1918. After the end of World War I, he returned to India and joined **Mohandās K. Gāndhī**'s nonviolent campaign for Indian independence. He completed his doctoral degree at the University of London in 1930 and died in Philadelphia in 1939.

DAYĀNANDA SARASVATĪ, SWĀMĪ (1824–1883). Founder of the **Ārya Samāj**, an important Hindu reform organization of the modern period. Born in Gujarat, in western India, to a **Śaiva** family. It is said that he began to question the use of images (**mūrtis**) in worship when, as a child, he kept a night vigil in a **Śiva temple** and saw mice eating the food offered to the deity. He left home to undertake renunciation (**sannyāsa**) at the age of 22, when his parents wanted to arrange a marriage for him. Wandering eventually to **Mathura**, Dayānanda studied the ***Vedas*** under his **guru**, Swāmī Virjānanda.

Dayānanda interpreted the *Vedas* as teaching a **monotheistic** doctrine and, much like **Ram Mohan Roy**, he did not find any Vedic warrant for later Hindu practices in texts such as the ***Purāṇas*** and sought to eliminate these later practices. He established the Ārya Samāj in order to promote a "purified" Vedic Hinduism with no use of images in worship and no **caste** prejudice. A **Hindu Nationalist**, Dayānanda was highly critical of **Christianity** and **Islam**, especially for the proselytizing activities of both Christian and Islamic missionaries in India. In addition to reforming Hinduism, another purpose of the Ārya Samāj was to neutralize missionary activities by these traditions, and a ritual of **conversion** was established to enable those who wished to become Hindu to do so. He found common cause with **Helena Petrovna Blavatsky** and **Henry Steele Olcott** of the **Theosophical Society**, who shared his vision of reviving ancient Indian traditions for the modern era. But he parted company with Blavatsky and Olcott when he heard that they had both undertaken a formal conversion to **Buddhism** in **Sri Lanka**.

DAYĀNANDA SARASVATĪ, SWĀMĪ (1930–). Not to be confused with the founder of the **Ārya Samāj**, the contemporary Swāmī Dayānanda Sarasvatī is the founder and the current head of the **Hindu Dharma Ācārya Sabhā** (or "Assembly of Hindu Religious Leaders") and the founder of the

Arṣa Vidyā Gurukulam in Saylorsburg, Pennsylvania. He is an adherent of the **Advaita** system of **Vedānta** in the tradition of **Śaṅkara**.

The Hindu Dharma Ācārya Sabhā has a membership of over 100 **ācāryas**, or leaders of **saṃpradāyas** (Hindu religious traditions) and is an attempt to bring greater institutional cohesion to Hinduism in order to advance a number of interests and concerns shared across many saṃpradāyas. Particularly noteworthy **actions** of the Hindu Dharma Ācārya Sabhā include a 2008 summit between the Sabhā and the chief rabbis of Israel in order to facilitate dialogue between Hinduism and Judaism and numerous proclamations that condemn proselytizing as a form of cultural violence against indigenous religions.

Arṣa Vidyā Gurukulam is an educational organization dedicated to the teaching of **Sanskrit** and Advaita **philosophy**.

DE, ABHAY CHARAN (1896–1977). The birth name of A. C. **Bhaktivedānta Swāmī Prabhupāda**.

DE, S. K. (1890–1968). Indologist; born in **Calcutta**; professor of English, **Sanskrit**, and Sanskrit **literature** at Calcutta University.

DEATH. In most Hindu traditions, death is seen as a transition from one lifetime to the next in the beginningless cycle of **rebirth** (a cycle known as **saṃsāra**). The ***Bhagavad Gītā*** (2:22) compares the transition from one body to another to the discarding of old, worn-out clothes for a new set of clothes, and **Ramakrishna**, in a vision to his wife, **Saradā Devī**, is said to have proclaimed that, in dying, he had merely moved "from one room to another." **Mohandās K. Gāndhī** described birth and death as two different sides of the same door. The nature of one's next life is determined by the quality of one's **karma**, the accumulated effects of one's moral **actions**, at the time of one's death. The ultimate goal of most Hindu systems is to achieve **liberation** from rebirth (**mokṣa**).

Reassuring though such a concept may be, however, Hindus, like the adherents of all other religions, experience profound grief at the passing of a loved one, and a variety of rituals exist for the purpose of assuaging this grief. The **antyeṣṭi**, or **Vedic** funeral, is conducted as soon as possible after death, and includes the **cremation** of the body of the deceased. The particulars of the ritual vary a great deal, depending on region and **caste**, but it often extends over the course of several days. There are also **ancestral rites**, such as the **śrāddha**, which occurs periodically and consists of making offerings of food and water to one's departed ancestors. These offerings are believed to become the food that one's ancestors consume in their next life.

It is not known precisely when or how the doctrine of rebirth arose in Hinduism. The first unambiguous reference to this process is found in the

Bṛhadāraṇyaka Upaniṣad (4.4.5–7), which was probably compiled around 500 BCE but likely contains material that had been handed down orally for many generations before that time. References to the afterlife in earlier Vedic texts suggest a shadowy afterworld, not unlike the ancient Greek Hades, and other **Indo-European** conceptions of the afterlife (though other Indo-European cultures, such as the that of the Celts, also developed a rebirth concept like that of Hinduism).

A distinction is also drawn between two afterlife destinations called the "Realm of the Fathers" (**pitṛloka**) and the "Realm of the Gods" (**devaloka**). As the idea of rebirth develops in the later Vedic **literature**, the realm of the fathers comes to be identified with eventual rebirth in the physical world, whereas the realm of the gods is interpreted as a path leading to eventual freedom from rebirth. Some scholars speculate that the origins of the ideas of karma and rebirth can be found in Vedic rituals, such as the **Agniṣṭoma**, which has the goal of leading to a rebirth in heaven (**svarga**). If the ritual actions, or *karmans*, are performed correctly, they lead to the desired goal; but if they are performed incorrectly, they can fail to bear fruit, or even bring about the opposite of the desired goal.

The theory is that this concept of correctly or incorrectly performed ritual action—"good" or "bad" karmans leading to a correspondingly good or bad result develops into the idea of ethically good or bad actions in life leading to similar, corresponding results in the world. The Vedic sacrificial arena essentially becomes extended to encompass all of life. Another theory is that the idea of rebirth was foreign to the Vedic traditions and was introduced through interaction with **śramaṇa** traditions, such as **Buddhism** and **Jainism**, which either arose from other Indo-European traditions, distinct from the Vedic, or represent an ancient indigenous Indian tradition, perhaps an ideology of the **Indus Valley civilization**. But this is all quite speculative.

DELHI, NEW DELHI. Capital of the modern Republic of India. The region has been settled since ancient times and is believed to be the site of the **Pāṇḍavas**' ancient city of **Indraprastha**. The city was the capital of the Turkish Delhi sultanate, which ruled most of northern India from 1206 to 1526, after which it was incorporated into the **Mughal Empire**. Delhi served as the Mughal capital from 1649 to 1857, after which the empire was formally dissolved and India came under the direct control of the British crown. The British administration was based in **Calcutta** until 1911, when it was moved to Delhi. New Delhi, the southern part of the greater metropolitan area, was mostly built in the 1920s. When India became independent in 1947, New Delhi remained its capital.

DEMON, DEMONIC. Word frequently used to translate the terms ***asura*** and ***rākṣasa***. The term is both accurate and inaccurate. It is accurate in the basic sense that asuras and rākṣasas are generally seen in Hindu sacred **literature** as evil beings, and as opponents of the **gods (devas)**. But there is no figure of ultimate evil in Hinduism comparable to Satan and his demonic minions. Asuras and rākṣasas are sometimes encountered in Hindu texts that behave in a good and noble fashion, such as the good rākṣasa **Vibhīṣana**, from the ***Rāmāyaṇa***, who is a devotee of **Rāma** and joins him in his war against **Rāvaṇa**. There are also times when the devas do not behave virtuously in relation to the asuras, such as when the devas trick the asuras out of their share of the elixir of life (**amṛta**) after getting their cooperation in the churning of the ocean. At the same time, there are resonances between the war in heaven between angels and demons depicted in Abrahamic religions such as **Christianity** and **Islam** and the conflict between the devas and asuras, the likely historical connection between the two being **Zoroastrianism**.

DESIRE. According to the ***Bṛhadāraṇyaka Upaniṣad*** (4.4.5–7) and subsequent systems of Hindu **philosophy**—particularly **Vedānta**—desire is a primary cause of bondage to the cycle of **rebirth**, which must be relinquished in order for **liberation (mokṣa)** to occur. The idea is that it is not merely **action**, or **karma**, as such that leads one to be reborn, but rather action that has been invested with desire. This is why the ***Bhagavad Gītā*** (3:4–8) recommends detachment from the fruits of action as a path to liberation (the idea being that a life of complete inaction is impossible). Desire as the fundamental cause of the cycle of rebirth, and thus of suffering, is also a major theme of **Buddhism** and the basis for the emphasis on **asceticism** in many Hindu traditions.

Because the **Vedic** ritual of sacrifice (**yajña**) is enjoined precisely so that one may fulfill one's desires, such rituals are rejected by the **śramaṇa** traditions and by Vedāntic texts such as the *Bhagavad Gītā* (2:42–44) as conducive to karmic bondage (as well as for the fact that such rituals, especially if they involve **animal sacrifice**, violate the principle of **ahiṃsā**, or nonviolence).

DEVA. Deity, god, literally "shining one." The earliest extant references to devas are from the ***Ṛg Veda***. The **Vedic** devas are usually associated with natural phenomena, such as **Sūrya** the sun god, **Uśā** the goddess of the dawn, **Soma** the god of the **moon** and the hallucinogenic plant of the same name, **Vāyu** the god of the wind, **Yama** the god of **death**, and so on. The lord of the Vedic devas is **Indra**, who is associated with thunder and is analogous to the Greek Zeus and the Norse Thor. Also of particular importance is **Agni**, the god of fire. Agni's special importance derives from his role as an intermediary between the human and divine worlds, due to the fact that all offerings to the devas are made through the medium of the sacred fire, which Agni personifies. Indra and Agni, respectively, are the most and second-most frequent objects of adoration in the hymns of the *Ṛg Veda*. Also of considerable importance is **Prajāpati**, whose name literally means the "father of offspring" and who is regarded as the creator of the universe—later known as **Brahmā**. The two chief deities of later Hinduism, **Viṣṇu** and **Śiva**, receive relatively little mention in the *Vedas* (the latter typically under the name **Rudra**).

Early in the Common Era, as the various systems of Hindu theology develop in a **monotheistic** direction (primarily centered on Viṣṇu or Śiva as the supreme deity—though **Śakti** and **Ganeśa** also have their followings in this regard), the Vedic devas come to be seen as lesser deities, analogous to the angels or angelic forces found in the Abrahamic religions, or as aspects, emanations, or powers of "higher" deities. Perpetually opposed to the devas are the demonic forces—the **asuras**, who are depicted as being in a state of constant warfare with the devas.

In addition to this meaning, though, the term *deva* also becomes a generic term for any deity, including the supreme deity. So Śiva, for example, is known by the epithet **Mahādeva** or "Great Deva," even by **Śaiva** traditions that regard him monotheistically as the Supreme Being, and not as a "mere" deva or demigod. Similarly, the feminine **Devī**, a term that refers originally to any female deva, becomes a proper name for the supreme **goddess** of the **Śākta** traditions, as does **Mahādevī** (Great Goddess).

DEVADĀSĪ. "Handmaiden of **God** (or of the **Gods**)"; **woman** employed as a dancer in a **temple** and is technically married to the deity of that temple. In the medieval period, Devadāsīs began to be exploited as prostitutes, bringing disrepute upon the **art** of **dance**, in which they were quite skilled. Indian classical dance has seen a revival in the modern period as the practice of forced prostitution has ceased to receive either religious or legal sanction.

DEVAKĪ. Mother of **Bālarāma** and **Kṛṣṇa**.

DEVALOKA. Realm of the **gods**; one of two possible afterlife destinations according to early **Vedic** thought, the other being the **Pitṛloka**, or realm of the ancestors. *See also* DEATH.

DEVĪ. Goddess; common epithet of the **Mother Goddess**.

DEVĪ MAHĀTMYA. "Glorification of the Great **Goddess**"; portion of the ***Markaṇḍeya Purāṇa*** (composed c. 250–550 CE) that describes the victories of the **Mother Goddess** over various **asuras**. Also known as the *Caṇḍīpaṭha*, it is recited during **Durgā Pūjā**.

DEVOTION. *See* BHAKTI.

DHARMA. Literally, "support." However, this important term has a range of meanings that include the order of the universe, the order of society, natural law, justice, religion, and personal duty. Contemporary Hindus often refer to Hinduism as *Hindu Dharma* or **Sanātana Dharma**. In this context, *dharma* refers to the Hindu way of life in its entirety and is often presented as a deliberate contrast with *religion*, dharma being seen as a more holistic and all-encompassing concept than religion, which has become a more privatized in modernity than it was in earlier periods of history. *Sanātana* means "eternal," and the implication of calling Hinduism *Sanātana Dharma* is that it reflects an unchanging and universal order of existence—in contrast with the Abrahamic religions, which are seen as being more localized and tied to history.

In the ***Ṛg Veda***, the preferred term for the universal order to which *dharma* refers is ***ṛta***, and regular performance of **Vedic** ritual is seen as essential to its maintenance. In the ***Dharma Śāstras*** and the epics (the ***Rāmāyaṇa*** and ***Mahābhārata***, composed around the beginning of the Common Era), the term *dharma* becomes preferred. With this shift in terminology, there is also a shift in emphasis from maintaining the cosmos through right ritual **action** to maintaining it by fulfilling social obligations. This idea of dharma as *duty* remains prevalent today.

In the *Dharma Śāstras*, dharma is largely identified with the duties connected to the system of **varṇas** (or **castes**) and **āśramas** (stages of life). Each varṇa (and the **jātis** that make up each varṇa) and each āśrama, of course, has its own distinct duties attached to it. Closely tied, therefore, with dharma is the concept of **svadharma**, or one's own dharma, which is a function of one's location in the caste system and the stage of life that one currently occupies.

The idea of svadharma adds a layer of complexity to dharma, as an ethical ideal, that does not necessarily obtain in more universalist, less particularized ethical systems. Understanding dharma is not simply a matter of learning a set of abstract rules that apply to everyone but of knowing the duties that apply to one's own specific circumstances. The *Dharma Śāstras* consist largely of an enumeration of duties associated with each caste and stage of life.

Universal moral norms, however, are also an important part of dharma, and are invoked in the *Dharma Śāstras*. These norms correlate closely with the **yamas**, or moral restraints, enumerated in the ***Yoga Sūtras*** of **Patañjali**: **ahiṃsā** (nonviolence), **satya** (truthfulness), **asteya** (nonstealing), **brahmacarya** (sexual restraint, chastity), and **aparigraha** (nonattachment). These same norms are shared by the **śramaṇa** traditions, **Jainism** and **Buddhism**. The *Dharma Śāstras* invoke these norms in dealing with moral dilemmas and difficult questions that arise in the course of applying the idea of dharma to concrete situations, such as conflicts between competing duties.

As the caste system has come under increasing critical scrutiny during the modern period, even being rejected by many Hindu thinkers, the concept of dharma has continued to evolve. Reflection on dharma in contemporary Hinduism conceives of dharma less as a matter of inheritance—of birth caste—and more as a kind of personal destiny or calling in life that one must discern over the course of one's lifetime. As the discourse of human rights has entered Hinduism, dharma has also been rethought in terms of a responsibility that all human beings have both to one another and to the larger environment.

Finally, dharma is one of the four goals of humanity, or **puruṣārthas** of classical Hindu thought, along with **kāma** (pleasure), **ārtha** (wealth), and **mokṣa** (**liberation** from the cycle of **rebirth**).

DHARMA ŚĀSTRAS. Authoritative texts on **dharma**; Hindu law books. Many of these texts exist, including the ***Manusmṛti***, the *Apastamba Dharma Śāstra*, the ***Yājñavalkya*** *Dharma Śāstra*, and others. They were composed roughly between 300 and 100 BCE.

DHĀTṚ. Early **Vedic** deity, one of the 12 **Ādityas**—sons of the goddess **Aditi** and the sage **Kaśyapa**. His name means both "order" and "sustainer," both of which connect him with the concept of **dharma**.

DHṚTARĀṢṬRA. Character in the ***Mahābhārata***; blind king; brother of **Paṇḍu**; father of **Duryodhana**, the chief villain of the epic, and the other 99 **Kauravas**; uncle of the **Pāṇḍavas**; husband of **Gāndhārī**. Dhṛtarāṣṭra is often criticized by commentators for being an overindulgent father and failing to reprimand Duryodhana's excessive hatred for and many plots against the Pāṇḍavas.

Dhṛtarāṣṭra speaks the first verse of the ***Bhagavad Gītā*** when he asks **Sañjaya**, his clairvoyant minister, to describe for him the events of the battle of **Kurukṣetra**. He is also mentioned briefly in the ***Bṛhadāraṇyaka Upaniṣad***, an independent reference to this character suggestive of his possible historicity.

DHYĀNA. Meditation; seventh of the eight stages or "limbs" of **Patañjali**'s eight-limbed (**aṣṭāṅga**) system of **yoga**. The sixth limb, **dharaṇā**, is concentration on a single object. **Dhyāna** is absorption in that object, with no awareness of any other phenomena.

Dhyāna involves the stilling of the waking, conscious **mind** so that deeper levels of consciousness can be experienced. The goal of dhyāna is **samādhi**—the eighth limb of Patañjali's system—which is complete absorption in the object of concentration, in which the distinction between subject and object vanishes.

The practice of dhyāna is shared by many of the Indic traditions and is especially prominent in **Buddhism**. In early Buddhism, the term *dhyāna* also refers to the **states of consciousness** to which the practice of dhyāna can lead. Interestingly, when Buddhism was transmitted to China, the term dhyāna was rendered as *ch'an*. When the tradition was transmitted to Japan, the term *ch'an* was transformed into *zen*.

DĪKṢĀ. Formal initiation into a spiritual discipline; performed by one's spiritual teacher or **guru**. Dīkṣā often involves the transmission of a secret **mantra** that the practitioner will use in **meditation** and not disclose to any other person. The mantra will possess the **guru-śakti**, or power of the spiritual lineage through which it has been transmitted.

DĪPĀVALI (DĪWALI). Festival of Lights; this holiday commemorates **Rāma**'s victory over **Rāvaṇa**. It is also a day that is especially sacred to **Lakṣmī**, wife of **Viṣṇu** and **goddess** of wealth and prosperity. The holiday is celebrated with the lighting of **dīyās**, or oil lamps, as well as, in the modern period, fireworks and strings of colored electric lights similar to Christmas lights. The festival occurs on the **Amavasya**, or new-moon day, of the month of **Kārtika** (late October to early November). In northern India, this date also marks the last day of the year. Those who wish to have Lakṣmī's blessings for the New Year leave a lamp burning outside of their home all night long (or an electric light). In **Bengal**, **Kālī pūjā** is celebrated on the night of Dīwali. In October 2007, after lobbying by the **Hindu American Foundation**, the U.S. Congress passed a resolution in recognition of the religious and historical significance of Dīwali.

In **Jainism**, Dīwali is celebrated as **Mahāvīra** Nirvāṇa Divāsa, the date on which the sage **Mahāvīra** attained his final **nirvāṇa** and left his body. It is said that the king of the region where Mahāvīra died proclaimed that lamps should be lit on that night because such a great light had gone out of the world.

DITI. Sister of **Aditi**, daughter of **Dakṣa**, and mother of the **Daityas**, a group of beings opposed to the **Vedic devas** (deities) and generally regarded as demonic.

DIVINE LIGHT MISSION. Hindu organization established by Sri Hāṃsā Mahārāj Ji in the early 1960s and taken over after his death in 1966 by his son, **Guru Mahārāj Ji**, who was only nine years old. Its basic theology is derived from the **Vallabha Vaiṣṇava** tradition. It was renamed "Elan Vital" in 1983.

DIVINE MOTHER. An alternative designation for the **Mother Goddess**.

DĪWALI. *See* DĪPĀVALI.

DĪYĀ. Oil lamp used in many Hindu rituals, such as **pūjā** and **āratī**, and on a very large scale during **Dīpāvali**, the festival of lights.

DOMESTIC RITUALS. A variety of Hindu rituals can be performed at home, and in fact it is probably accurate to say that the home is a more central location than the **temple** for Hindu religious activity. The typical Hindu home will have a room, or at least a small space, dedicated exclusively to religious activity: a shrine or altar before which the daily **pūjā** and **meditation** can be performed. The most common domestic ritual is a morning pūjā performed as soon as one has risen from bed and bathed. The ideal time for such a pūjā is early in the morning, just before dawn, during the **Brāhma-muhurta**. **Brahmins** will often recite the **Gāyatrī mantra** at this time or as the sun is rising. Some Hindus also perform an evening pūjā, at sundown. Other pūjās frequently held at home include the **Satyanarāyaṇa Pūjā**, performed every full-moon day (**purṇima**), and a weekly pūjā to **Lakṣmī**, which is usually performed by the **women** in the home. More elaborate and large-scale rituals performed at home typically require one to employ a priest—such as the **Gṛha-praveśa**, or "entering the home," a ceremony for blessing a new house. Detailed instructions for the performance of domestic rituals are contained in a set of late **Vedic** texts called the ***Gṛhya Sūtras***, which were likely composed around 300 BCE.

DONIGER, WENDY (1940–). Indologist and Sanskritist who has been a professor at the University of Chicago since 1978. Doniger's title is **Mircea Eliade** Distinguished Service Professor of the History of Religions. She is located jointly in the University of Chicago's Divinity School, its Department of South Asian Languages and Civilizations, and its Committee on Social Thought. She has two doctoral degrees—one from Harvard University (1968) and one from Oxford University (1973). Much of Doniger's work has focused upon the interpretation of Hindu sacred **literature**, though she has also done a good deal of translation of **Sanskrit** texts—most notably of selected hymns from the ***Ṛg Veda*** and of the ***Manusmṛti***. Her interpretations of Hindu texts have proven controversial due to her application of Freudian psychoanalytic theories. Many in the Hindu community have found her work and that of her students who have followed a similar line of interpretation to be objectionable—most notably **Rajiv Malhotra**, who has accused Doniger and her students of neocolonialism. However, much of this same work has met with great scholarly acclaim, making Doniger a polarizing figure.

DRAUPADĪ. Character in the ***Mahābhārata***; wife of the five **Pāṇḍava** brothers. In one of the more unusual scenes in the epic, though it is **Arjuna** who wins Draupadī's hand in marriage, his mother, **Kuntī**, requires him to share Draupadī with his four brothers. (She had told him, "Whatever you have won, you must share with your brothers," before she had seen that Arjuna had won a bride, and a mother's word must be obeyed.) In another account, Draupadī's situation is depicted as the result of a wish she made in a past life, in which she prayed five times for a husband.

Draupadī is central to the main plotline of the ***Mahābhārata***. When **Yudhiṣṭhira** gambles away his own freedom and that of his brothers, losing all of his belongings to **Duryodhana**, he stakes Draupadī to win everything back, losing her in the process as well. Draupadī challenges this outcome, arguing that Yudhiṣṭhira had no right to gamble away his wife, as though she were a material possession, particularly given that he had already lost himself when he staked her. When none of the assembled elders will rise to her defense, due to their loyalty to Duryodhana's father, who is presiding over the entire proceedings, Duryodhana, his brothers—the **Kauravas**—and **Karṇa** try to molest her. When Duryodhana's brother Duḥśāsana tries to strip off her clothing, Draupadī takes refuge in **Kṛṣṇa**, who performs a miracle that consists of covering her with an infinite cloth that cannot be removed. This supernatural event frightens the Kauravas; their father **Dhṛtarāṣṭra**, who has been silent up to this point, grants her any boon that she wishes to request. She asks for the freedom of her husbands and that all their belongings be returned. Dhṛtarāṣṭra grants this and Draupadī's own freedom as well. She thus saves her husbands when they were helpless to save either her or themselves. The insult that she suffers at the hands of the Kauravas, however, heightens the tensions between the two families, and both Draupadī and **Bhīma** swear vengeance. This vengeance is achieved at the battle of **Kurukṣetra**, at which all of the Kauravas are killed. Duḥśāsana is killed by Bhīma and Draupadī washes her hair in his blood. Duryodhana dies by Bhīma's hand as well.

In southern India, Draupadī is regarded as an incarnation of the **Mother Goddess** and is worshiped as such. The famous image of Hindus walking across hot coals is part of her worship, where devotees vow to perform this act if she will answer their prayers.

Commentators often contrast the strong, fierce, and outspoken Draupadī with the relatively meek and submissive **Sītā**, the analogous chief female protagonist of the other major Hindu epic, the ***Rāmāyaṇa***. Some contemporary interpreters see in Draupadī a critique of traditional Hindu patriarchy and as expressing the possibility of an indigenous Hindu feminism based on the concept of **dharma**. Her successful invocation of Kṛṣṇa also represents the power of **bhakti**. *See also* WOMEN.

DRAVIDIAN. Language family predominant in the southern half of India that includes Kannada, Malayalam, **Tamil**, and Telugu; distinct from the **Indo-European** languages that predominate in northern India (such as **Hindi**

and **Bengali**), all of which are closely related to **Sanskrit**. In keeping with the conflation of culture and ethnicity introduced by 19th-century **Indologists**—who spoke not only of Indo-European culture but also of an Indo-European or **Āryan** "race"—the term *Dravidian* has come to refer not only to the languages of southern India but to the people who speak those languages as well. This has led to a northern and southern political division that is based on the **Āryan Invasion Theory**, with its implication that northern Indian languages (and the people who spoke them) invaded and ousted an indigenous Dravidian population some time prior to 1500 BCE. This division has most often been played out in the form of controversies over the Indian government's promotion of Hindi in southern India. Indeed, English is preferred in southern India over Hindi as a medium of communication.

DREAM. The dream state is the second of the four **states of consciousness** enumerated in the ***Upaniṣads*** and in **Vedānta philosophy**. The dream state (*taijasā*, or "brilliant") is differentiated from the waking state (*vaiśvānara*, or "omnipresent") by the fact that the objects that appear in it are generated by the mind (**manas**) rather than by one's sensory organs (**indriyas**). These objects, however, are often of the same kind as those that one experiences in the waking state and can be just as convincing while one is in the dream state. Particularly in **Advaita Vedānta** and **Buddhism**, waking consciousness is said to be dreamlike in the sense that its objects are not ultimately real—being merely conceptual constructs—in contrast with pure, **non-dual** awareness.

DROṆA. Character in the ***Mahābhārata***; a highly gifted warrior, and **guru** of both the **Pāṇḍavas** and the **Kauravas**. Although born a **Brahmin**, Droṇa performed the duties of a **kṣatriya**. Despite this violation of the principle of **svadharma** on his own part, Droṇa did not allow **Ekalavya**, a lower-caste man who wanted to be his student, to similarly do the duty of a **caste** to which he was not born. It is said that this was because Droṇa did not want his favorite pupil, **Arjuna**, to have any rival. Though fond of the Pāṇḍavas, and of Arjuna in particular, Droṇa was required by his oath of loyalty to the Kaurava throne to fight in the battle of **Kurukṣetra** on the Kaurava side. As Arjuna's guru, Droṇa was one of the persons whom Arjuna was hesitant to fight at the start of the battle, as narrated in the ***Bhagavad Gītā***. Droṇa's slaying occurred in a dishonorable fashion. An elephant was slain whose name was **Aśvatthāma**, which was also the name of Droṇa's beloved son. Hearing that "Aśvatthāma has been slain," Droṇa laid down his arms in mourning and was struck down. Even though the statement "Aśvatthāma has been slain," was technically true, it was said with the intent and effect of creating deception, and was thus dishonorable—as was striking Droṇa after he had laid down his arms. In reference to this episode of the *Mahābhārata*, the phrase "Aśvatthāma has been slain," has entered Hindu parlance as a reference to any statement that, while technically true, is nevertheless said with deceptive intent.

DUMÉZIL, GEORGES (1898–1986). Scholar of **Indo-European** language and culture; developed the theory of a tripartite division of Indo-European societies that is reflected in the area of religion. This division is present in traditional Hindu society in the form of the top three **castes**, or **varṇas**, which are regarded as **twice born**—**Brahmins**, **Kṣatriyas**, and **Vaiśyas**—all of which have parallels in other Indo-European cultures. In regard to **Indology**, Dumézil's most famous work is his study of the ***Mahābhārata***.

DURGĀ. Literally, "She who is difficult to approach," or alternatively, "She who makes evil go away"; popular form of the **Mother Goddess**, particularly in **Bengal**. According to the ***Devī Mahātmya***, when the seemingly invincible Buffalo Demon (or **Mahīṣāsura**) had conquered the world, the **gods**, who could not defeat him, approached **Viṣṇu** for help. On Viṣṇu's advice, the gods combined their energies, and Durgā emerged.

Durgā thus represents the combined power, or **śakti**, of all of the other deities. In the **Śākta** tradition, she is a manifestation of the supreme deity—the

Durgā, a form of the Mother Goddess and slayer of the Buffalo Demon.

Mother Goddess in a fierce form to save the world from evil. She is depicted riding upon a lion and having 10 arms and hands, with a different weapon in each hand—each weapon representing one of the deities whose powers went into making her up. She is spearing the Buffalo Demon in the side and her lion is attacking the water buffalo that is the Buffalo Demon's vehicle. In many representations, especially those used during **Durgā Pūjā**, she is accompanied by her children, the deities **Gaṇeśa**, **Lakṣmī**, **Sarasvatī**, and **Kārttikeya**.

DURGĀ PŪJĀ. Ten-day festival in honor of the **Goddess Durgā** and commemorating the various fierce manifestations of the **Mother Goddess** who appear on Earth to destroy the forces of evil; especially popular in **Bengal**. It corresponds to **Daśahra**, the 10-day festival celebrated in the **bright half** of the month of **Āśvina** that, in northern India, is celebrated in honor of **Rāma**'s defeat of **Rāvaṇa**.

DURVĀSA. Sage; son of the sage **Atri** and his wife, Anasuya. In the ***Mahābhārata***, he gave **Kuntī** a **mantra** that enabled her to bear semi-divine children. Durvāsa also cursed **Śakuntalā** to be forgotten by her lover. *See also* KĀLIDĀSA.

Priest performing Durgā Pūjā.

DURYODHANA. Main villain of the ***Mahābhārata***, eldest of the 100 sons of King **Dhṛtarāṣṭra** and Queen **Gāndhārī**.

DUSSEHRA. Popular alternate spelling of **Daśahra**. *See also* DURGĀ PŪJĀ.

DVAITA VEDĀNTA. Dualistic **Vedānta**; system of Vedānta **philosophy** developed by the **Vaiṣṇava ācārya Madhva** (1238–1317). Born near **Udipi** in **Karnataka**, where he spent most of his life, Madhva is believed by his devotees to be the third incarnation or **avatāra** of **Vāyu**, the **Vedic god** of the wind (the first two incarnations being **Hanuman** and **Bhīma**). A devout **Vaiṣṇava**, Madhva was highly critical of the **Advaita Vedānta** of **Śaṅkara**, seeing it as diminishing the significance of **bhakti** and as relegating **God** to a role subordinate to an impersonal reality (**Nirguṇa Brahman**). Madhva sees Brahman as identical to **Viṣṇu**, the supreme deity, and the **jīva**, or individual soul of a living being, as an eternally existing reality distinct from Viṣṇu. **Liberation**, or **mokṣa**, therefore does not involve an actual metaphysical union between the devotee and the divine (or, as in Advaita Vedānta, a realization that the distinction between the devotee and the divine is an illusion). The devotee and the divine are forever distinct. "Union" with the divine is a union of wills, of complete subordination of the will of the individual soul to the will of God (**Īśvara-praṇidhāna**). The individuality of one who attains liberation is not effaced. Liberation, rather, consists of residing for eternity in **Vaikunṭha**, or heaven, with God, a place of infinite bliss. Unusually for a Hindu tradition, Dvaita Vedānta teaches that it is possible that some souls may never reach liberation and remain eternally separated from God. Madhva's thought was highly influential within the bhakti movement, particularly upon such later thinkers as **Caitanya** and, in the modern period, **Bhaktivedānta Swāmī Prabhupāda**. The **Gauḍīya Vaiṣṇava** tradition of **Bengal** bears the stamp of Madhva's thought, as does the **International Society for Krishna Consciousness** (ISKCON).

DVĀRAKĀ. Site in Gujarat, on the western coast of India; believed to be the capital of **Kṛṣṇa**'s kingdom and a major site of pilgrimage for this reason. One of the four **maṭhas** or monasteries established by **Śaṅkara** is located in Dvārakā. A considerable number of ruins are present on the ocean floor just off the coast of Dvārakā. Interestingly, according to the ***Mahābhārata***, Dvārakā sank into the ocean after the accidental death of **Kṛṣṇa** at the hands of a hunter, with **Arjuna** leading a group of refugees away from the doomed city. Archaeologists estimate that the submerged portion of the city likely sank into the ocean around 1500 BCE. If this site can, indeed, be identified with Kṛṣṇa's Dvārakā, this suggests a likely date for whatever historical events form the basis of the main narrative of the *Mahābhārata*.

DVIJA. Twice born; term for the top three **castes**, or **varṇas**, of the caste system due to their employment of the **upanayana**, or **sacred thread** ceremony—a coming-of-age ritual that is likened to a "second birth" and marks one's entry into the first of the four stages of life or **āśramas**. Although all three of the upper castes are eligible to undergo this ritual according to the ***Dharma Śāstras***, it became increasingly common over the centuries for only **Brahmins** to undergo this ritual, the term *twice-born* became virtually synonymous with *Brahmin*.

DWARF AVATĀRA. *See* VĀMANA.

DYAUḤ PITṚ. "Heavenly Father"; a **Vedic** deity whose name is cognate with those of other **Indo-European** father deities, such as Zeus and Jupiter, and with the Latin *deus*, a generic term meaning "**god**." Dyauḥ Pitṛ seems to have many of the attributes of these other Indo-European father deities (and of others, such as the Norse Odin). A relatively obscure deity in the ***Vedas***, he is mentioned infrequently. He is the husband of **Pṛthvī** (also known as **Bhūdevī**), the **goddess** of the **Earth**, and father of **Indra**, **Agni**, and **Uṣā**, the gods and goddess, respectively, of the sky, fire, and the dawn. *See also* DEVAS.

E

EARTH. One of the elements (**mahābhūtas**) making up the physical universe according to **Vedānta philosophy**; also the **goddess** of the earth, wife of **Dyauḥ Pitṛ**, the heavenly father. *See also* BHŪ; BHŪDEVĪ; PṚTHVĪ.

EKA. One; "**the One**"; the supreme reality or absolute that underlies all existence. In the ***Ṛg Veda*** it is said that the One is the reality behind the appearance of diversity that gives rise to the world of phenomena. It is also said that the many **devas** or deities are all names for the One (*Ṛg Veda* 1.164.46)—"Reality is one, but the wise speak of it in many ways." In the ***Upaniṣads***, the ultimate reality—**Brahman**—is frequently said to be "One alone, without a second." Such Vedic references to the One are the basis for the view that an ancient thread of **monotheism** underlies the Hindu practice of **polytheism**, the idea being that what appear to be many deities are forms, aspects, or manifestations of the One. Though this view is certainly ancient in Hinduism, it has been reemphasized in the modern period in response to the criticisms of **Christian** and **Islamic** missionaries.

EKADANTA. One-toothed. Epithet of **Gaṇeśa**, who is given this name due to the fact that he is typically depicted as missing one tusk (or more commonly, with a broken tusk). According to one account, Gaṇeśa lost this tusk during a conflict with **Paraśurāma**. According to another account, he broke off the tusk to use it as a writing implement when **Vyāsa** was dictating the ***Mahābhārata*** to him. According to yet another account, he broke it off and flung it at the **moon** in anger when the moon laughed at him for falling off of his **vahana**, or vehicle, the mouse.

EKĀDAŚĪ. Eleventh; the 11th day of either the **bright half** or **dark half** of a month (that is, the 11th day after either **Amavasya**—the new-moon day—or **Purṇima**—the full-moon day). Many **Vaiṣṇavas** fast or hold a special **pūjā** (or worship ceremony) on this day. *See also* CALENDAR, HINDU.

EKALAVYA. Character from the ***Mahābhārata***. Ekalavya was a boy from one of the lower castes who wished to study with the great martial arts teacher

Droṇa in order to become a warrior. Droṇa rejected Ekalavya because of Ekalavya's low **caste** status. Undaunted, Ekalavya fashioned an image or **mūrti** of Droṇa and took it as his teacher, training before the image and showing it the devotion that one would normally show to one's teacher, or **guru**. Ekalavya progressed quickly in this fashion and his fame began to spread. Droṇa, hearing of Ekalavya's prowess, confronted him and demanded the customary payment that a student would give to a teacher, given that Ekalavya claimed Droṇa as his teacher. After Ekalavya promised to pay Droṇa in any way he requested, Droṇa demanded Ekalavya's thumb in payment, which Ekalavya cut off and surrendered to Droṇa without hesitation. This of course prevented Ekalavya from living as a warrior, for without a thumb he would be unable to perform the basic duties of a warrior, such as stringing a bow, holding a sword, and so on. In the modern period, Ekalavya has become a symbol of protest for the **Dalit** movement, who perceive the cruel behavior of Droṇa as emblematic of their suffering under the caste system. To compound Droṇa's behavior, it is also pointed out that Droṇa was not only engaging in **casteism**, or caste prejudice in the way he treated Ekalavya, but that he was behaving hypocritically as well, since Droṇa himself was a **Brahmin**, not a **kṣatriya**, or warrior, although he had adopted a vocation as a warrior.

EKNĀTH (1533–1599). Author and devotee of **Kṛṣṇa** from Maharashtra; widely known in Maharashtra as *Sant Eknath*. Like other adherents of the **bhakti** movement, Eknath, a **Brahmin** by birth, was opposed to **casteism** and once saved the life of a drowning **Dalit** child. A prolific writer, his best-known work is his *Eknāthi Bhāgavata*, a commentary on the ***Bhāgavata Purāṇa***.

ELEMENTS. The five elements are earth (**pṛthvī**), air (**vāyu**), fire (**agni**), water (**ap**), and space (**ākāśa**). According to the **Vaiśeṣika** system of philosophy (**darśana**), the first four of these elements are atomic and compounded in nature—unlike the self (**ātman**), which is atomic but not compounded, and space (ākāśa), which is neither atomic nor compounded. *See also* MAHĀBHŪTAS.

ELEPHANTA. Island near Mumbai (Bombay) with a large **temple** dedicated to **Śiva**. Its most famous image is of the **Trimūrti**, or three forms of the supreme deity—**Brahmā**, **Viṣṇu**, and **Śiva**. The temple dates to the period between the fifth and eighth centuries of the Common Era. Portuguese colonists named it after a large stone elephant that is one of the first features of the temple complex that one sees when landing on the island.

ELIADE, MIRCEA (1907–1986). Renowned Romanian historian of religions. Eliade studied **Sanskrit** and Indian **philosophy** at **Calcutta** University from 1928 to 1931 under the tutelage of **Surendranāth Dasgupta**. After teaching at the University of Bucharest and at the Sorbonne in Paris, he became a professor of the University of Chicago, where he established himself as a major figure in the study of the history of religions. He taught at the University of Chicago's Divinity School from 1957 to 1985. A prolific author not only in the area of religious studies but also of philosophy and fiction, his most famous works include *The Sacred and the Profane* and *Yoga: **Immortality** and Freedom*. **Wendy Doniger** currently holds the chair endowed in his name. *See also* INDOLOGY.

ELLORA (ELŪRĀ). Extensive site of numerous Hindu, **Buddhist**, and **Jain temples** and monasteries. Numerous caves dot the region, many of which have been used as sites for **meditation** through the centuries, being at various times extended and connected for the use of whole communities of monks. Among the more famous Hindu temples located at this complex is the **Kailāsa** temple, which is twice the size of the Parthenon in Greece and was carved from a single piece of rock. It was carved in the eighth century CE and is named after the mountain on which **Śiva** is believed to reside in the **Himālayas**.

EMERSON, RALPH WALDO (1803–1882). American author, philosopher, Unitarian minister, and a founding figure of the **transcendentalist** movement, which could be seen as the first wave of interest in Hindu thought in North America. Through his familiarity with early English translations of the ***Upaniṣads*** and the ***Bhagavad Gītā***, Emerson was deeply influenced by **Vedānta philosophy**. This influence is most pronounced in some of his **poetic** works, such as "Brahma," which includes direct quotations from the *Bhagavad Gītā*. *See also* THOREAU, HENRY DAVID.

ENLIGHTENMENT. Common English term for the state of heightened awareness that, in many Indic religious traditions, is a necessary precondition for **liberation** from **rebirth** (or **mokṣa**) and that is frequently used as a synonym for such liberation. Also known in contemporary Hindu traditions as **God-realization**, enlightenment consists of the direct awareness that **Brahman** and **ātman** are one and the same: that the fundamental basis of one's identity is the same as the ultimate reality that is the basis of all existence. It is the experiential discovery of the ground of all being as the basis of one's own being. It is not merely a cognitive awareness of this unity—an act of mental assent to the proposition that such unity is the case—but a direct, experiential awareness (**anubhāva**).

According to the **Advaita Vedānta** tradition, assent to the proposition of the unity of Brahman and ātman is a condition for the direct awareness that follows it, and the source of this proposition, is the Hindu **scriptures**. In **Neo-Vedānta**, the awareness itself is emphasized more than its scriptural source. Although Advaita Vedānta, **Jainism**, and **Buddhism** tend to conceive of enlightenment in impersonal terms, as the realization of an abstract **truth**, the more **bhakti**-oriented, theistic Vedānta traditions see it as coming to know **God**. *See also* VEDĀNTA.

ETAŚA. Vedic sage whose life was saved by **Indra**; also the name of one of the horses that pull the flying **chariot (vimāna)** of the sun **god, Sūrya**.

F

FASTING. A common form of **ascetic** practice, especially popular among laywomen, and often practiced to fulfill a specific wish. *See also* VRATA.

FIRE SACRIFICE. *See* AGNIṢṬOMA.

FISCHER, LEOPOLD. *See* AGEHĀNANDA BHĀRATĪ, SWĀMĪ.

FISH AVATĀRA. *See* MATSYA.

FIVE M'S. Five substances consumed or activities performed in the ceremonies of the Vāmācāra or **Left-Handed** tradition of **Tantra** that are normally regarded as impure. This tradition involves participation in activities normally considered impure in the name of demonstrating the principle of nonduality (**advaita**): that both purity and impurity are illusory constructs, the reality being that all is **Brahman**. The substances or activities in question are called the "five M's" because the words for them all begin with the letter m: madya (alcohol), māṃsa (meat), **matsya** (fish), **mudrā** (grain), and maithunā (sexual intercourse—although in this context, it refers specifically to sexual intercourse with a partner who is not one's spouse, because sexual intercourse is otherwise not regarded as inherently impure, being a natural and normal activity for non**ascetics**).

Mudrā (grain) is an unusual member of this set of items, since it is not normally regarded as impure, though it is forbidden by some religious fasts (**vratas**). It is possible that this term refers to specific symbolic gestures performed in the context of the ritual (as when it refers to the hand gestures of deities when depicted in **mūrti** form or when employed in specific forms of **meditation**).

FOUR GOALS OF HUMANITY. Physical pleasure (**kāma**), wealth (**artha**), virtue (**dharma**), and **liberation** from the cycle of **rebirth** (**mokṣa**). *See also* PURUṢĀRTHA.

FOUR STAGES OF LIFE. The student stage (**brahmacarya**), the householder stage (**gārhasthya**), the stage of withdrawal or retirement (**vanaprastha**), and renunciation (**sannyāsa**). *See also* ĀŚRAMA.

FOUR YOGAS. Four spiritual disciplines that can be practiced either individually or jointly in the pursuit of **mokṣa**. Although developed in a variety of Hindu texts through the centuries, the yogas were first codified and theorized as four distinct disciplines in the modern period by **Swāmī Vivekānanda**. They are the yogas of action (**karma yoga**), of wisdom (**jñāna yoga**), of devotion (**bhakti yoga**), and of **meditation** (**dhyāna** or rāja yoga). As conceived by Vivekānanda, each **yoga** (or combination of yogas) is suited to a different personality type. Karma yoga is working selflessly for the good of others with no thought of personal reward and is suited to an activist temperament. Jñāna yoga is for the intellectual, the philosopher, and consists of discerning and differentiating between what is real and what is unreal. Bhakti yoga is intense love and longing for a personal form of the divine and manifests in a relationship with **God**, as a servant, friend, spouse, parent, or child. Dhyāna yoga is the practice of meditation. The subsequent tradition of **Neo-Vedānta** tends to emphasize the idea of practicing all four yogas as aspects of a total, holistic approach to the spiritual life.

FUNERAL. *See* ANCESTRAL RITES; ANTYEṢṬI.

G

GADAR MOVEMENT. *See* GHADṚ MOVEMENT.

GAṆAPATI. Lord of hosts, an epithet of **Gaṇeśa**. The gaṇas, or hosts, refer to groups of demigods under Gaṇeśa's command.

GĀṆAPATYA. Branch of Hinduism devoted to the worship of **Gaṇeśa** as the supreme form of the divine, analogous to **Vaiṣṇava** worship of **Viṣṇu**, **Śaiva** worship of **Śiva**, and **Śākta** worship of the **Mother Goddess**. Though not as widespread as these movements, the Gāṇapatya tradition has made its presence felt in the universal popularity of Gaṇeśa.

The worship of Gaṇeśa probably began as a Śaiva practice—a logical development, given that Gaṇeśa is the son of Śiva and **Śaktī** (or **Pārvatī**, as the Mother Goddess is also known). In the ninth century, **Śaṅkara** declared Gaṇeśa to be one of five possible deities of choice, or **iṣṭadevatās**, in his system of five objects of worship (**pañcayātana pūjā**), alongside Śiva, Śakti, Viṣṇu, and **Sūrya**. The inclusion of Gaṇeśa in this system as an equal to such "high" deities as Śiva, Śakti, and Viṣṇu suggests the Gāṇapatya sect already existed in some form in Śaṅkara's time.

In the modern period, largely due to **Bal Gangadhar Tilak**'s promotion during the movement for Indian independence of **Gaṇeśa pūjā** as a symbol of national unity, the worship of Gaṇeśa has become a pan-Hindu phenomenon, with members of all the major sects honoring Gaṇeśa as the remover of obstacles at the outset of any large undertaking.

GANDHA. Scent; the sense of smell; attribute of the **earth element (pṛthvī)** according to **Vaiśeṣika philosophy**. *See also* MAHĀBHŪTAS.

GĀNDHĀRĪ. Character in the ***Mahābhārata***; wife of **Dhṛtarāṣṭra** and mother of the **Kauravas**. After the climactic battle of the epic, in which all of her sons are slain by the army of the **Pāṇḍavas**, Gāndhārī curses **Kṛṣṇa** for his role in the battle as advisor to the Pāṇḍavas. Gāndhārī's curse eventually results in Kṛṣṇa's accidental **death** in the forest at the hands of a hunter.

GANDHARVAS. Celestial musicians, a category of divine being said to possess great physical strength. The word is cognate with the Greek *centaur*.

GĀNDHĪ, MAHĀTMA. *See* GĀNDHĪ, MOHANDĀS K.

GĀNDHĪ, MOHANDĀS K. (1869–1948). Hindu reformer and leader of the nonviolent movement for Indian independence; often called **Mahātma** (Great Soul). He was born to a **Vaiśya** family in Gujarat, on the western coast of India. His family religious tradition was **Vaiṣṇava**, though he had a strong exposure in his early years to **Jainism** as well. At the age of 13 he entered into an arranged **marriage** with the equally young Kasturba Kapadia. At 18, he traveled to London to study law, against the wishes of his **caste** elders. With an intense interest in religion and **philosophy**, he had many conversations in England with both Christians and **Theosophists**. Through a translation of the ***Bhagavad Gītā*** given to him by a British Theosophist, he rediscovered his Hindu roots. He moved to South Africa in 1891, where he experienced intense racial prejudice for the first time, leading to his political awakening. While in South Africa, he agitated for equal treatment of Indians as citizens of the British Empire.

Only after returning to India in 1914 did Gāndhī begin to see imperialism itself as the root of the problems facing Indians. After touring the country extensively in order to learn firsthand about the concerns of his countrymen, he joined the movement for Indian independence.

Advocating **nonviolent** methods of protest and also adopting the lifestyle of a **sannyāsī** (taking a **brahmacarya** vow, though he was still married to Kasturba), Gāndhī began to have a wide following among the common people of India, especially in rural areas and villages. Unlike other independence leaders, whose English educations made them culturally Westernized, and so remote from common people, Gāndhī embraced and practiced village traditions. At the same time, though, many of the stands he took on a variety of issues were controversial, even among Indians, and several attempts were made on his life. For his activism he was jailed a number of times by the British authorities. Gāndhī was also a leading figure of the Indian National Congress, the main party that was working for Indian political independence.

Gāndhī called his philosophy **satyāgraha**, or "soul force," although the literal meaning of this term is "holding fast to the **truth**." Having some resonance with the epic concept of the vow of truth—in which the truth of a character's words give his or her vow particular effectiveness—the idea behind satyāgraha is that the truth always prevails, and that one who is faithful to truth will also prevail, despite adversity and opposition. The nonviolent activist who adheres to methods that are in harmony with the ends he pursues is behaving in a manner consistent with truth. The inherent power of truth will therefore ensure the ultimate success of the activist's cause. The idea of the harmony of ends and means is also connected with the idea of **karma**, that like **actions** produce like effects. Therefore only just means can produce just results.

Gāndhī viewed the pursuit of truth and the practice of nonviolence (**ahiṃsā**) as inseparable from one another, seeing truth and nonviolence as different sides of the same coin, truth being the interconnected and ultimately unified nature of all beings (his interpretation of **Advaita Vedānta**) and nonviolence being the implication of this truth in practice. He also underwent a shift in his thinking over the course of his lifetime from the idea that "**God** is truth" to the idea that "Truth is God." The significance of this shift is that, whereas by holding that "God is truth" one might identify one's own idea of God with the truth, by holding that "Truth is God" one is committed to pursuing the truth wherever it may lead.

In terms of Indian independence, Gāndhī's methods were in one sense effective, creating global sympathy for his movement. Utilizing boycotts and marches, Gāndhī was able to put the brutality of imperialism on display, with peaceful demonstrators facing the harsh blows of the British police in front of the world media. On the other hand, it is still debated today whether the eventual withdrawal of the British from India was due more to the independence movement or to other circumstances, such as World War II and the gradual realization among the European powers that far-flung colonial empires, in the end, were more of an economic drain than a boon.

Gāndhī's understanding of Indian independence, or self-rule (*swarāj*), was holistic and informed by Hindu traditions, as well as by Jainism, **transcendentalism**, and **Christianity**. He saw political **liberation** as one component of the liberation of the whole person—like liberation in the classical Hindu sense, as **mokṣa**, with a collective dimension distinct from the individualism of traditional **yoga** philosophies. He therefore placed a great deal of emphasis on purification and the moral perfection of the Indian community.

In addition to working for Indian independence, Gāndhī sought to end the practice of **Untouchability**—though he did not advocate the total abolition of caste, which led to a rift between himself and **Bhīmrao Ambedkar**. Gāndhī also advocated interreligious harmony, particularly between Hindus and Muslims, the many divisions between these two religious communities having been successfully exploited by British divide-and-rule policies, ultimately leading to the partition of India and Pakistan. These are two areas in which Gāndhī received, and continues to receive, considerable criticism; his actions on behalf of **Dalits** and Hindu–Muslim unity ultimately failed to resolve these issues.

On a number of occasions Gāndhī undertook **fasting**—in effect, going on a hunger strike—to persuade his followers to behave as he wished: to renounce violence against the British, to treat people of the lower castes as equals, or to renounce the Hindu–Muslim conflict.

India became independent on 15 August 1947, an event that was widely seen as a triumph for Gāndhī and his methods. Many, however—including Gāndhī himself—did not view it this way, the euphoria of independence being overshadowed by the violence of partition. On 30 August 1948, Gāndhī was assassinated by Nathuram Godse, a **Hindu Nationalist** who blamed Gāndhī for the violence suffered by Hindus during the partition.

Though widely revered globally today, Gāndhī has also been subject to criticism, some of it during his lifetime. In addition to the criticisms already mentioned—that his denunciation of **casteism** was insufficiently radical and that he did not do enough to stop the partition of India and Pakistan—he was heavily criticized for testing his commitment to celibacy by sleeping next to naked young women (a test he did pass, by all accounts). At the same time, even some of his harshest critics acknowledge Gāndhī's transformative leadership and the power of his vision of peace and justice.

GAṆEŚA. Popular Hindu deity; elephant-headed remover of obstacles. As one of the sons of **Śiva** and **Pārvatī** (the other being **Karttikeya**), Gaṇeśa has long been an object of devotion in **Śaiva** traditions. In modern Hinduism, however, he has become a popular pan-Hindu deity. As the remover of obstacles, he is traditionally evoked at the beginning of any new venture, including at the commencement of a **pūjā**, or worship ceremony, for any deity. There is also a **Gāṇapatya** tradition that is centered on the worship of Gaṇeśa as the supreme deity, just as the Śaiva traditions are centered on Śiva and **Vaiṣṇavism** is centered on **Viṣṇu**.

There are many differing accounts of how Gaṇeśa came to have an elephant head. In one account, Pārvatī creates Gaṇeśa from the residue left behind after her bath. This occurs while Śiva is away from home. Pārvatī assigns her newly formed son the task of guarding the door to her chamber while she is bathing, ordering him not to allow anyone to come in, but neglecting to make an exception in the case of her husband, Śiva. When Śiva returns, he is angered to find this creature, Gaṇeśa, forbidding him from entering his wife's room. He therefore beheads Gaṇeśa. Pārvatī, greatly distressed at this, tells Śiva that he has killed his son. The repentant Śiva then searches for the best head he can find for Gaṇeśa, and takes the head of **Airāvata**, the elephant mount of **Indra**, the lord of the **devas**, placing it upon Gaṇeśa's neck and bringing him back to life.

In another account, Gaṇeśa loses his original head when his mother, Pārvatī, is insistent that all the other **gods** look at her beautiful new baby. Unfortunately, **Śāni**, the presiding deity of the planet Saturn, is cursed with an evil eye. Śāni's gaze causes the infant deity's head to fall off, requiring it

Gaṇeśa, remover of obstacles and son of Śiva and Śakti.

to be replaced with the head of an elephant (dutifully supplied this time not by Śiva, but by **Viṣṇu**). Finally, there is another account in which Gaṇeśa is simply born with the head of an elephant, with no particular reason being given. Gaṇeśa's vehicle is **Mūśaka**, the mouse.

Symbolically, Gaṇeśa's elephant head represents both divine wisdom (because the elephant is a wise animal, with a long memory) and strength (given the great strength of elephants). He also has a pot belly, which is said to represent divine expansiveness, and is fond of sweets, which are the favored offering to present during his pūjā.

The worship of Gaṇeśa was popularized in the modern period by **Bal Gangadhar Tilak** (1856–1920) in Maharashtra to promote Hindu pride and unity. The annual Gaṇeśa Pūjā that he instituted is a very popular event in the city of Mumbai (Bombay).

GAṆEŚAPURI ĀŚRAMA. Indian center of the **Siddha Yoga** movement; established in the village of Gaṇeśapuri, on the outskirts of Mumbai (Bombay) in 1949 by a **sannyāsī** named **Swāmī Nityānanda** (1897–1961), founder of the Siddha Yoga **saṃpradāya** and **guru** of **Swāmī Muktānanda** (1908–1982), who brought the practice to the West. The lineage is now led by **Swāmī Chidvilāsānanda (Gurumayī)**.

GAṄGĀ. The most sacred river in Hinduism; also the name of the **goddess** who is the personification of this river. Flowing from the northwestern reaches of the **Himālayas**, where it is fed by melting glaciers, and emptying into the Bay of **Bengal** in the east, many sacred pilgrimage sites are located along the course of this river, including **Haridwār**, **Rishikesh**, **Prayāga (Allahabad)**, and **Banaras**, two of which (Haridwar and Prayāga) are traditional locations for the **Kumbha Melā** festival. Many devout Hindus believe a prayerful bath in the Gaṅgā (or Ganges) can be both physically and spiritually purifying. It is customary, if possible, to have one's ashes immersed in the Gaṅgā after **cremation**, and many cremation grounds are located near the **ghāṭs**, or stairs leading into the river at various sites, in order to facilitate this custom.

According to Hindu sacred **literature**, the Gaṅgā is an extension of a celestial river that corresponds to the Milky Way. The river was brought to the Earth by the **asceticism** of Bhagiratha, a king whose ancestors had been cursed by a sage. Bhagiratha wanted to find a way to cleanse his ancestors of this curse, and so prayed for the Gaṅgā's descent. Fearing that the force of the river's descent to the Earth might destroy the world, **Śiva** agreed to catch the river on his head, letting it then flow gently down his matted hair and onto the Earth. Śiva, in this image, represents the Himālayas, from where the river flows and where Śiva is also believed to reside, on Mount **Kailāsa**.

In the ***Mahābhārata***, King Śantanu of the **Bhārata** dynasty falls in love with the goddess Gaṅgā when he encounters her in the forest while on a hunting expedition. She agrees to marry him on the condition that he must not question anything she does, or she will leave him. Unbeknownst to Śantanu, however, a set of **Vedic** deities, the eight **Vasus**, have been cursed to be reborn as human beings by the sage **Vasiṣṭha** because they stole his cows. Gaṅgā agrees to help the Vasus escape the limits of the human form by giving birth to them and then drowning them in her waters. One by one, Gaṅgā gives birth to healthy baby sons, and then, to Śantanu's horror, drowns them immediately after birth. But he remembers his promise not to question his wife's **actions** and remains silent. The eighth time, however, he intercedes and asks Gaṅgā to spare their child. She agrees but then leaves him because he has broken his promise. This child grows up to be **Bhīṣma**, the wise elder of the Bhārata dynasty throughout most of the epic. In terms of **karma**, it is said that Bhīṣma lived such a long life and witnessed as much suffering as he did due to the fact that, among the Vasus, he was the one who instigated the theft of the cows.

In the contemporary period, the excessive pollution suffered by the sacred Gaṅgā has become a major issue and a source of much controversy, with calls by both religious and secular organizations for the government of India to address the ecological crisis. On top of the pollution issue, recent studies have also suggested that global warming may be melting the glaciers on which the river depends at such a rate that the river itself may one day dry up completely. This would be a major disaster, not only from a religious point of view but also because millions of people depend upon the Gaṅgā as their main source of drinking water.

GANGES RIVER. *See* GAṄGĀ.

GARBHA. Literally "womb" or "embryo"; a folk **dance** especially popular in Gujarat. The dancers, who are usually (but not always) **women**, form a circle and make sweeping gestures. Each gesture ends with either the clapping of the hands or the striking together of two sticks. It is a joyful, celebratory dance, performed on festive occasions.

GARBHA-GṚHA. Innermost chamber of a **temple**, where the main image (**mūrti**) of its central deity is enshrined. Typically only the temple priests are permitted to enter this chamber, although devotees may look inside when the doors are open for **darśana** (viewing of the image). Not all temples have a garbha-gṛha with closing doors. In these temples, the main mūrti is either always on display or is covered with a curtain.

GĀRHASTHYA. The **householder** stage of life; the second of the four stages of life or **āśramas**. This stage of life is characterized by marriage, child-rearing, and economically productive activity. One formally enters this stage by means of one's wedding ceremony.

GARUḌA. "Devourer" (of serpents); the divine eagle; servant and vehicle of **Viṣṇu**, and a popular subject of Hindu **temple art**. Symbolically, Garuḍa is represented in **pūjā**, or ritualistic worship, by a bell. Through his symbolic presence, Garuḍa serves to protect the worship ceremony from evil influences.

GAUḌAPĀDA (fl. 8th century CE). Guru of **Govinda**, who was the guru of **Śaṅkara**, thus making Gauḍapāda Śaṅkara's "grand-guru"; early exponent of **Advaita Vedānta**, whose best-known work is his commentary (**bhāṣya**) on the ***Maṇḍukya Upaniṣad***. Of particular note is Gauḍapāda's extensive use of **Buddhist** terminology and styles of argumentation in this text, albeit in the service of a thoroughly **Vedāntic** thesis—*ajātivāda*, the doctrine of nonorigination, according to which all change is an illusion, the sole reality being the eternal and changeless **Brahman**, identical to the self (**ātman**). His name suggests that Gauḍapāda was from **Bengal**, a major Buddhist center.

GAUḌĪYA VAIṢṆAVA. Vaiṣṇava tradition of **Bengal**. **Caitanya** (1486–1533) started this branch of Vaiṣṇavism. Though sharing with the **Dvaita Vedānta** of **Madhva** a very strong emphasis on **bhakti** and the belief that

Kṛṣṇa is the supreme reality, the Gauḍīya Vaiṣṇava tradition, following the theology of the **Gosvāmins**, claims the relationship of the world to the divine is *acintya-bhedābheda*, or "inconceivable difference and identity," rather than a pure difference, as Madhva affirms (much less a pure identity, as **Śaṅkara**'s **Advaita Vedānta** claims). The **International Society for Krishna Consciousness** of **Bhaktivedānta Swāmī Prabhupāda** is a continuation of this tradition.

GAURĪ. Benevolent rain **goddess**, associated with agriculture and human flourishing in general; usually depicted as a form of the **Mother Goddess** and wife of **Śiva**, but also as the wife of **Varuṇa**, the **Vedic** ocean deity.

GAUTAMA. One of the Seven Sages (**Saptarṣi**) presiding over the cosmos. *Gautama* is also the **gotra** name of the **Buddha**, Siddhārtha Gautama (c. 490–410 BCE), but the two figures should not be confused with one another.

Haridrumata Gautama is also the name of the sage in the ***Chandogya Upaniṣad*** who accepts the boy **Satyakāma** as his student, despite the boy's low birth **caste** status, because the boy is honest about his background, and honesty is a trait of an ideal **Brahmin**.

GAYĀ. Town in the northeastern Indian state of Bihar; sacred place of pilgrimage that is especially dedicated to the making of offerings to one's ancestors (**śrāddha**). Gayā is near Bodh Gayā, a sacred place of pilgrimage for **Buddhists** for being the location where the **Buddha** attained **enlightenment** (**nirvāṇa**) under a banyan tree. Interestingly, the site of the offerings to the dead at nearby Gayā is also under a sacred banyan tree. Which sacred location came first is a subject of some contention and speculation among scholars.

GĀYATRĪ. "Song of protection"; name of a famous **mantra** of the ***Ṛg Veda*** (3.62.10), as well as the **poetic** meter in which it was composed; later personified as a **goddess** with five heads who is a wife of **Brahmā**. The mantra is a hymn to the solar deity **Savitṛ** and is traditionally recited by **Brahmins** at dawn. The chanting of the Gāyatrī mantra as a daily practice for all people is also promoted by the **Ārya Samāj**.

The mantra reads: *Oṃ bhūr bhuvaḥ svaḥ, Tat savitur vareṇyam, Bhargo devasya dhīmahi, dhiyo yo naḥ pracodayāt*. It means, "Om. Oh, earth! Oh, sky! Oh, heavens! Let us reflect upon the beautiful light of the god Savitṛ. May he guide our thoughts."

The five-headed goddess who personifies this mantra became the wife of Brahmā when Brahmā was holding a sacrifice (**yajña**). A **householder** who performs a sacrifice must be accompanied by his wife. But Brahmā's wife, **Sarasvatī**, was late for the ritual, which also had to be performed at the astrologically correct time. **Indra** then presented Brahmā with Gāyatrī, who

Goddess Gāyatrī, embodiment of the Gāyatrī Mantra.

served as Brahmā's wife for the purpose of the sacrifice. The deeper symbolism of the story seems to be that the Gāyatrī mantra is just as indispensable to the ritual of sacrifice as is the presence of one's spouse.

GĀYATRĪ MANTRA. *See* GĀYATRĪ.

GHADṚ MOVEMENT. Early 20th-century movement among Indian immigrants in North America to support the violent overthrow of the British government in India. It sought to foment rebellion among Indians serving in the British army and to gain support from the United States in the cause of Indian independence. The movement, which was led by **Har Dayal** (1884–1939), suffered major setbacks when the United States entered World War I as an ally of Great Britain. Dayal was arrested and then fled to Germany. Many of the Indian immigrants in the United States and Canada returned to India to help with the revolution, but the British government was aware of their plans and arrested them. At the end of World War I, Dayal returned to India, where he renounced violence and joined **Mohandās K. Gāndhī**'s nonviolent independence movement. The Ghadṛ movement ceased to be a major force at this point and dissolved when independence was achieved in 1947.

GHĀṬ. (**Sanskrit**: ghaṭṭa.) Set of stairs leading into a sacred river, such as the **Gaṅgā**, to facilitate bathing for pilgrims.

GHEE. Clarified butter; substance frequently offered in a **Vedic yajña** and also in **pūjā**, or worship. In the latter case, it is usually mixed with other sacred items, such as honey, milk, and yogurt. When offered as part of a Vedic ritual, such as a **homa** or **havan**, it is not mixed with anything else and is placed directly in the sacred fire with special spoons designed for that purpose.

GHOSE, AUROBINDO (1872–1950). Better known as Sri Aurobindo; freedom fighter for Indian independence and later a major philosopher, Hindu reformer, and advocate of a system of **yoga** known as "integral yoga." Trained in Western philosophy, Aurobindo's writings seek to unite and integrate both Western and Indian metaphysical themes.

Born into a wealthy **Bengali Brahmin** family, Aurobindo was sent to England for his education in 1879, where he studied in Cambridge University. In 1893, he returned to India where he served as a minister for the Mahārāja of Baroda, Gujarat. But wanting to strengthen his ties to his Bengali heritage, he moved to **Calcutta** in 1906.

Both during his service in Baroda and subsequently, in Calcutta, Aurobindo was drawn to the cause of Indian independence. Aligning himself with the militant **Hindu Nationalists**, such as **Bal Gangadhar Tilak**, Aurobindo advocated violent revolution. As a result of his political activities, the British government arrested Aurobindo in 1908 on the suspicion that he was connected with an antigovernment bombing. Although he was acquitted in the bombing case, he was imprisoned for a year for sedition. During the period of his imprisonment, he practiced yoga extensively and wrote of experiencing a number of powerful spiritual visions at this time, including visions of **Kṛṣṇa** and **Swāmī Vivekānanda**, who had died just a few years earlier (in 1902). In 1910, after his release from prison, he announced his retirement from politics. Moving to the French colony of Pondicherry, he dedicated himself to spiritual practice and philosophical writing, developing his system of integral yoga. A prolific author, his writings include *Integral Yoga*, *The Synthesis of Yoga*, *The Secret of the Veda*, *Essays on the Gita*, *Rebirth and Karma*, and the monumental *The Life Divine*.

One of the major themes of Aurobindo's writing is the integration of Western thought, with its emphasis on the **material** world and the evolution of **mind** from matter, and Indian thought, with its emphasis on pure consciousness and what Aurobindo calls the "involution" of mind into matter. These two complementary processes are really one process viewed from different perspectives, according to Aurobindo's account. The term "involution" is drawn from the writings of Swāmī Vivekānanda, and Aurobindo says several times that he sees himself as building on and continuing the work that was begun by Vivekānanda and his master, **Ramakrishna**, both of whom sought to reconcile the concepts of the absolute realm of spirit and the relative realm of time, space, matter, and change. In *Rebirth and Karma*, he also articulates the idea—which is now common among Westerners who believe in **rebirth**—that reincarnation is a learning process for the soul. Aurobindo dedicated his life to bringing divine awareness or "supermind" into the realm of concrete, physical expression through the practice of yoga. Before his death, he claimed to have achieved this manifestation within himself.

Aurobindo also popularized an approach to the ***Vedas*** that was a striking contrast with the dominant **Indological** paradigm of his time. Rather than seeing the early **Vedic literature** as the relatively primitive nature **poetry** of a nomadic society that gradually develops into the more sophisticated **Vedānta** philosophy of the ***Upaniṣads***, he suggests that the early Vedic poems already presuppose the fully developed **philosophy**, presenting it in a symbolic form. It is only as the key to this ancient symbolic code is forgotten that Vedic philosophy needs to be articulated more explicitly in the *Upaniṣads*, which are thus seen as an unpacking of what was already present in the early Vedic texts, rather than as an evolutionary development from them.

Aurobindo attracted many followers, including Westerners, the most famous of whom was a French woman named Mira Richard, to whom Aurobindo and his followers referred as "the Mother." Aurobindo saw Richard as an incarnation of **Śakti**, the **Mother Goddess** and feminine energy of **creation**. Richard took over Aurobindo's community after his death in 1950.

GĪTAGOVINDA. "Song of the Cowherd." This highly **bhakti**-infused 12th-century **Sanskrit poem** by the **Bengali Vaiṣṇava** author **Jayadeva** uses the love affair between **Rādhā** and **Kṛṣṇa** to depict the bond of love between the soul of the **devotee** and **God**. The text is highly erotically charged and has been compared by some with the biblical *Song of Solomon*. It is based on the ***Bhāgavata Purāṇa***.

GOBIND SINGH, GURU (1666–1708). Tenth and final **guru** in the lineage of gurus of **Sikhism**. In response to the fierce persecution suffered by the Sikh community under the **Mughal** emperor Aurangzeb, Gobind Singh established the *khalsa*, or community of Sikh warriors, marked by the "Five K's," or five items whose names, in Punjabi, start with the letter K: *keś*, or long hair; *kangha*, a special comb with which the hair is tied on top of the head; *kara*, a circular steel bracelet; *kacha*, an undergarment ensuring preparedness for battle; and the *kirpan*, a sword or dagger. Gobind Singh's father, Guru Tegh Bahadur, had been beheaded by Aurangzeb, and Gobind Singh himself had to spend much of his time in hiding. Knowing that he might not survive in the ongoing conflict, he designated the sacred text of the Sikhs, the *Ādi Granth*, the perpetual guru of the community after his **death**. *See also* NĀNAK, GURU.

GOD. The concepts of divinity in the various Hindu traditions vary greatly. Hindu texts express positions ranging from atheism, to **monotheism**, to **polytheism**, to panentheism (the idea that God is present within all beings, and that all beings, in turn, dwell in God), to pantheism (the idea that God simply *is* all beings). Translating Hindu concepts of God into English is further complicated by the fact that there are a variety of **Sanskrit** terms that can be translated as "God" that all have quite distinct meanings in their original Hindu contexts. A **deva**, for example, is a powerful and long-lived being in charge of a particular aspect of the universe: such as **Agni**, the god of fire; or **Sūrya**, the god of the sun; or **Yama**, the god of **death**.

Because there are many devas, corresponding to many different aspects of reality, translating *deva* as "god" communicates a polytheistic view of Hinduism. If one speaks of "the **gods**" in the plural in a Hindu context, one is typically referring to the devas. If, however, one translates *deva* as "angel" (which may be a more appropriate analogue), then one gets a picture of Hinduism as a tradition with a view of divinity closer to those of the monotheistic Abrahamic traditions. God, in the singular, in a monotheistic sense, corresponds to the Sanskrit terms **Īśvara** or **Bhagavān**. Some of the Hindu traditions, such as **Vaiṣṇavism** and **Śaivism**, do conceive of God in this way (with the one supreme deity being identified with either **Viṣṇu** or **Śiva**, and other deities, the devas, playing a role similar to that of angels in the Abrahamic traditions). But there is also the idea in Hinduism of panentheism—of divinity as an all-pervasive presence that corresponds to the **Vedāntic** concept of **Brahman**. God, as Brahman, is an omnipresent energy and consciousness that can be approached and experienced either as the supreme deity, in a monotheistic sense, or through various manifestations that correspond to the many devas. One could call this a monotheistic polymorphism—the idea of one supreme divine reality that takes many forms.

Because Brahman is present in *all* beings, then all beings—including ourselves—are at least potentially divine, or divine in our true, inner nature that will only be fully realized when we become **enlightened**.

On the other hand, because most Hindu traditions see the universe as eternal, with no specific beginning in time but rather as undergoing an ongoing process of emergence, existence, and dissolution, there is no creator God in an absolute sense, as there is in the Abrahamic traditions, who creates the universe *ex nihilo*. So in this sense, Hinduism can even be seen as atheistic. *See also* GODDESS.

GODDESS. In Hindu traditions, far from being limited to the male form, divinity also manifests in a great variety of female forms. As with Hindu **gods**, one can conceive of the goddesses of Hinduism in **polytheistic**, **monotheistic**, or panentheistic senses. **Devī**, the feminine form of the **Sanskrit** word **deva**, can simply refer to a female deva—one of many goddesses in a polytheistic sense. **Vedic** goddesses, like their male counterparts, are largely identified with or preside over natural phenomena, such as **Uṣā**, the goddess of the dawn, and **Sarasvatī**, the goddess of the river of the same name (who is identified in later Hindu traditions as the goddess of wisdom). In the **Śākta** tradition, though, *Devī* is a proper name for the Goddess in the singular, in a monotheistic sense, as the supreme deity of the entire universe: the **Mother Goddess**. Devī, or **Mahādevī** (Great Goddess) is identified in many Hindu traditions as the wife of **Śiva**. She has many forms, such as the docile wife and mother, **Pārvatī**; the warrior goddess, **Durgā**, who defeats **demonic** beings and drives away evil; and the fierce, demon-slaying **Kālī**.

In her role as **Śakti**, the power of **creation**, the Goddess can also be identified with all of the many goddesses of the Hindu pantheon, who are seen as her various forms or manifestations. Goddesses such as **Lakṣmī** and Sarasvatī are also called *śaktis*, or power centers, of the deities that are their husbands—**Viṣṇu** and **Brahmā**, respectively. In this role, the Goddess and her various personae are seen as the energizing principle, in the absence of which their corresponding male gods would be incapable of effective activity. The divine pairing of Śiva and Śakti, in particular, is often presented, especially in Śākta texts, as a composite being, with the **God** and Goddess ultimately inseparable from one another as parts of an internally differentiated, but finally unitary, godhead. In its affirmation of internal relations within the godhead, this concept is not unlike the **Christian** idea of the trinity.

Finally, the supreme Mother Goddess is identified, in **Tantric** traditions (and in **Neo-Vedānta**, which is strongly informed by the Tantric background and sensibility of **Ramakrishna**), with **Brahman**, the absolute, as it appears from the perspective of **māyā**, the universe of time and space. Ramakrishna states that "Kālī is verily Brahman, and Brahman is verily Kālī. It is one and the same Reality. When we think of It as inactive . . . then we call it Brahman. But when It engages in . . . activities, then we call It Kālī or Śakti." This statement implies a pantheistic or panentheistic understanding of the Goddess as being manifested within all beings. This understanding is also present in the ancient Śākta scripture, the ***Devī Mahātmya*** or ***Caṇḍī*** *Paṭh*, with its refrain of **mantras** that refer to "The Goddess who dwells within all beings."

Somewhat ironically, there is no clear relationship between the worship of female deities, to the point of identifying the supreme reality as the Goddess, and the treatment of actual Hindu **women** historically. Patriarchy has coexisted with Goddess-worship in Hindu practice and the worship of the Goddess (and various goddesses) has not been seen as the basis for a feminist critique of patriarchy until the modern period. It is also not at all clear that Goddess-worship has been in any way harmful to women. Rather, the two phenomena—Goddess-worship and patriarchy—seem to be independent variables. Again, this situation has begun to change in the modern period, with Hindu feminists utilizing the discourse of Goddess-worship as a starting point for a critique of patriarchy. But this is a relatively recent development.

GODS. Deities; divine beings. When referring to "gods" in the plural, in a **polytheistic** sense, one is typically referring, in a Hindu context, to the **devas**. These deities can be seen as distinct beings—superpowerful entities in charge of some aspect or other of the natural world, such as **Agni**, the god of fire; or **Sūrya**, the god of the sun; or **Yama**, the god of **death**. But they can also be seen as forms or aspects of one supreme deity—**God** in a **monotheistic** sense, performing various roles and taking on various personalities for the purpose of maintaining the universe. This understanding most commonly applies to what one could call the "high gods"—deities like **Viṣṇu**, **Śiva**, and the **Mother Goddess**, who are widely seen as the one God, of whom all the other gods are either forms or aspects. The gods can also be seen as subordinate demigods or angels, ultimately answering to the **One**. It is also possible, finally, to see all personal forms of divinity as manifestations of a higher energy or consciousness—**Brahman**—that is ultimately impersonal.

GOD-REALIZATION. Brahma-**nirvāṇa**; the state of ultimate realization that liberates one from the cycle of **death** and **rebirth**. In **Advaita Vedānta**, this realization consists of the direct awareness that **Brahman** and **ātman** are one: that the individual self and the ultimate reality at the basis of all existence are not separate entities.

According to Advaita Vedānta, the differentiation between Brahman and ātman is a mere appearance, or **māyā**. One therefore does not "become" one with the divine so much as realize that one was never separate from the divine in the first place. But in more dualistic, theistic forms of **Vedānta**, there is a real metaphysical distinction between the individual and the divine. God-realization in these traditions is therefore conceived as a loving union or harmonizing of wills between the individual devotee and **God** in the form of **bhakti**—a relationship of devotion and of absolute dependence of the devotee upon the divine—not a realization of a literal metaphysical unity. *See also* MOKṢA.

GOLDEN AVATĀRA. Epithet of **Caitanya**.

GOLDEN EMBRYO. *See* HIRAṆYAGARBHA.

GOLOKA. "Cow world"; name for **Kṛṣṇa**'s celestial realm, also known as **Vaikuṇṭha.**

GONDA, JAN (1905–1991). Dutch **Indologist**; professor of **Sanskrit** from 1932 to 1970 at the University of Utrecht. A prolific author, Gonda published a wide variety of articles throughout his lifetime on many Indological subjects.

GOPĪ. "Cowherdess"; "milkmaid"; literally "cowgirl," though the cultural connotations of this word in English make it an odd fit as a translation. It refers specifically to a group of women in the **Vraja** region who, according to the ***Bhāgavata Purāṇa***, were the lovers and playmates of **Kṛṣṇa** in his youth. **Rādhā** was the foremost among the gopīs and the special beloved of Kṛṣṇa. Their relationship is detailed in the ***Gītagovinda***, a work by the 12th-century **bhakti poet Jayadeva**. In **Vaiṣṇava** theology, the deep mutual affection between Kṛṣṇa and the gopīs is an ideal model of bhakti, or devotion, being seen as very spontaneous and free from concern for social conventions. Vaiṣṇava practice is aimed at cultivating a devotion to Kṛṣṇa like that of the gopīs. The practitioners—men and women alike—are encouraged to visualize themselves as the gopīs. This can be done mentally or, in some cases, through an actual enactment of female roles.

GORAKHNĀTH (fl. 12th century CE). **Śaiva** sage and second **guru** in the lineage of the **Nāth Yogīs**; founder of the **Kāṇphaṭa** sect of ascetics; also credited with the creation of **Haṭha Yoga**. Gorakhnāth is regarded as a **siddha**, or a perfected, **enlightened** being.

GOSVĀMINS (fl. 16th century CE). Literally "cow masters"; **Vaiṣṇava** theologians. The Gosvāmins were six of the immediate disciples of **Caitanya**, at whose command they all settled in the **Vraja** region, in **Vṛndāvana**, where **Kṛṣṇa** is said to have resided during his youth. The theology of the Gosvāmins is foundational for the **Gauḍīya** tradition of **Vaiṣṇavism** and the theology of the **International Society for Krishna Consciousness** (ISKCON).

Like the **Tantric Śaiva** philosopher **Abhinavagupta**, the Gosvāmins see **rasa**, or aesthetic experience, as being akin to the experience of **mokṣa**, and as itself a potentially liberating phenomenon. The Gosvāmins applied this basic Tantric insight to the practice of **bhakti**, arguing that listening to and visualizing oneself as a participant in the stories of Kṛṣṇa and his earthly activities can evoke an aesthetic experience that, by Kṛṣṇa's grace, can lead to the state of **liberation**. One can visualize oneself as Kṛṣṇa's servant, parent, friend, or lover. All four relationships are commended, though the last is often seen as the highest and best, being modeled on the relationship between Kṛṣṇa and the **gopīs** (and Kṛṣṇa and **Rādhā** in particular).

GOTRA. A name identifying one as a descendant of one of the Seven Sages (**Saptarṣi**) presiding over the cosmos. Traditionally, persons with the same gotra cannot marry one another, being regarded as blood relatives. A large number of gotra names (49 according to some accounts) have been generated from the original seven, each of which is believed to trace back to an ancient sage. Gotra names are largely, but not exclusively, applied to **Brahmins**.

If one does not know one's gotra name (or have a gotra name), one uses the gotra of **Kaśyapa**, who is held to be the father of all of humanity. Gotras are traditionally used in ritual contexts in order to identify the participants.

GOVARDHANA, MOUNT. Mountain near **Mathurā**, in the **Vraja** region of northern India, that is sacred to **Vaiṣṇavas** for its association with the youth of **Kṛṣṇa**. Kṛṣṇa is said to have lifted the mountain singlehandedly and used it to shelter the local residents from a rainstorm that had been sent by **Indra**. This event is a popular **artistic** subject, the mountain often shown being held up by Kṛṣṇa with only his little finger. The mountain is a popular pilgrimage site, being an essential stop on the larger tour of sacred sites in the Vraja region.

GOVINDA. "Cow-finder"; "cowherd"; epithet of **Kṛṣṇa**, who performed this particular duty in his youth. The image of Kṛṣṇa gently caring for his herds is a popular symbol for divine benevolence, analogous to the **Christian** image of Jesus as the "Good Shepherd."

GRĀMA-DEVATĀ. Town or village deity; the presiding deity of a town or a village.

GṚHA-PRAVEŚA. Entry into the house; a **Vedic** ritual held to bless a new home, drive away negative forces, and ensure the health, happiness, and prosperity of all who dwell in it.

GṚHASTHA-ĀŚRAMA. The **householder** stage of life; the second of the four stages of life, or **āśramas**. The Gṛhastha-āśrama is characterized by marriage, child-rearing, and economically productive activity.

GṚHYA SŪTRAS. A set of texts that explain how to perform **Vedic domestic rituals**; probably composed around 300 BCE.

GUṆA. Quality. According to the **Sāṃkhya** and **Yoga** systems of **philosophy**, as well as the ***Bhagavad Gītā***, all natural phenomena are made up of a combination of three basic guṇas: **sattva** (clarity, luminosity), **rajas** (dynamism), and **tamas** (inertia). In some texts, the term *guṇa* refers to any good quality. **God** is therefore referred to as *guṇāśraya*, or "abode of good qualities." As such, both God and the world are regarded in **Vedānta** as making up **Saguṇa Brahman**, or "**Brahman** with qualities." **Advaita Vedānta** contrasts Saguṇa Brahman with **Nirguṇa Brahman**, or "Brahman without qualities."

GUPTA. Hindu royal dynasty that ruled much of northern India from 320 to 550 CE; the second of the three premodern Indian empires that controlled a substantial portion of the subcontinent, the first being the **Maurya** Empire and the third being that of the **Mughals**. In contrast with many dynasties that preceded them—most notably that of the Mauryas—which gave heavy patronage to **śramaṇa** traditions such as **Buddhism** and **Jainism**, the Guptas were patrons chiefly of the **Brahmins**.

The Gupta period saw a massive burst of creativity in the areas of **artistic** and textual production. Many classic Hindu texts, like the ***Purāṇas*** and the ***Dharma Śāstras***, date to this era, as do the plays and poems of **Kālīdāsa**, who is sometimes called the "Shakespeare of **Sanskrit**."

GURU. Teacher, spiritual teacher; literally, one who is "heavy" or "weighty," important. Traditionally, a **brahmacarin** or **sannyāsin** lives for a period of time in his guru's **āśrama**, or place of spiritual retreat, which is typically in a remote location, away from the distractions of society. A guru will often be affiliated with a particular teaching lineage, or **saṃpradāya**. The disciples or students of a guru are called **śiṣyas**. A guru who is the leader, or **ācārya**, of a saṃpradāya will choose one of his śiṣyas to succeed him as guru after his physical **death**. The tradition of succession from guru to śiṣya is called the **guru-śiṣya-paraṃpara**. This idea of a teaching lineage is roughly analogous to the concept of apostolic succession in the Roman Catholic Church. In **Tantric** traditions and in **Neo-Vedānta**, the guru–śiṣya relationship is fairly formalized. One formally enters into this relationship, taking a particular teacher as one's guru and being accepted by that teacher as that teacher's śiṣya, by taking **dīkṣa**, or initiation, from that person. Initiation typically involves the guru giving the new śiṣya a **mantra** for the śiṣya to use for the purpose of **meditation**. In many traditions, this mantra is secret—not to be revealed by the śiṣya to anyone, under any circumstances. A secret mantra given by one's guru is said to be particularly potent—to possess **guru-śakti**, the power of the entire teaching lineage.

GURU PŪRṆIMĀ. Full-moon day of the Hindu month of **Āṣāḍha** (which corresponds roughly to the period from mid-June to mid-July); holiday devoted especially to paying respect to one's **guru**, or spiritual teacher.

GURU-ŚAKTI. The collective spiritual power of a **saṃpradāya**, or lineage of teachers and students, which is passed down from **guru** to disciple through the act of **dīkṣā**, or initiation.

GURU-ŚIṢYA-PARAṂPARĀ. Literally, "teacher-disciple from one to the other"; the teacher–disciple lineage; tradition; the unbroken succession of a spiritual tradition from teacher (or **guru**) to student (**śiṣya**). The student, in time, becomes the teacher to another group of students to whom the lineage is then passed. Those students themselves become teachers to other students, and so on.

GURUMAYĪ (1955–). Swāmī Chidvilasānanda, the current **guru** of the **Siddha Yoga** lineage, which was established by **Swāmī Nityānanda** (1897–1961) and was perpetuated and popularized by **Swāmī Muktānanda** (1908–1982). Born Malti Shetty, Gurumayī's parents were devotees of Swāmī Muktānanda during her childhood and frequent visitors to Muktānanda's **Gaṇeśapuri Āśrama**. Initiated into the tradition through the ritual of **śaktipat** at the age of 14, she became Muktānanda's English translator and accompanied him on three world tours.

In 1982, Shetty took her ascetic vows and joined the **Sarasvatī** branch of the **Daśanāmi Order**, taking the name Swāmī Chidvilasānanda ("Bliss of the Play of Consciousness"). Before he died in 1982, Swāmī Muktānanda designated both Gurumayī and her brother, Swāmī Nityānanda (Subhash Shetty), as his co-successors in leading the Siddha Yoga movement and organization. However, in 1985, Gurumayī became the sole head of Siddha Yoga after a controversial falling out with her brother. Theologically, Siddha Yoga draws on both **Kaśmīr Śaivism** and **Vedānta**. Having a heavily **Tantric** emphasis, the practice centers around the experience of the **kuṇḍalini** energy through the mediation of the guru, who is a major object of **devotion**.

GURUVĀRA. Thursday, the day of the week that is governed by the planet Jupiter. The presiding deity of the planet Jupiter is the sage **Bṛhaspati**, the **guru** of the **Vedic** deities, or **devas**—hence the name *Guruvāra* for this day. *See also* CALENDAR, HINDU.

GURUVAYŪR. Town in the coastal state of **Kerala**, in southern India; a pilgrimage center famous for its **temple** to **Kṛṣṇa** in his infant form. Every year a series of eight **dance** dramas is performed in the **Kūṭiyāṭṭam** style that depicts events from Kṛṣṇa's life.

GWALIOR. Town located in the northern part of the central Indian state of Madhya Pradesh. Historically it has been a site of great military importance and the capital city of several Indian kingdoms from the 15th century to the modern period.

H

HALEBID. Site located in southern **Karnataka**; home to a variety of **temples** dating to the 11th and 12th centuries CE. The temples, built by the Hoysala dynasty, are among the most elaborately carved Hindu temples in India, with walls and pillars that appear to be almost alive with motion, due to practically every space upon them being carved with realistic figures of deities enacting scenes from the Hindu scriptures.

HANUMAN. Ape deity, helper of **Rāma**, and general of the animal army that assists Rāma in his siege upon **Laṅka** in the ***Rāmāyaṇa***. Hanuman is said to represent the ideal of **bhakti**. His profound devotion to Rāma enables him to perform great feats of strength that include leaping across the ocean

Hanuman, ape deity and helper of Rāma, symbol of the power of devotion.

from India to Laṅka to discover the fate of **Sītā** and lifting an entire mountain in order to bring a healing herb to **Lakṣmaṇa**, who has been wounded in battle. Though a devotee of Rāma, and often represented iconographically with Rāma, Sītā, and Lakṣmaṇa as a loyal servant bowing or kneeling at their feet, for many Hindus, Hanuman is a deity in his own right. According to one **Vaiṣṇava** tradition, Hanuman is an **avatāra** of **Śiva** who came to Earth to assist Rāma in his struggle with the wicked **Rāvaṇa**. Hanuman's great physical strength is also attributed to the fact that he is the son of the wind god, **Vāyu**.

HARA. Destroyer. Also the destroyer of evil, or the destroyer of the universe at the end of a cosmic cycle, in order that a new universe might emerge to take its place. Epithet of **Śiva.**

HARAPPA. Location in modern Pakistan and site of one of the two largest cities of the Harappan, or **Indus Valley**, or **Indus-Sarasvatī civilization**, the other major site being **Mohenjo-Daro**. *See also* HARAPPAN CIVILIZATION.

HARAPPAN CIVILIZATION. Also known as the **Indus Valley** or **Indus-Sarasvatī civilization**. The largest Harappan site is located at **Mohenjo-Daro**. Both Harappa and Mohenjo-Daro had populations ranging from 40,000 to 50,000, making them by far the largest cities of the ancient world. The civilization as a whole had a massive population, for its time, of over 5,000,000.

The Harappan civilization was at the height of its technological development from 2600 to 1900 BCE, although it displays archaeological continuity with other sites in the region, such as Mehrgarh, that date from as early as 7000 BCE. There is a great deal of fascination with this civilization because of its high level of technological advancement, the fact that its **script** has not yet been deciphered, and the fact that certain practices—and perhaps corresponding concepts—of Hinduism may have originated with this civilization.

It was believed at one time that this civilization had been destroyed in the **Āryan invasion**, but this idea has since been discredited, the dominant theory now being that the civilization declined due to earthquakes and floods.

HARDWĀR (HARIDVĀRA). "Door to **Hari (Viṣṇu)**"; "Viṣṇu's Gate"; popular and very holy pilgrimage site on the river **Gaṅgā**. Hardwār is one of the sites of the **Kumbha Melā**. The sage **Kāpila** is believed to have practiced **asceticism** here. It also has a Viṣṇu **temple** featuring a stone bearing his footprints. **Dakṣa**'s sacrifice, which was destroyed by **Śiva** after **Satī** immolated herself, is also said to have occurred on the site of Hardwār. Finally, Hardwār is one of several sites on the Gaṅgā where it is believed to be especially auspicious to deposit the ashes of one's departed loved ones and perform the **śrāddha** rite in honor of one's ancestors. *See also* ANCESTRAL RITES.

HARE KRISHNA MOVEMENT. Popular name for the **Gauḍīya Vaiṣṇava** tradition brought to the West by **Bhaktivedānta Swāmī Prabhupāda**. *See also* INTERNATIONAL SOCIETY FOR KRISHNA CONSCIOUSNESS.

HARI. "Remover of sins"; also "yellowish green"; epithet of **Viṣṇu**.

HARIHARA. Composite deity made up of both **Viṣṇu** (**Hari**) and **Śiva** (**Hara**). The right half of the deity depicts Śiva and the left half depicts Viṣṇu. Harihara symbolizes the ultimate unity of the two deities and the religious traditions centered upon them. Śiva represents the forces of entropy and chaos in the universe and Viṣṇu represents the forces of order. In these terms, Harihara represents a state of balance between the two.

One of the oldest representations of Harihara dates from the sixth century of the Common Era and is located at **Bādāmī**, in the southern Indian state of **Karnataka**.

HARIJAN. "Children of God"; a term that was coined by **Mohandās K. Gāndhī** for the **Untouchables** and other persons of low **caste**. This term was rejected by **Bhīmrao Ambedkar** as patronizing. The term *Dalit*—"the oppressed"—also employed by members of these castes, emphasizes the suffering this group has endured as a result of **casteism**. Both terms—*Harijan* and *Dalit*—have their own political implications, and use of one or the other seems to map onto the attitude of the person employing it toward Hinduism and the degree to which it is seen to be in need of either reform or complete rejection. This, however, is difficult to verify in a scientific fashion, and one does find persons who use the two terms interchangeably. The formal term preferred by the government of India is **Scheduled Castes**.

HARIVAṂŚA. "Lineage (or genealogy) of Hari (**Viṣṇu**)"; a three-part **Sanskrit** text that is often appended to the ***Mahābhārata*** and is sometimes regarded, because of its subject matter, as one of the ***Purāṇas***. The first section of this work presents the history of the **Yadava** clan, of which **Kṛṣṇa** was a member. The second section focuses specifically on the life of Kṛṣṇa, particularly the episodes of his youth that are not covered in depth in the *Mahābhārata*. The third section consists of prophecies regarding the rest of the current era, or **Kali Yuga**, which begins with Kṛṣṇa's **death**.

HARRISON, GEORGE (1943–2001). Member of the Beatles who was known for his deep interest in Hinduism and particularly for his roles in promoting both the **Hare Krishna movement** and the practice of **Transcendental Meditation** among his fans in Europe and North America, as well as his promotion of Indian classical **music**, notably the sitar. He was associated, along with the other Beatles, with the **Maharishi Mahesh Yogi**, but his more enduring relationship was with **Bhaktivedānta Swāmī Prabhupāda**.

Harrison's interest in Hinduism was sparked by an interest in Indian music, which prompted him to befriend **Ravi Shankar**, from whom he learned to play the sitar. Hindu themes were a prominent part of Harrison's song lyrics from 1967 until his death in 2001, his most famous Hindu-influenced song being his 1970 hit, "My Sweet Lord."

HARṢA (590–647 CE). Harṣa is regarded, along with Aśoka and **Akbar**, as one of the great emperors of Indian history. After the decline of the **Gupta** dynasty, the second great empire after that of the Maurya to unite much of the Indian subcontinent, Harṣa succeeded in developing a large and prosperous kingdom, in which education and culture could thrive. The period of Harṣa's reign is one of the best documented in ancient Indian history, being covered in great detail in two texts composed during his time: the *Harṣa Carita*, or biography of Harṣa, written by the **Sanskrit poet** Bāṇa, and the travelogue of Xuanzang, a Chinese Buddhist monk who traveled extensively in India during Harṣa's reign, writing in vivid detail about India's natural features, society, and forms of political administration.

One reason for Harṣa's success was his longevity. A talented administrator, he was able to oversee his kingdom for 41 years, ruling from 606 to 647 CE. He died without an heir, however, and did not leave a strong administrative structure to succeed him, relying on his own talents and the force of his personality to rule his kingdom. It therefore suffered the same fate of other Indian empires and disintegrated into a number of small kingdoms after his **death**.

Harsha hailed from what is now the state of Haryana, in northwestern India, from the city of Thanesar, though he later moved his capital to the city of Kanyakubja, now known as Kannauj, in what is now the state of Uttar Pradesh, on the banks of the **Gaṅgā**. The early years of his reign were preoccupied with warfare with Śaśaṅkha, king of Gauḍa, in what is now **Bengal**.

Like Aśoka before him and Akbar to follow, Harṣa practiced a policy of tolerance toward all the religions practiced in his realm, giving patronage to **Buddhism**, **Jainism**, and the various Hindu sects. Harṣa himself came from a **Śaiva** family. But he was also a generous patron of Buddhism, particularly Mahāyāna Buddhism. In Xuanzang's account, Harṣa's conflict with Śaśaṅkha is cast as a religious war between Buddhism and **Śaivism**, with Śaśaṅkha being depicted as an archpersecutor of the Buddhists and Harṣa as their champion. Scholars suspect, however, that this is a biased account, given the prevalence of mixed religious allegiances in ancient India. Harṣa continued to support Śaivism while also supporting Buddhism, and some of the most prominent Buddhist educational institutions in India, such as the great monastic university of Nalanda, were in Śaśaṅkha's kingdom.

A play written by Harṣa, *Nāgānanda*, reflects Harṣa's mixed religious allegiance. The play is essentially a Buddhist one, being a retelling of a *Jātaka* tale, or story of one of the Buddha's past lives. But Harṣa makes the goddess **Gaurī**, the wife of Śiva, a prominent figure in his play—an incorporation that is his own innovation.

HAṬHA YOGA. Literally "the **Yoga** of Force"; system of physical postures, stretches, and breathing exercises attributed to the 12th-century **Nāth Yogī** ascetic **Gorakhnāth**. When most Westerners use or hear the term **yoga**, they usually have this system in mind. The original purpose of this system is not, however, the pursuit of physical health as an end in itself but to prepare the physical body for higher yogic disciplines like **meditation** and the **Tantric** practice of raising the **Kuṇḍalinī**.

Starting in the early 20th century and continuing to the present day, many innovations have been made in Haṭha Yoga. A number of the stretches and **āsanas** used in contemporary Haṭha Yoga are not part of Gorakhnāth's original system, and many of these innovations have come from the West. *See also* AṢṬĀṄGA YOGA.

HAVAN. Literally "offering"; a **Vedic** ritual of sacrifice (**yajña**) of **ghee** and aromatic powders into the sacred fire (**Agni**). This ritual, intended for purification, is a variant of the ancient **Agnihotra** yajña. Traditionally the preserve of orthodox **Brahmins**, popular and widespread practice of this ritual on a regular basis has been heavily promoted in the modern period, particularly by the **Ārya Samāj**.

HEAVEN. *See* SVARGA; VAIKUṆṬHA.

HELL. *See* NARAKA; PĀTĀLA.

HIMĀLAYA. Abode of snow; the Himālayan mountain range that forms the northern boundary of the Indian subcontinent. The Himālayas are religiously significant to Hindus for several reasons. The home of **Śiva** and **Pārvatī**, Mount **Kailāsa**, is located in this mountain range. The melting snows of the Himālayas are also the source of many sacred rivers, including the **Gaṅgā**. These mountains have been a popular destination for **sannyāsins** who dwell and practice **meditation** within Himālayan caves.

HINDI. One of India's many official languages; mother tongue to roughly 40 percent of the people of India and medium of a popular film and **music** industry. It should not be confused with the term *Hindu*.

HINDU. *See* HINDUISM.

HINDU AMERICAN FOUNDATION (HAF). Organization established in 2004 in order to advocate for the Hindu community in the United States and globally. Modeling itself on such minority advocacy groups as the Anti-Defamation League, the Hindu American Foundation has published reports on violations of the rights of Hindus around the world, as well as a report on anti-Hindu hate speech on the Internet. It has also produced and circulated **literature**, aimed primarily at journalists, that is intended to correct common misconceptions about Hinduism. Most controversially, the HAF was party to a legal dispute over the representation of Hinduism in high school textbooks in the California school system. This, in turn, led to accusations by some scholars that members of the foundation had **Hindu Nationalist** leanings. The stated goals of the Hindu American Foundation, though, emphasize this organization's strong commitment to the shared Hindu and American ideals of tolerance and pluralism, which would seem to be incompatible with such a political orientation.

HINDU CALENDAR. *See* CALENDAR, HINDU.

HINDU DHARMA ĀCĀRYA SABHĀ. Organization of **ācāryas**, or leaders of Hindu **saṃpradāyas**, or denominations, established in 2002 by **Swāmī Dayānanda Sarasvatī (1930–)**. The Hindu Dharma Ācārya Sabhā has a membership of over 100 ācāryas and is an attempt to bring greater institutional cohesion to Hinduism in order to advance a number of interests and concerns shared across many saṃpradāyas. Noteworthy **actions** of the Hindu Dharma Ācārya Sabhā include a 2008 summit between the Sabhā and the chief rabbis of Israel in order to facilitate dialogue between Hinduism and Judaism, as well as many proclamations that condemn religious proselytizing as a form of cultural violence against indigenous religions.

HINDU MAHĀSABHĀ. Hindu Nationalist organization established in 1909 by Pandit Mohan Malaviya with the assistance of other members of the **Ārya Samāj**. During the struggle for Indian independence, the Hindu Mahāsabhā advocated violent revolution. It subsequently became a political party, but it has recently been eclipsed by the **Bharatīya Janatā Party** (BJP) as the primary voice of Hindu Nationalism in India. It has close ties to other Hindu Nationalist groups, such as the **Rāṣṭrīya Svayamsevak Saṅgh** (RSS) and the **Viśva Hindu Pariṣad** (VHP).

HINDU NATIONALISM. Also known as **Hindutva**; political ideology loosely united around the concept of India as a Hindu state. Hindutva, or "Hinduness," as defined by **Vinayak Damodhar Savarkar (1883–1966)** in an essay of the same name, is a conception of Hindu identity that conflates it with Indian identity. According to Savarkar, a Hindu is one who is of Indian descent, who claims India as his or her homeland, and who adheres to a religion of Indian origin. Indians who do not practice a religion of Indian origin are often seen by Hindu Nationalists as less Indian than self-identified Hindus. But though Savarkar's definition would seem to preclude the possibility of non-Indians being Hindu, non-Indian Hindus are generally welcomed as Hindus by Hindu Nationalists as persons sympathetic to Hinduism.

Hindu Nationalism has been widely criticized both by political opponents within India and by scholars globally. As an ideology that advocates an identification of Indian-ness with Hinduness, Hindu Nationalism is at cross-purposes with the ideal of secularism on which the Indian constitution is based, according to which all religions are welcome in India and all Indians are free to practice whichever religion they choose. Some within the Hindu Nationalist movement, however, openly advocate a Hindu state.

There is also a close association of militant Hindu Nationalist rhetoric with actual violence against religious minority communities in India, especially Muslims. **Mohandās K. Gāndhī** was assassinated by Nathuram Godse, a Hindu Nationalist who felt Gāndhī had betrayed the Hindu community by allowing the partition of India and Pakistan. Hindu Nationalists, for their part, criticize what some call the "pseudo-secularism" of the Indian government, whose protection of minority communities the Hindu Nationalists regard as appeasement carried out at the expense of the Hindu majority. The Hindu Nationalist organizations, forming a loose coalition known as the **Saṅgh Parivar**, include such groups as the **Rāṣṭrīya Svayamsevak Saṅgh** (RSS), the **Viśva Hindu Pariṣad** (VHP), and the **Bharatīya Janatā Party** (BJP).

HINDUISM. The religion practiced by Hindus is a highly internally diversified family of traditions that were generally not, until the modern period, seen as forming one unified whole. The word *Hindu* itself is derived from the Persian pronunciation of *Sindhu*, the **Sanskrit** name for the river known to the Greeks as the **Indus**. This was the term for the people of India among non-Indians for many centuries. The word simply meant "Indian" and had no specifically religious connotations until the time of **Al-Bīrūnī** (973–1048), an Arab Muslim scholar who traveled in India and wrote extensively about Indian religious customs in his *Kitab al-Hind* ("Book of India"). Al-Bīrūnī's account of the "religion of the Hindus" remained an authoritative source outside India for many centuries, until more detailed studies were made by Christian missionaries and other European scholars during the period of British colonial rule.

But as more detailed knowledge of Indian religiosity emerged, it became clear that not all Indians practiced the same religion, and a great deal of religious variety was present in the subcontinent. Some Indians practiced religions brought to India from outside—traditions such as **Islam**, **Christianity**,

Judaism, and **Zorastrianism**. The religions native to India included some traditions that affirmed the sanctity of the ***Vedas*** (**Vaiṣṇava**, **Śaiva**, **Śākta**, and **Smārta** traditions) and some that did not (**Jainism, Buddhism**, and **Sikhism**). Over time, scholarly and popular usage has come to define *Hinduism* as Vedic religion, although **Hindu Nationalists** continue to use the term *Hindu* to refer to all traditions of Indic origin (despite the objections of many Jains, Buddhists, and Sikhs). In 1995, the Supreme Court of India defined Hinduism as "Acceptance of the ***Vedas*** with reverence; recognition of the fact that the means or ways to salvation are diverse; and the realization of the **truth** that the number of gods to be worshiped is large, that indeed is the distinguishing feature of Hindu religion." Whether one must be born a Hindu or can "convert," becoming Hindu despite being born in another tradition, remains a disputed question.

The foreign origins of the terms *Hindu* and *Hinduism*, combined with the fact that the definitions of these terms was largely a function of a colonial scholarly discourse, has led some scholars to argue that these terms are not appropriate. Some Hindus have come to the same conclusion, preferring to refer to their traditions collectively not as *Hinduism* but as ***Sanātana Dharma***.

HINDUPHOBIA. Aversion to Hindus or to Hinduism; cultural bias, possibly ethnically motivated, against Hindus, Hinduism, or both. This term was first coined by independent scholar **Rajiv Malhotra** in response to what he perceived as anti-Hindu bias in academic writing on Hinduism. The term has also been used by the **Hindu American Foundation** to describe the anti-Hindu rhetoric of **Christian** fundamentalist organizations as found on the Internet. The term is controversial, with academic scholars of Hinduism and religious groups that have been accused of Hinduphobia objecting that legitimate disagreements or differences of interpretation have been placed by Hindu critics on the same level as racist hate speech. At the same time, some writing on Hinduism, particularly on the Internet, clearly exhibits an anti-Hindu bias. It seems that Hinduphobia can sometimes be in the eye of the beholder and can sometimes be a genuine phenomenon.

HINDUSTĀN. "Land of the Hindus" or "Land beyond the Hindu (the **Sindhu** or **Indus**) River"; Persian name for India, still frequently in use among speakers of **Hindi** and Urdu.

HINDUTVA. *See* HINDU NATIONALISM.

HIRAṆYAGARBHA. "Golden Embryo." According to several **creation** stories in the **Vedic literature**, the cosmos emerged from a golden egg floating on an infinite ocean of nonexistence. According to some accounts, **Brahmā** emerged from this egg and began the process of creation.

HIRAṆYAKAŚIPU. "Golden-robed"; one of the **Daityas** (sons of **Diti**). Personifying ignorance, he is said to have ruled over the entire Earth. He held a deep hatred for **Viṣṇu**. Annoyed by his son **Prahlāda**'s equally deep devotion to Viṣṇu, Hiraṇyakaśipu taunted Prahlāda. Once, asking Prahlāda where Viṣṇu could be found, Prahlāda answered that Viṣṇu (whose name means "all-pervasive") was everywhere, even inside a nearby stone pillar. On hearing this, Hiraṇyakaśipu kicked the pillar. The pillar then broke open and Viṣṇu, in the form of the **Narasiṃha**, or man-lion **avatāra**, came forth. The man-lion grabbed Hiraṇyakaśipu, placed him on his lap, and slew him. This event occurred at dusk. The circumstances surrounding the **death** of Hiraṇyakaśipu were a result of the fact that he was magically protected from any attack by man or beast (the Narasiṃha was neither), on the ground or in the air (which is why Narasiṃha held him in his lap), and by day or night (making dusk and dawn times of vulnerability for him).

HIRAṆYAKṢA. "Golden-eyed"; one of the **Daityas** (sons of **Diti**). Personifying, like his brother **Hiraṇyakaśipu**, ignorance that is overcome by divine wisdom, Hiraṇyakṣa is said to have cast the Earth into the cosmic ocean, from which it was rescued by the boar **avatāra** of **Viṣṇu**—**Varāha**—who then slew Hiraṇyakṣa (thereby evoking Hiraṇyakaśipu's enmity).

HIRIYANNA, M. (1871–1950). Indologist. Based in Mysore, **Karnataka**, Hiriyanna authored numerous works on Indian **philosophy**, particularly **Vedānta**. His most famous work is probably his *Outlines of Indian Philosophy*.

HOLĪ (HOLIKĀ). Spring festival held on the **Pūrṇimā** (full-moon day) of the lunar month of **Phalguna** (February–March), celebrated by both Hindus and **Sikhs**. This playful festival is celebrated by throwing brightly colored powders and liquids on friends, family members, and passersby. It is a celebration of the renewal of life at springtime.

The name of the festival comes from the name of a female demon, the sister of **Hiraṇyakaśipu**, who sought to burn her nephew **Prahlāda**, a devotee of **Viṣṇu**, to **death**. Prahlāda was spared, and it was Holikā who ended up burning to death—an event that this holiday commemorates.

HOLY MOTHER. Epithet of **Saradā Devī**.

HOMA. A very basic **Vedic** sacrifice (**yajña**) that consists of the ritual offering of **ghee** (clarified butter) to **Agni** (the sacred fire); part of the daily **Agnihotra** ritual traditionally performed by orthodox **Brahmins** and promoted for widespread practice in the modern period by the **Ārya Samāj**. *See also* HAVAN.

HOPKINS, E. WASHBURN (1857–1932). Indologist; author of a number of works on the ***Mahābhārata*** and professor of **Sanskrit** at Yale University from 1895 to 1926. By his own account, Hopkins had a decidedly negative view of **Jainism**, which he once infamously said "has indeed no right to exist."

HORSE SACRIFICE. *See* AŚVAMEDHA.

HOTṚ. Brahmin priest whose role in the **Vedic** sacrifice, or **yajña**, is to chant selected verses from the ***Ṛg Veda*** as appropriate to the ritual context.

HOUSEHOLDER. *See* ĀŚRAMA; GĀRHASTHYA.

HUXLEY, ALDOUS (1894–1963). English author and adherent of **Vedānta**. Huxley's best-known works include *The Perennial Philosophy*, *Brave New World*, and *The Doors of Perception*. Huxley immigrated to the United States in 1937. His close association with Vedānta—specifically, the **Neo-Vedānta** tradition of **Ramakrishna** and **Swāmī Vivekānanda**—began in 1939, when he met **Swāmī Prabhavānanda**, the founder and head of the **Vedānta Society** of Southern California. Huxley received **dīkṣā**, or formal initiation into the Vedānta tradition, from Prabhavānanda and began a regular practice of **meditation**.

Vedāntic themes pervade Huxley's writings—sometimes in a very obvious way, at other times more subtly. He was fascinated, even before his practice of Vedānta, with the hidden potentials of the human **mind** and had a deep interest in psychic research. He was among the early advocates of using psychedelic drugs to expand consciousness and one of the heroes of the countercultural movement of the 1960s.

Huxley is at his most Vedāntic in *The Perennial Philosophy*, where he advocates the idea of a universal wisdom present in the teachings of the mystics of all the world's great religious and philosophical traditions—"the metaphysic that recognizes a divine Reality substantial to the world of things and lives and minds; the psychology that finds in the soul something similar to, or even identical with, divine Reality; the ethic that places man's final end in the **knowledge** of the immanent and transcendent Ground of all being." This idea of a **perennial philosophy** is close to the Neo-Vedānta tradition's teaching of religious pluralism, which is based upon the multireligious practices of Sri Ramakrishna, according to which many traditions contain deep **truths** and can serve as vehicles toward **God-realization**. Critics, however, argue that the many quotations from various traditions that Huxley cites have been taken out of their original contexts.

I

ICONOGRAPHY. *See* DARŚANA; IMAGES IN WORSHIP; MŪRTI.

ILĀ. The **goddess** of the **Earth**, the wife of **Dyauḥ Pitṛ**, the heavenly father. *See also* BHŪ; BHŪDEVĪ; PṚTHVĪ.

IMAGES IN WORSHIP. Images, or **mūrtis**, have been an integral part of Hindu ritual for millennia. The specific ritual significance of the apparently religious images of the **Indus Valley civilization** is not clear. But resemblances to later imagery are suggestive of some continuity between that ancient culture and later Hindu practice. Though there is occasional mention of the physical appearance of some of the **devas** or deities of **Vedic** religion, physical evidence suggests that Vedic religious practice was centered not on concrete images but on the sacred fire. By the Common Era, though, images of the Hindu deities constructed from a wide array of materials—stone, clay, wood, marble, and metal—are very much in evidence, and continue to play an important role to the present time.

The theology behind **mūrti-pūjā**, or image worship, is developed most fully by the **Vaiṣṇava Vedāntic ācārya Rāmāṇuja**. According to Rāmāṇuja's thought, as in the Abrahamic monotheistic traditions, **God** is all-pervasive. But in order to accommodate human devotees, God is willing to take on a physical form, becoming embodied in such a form in order to facilitate **bhakti** (devotion). When an image in a **temple** is consecrated, it becomes the "seat" or "abode" of the deity it represents. Devotees can then approach the deity as they would a respected human guest, offering gifts of food, flowers, water for drinking and bathing, clothing, incense, and so on. It is not that the image itself is divine, any more (or less) than any other object is divine, divinity being omnipresent. But such a practice allows human beings to express their devotion and to increase that devotion by the process of worship (**pūjā**). Because the use of images in worship is forbidden in the Abrahamic traditions, this Hindu practice has historically evoked very negative reactions from **Christians** and Muslims who have encountered it. The prevention of "idolatry" has been used as an ideological justification for the destruction of Hindu temples, and the association of the religious use of images with superstition has been used as a rhetorical device to denigrate Hinduism as less rational than "pure" Abrahamic **monotheism**.

In the modern period, many Hindu reformers, such as **Rām Mohan Roy** (1772–1833) and **Swāmī Dayānanda Sarasvatī** (1824–1883), have absorbed these criticisms of the use of images in worship. When combined with the fact that the Vedic **literature** does not appear to endorse (nor even to be aware of) such practices, these reformers have shown a kind of Protestant zeal to put an end to Hindu "idolatry" in the name of "purifying" the tradition. But the organizations established by Roy and Dayānanda—the **Brahmo Samāj** and **Ārya Samāj**, respectively—have been outliers in this regard, with mainstream Hindus continuing to practice mūrti-pūjā, though this practice is frequently accompanied by a defensive effort to explain its significance in monotheistic terms.

IMMORTALITY. Amṛta; elixir of life churned from the cosmic ocean by the **devas** and **asuras**. As an objection of religious aspiration, immortality is characterized in some **Vedic** texts not as literal deathlessness, but as a long, full, and healthy life span, perhaps of a hundred years. Even the **gods** of Hinduism are not literally deathless but live only for the length of a **kalpa**, or cosmic epoch, merging back with the rest of the universe in the great dissolution that ends one of these vast periods.

The doctrines of **karma**, **rebirth**, and **mokṣa**, or **liberation** from rebirth, require one to approach the topic of immortality in different terms when looking at Hinduism and other Indic traditions than one might normally expect from a conventional Western point of view. An unending existence in a physical body is not seen, in most Hindu traditions, as a particularly desirable thing. The goal, rather, is being free from **death** by being free from rebirth. Immortality is therefore conceived, such as in the famous prayer from the ***Upaniṣads*** that asks, "Lead from the unreal to the real; lead me from darkness to light; lead me from death to immortality," not as a state of unending physical existence but as freedom from rebirth. Only the soul (**ātman**, **jīvātman**) is truly immortal in the sense of being completely free from death. It is the temporary, periodic identification of the soul with a body that makes it experience death. If the soul ceases to identify with a body, it is free from this experience.

INDO-ĀRYAN. Subset of the **Indo-European** language family consisting of **Sanskrit** and the other northern Indian languages related to it. Early Indo-Āryan includes **Vedic** and classical **Sanskrit**. Middle Indo-Āryan consists of the various **Prākrit** vernacular languages commonly used in ancient and early medieval India—including the Pālī and Ardha-Māgadhī languages of the **Buddhist** and **Jain** scriptures, respectively. Late Indo-Āryan includes modern northern Indian languages such as **Hindi**, Bengali, Marāthi, and Gujarati, among others. The term *Indo-Āryan* does not refer to an ethnic group but only to language and culture. *See also* ĀRYAN.

INDO-EUROPEAN. Language family that includes **Sanskrit** and the other languages of northern India that are related to it, as well as a host of languages spoken in other parts of Eurasia, including ancient and modern Iranian and Persian, Armenian, Hittite, Greek, Latin (and the Romance languages derived from it), and the Celtic, Germanic, and Slavic languages. The close affinities between these languages and the cultures in which they are spoken form the basis for their being regarded as a "family." Speculation regarding the origins of this family and close studies of the extent of the affinities between them and of non-Indo-European "substrate" elements contained within them have led to the theory that all of these languages are derived from a common source dubbed "Proto-Indo-European" by linguists. The explanation given for the dispersal of Proto-Indo-European linguistic and cultural elements across Eurasia is an actual movement of peoples from a presumed homeland. Though an undisputed consensus has not yet been reached, scholars generally maintain that this homeland was located somewhere in the vicinity of the Black and Caspian Seas, in Central Asia.

The location of the Indo-European homeland is a matter of contention in the study of India, due to the belief among some Hindu scholars that the Indo-European homeland must have been India, and that Sanskrit is the oldest Indo-European language (possibly Proto-Indo-European). The latter claim is unlikely to be true, given the presence of non-Indo-European substrate elements in Sanskrit. But critics of a Central Asian homeland point to ambiguities in the evidence that could support either an east-to-west or a west-to-east migration pattern. The entire conversation is highly politically charged, in part due to the fact that the idea of an Indo-European homeland became bound in the early part of the 20th century with Nazi ideology and the concept of a "pure, white race." *See also* ĀRYAN; ĀRYAN INVASION THEORY; ĀRYAN MIGRATION THEORY; INDO-ĀRYAN; OUT OF INDIA THEORY.

INDOLOGISTS, INDOLOGY. Indology is the academic study of India and of Indian culture, with an Indologist being a scholar who pursues Indology. This term has largely been superseded in North America by the term "South Asian Studies" (due to the fact that the modern-day Republic of India does not exhaust the region still widely known as the Indian subcontinent). Drawing on a wide range of disciplines, including anthropology, archaeology, history, linguistics, **philosophy**, and religious studies, Indology was one of the first "area studies" to develop in Western universities.

One of the first Indologists was **Sir William Jones** (1746–1794), who founded the **Royal Asiatic Society** in **Calcutta** in 1784. A brilliant linguist, Jones was one of several scholars who discovered the **Indo-European** language family, discerning the similarities between **Sanskrit** and both ancient and modern European languages. Early Indologists focus much of their work on the translation of ancient Indian texts, such as the ***Bhagavad Gītā*** (translated in 1785 by Charles Wilkins) and the ***Ṛg Veda*** (translated between 1850 and 1888 by **Horace Hayman Wilson**).

Friedrich Max Müller (1823–1900), a giant in the field of Indology, oversaw the translation of numerous Sanskrit texts through his *Sacred Books of the East* series. He is also known for developing the **Āryan Invasion**—later modified to the **Āryan Migration**—theory of **Vedic** origins. Müller was also the first Western scholar to become aware of **Ramakrishna**, writing one of the first works in a European language on the life and teachings of this Hindu saint.

A multitude of other scholars—American, European, and Indian—have contributed to the field of Indology through the years. Prominent names include, but are by no means limited to, **A. L. Basham**, **Norman Brown**, **R. N. Dandekar**, **S. N. Dasgupta**, **S. K. De**, **Wendy Doniger**, **Georges Dumézil**, **Mircea Eliade**, **M. Hiriyanna**, **S. Radhakrishnan**, **Romila Thapar**, **J. A. B. Van Buitenen**, and **Robert Charles Zaehner**.

In its earliest stages, Indology was closely tied to the colonial enterprise, and area studies in general remain heavily funded by government interests, including the Departments of Defense and State. This historical inheritance has led, in recent decades, to a good deal of self-critical scholarship and reflection on the ideological assumptions and effects of Indological scholarship—a conversation recently joined by independent Hindu scholars such as **Rajiv Malhotra** who have questioned the validity of much academic scholarship on Hinduism, a topic that has become highly politically charged. *See also* GONDA, JAN; HOPKINS, E. WASHBURN; KANE, P. V.; INGALLS, DANIEL H. H.; MAJUMDAR, R. C.; RAGHAVAN, V.; RAMANUJAN, A. K.; SUKTHANKAR, V. S.

INDRA. Lord of the **devas**, or **Vedic** deities; god of thunder and lightning who rides a **chariot** through the sky, destroying monsters with his thunderbolt weapon; one of the 12 **Ādityas** (sons of **Aditi**). Indra is mentioned more frequently than any other deity in the ***Ṛg Veda***, indicating his importance in ancient Vedic religion, though he is a figure of less importance in later Hinduism (playing relatively minor roles in the ***Purāṇas***, ***Rāmāyaṇa***, and ***Mahābhārata***). Along with his fellow deities **Agni**, **Varuṇa**, and **Yama**, Indra is one of the four **Lokapālas**, or "World Guardians." Apart from guarding the realms of fire, the ocean, the underworld, and the sky, respectively, these four deities are frequently invoked early in ritualistic worship, or **pūjā**, in order to help ensure that the ritual will be completed without mishap.

In the ***Vedas***, Indra is most famous for destroying the demon **Vṛtra**, who had trapped the world's waters and its cows inside his mountain cave. Indra destroys Vṛtra and sets the waters and cows free, allowing the Earth to flourish. He is in many ways comparable to other **Indo-European** sky deities, such as the Greek Zeus and the Norse Thor. The latter's slaying of the Midgard serpent strongly resembles the battle between Indra and Vṛtra. *See also* INDRA-DHVAJA FESTIVAL; JARJARA.

INDRA-DHVAJA FESTIVAL. Festival celebrating **Indra**'s victory over the forces of evil and chaos. A *dhvaja* is a banner or flag, and the celebration of this festival includes the setting up of a large pole representing Indra's flagpole. The festival is held on the full-moon day or **Pūrṇimā** of the lunar month of **Kārtika** (October–November).

INDRAPRASTHA. Ancient capital of the **Pāṇḍavas**' kingdom in the ***Mahābhārata***, located in the general vicinity of **New Delhi**.

INDRIYAS. The senses; in most forms of **yoga**, the senses need to be restrained—that is, brought under the control of the **mind**. In **Tantra**, the senses can be used as a medium to experience divine realities, and thus to transcend themselves.

INDUS RIVER. *Indus*, from which India gets its name, is the Greek name for the river **Sindhu**, which flows from the **Himālayas** to the Arabian Sea through the middle of what is now Pakistan. The **Indus Valley civilization** was centered on this river.

INDUS VALLEY CIVILIZATION. Also known as the **Indus Valley**, the **Harappan**, or the **Indus-Sarasvatī civilization**. The largest and longest-known sites connected with this civilization are located at **Mohenjo-Daro** and **Harappa** in the Indus River valley in contemporary Pakistan. Both of these cities had populations, at the height of the Indus civilization, ranging from 40,000 to 50,000, making them by far the largest cities of the ancient world. Comparable cities in the ancient Near East had populations of, on the high side, 10,000. The civilization as a whole had a massive population for its time, over 5,000,000. The cities were planned in advance, rather than growing organically from a smaller habitation, and indicate a high degree of engineering ability.

The Indus Valley civilization was at the height of its technological development from 2600 to 1900 BCE, although it displays archaeological continuity with other sites in the region, such as Mehrgarh, that date from as early as 7000 BCE, and with later sites that extend into the first millennium before the Common Era. There is much fascination with this civilization because of its high level of technological advancement, the fact that its **script** has not yet been deciphered, and the fact that certain practices—and perhaps corresponding concepts—of Hinduism may have originated with this civilization. Figures that appear to be seated in **yoga** postures are represented on clay seals from this culture, as well as figures evocative of both **Śiva** and the **Mother Goddess**, though the precise meaning of these images is a matter of some dispute and will likely remain so until the Indus script is deciphered. Ritual bathing and cleanliness also seem to have been a major preoccupation of this civilization, with a good deal of engineering activity being devoted to the building of public baths, sanitation, and irrigation.

Compared to other ancient civilizations of the same period, the Indus civilization extended over a vast area and engaged in overseas trade extending to Mesopotamia and the Arabian Peninsula, as well as into Central Asia. Indus-manufactured items have been discovered in all of these regions. The civilization's center of gravity, though, was the fertile valley formed by the Indus and the Gaggar-Hakra, or **Sarasvatī**, rivers.

It was believed at one time that this civilization had been destroyed in an **Āryan invasion**, but this idea has since been discredited, the dominant theory now being that the civilization declined due to earthquakes and floods that led the Indus to change its course and the Sarasvatī to go underground and, in some areas, dry up completely. Any **Āryan** migrants into the region after 1900 BCE would have encountered a civilization already very much on the decline.

INDUS-SARASVATĪ CIVILIZATION. Alternative designation for the **Indus Valley civilization** that emphasizes the fact that many of this civilization's settlements were centered not only on the **Indus** but also on another river, the Gaggar-Hakra, which once flowed adjacent to it and is identified by many scholars with the **Sarasvatī** River of the **Vedic** scriptures. Due to dramatic geological and meteorological changes, this river dried up around 1900 BCE, a development that was likely a major factor in the decline of the civilization.

INGALLS, DANIEL H. H. (1916–1999). Indologist. Taught **Sanskrit** at Harvard from 1956 to 1979, authoring many works on Indian **literature** and **philosophy**.

INTERNATIONAL SOCIETY FOR KRISHNA CONSCIOUSNESS (ISKCON). Gauḍīya Vaiṣṇava organization established by **Bhaktivedānta Swāmī Prabhupāda** in 1965. Bhaktivedānta first arrived in New York and found a home with a group of young people who were part of the countercultural movement of that period. It was largely from this movement that the following of ISKCON, the **Hare Krishna movement**, was first drawn, though it has since become somewhat more of a mainstream group, particularly as more Indian families have joined it, and a generation has grown up within the movement.

ISKCON is one of the first Hindu organizations, after the **Vedānta Society**, to have a large non-Indian following. Unlike other largely non-Indian Hindu organizations, ISKCON, in its early days, insisted that its adherents adopt Indian cultural norms—modes of dress, hairstyles, names, and so on. This has been emphasized less in recent years, as leaders of ISKCON have sought to increase the appeal of the tradition, working against common stereotypes of robed and bald-headed devotees chanting **mantras** in airports and on street corners. The organization has put a good deal of emphasis on charitable work and taking effective **action** to address cases of abuse that occurred after the time of Bhaktivedānta, but before the contemporary period. *See also* BHAKTI; HARRISON, GEORGE; KṚṢṆA.

ĪŚA. Lord, ruler, master, **God**. Epithet of **Śiva**.

ĪŚA UPANIṢAD. Also known as the *Īśavasya Upaniṣad*, this brief text is traditionally listed first among the ***Upaniṣads***, although most scholars agree that it is not the oldest of the *Upaniṣads* (that distinction belonging to the ***Bṛhadāraṇyaka Upaniṣad***). The *Īśa Upaniṣad* contains some of the basic concepts that would later become central to the various systems of **Vedānta philosophy**. It is theistic, referring to the all-pervasive Lord (**Īśa**, from whom the text takes its title). It also contains a possible allusion to the idea of **karma yoga** and affirms the idea of **Brahman** as a reality beyond all dualistic logical conceptions.

ISHERWOOD, CHRISTOPHER (1904–1986). English author, adherent of **Vedānta**. Better known in literary circles for his novels, Isherwood's writings on Vedānta include a biography of **Ramakrishna** entitled *Ramakrishna and His Disciples*, *My Guru and His Disciple*, and, in collaboration with **Swāmī Prabhavānanda**, translations of Hindu texts, (including the principle ***Upaniṣads***, the ***Bhagavad Gītā***, and the ***Yoga Sūtras*** of **Patañjali**). Isherwood immigrated to the United States in 1939. His close association with Vedānta—and specifically, the **Neo-Vedānta** tradition of Ramakrishna and **Swāmī Vivekānanda**—began that same year when he met Swāmī Prabhavānanda, the founder and head of the **Vedānta Society** of Southern California. Isherwood received **dīkṣā**, or formal initiation into the Vedānta tradition, from Prabhavānanda, who became his **guru**.

ISLAM. The world's second-largest religion, in terms of the number of its adherents, and a member, along with Judaism and **Christianity**, of the Abrahamic family of traditions, sharing a common worldview that includes **monotheism**, divine revelation and divine intervention in human history, a single lifetime, a day of judgment, and an everlasting afterlife either in a heavenly paradise or a hellish state of punishment (though exceptions and variations in regard to this basic worldview can be found across all three of these traditions).

Historically, relations between Hindus and Muslims (practitioners of Islam) have oscillated between periods of peaceful coexistence and periods of communal violence. Initial contacts between Muslims and Hindus were peaceful, being largely a function of trade with Arab merchants along the coasts of India. During this period, in the latter half of the first millennium of the Common Era, some Hindus from the lower **castes** became converts to Islam in order to escape the inequities of the caste system—though the practice of caste is so pervasive in India that, within a few generations, these Muslim converts had again organized themselves into castes, as Christians had done previously and continue to do even today. Much like the initial coming of Christianity to India, these conversions did not have a major impact on the dominant Hindu community.

In succeeding centuries, however, waves of invasion—first by Arabs, then Turks, and finally the **Mughals**, often using Islam as an ideological justification for destruction of **temples** and monastic institutions and displacement of Hindu kings—created a situation of deep distrust between the two communities.

Under Mughal rule, though—particularly the reign of **Akbar**, which lasted from 1556 to 1605—the situation began to change. The Mughal policy of tolerance created the conditions for a hybrid Hindu–Islamic culture to emerge, leading to an amazing burst of creative activity in the visual **arts**, **music**, architecture, and religion itself. Specifically in regard to religion, the **Sant** movement—a fusion of Islamic **Sufi** mysticism with Hindu **bhakti** traditions—emerged, emphasizing the common thread of devotion and longing for the divine uniting the otherwise dramatically different religions of Hindus and Muslims. Mystics like **Kabīr** taught the unity of Āllāh (the one **God** of Islam) and **Rāma**. A third tradition, **Sikhism**, arose from this movement, with the teaching of **Guru Nānak** that, in the eyes of God, "There is no Hindu and there is no Muslim." **Syncretism** occurred on a massive scale, as Hindus and Muslims celebrated one another's holy days and borrowed one another's practices and concepts. The only substantial interruption of this period of relative harmony came during the reign of the Mughal emperor Aurangzeb, which lasted from 1658 to 1707. Aurangzeb favored the forcible conversion of Hindus to Islam and engaged in fierce campaign of persecution of both Hindus and Sikhs.

The colonial period and the British "divide and rule" policy that set members of different communities against each other reinforced the sense of separate communal identities and mutual suspicion between Hindus and Muslims. Both Islamic and **Hindu Nationalism** emerged in the late 19th and early 20th centuries, fueling hostile feelings between the two communities. These hostilities culminated with the partition of India and Pakistan when British rule ended in 1947.

Relations between Hindus and Muslims continue to be highly fraught today. Both Hindu minorities in Pakistan and Bangladesh and the Muslim minority in India have, at different times, experienced persecution. India and Pakistan have fought three wars and both have had nuclear weapons since 1998. Particularly low points in Hindu–Muslim relations have been 1992, when the **Babrī Masjīd** was demolished in **Ayodhyā** by Hindu Nationalists, and 2002, when horrific riots broke out between Hindus and Muslims in the state of Gujarat. At the same time, one may observe that these outbreaks of violence take place against a background of largely peaceful coexistence.

IṢṬADEVATĀ. Chosen deity, preferred deity, chosen ideal. Based on the idea that **Brahman**, being infinite, is beyond human conception, the **Smārta** and **Neo-Vedānta** traditions of Hinduism teach that Brahman can be approached through a personal form to which it is easier for human beings to relate. The form will vary according to the needs of the **devotee**, but typically takes the shape of one of the Hindu deities, though the deity can also be a saintly historical personage—or even, in more liberal forms of Hinduism, a non-Hindu figure, such as Jesus or the **Buddha**. **Ramakrishna** compares the iṣṭadevatā to a hole in a high wall that surrounds a beautiful garden. People who wish to see the garden have to peek through the holes in this wall. The holes will be located at varying heights, to suit the needs of the various people looking in, but the beautiful garden to which these various holes grant them access is one and the same. In the same way, the one universal Brahman is accessed by different types of devotee by means of the various iṣṭadevatās. *See also* GOD; GODS.

ĪŚVARA. The Lord, **God**. This is the term by which the Supreme Being is generally designated in Hindu philosophical writings when God in the abstract is under discussion. Both **Viṣṇu** and **Śiva** are frequently designated by this term in the sectarian writings of their respective devotees in the **Vaiṣṇava** and **Śaiva** traditions. The other term frequently used for God in the generic sense is **Bhagavān**, the Blessed One.

ĪŚVARA-PRAṆIDHĀNA. Contemplation of the Lord; fifth of the **niyamas**; a major component of the **yoga** system developed by **Patañjali**. *See also* AṢṬĀṄGA YOGA; *YOGA SŪTRAS*.

ITIHĀSA. History, literally "thus it was." This term usually refers to the two primary epics of Hindu **literature**—the ***Rāmāyaṇa*** and the ***Mahābhārata***.

IYER, E. KRISHNA (1897–1968). Artist chiefly responsible for reinvigorating Indian classical **dance**—specifically **Bharata-nāṭyam**. A **Brahmin** from **Tamil** Nadu, Iyer first trained in and practiced **law** and participated in the Indian independence movement prior to devoting himself to the revival of classical dance. Through his efforts and those of a variety of dedicated artists who have come since, Indian classical dance has emerged as a highly respected art form after centuries of disrepute.

J

JAGADDHĀTRĪ. Form of **Durgā**. *See also* AMBĀ.

JAGANNĀTHA. Lord of the Universe, **God**, epithet of **Viṣṇu**. The particular **mūrti** or image to which this term refers is located at a famous **mandir**, or **temple**, in the city of **Puri** in the state of **Orissa**. Controversially, the administration of this temple does not permit entry by non-Hindus. Non-Indian **devotees**, whom the administration does not regard as truly Hindu, have frequently objected to this practice. The central image of the temple is carried out in procession once a year on a very large cart modeled on a **chariot** or **ratha**. The massive size of this cart, and the inherent difficulty of controlling it once it is in motion, gave rise to the English word "juggernaut."

JAGAT. Literally, "flow" or "process"; the universe and the entities constituting it, in contrast with **God**, or **Īśvara**, its lord and controller. According to the **Viśiṣṭādvaita** of the **Vedāntic ācārya Rāmāṇuja**, God and the world together make up a greater unity—**Brahman**. If one were to draw an analogy between Brahman and a person, God could be said to be the person's **soul**, and the world (jagat) the person's body.

JAIMINI. Author to whom the ***Pūrvamīmāṃsā Sūtra*** is attributed and founder of the **Pūrva Mīmāṃsā** system of classical Indian **philosophy**. Pūrva Mīmāṃsā, or "earlier exegesis" is a continuation of the ancient, orthodox system of Vedic **Brahmanism**, with a very strong emphasis on the correct performance of **Vedic** ritual and a corresponding emphasis on the correct pronunciation of the **Sanskrit** verses of the ***Vedas*** during a ritual performance. This emphasis on Sanskrit led to the development of an elaborate linguistic philosophy on the part of the Mīmāṃsakas. The term *Pūrva Mīmāṃsā* contrasts this school of thought with later, or **Uttara Mīmāṃsā**—more widely known as **Vedānta**. The system of Jaimini emphasizes the earlier, ritualistic portion of the *Vedas*, while Vedānta emphasizes the later Vedic **literature**, the ***Upaniṣads***, and their teaching of **Brahman**.

JAINISM. Śramaṇa tradition that is traced, in its current form, to **Mahāvīra** (c. 499–427 BCE), though according to Jain tradition Mahāvīra is the 24th in a series of **enlightened** beings, or **Tīrthaṅkaras**, who have been teaching the same **truths** for millennia, and there is some evidence that Mahāvīra's teaching is a continuation of an earlier, proto-Jain tradition. Along with **Buddhism**, Jainism is one of the only two surviving śramaṇa traditions that thrived in northern India in the first millennium before the Common Era. Other śramaṇa groups, such as the **Ājīvikas**, had died out by the 13th century CE, as had Buddhism in India (though it had already spread across Asia by this time).

The Jains are known primarily for their profound commitment to nonviolence, or **ahiṃsā**, which Jain ascetics practice to the greatest extent humanly possible, sometimes wearing a face mask, or *muhpattī*, to avoid accidentally inhaling or ingesting insects or microorganisms, and sweeping the ground in front of them as they walk to avoid doing even accidental harm to small living things. Another central Jain value is **aparigraha**, or nonpossessiveness, which some Jain ascetics—the monks of the "sky-clad" or *Digambara* sect, practice to the extent of giving up even the wearing of clothing. Finally, the third "pillar" of Jainism is *anekānta-vāda*, or "non-one-sidedness," which consists of the view that there is some truth in all perspectives. No tradition is completely wrong (though the teachings of the Tīrthaṅkaras are held to be absolutely true).

Jainism shares many core ideas of Hinduism, such as the doctrines of **karma** and **rebirth** and the aspiration for **liberation** (**mokṣa**) from the cycle of rebirth as a central salvific goal. Jainism is distinctive in seeing karma as a material substance that adheres to the soul (**jīva**) and in the relentless logic it applies to the questions of karmic merit and demerit, with very specific conceptions of which **actions** produce particular effects.

Jainism shares with other śramaṇa traditions, such as Buddhism, a rejection of the claims of **Brahmanism** regarding the sanctity of **caste** and the authority of the ***Vedas***. Specifically, it rejects the idea that birth caste is a reflection of one's spiritual attainment (with its implication that the **Brahmins** are the most evolved of human beings) and **Vedic** injunctions to perform **animal sacrifice**. Jainism was an ideological rival of Brahmanism for many centuries. But as Hinduism coalesced from many Indic traditions, some Jain concepts and practices were assimilated into it. For example, though nominal affirmation of the authority of the *Vedas* continues, practices such as animal sacrifice gradually fell by the wayside, being replaced by **vegetarianism** under the influence of the concept of ahiṃsā. Jain practice in regard to nonattachment has influenced Hindu practices, such as fasting, and there are Hindu orders of naked monks not unlike the Digambaras of Jainism. Though the caste system continues to be practiced, movements that affirm the irrelevance of caste to the spiritual path, such as **bhakti** and **Tantra**, have many Hindu followers.

And the Jain teaching of the relativity of perspectives finds an echo in the **Neo-Vedāntic** teaching that truth can be found in many religions.

Jainism was especially influential on the life and teachings of **Mohandās K. Gāndhī**, who grew up in a region of India (Gujarat) with a strong Jain presence. The central Jain ethical principle of nonviolence can be found not only in the teachings of Gāndhī but also in Hindu texts such as the ***Yoga Sūtras*** of **Patañjali** and the ***Dharma Śāstras***. Even though the Jain community is, numerically, relatively small (there being roughly four and a half million Jains in the world today), the Jains have had a disproportionate influence on the dominant Hindu culture that has surrounded them. This influence is probably a result of several factors, including the relative wealth of this largely mercantile community and the respect evoked by the rigorous **asceticism** and profound commitment to nonviolence exhibited by Jain monks and nuns. *See also* VRATA; YAMAS.

JAMADAGNI. Father of **Paraśurāma**, a wrathful **avatāra** of **Viṣṇu** who is said to have slain the entire **kṣatriya** (or warrior) **caste** in vengeance for Jamadagni having been killed by a kṣatriya, Arjuna Kārtavīrya (not the **Pāṇḍava** hero **Arjuna** of the ***Mahābhārata***). It is said that Jamadagni and Paraśurāma were **Brahmins** of the **Bhārgava** clan. After all the kṣatriyas were slain by Paraśurāma, they had to be replaced by Brahmins. It is thus believed that all living kṣatriyas are actually descended from Brahmins.

JANAKA. Ancient king of Mithilā, in northeastern India; represented in the ***Upaniṣads*** as engaging in frequent discourse with wise sages such as **Yajñavālkya**; represented in the ***Rāmāyaṇa*** as the father of **Sītā** and father-in-law of **Rāma**. In the **Vedānta** tradition, Janaka is said to have been liberated while still alive (**jīvanmukta**). His attainment of this goal while remaining a **householder** involved with kingly duties is used to illustrate the point that it is not necessary to practice renunciation in a formal sense (**sannyāsa**) in order to be liberated. What is essential is *inner* renunciation, an attitude of detachment from the fruits of **action**. At the same time, it is emphasized that Janaka is unusual in this regard and likely practiced sannyāsa in previous lifetimes.

JANMĀṢṬAMI. Also known as **Kṛṣṇa Janmāṣṭami**, the birthday of Kṛṣṇa. It is the eighth (aṣṭami) day of the **dark half** (**kṛṣṇa pakṣa**) of the month of **Bhādra** in the Hindu lunar calendar, which corresponds roughly with the month of August in the solar calendar.

JAPA. The practice of repeating a **mantra**—either aloud but quietly, or purely mentally and silently—while keeping track of the number of repetitions on a string of beads known as a **māla**, or sometimes as a japa māla. In most traditions, it is recommended that the practitioner repeat the mantra in units of 108, thus giving rise to the need for a method of keeping track of the number of repetitions. In addition to the māla, there are also ways of keeping track of one's mantra repetitions using one's fingers.

JARJARA. Flagpole of **Indra**, brought onto the stage in traditional Indian theater as a way of invoking Indra's protection. This practice is prescribed by the ***Nāṭya Śāstra***, the authoritative textual guide to traditional Indian theater and **dance**.

JATAYU. Character in the ***Rāmāyaṇa***; eagle who attempts to rescue **Sītā** from **Rāvaṇa** in the course of her abduction. As Rāvaṇa abducts Sītā in his flying **chariot** (**vimāna**), Jatayu attacks and tries to pull her away.

JĀTI. Birth **caste**; hereditary occupational group to which one is born. The jātis are the "subcastes" into which the four main castes, or **varṇas**, are divided. Far more than one's varṇa, it is one's jāti that forms the actual, living communal unit that determines one's caste identity. Relative to jāti, varṇa is more or less an abstraction. In contrast with the four varṇas, there are dozens of jātis. The location of each jāti within the larger caste hierarchy varies a great deal in different regions of India.

JAYADEVA (fl. 1200 CE). Bengali author of the ***Gītagovinda***, a **bhakti** text that uses the love affair between **Rādhā** and **Kṛṣṇa** to depict the bond of love between the soul of the **devotee** and **God**. The text is highly erotically charged and has been compared by some with the biblical *Song of Solomon*.

JĪVA. Literally "life force." The individual, reincarnating soul, contrasted, in **Advaita Vedānta**, with the **paramātman**, or supreme soul, with which all the individual souls are ultimately one. Non-Advaita systems of **Vedānta**, with their greater emphasis on theistic realism and a strong distinction between the individual **devotee** and **God**, claim that the jīvas always remain numerically distinct from **God**, or **Īśvara**, their union being one of love and a harmonizing of wills, rather than an actual obliteration of difference. **Jainism** distinguishes between the jīva in its mundane state, polluted by obscuring **karma**, and the soul in its inherent, perfected state, which it realizes upon **enlightenment**, which consists of infinite **knowledge**, bliss, and freedom. Jains also use the term *paramātman* to refer to the enlightened jīva. *See also* ĀTMAN.

JĪVANMUKTA. An **enlightened** being. One who is in the state of **jīvanmukti**.

JĪVANMUKTI. The state of being liberated while still alive, prior to the **death** of the body. The possibility of attaining **mokṣa** while still alive is denied by many Hindu schools of thought—those more theistically and devotionally oriented traditions that think of **liberation** as residing eternally in **heaven** with **God** (usually conceived as residing in **Vaikuṇṭha** with **Kṛṣṇa**). Clearly this is a conception of mokṣa as a postmortem state. In **Advaita Vedānta**, however, where mokṣa consists of the realization of the identity of the **ātman** and **Brahman**, such a realization is seen as being possible while one is still alive. The body of a **jīvanmukta** continues to survive after mokṣa due to **prarabdha karma** of a kind that does not interfere with a correct perception of reality. Such a being appears to others who are not **enlightened** as a human being engaged in the usual activities of life, such as eating, drinking, sleeping, and so forth. Such a being can even be physically injured or become ill. But from the perspective of that being, all is Brahman, and there is no distinction to be made between self and other, or among various karmic states. The activities of such a being are therefore entirely spontaneous and reflective of the nature of Brahman. In many respects, this conception is like that of an enlightened being in the **Buddhist** tradition.

JĪVĀTMAN. *See* JĪVA.

JÑĀNA. "Knowledge"; "wisdom"; cognate with the Greek *gnosis*. **Advaita Vedānta** teaches that knowledge is constitutive of **mokṣa**, or **liberation** from the cycle of **rebirth**—specifically, the knowledge that the individual self, or **ātman**, and the universal reality, or **Brahman**, are one and the same. The **Neo-Vedānta** of **Ramakrishna** and **Swāmī Vivekānanda** teaches that wisdom is one of four possible **yogas** or **mārgas** (paths) that can lead to liberation (along with devotion, or **bhakti**; work, or **karma**; and **meditation**, or **dhyāna**). Support for both views, as well as endorsements of the sole efficacy of the other paths, can be found in the Hindu **scriptures**. *See also* FOUR YOGAS; YOGA.

JÑĀNA KANDA. Literally "wisdom portion"; the ***Upaniṣads***; the final portion of the ***Vedas***, devoted to knowledge of **Brahman**, as distinct from the earlier "**action** portion" or **Karma Kanda**, consisting of ritualistic texts focused on sacrificial performance. *See also* VEDĀNTA.

JÑĀNA MĀRGA, JÑĀNA YOGA. "Path or way of knowledge"; "spiritual discipline of knowledge." *See* JÑĀNA.

JÑĀNASAMBANDAR (639–655). A precocious **Tamil Śaiva** devotee who is said to have sung songs of devotion to **Śiva** at the young age of three. His father carried him to various Śaiva **temples**, where the boy gave sermons and is also said to have performed miracles. Jñānasambandar dismissed traditional concerns regarding **astrology**, claiming that faith in Śiva could override negative astrological influences.

JÑĀNEŚVARA (1275–1296). Bhakti poet from Maharashtra; a **Brahmin**; best known for his exposition of the ***Bhagavad Gītā***. Drawing upon the **Vaiṣṇava**, **Śaiva**, and **Śākta** traditions, he commented upon the *Gītā* but also wrote of the essential unity of **Śiva** and **Śakti**, asserting that, "Without the **God** there is no **Goddess**, and without the Goddess there is no God."

JONES, SIR WILLIAM (1746–1794). One of the first **Indologists**. Jones discovered the **Indo-European** family of languages and cultures, being the first to recognize the strong similarities between **Sanskrit** and European languages such as Greek and Latin. He established the **Royal Asiatic Society** in **Calcutta** in 1784, thus formally initiating the study of Indology as an academic discipline. He translated the ***Manusmṛti*** ("Laws of Manu"), the ***Gītagovinda*** of **Jayadeva**, and **Kālidāsa**'s play, the *Abhijānaśakuntala* or "Recognition of **Śakuntalā**."

JYAIṢṬHA. Month of the **Hindu calendar** that corresponds roughly to the period from mid-May to mid-June.

JYOTIṢA. *See* ASTROLOGY.

K

KABĪR (1440–1518). Sant poet who is revered by both Hindus and Muslims. Born into a **caste** of weavers in **Banaras**, his name is Muslim. It is likely that his entire caste converted as a group to **Islam** prior to his birth. Although he uses Islamic terminology, Kabīr's writings show a greater familiarity with the ***Rāmāyaṇa*** than with Islam. Kabīr himself did not hold exclusive religious identity in high regard, ridiculing institutional features of both Hinduism and Islam that kept their followers apart. He advocated devotion (**bhakti**) to a formless divinity, beyond limiting qualities and attributes. In emphasizing the formless (**nirguṇa**) nature of the divine, his teaching is like **Advaita Vedānta**. But his emphasis on personal devotion places him closer to theistic bhakti traditions and to Islam. A major influence on the broader Sant movement, and on **Sikhism**, many of Kabīr's writings are preserved in the sacred scripture of the Sikhs, the *Ādi Granth*. His belief in the oneness of Āllāh and **Rāma** and emphasis on personal devotion over institutional affiliation and formal ritual anticipate modern Hindu teachers like **Ramakrishna**.

KAILĀSA, MOUNT. Mountain in the central **Himālayas**, located within the modern boundaries of Tibet, and traditionally believed to be the home of **Śiva** and **Śakti**. It is a popular, if difficult to reach, pilgrimage site. It is near Lake **Manosarovar**, also a sacred site.

KAIVALYA. Literally "isolation"; a term used in the **Sāṃkhya** and **Yoga** systems, as well as in **Jainism**, for the state of **mokṣa**, or **liberation** from the cycle of **rebirth**, a state characterized in these traditions as the separation of the soul (**puruṣa**, **jīva**, or **ātman**) from matter, or the phenomena of nature (ajīva, **prakṛti**) with which it has come to be identified. According to Sāṃkhya and Yoga, the identification of the soul with matter is merely apparent, to be overcome (in the Sāṃkhya system) by right understanding of the nature of the soul as pure consciousness, or (in the Yoga system) through the experience of **samādhi**, or **meditative** absorption in this consciousness. This is in contrast with the Jain tradition, which sees the soul as having become actually entangled with matter, from which it needs to separate itself through **ascetic** practice—though the Digambara **ācārya** Kundakunda (from the middle of the first millennium of the Common Era) holds a view that is closer to that of Sāṃkhya and Yoga.

KĀLĀMUKHA. "Black face"; a south Indian **Tantric Śaiva ascetic** lineage; a subset of the **Paśupata** tradition of **Śaivism**. Their name comes from the black **tilak**, or sectarian mark, that they wear on their foreheads.

KĀLĪ. "Black **Goddess**"; fierce form of the **Mother Goddess** in her role as slayer of the demonic. She is traditionally depicted as having four arms. Her right hands are shown in the **abhaya-mudrā** and **dāna-mudrā**—the gestures of fearlessness and generosity. This is her benevolent aspect. Her left hands are shown carrying a ferocious-looking sword and the head of a demon. Her skin is black and her tongue, red with blood, is sticking out of her mouth. She is wearing a garland of skulls and a skirt of arms and heads of demons she has slain. She is standing on the prone and apparently unconscious body of **Śiva**, her husband. Despite her fierce appearance—evocative, to many non-Hindus, of the demonic—Kālī is seen as a benevolent deity who is fierce in order to protect her devotees from evil. Her iconography depicts a moment from a battle depicted in the ***Devī Mahātmya*** during which she was fighting a demon known as Raktabīja, or "blood seed." Each drop of Raktabīja's blood that spilled on the ground would transform itself into a completely new Raktabīja. Spilling this demon's blood in battle therefore served only to create an entire army of Raktabījas. It is for this reason that Kālī used her tongue to catch or lick up every drop of the blood of this demon that was spilled in the course of her battle with him. This is why she is depicted with a long, bloody tongue sticking out of her mouth. It is also said that her husband, Śiva, fearing that in her blood frenzy she would destroy the world, laid down on the battlefield as if dead. In her **dance** of destruction, Kālī stepped on top of him. Realizing, abruptly, that she was standing on her (possibly dead) husband, Kālī ceases her destruction and transforms back into the gentle **Pārvatī**. This moment is captured in her **mūrti**, or iconographic representation.

Kālī is especially popular in **Bengal** where **Tantric** and **Śākta** traditions are quite strong. She was the preferred deity (**iṣṭadevatā**) of the Bengali saint **Ramakrishna**, who was intensely devoted to her. Her **pūjā** is traditionally performed at midnight on the **Amavasya**, or new-moon day, of the month of **Kārtika** (which corresponds to the period from late October to early November). This is the same night on which most Hindus in northern India celebrate **Dīpāvali**, or Dīwali.

The **Kālīghāṭ**, in **Calcutta** (Kolkata), is one of the few remaining places in India where **animal sacrifice** still occurs, with goats being offered to Kālī. But these sacrifices are controversial, and in many places (especially outside of India), the sacrificial goat has been replaced with a gourd, banana, cucumber, or other **vegetarian** offering. The **Ṭhags**, or Thugs, used to offer human sacrifices to Kālī. These were usually unwitting travelers who would hire the Ṭhags as tour guides. The Ṭhags would then take them to an isolated place and strangle them. Although the basis of the film *Indiana Jones and the Temple of Doom*, the actual Ṭhag cult consisted of a small group of men, not

Kālī, fierce form of the Mother Goddess and slayer of demons.

the elaborate **temple** community depicted in the sensationalist film. Human sacrifice is not condoned in any mainstream Hindu sect, or even in mainstream Tantric or Śākta thought.

Ramakrishna identified Kālī with **Brahman** in its active form, as the energy of **creation**. "Kālī is verily Brahman, and Brahman is verily Kālī. It is one and the same Reality. When we think of It as inactive . . . then we call it Brahman. But when It engages in . . . activities, then we call It Kālī or Śakti."

KALI YUGA. The fourth, last, and worst of the progressively more unfortunate ages or **yugas** into which a cosmic epoch, or **kalpa**, is divided. We are presently experiencing the Kali Yuga of our current cosmic epoch. According to Hindu traditions, the Kali Yuga began with the death of **Kṛṣṇa**, shortly after the ***Mahābhārata*** war. Hindu texts date the death of Kṛṣṇa around 3021 BCE, in terms of the predominant global dating system. But mainstream scholarship on Hinduism regards this date as too early for the *Mahābhārata* war, which tends to be placed at either 1500 BCE (the approximate date of the sinking of **Dvārakā**) or 950 BCE (based on archaeology in northern India, where most of the epic's main narrative occurs).

KĀLĪBĀRĪ. "House of **Kālī**"; **Bengali** generic term for a temple to the **goddess** Kālī.

KĀLIDĀSA (fl. 4th–5th centuries CE). "Servant of Kālī"; **poet** and playwright regarded by many as the "Shakespeare of **Sanskrit**." Flourishing during the reign of the **Gupta** dynasty and the "Hindu Renaissance" that the Gupta emperors helped to facilitate, little is known of Kālidāsa's life. Religiously, his work reflects an eclectic sensibility, drawing on both **Vaiṣṇava** and **Śaiva** narratives from the ***Mahābhārata***, the ***Rāmāyaṇa***, and the ***Purāṇas***. His most famous work is the *Abhijñānaśakuntala* ("The Recognition of **Śakuntalā**"), a play based on an episode from the *Mahābhārata*. Kālidāsa's Sanskrit is highly refined and distinctive in style, making extensive use of puns, nature imagery, and references to traditional Hindu **literature**. *See also NĀṬYA ŚĀSTRA*.

KĀLĪGHĀṬ. Famous **Kālī temple** in **Calcutta** (Kolkata), for which the city is named. One of the few places where **animal sacrifice** is still practiced.

KALKIN. Tenth **avatāra** of **Viṣṇu** and the last to appear in the current cosmic epoch. Kalkin will appear at the end of the **Kali Yuga** and fight in a final cataclysmic battle of good against evil. Destroying the forces of chaos (**adharma**), he will reestablish order (**dharma**) and a new series of **yugas** will begin. Kalkin is usually depicted as a warrior riding on a white horse and carrying a sword.

KALPA. *See* WORLD AGES; YUGA.

KĀMA. Desire; sensory enjoyment; erotic love. Along with wealth and power (**artha**), virtue (**dharma**), and **liberation** (**mokṣa**), kāma is one of the four goals of humanity, or **puruṣārthas**.

KĀMADEVA. "God of (erotic) love"; Cupid-like deity who shoots flower arrows into the hearts of human beings, causing them to fall in love. Kāmadeva once sought to shoot **Śiva** in the heart while he was **meditating**, but before he could do so, Śiva opened up his "**third eye**," burning Kāmadeva to a crisp with the heat of his accumulated tapas, or ascetic power. Kāmadeva therefore no longer has a body and is for this reason known as **Anaṅga** ("he who has no limbs, or body"). This episode illustrates the conflict between **kāma** and **asceticism**, since one who wishes to pursue **mokṣa**, or **liberation** from the cycle of **rebirth**, must renounce attachment to sensory pleasure.

KĀMADHENU. "Wish-fulfilling cow"; daughter of **Dakṣa** and the wife of **Kaśyapa**; one of the treasures to emerge from the ocean when it was churned by the **devas** and the **asuras** in their search for the elixir of life (**amṛta**). The Kāmadhenu can grant any wish to her owner. *See also* COW, SACRED.

KĀMA SŪTRA*.** **Sanskrit** text composed around 300 CE by **Vātsyāyana** Mallanaga; a scholarly treatise on **kāma**, a term whose meaning encompasses the concepts of sensory pleasure—especially sexual pleasure—desire, and erotic love. Like Sanskrit treatises on the other four goals of humanity (**puruṣārthas**), such as the ***Artha Śāstra and the various ***Dharmas Śāstras***, the *Kāma Sūtra* approaches its topic in a detailed, systematic fashion.

Although long considered scandalous—then later, fashionable—in the West, due to its explicit and frank discussions of sexuality and various ways of both experiencing and heightening sexual pleasure, the traditional Hindu attitude toward sexuality that this text reveals is notable for its nonjudgmental understanding that sexuality is a natural part of the human condition. Although the **ascetic** traditions of Hinduism focus on transcending sexual desire as a way of attaining **mokṣa**, or **liberation** from the cycle of **rebirth**, there is no assumption that an ascetic orientation can or should be expected of all people. For those who are still "in the world" and not focused on mokṣa, worldly pursuits like kāma, **artha** (wealth), and **dharma** (virtue) are perfectly appropriate, and indeed recommended. The *Kāma Sūtra* is also of interest to historians for the considerable light that it sheds on ancient Indian society—particularly the wealthy class, who appear to have spent a good deal of time in leisure and social activities.

KĀṂSA. Character in the ***Bhāgavata Purāṇa***; king and wicked uncle of **Kṛṣṇa** who wanted to slay Kṛṣṇa just after his birth because of a prediction that Kṛṣṇa would one day slay him and take control of his kingdom. Kāṃsa was not the legitimate son of his father, King Ugrasena of **Mathurā**, but rather the son of an **asura** who had taken Ugrasena's shape and slept with his wife. Having his father's demonic nature, Kāṃsa overthrew the king, imprisoning him and usurping the kingship. Kṛṣṇa, true to the prophecy, did slay Kāṃsa when he reached adulthood. Like King Herod, as depicted in the New Testament, Kāṃsa sought to prevent his eventual slaying by Kṛṣṇa by having all the male children in his kingdom slain.

KAṆĀDA. Sage to whom the **Vaiśeṣika darśana**, or system of Indian **philosophy**, is attributed. Kaṇāda probably lived around 300 BCE.

KĀÑCĪPURAM. City in **Tamil** Nadu; sacred site of pilgrimage; known for its many **temples**, such as the **Śaiva** Kailāsanātha temple and the **Vaiṣṇava Vaikuṇṭha** Perumal. It is also the location of one of the monastic centers, or **maṭhas**, established by **Śaṅkara**—the Kāñcī Kāmakoti Pīṭa.

KANE, P. V. (1880–1972). Indologist; professor of **law** and vice-chancellor of Bombay University; author of the five volume *History of Dharmaśāstra*.

KANNAPPA (fl. 6th–11th centuries CE). One of the 63 **Nāyanārs**—saints and **bhakti poets** revered in the **Tamil Śaiva** tradition. It is said that Kannappa (which means "he who gave his eyes") offered his eyes to **Śiva**, plucking them out upon noticing that the eyes in an image of the deity appeared to be bleeding, his intention being to replace the image's eyes with his own. Śiva, being pleased with this profound devotion, restored his sight. It is also said that Kannappa was a hunter by **caste**—an example of the widespread appeal of the bhakti movement, which emphasized personal devotion over birth caste as a measure of one's spiritual advancement.

KĀṆPHAṬA. "Split-ear"; alternative name for the **Nāth Yogīs**, a **Tantric Śaiva** lineage of **ascetics**. The name *Kāṇphata* refers to the large earrings that these ascetics wear. The second leader of the lineage, **Gorakhnāth**, is attributed with inventing **Haṭha Yoga**.

KANYĀKUMĀRĪ (CAPE COMORIN). The southernmost tip of India. It derives its name ("Place of the Young Maiden") from the belief that it was here that the **Mother Goddess**, as a young girl, performed **ascetic** practice in order to win the hand of **Śiva** in marriage. The Kumārī Amman **temple**, located here, commemorates these practices.

There are also memorials to more recent Hindu sacred figures at Kanyākumārī. There is a shrine to **Mohandās K. Gāndhī** near the shore, where his ashes were kept prior to being immersed in the Indian Ocean. Just off the coast is Vivekānanda Rock, to which **Swāmī Vivekānanda** is said to have swum and where he practiced **meditation** in 1892, before setting off on his first major speaking tour. A small shrine to Vivekānanda is now located on the rock, to which regular boat rides are available for pilgrims and tourists.

KĀPĀLIKA. "Skull bearer"; a south Indian **Tantric Śaiva ascetic** lineage; a subset of the **Paśupata** tradition of **Śaivism**. Their name comes from their unusual begging bowls, which are made from the hollowed out tops of human skulls. This is in keeping with the **philosophy** of non-dualism that they seek to embody, which perceives traditional ideas of purity and impurity as part of the realm of duality, and so ultimately delusory.

KĀPILA. Highly revered sage attributed with creating the **Sāṃkhya** system of Indian **philosophy**. Kāpila is mentioned prominently in the ***Bhagavata Purāṇa***, where he is said to be an **avatāra**, or incarnation, of **Viṣṇu**, and is attributed with a theistic version of the Sāṃkhya system (though historically most Sāṃkhya texts are nontheistic, presenting a worldview close to that of **Jainism**). He is also mentioned in the ***Bhagavad Gītā*** as the best of sages (10:26). Kāpila is associated with the northeastern Greater Māgadha region of India, where Jainism and **Buddhism** were both prominent in ancient times. The city where the **Buddha** grew up—Kāpilavastu—is named in honor of this sage.

KARMA. "**Action**"; "work"; principle of cause and effect, by which actions of a certain moral character produce effects of a corresponding nature within the agent who performs them—with benevolent, kind actions leading to happiness for the one who performs them and harmful, violent actions similarly leading to suffering; also, the effects themselves—as in "good" karma (**puṇya** karma) and "bad" karma (**pāpa** karma).

The reciprocal process of intentional moral actions producing like effects fuels the perpetual cycle of **rebirth (saṃsāra)**, release from which (**mokṣa**) requires one to in some way negate or transcend the principle of cause and effect. The various Indic traditions often present themselves as strategies for achieving this negation or transcendence. The ***Bhagavad Gītā***, for example, presents a **yoga** of action (**karma yoga**) that aims at mokṣa through engaging in action without attachment to the results. On this understanding, it is not action itself, but the **desire** that motivates it, which brings about karmic effects.

KARMA KANDA. Literally "**action** portion"; the ***Saṃhitās*** and ***Brāhmaṇas***; the early portion of the ***Vedas***, consisting of ritualistic texts focused on sacrificial performance, as distinct from the later "wisdom portion" or **Jñāna Kanda**, devoted to knowledge of **Brahman** and consisting of the ***Upaniṣads***. *See also* MĪMĀṂSĀ.

KARMA MĀRGA, KARMA YOGA. "Path or way of **action**"; "spiritual discipline of action." As explained by the ***Bhagavad Gītā***, the path of action aims at **mokṣa** (freedom from the cycle of **rebirth**) through engaging in virtuous action without attachment to the results. On this understanding, it is not action itself but the **desire** that motivates action that brings about karmic effects. The **Neo-Vedānta** of **Ramakrishna** and **Swāmī Vivekānanda** teaches that the way of action is one of the **four yogas** or **mārgas** (paths) that can lead to **liberation** (along with devotion, or **bhakti**, wisdom, or **jñāna**, and **meditation**, or **dhyāna**). *See also* YOGA.

KARṆA. Character in the ***Mahābhārata***. Karṇa is a particularly tragic character. His mother, **Kuntī**, gave birth to him secretly, having tested the secret **mantra** given to her by the sage **Durvāsa**, by which she could call upon any deity of her choosing and bear a child by that deity. Calling the sun **god**, **Sūrya**, Kuntī gave birth to Karṇa, who had the characteristics of his divine father. As a young, unmarried mother, Kuntī, in shame, sent the infant Karṇa down a river in a basket, where he was found by a childless charioteer and his wife, who raised the child lovingly as their own. As an adult, Karṇa was rejected by the **Pāṇḍavas** on the basis of **caste** prejudice, since they believed he was the son of a lowly charioteer. **Duryodhana**, however, perceiving Karṇa's power, made him a king, thus securing him as a perpetual ally. Though the eldest brother of the Pāṇḍavas, Karṇa gave his loyalty to Duryodhana, thus obligating him to face his brothers in battle and die in combat at the hands of **Arjuna**. The Pāṇḍavas, though, were unaware of his identity until after his **death**.

KARNATAKA. State in southern India, just north of **Kerala** and **Tamil** Nadu and west of Andhra Pradesh, on the western coast of the Deccan peninsula; location of a number of important Hindu kingdoms of ancient times, including the **Cālukyas** (c. 550–880 CE), the Hoysalas (950–1343), and the Vijayanāgara empire (1336–1646). All of these kingdoms were patrons of the **arts**, sponsoring the construction of some of the most beautiful and elaborate Hindu **temples** ever built, including the temple complexes of **Belur**, **Halebid**, and **Bādāmī**, among others. Karnataka has also been a home to **Jainism**, particularly the Digambara sect, whose monastery at Śravaṇa Beḷgola houses a massive stone monument of the Jain saint Bāhubali, a product of the Hoysala era. Karnataka's contributions to the **bhakti** movement include the **Śaiva** bhakti **poet Basava** (1134–1196), the founder of the **Vīraśaiva** or **Liṅgāyat**

tradition, and the **Vaiṣṇava ācārya Madhva** (1238–1317). The author and **Indologist A. K. Ramanujan** (1921–1993) hailed from Karnataka as well.

KĀRTIKA. Month of the **Hindu calendar** that corresponds roughly to the period from mid-October to mid-November.

KĀRTTIKEYA. "Of the Kṛttikās (the Pleiades)"; son of **Śiva** and **Pārvati** and brother of **Gaṇeśa**; also known as **Skanda**, **Subramaṇya**, **Murugan**, **Kumāra**, and **Ṣaṇmukha**. The last name, which means "having six faces," is due to his having been born with six heads and 12 arms, though he is not always depicted in this way. In fact, he is widely regarded as a very handsome deity, often appearing as a young boy (the meaning of the name *Kumāra*). According to one tradition, he was raised by the six goddesses who are the main stars making up the Pleiades, hence the name *Kārttikeya*. A warrior deity, he is associated with the planet Mars and is regarded as a divine general, analogous to Michael in the **Christian** tradition, who leads the armies of heaven in battle against their demonic enemies, the **asuras**. Kārttikeya's vehicle is the peacock (**māyurī**). For this reason, he is known in Mahāyāna **Buddhism** as *Mahāmāyurī*, "the Great Peacock," and is a guardian of Buddhism and Buddhist holy sites.

KĀŚĪ. Alternative name for **Banaras**; the name for this city most often used in ancient sources.

KASHMIR, KAŚMĪR. Region in the extreme north of India; currently an area disputed by India and Pakistan, as well as by a movement for independence from both countries. Known for its breathtaking beauty, Kashmir is located in the **Himālayas** and has a large number of lakes and forests. The region is named for the sage **Kaśyapa**, who is believed to have lived there. The dominant religion in the region has historically been **Śaivism**—specifically the **Tantric Kaśmīr Śaiva** tradition. Kashmir was the birthplace of one of the greatest theologians and systematizers of Śaiva thought, **Abhinavagupta**. **Buddhism** was also prominent in Kashmir for many centuries, from which it spread to Central Asia. Since the Middle Ages, it has been a major center for **Islam** as well—particularly **Sufism**—and, until recently, was famous for peaceful coexistence between Hindus and Muslims.

KAŚMĪR ŚAIVISM. Collective term for a variety of **Tantric Śaiva** systems of thought and practice either originating or traditionally prominent in **Kaśmīr**. Prominent among these are the **Kaula Tantra** system of **Abhinavagupta** (950–1020), the Trika system, and the Krama system. The Trika, or "triadic," system focuses on a trio of **goddesses** who are all manifestations of **Kālī** or **Śakti**, the divine energy of **Śiva**. The rituals of this system include offerings of the **Five M's**, or traditionally impure substances utilized to embody the **truth** of nonduality: that there is truly nothing impure in the world if all is one. One of Abhinavagupta's innovations was to develop a system of contemplative visualization of these practices, so they did not have to actually be physically practiced in order for one to experience their spiritual benefits. The Krama, or "Steps," system similarly utilized practices such as the Five M's, which were also transformed into visualization exercises by Abhinavagupta. One of the results of Abhinavagupta's work was that Kaula Tantra eventually superseded and absorbed the other two systems.

KAŚYAPA. Literally, "tortoise"; **Vedic** sage believed to be the father of all humanity, as well as many of the deities, or **devas**, of the *Vedas*. He was married to 13 of the daughters of **Dakṣa**, including **Aditi**, with whom he fathered the 12 **Ādityas**, and both **Diti** and **Dānu**, with whom he fathered the **Daityas** and **Dānavas**, respectively. He is mentioned frequently in the ***Athārva Veda***. Because of his role as father of all human beings, whenever one is not aware of one's **gotra** name (a name that connects a person as a descendant to a Vedic sage, or **ṛṣi**), one uses the name *Kaśyapa*.

KAṬHA UPANIṢAD. One of the principle ***Upaniṣads***, probably composed between 400 and 300 BCE. The text consists primarily of a dialogue between a boy named **Nāciketa** and **Yama**, the **god** of **death**. Seeking to know the secret of **immortality** and what occurs after death, Yama reveals to him the **Vedāntic** doctrine of death, **rebirth**, and **mokṣa**, or **liberation** from rebirth. The text dwells at length on the nature of the soul (**ātman**) and contains a famous metaphor of the body as a **chariot**, with the horses that pull the chariot being the senses, the driver being the **mind**, and the self being the rider within the chariot.

KATHAK. Style of classical Indian **dance** developed in Uttar Pradesh, northern India. Kathak is known especially for the complex hand motions that it involves.

KATHAKALI. Style of classical Indian **dance** developed in **Kerala**. This dance style is traditionally performed only by men. It is well known for the very elaborate makeup and costumes that its performers wear.

KAULA TANTRA. System of **Tantric** practice aimed at realizing one's unity with **Śiva** through the elevation of the **Kuṇḍalinī** energy from the **mūladhāra cakra** at the base of the spine to the **sahāsrara cakra** or "thousand-petaled lotus," which, when energized by the rising energy, produces a blissful state that, according to this system, advances one quickly toward **en-**

lightenment. In the pursuit of this goal, Vāmācāra or **Left-Handed Tantric** practices such as the **Five M's** are employed.

Abhinavagupta (950–1020), the most prominent theologian of this tradition of **Kaśmīr Śaivism**, reinterpreted its Left-Handed practices as contemplative visualization exercises, making their spiritual benefits available without requiring aspirants to actually physically practice them.

KAURAVA. "Descendant of Kuru"; member of the **Kuru-Pañcāla** dynasty, the royal family whose misadventures are recounted in the ***Mahābhārata***. Though both branches of this family whose conflict is presented in the *Mahābhārata* are technically Kauravas, in order to distinguish the two groups, the sons of **Paṇḍu** are referred to as the **Pāṇḍavas** and their opponents as the Kauravas.

KAUṢĪTAKI UPANIṢAD. One of the principle ***Upaniṣads***, and a relatively early one, likely composed, in its current form, in the fifth century before the Common Era, around the same time as the ***Bṛhadāraṇyaka Upaniṣad*** and ***Chāndogya Upaniṣad***.

KAUṬILYA (c. 350–283). Author to whom the ***Artha Śāstra***, an ancient **Sanskrit** text of political science, is attributed; a **Brahmin** and chief political advisor to Candragupta **Maurya**; also known as Canakya. In later Sanskrit **literature** and in the Hindu popular imagination, Kauṭilya is depicted as a clever, wily figure—an ancient Indian Machiavelli. Following Kauṭilya's advice, the warrior Candragupta conquered most of northern India and established the first imperial dynasty to unite much of the subcontinent under a single government. Candragupta's grandson, Aśoka—known for his conversion to **Buddhism**—expanded the Mauryan Empire to its greatest geographic extent.

KĀVYA. Sanskrit poetics. *See also* POETRY.

KERALA. State on the southwestern coast of India; home to the majority of **Christians** in India. Kerala was the birthplace of **Śaṅkara** (788–820), the primary exponent of the **nondualistic** or **Advaita** form of **Vedānta** and founder of the **Daśanāmi Order** of Hindu monks. It is also the location of **Sabarimalai** hill, which is sacred to the followers of the deity **Ayyappan**. Kerala is believed to be the birthplace of **Paraśurāma**, the sixth out of the traditional list of 10 **avatāras** of **Viṣṇu**. The **guru Amritānandamayī Mātā** also hails from Kerala.

KETU. One of the **navagrahas**; companion of **Rāhu**. Rāhu was an **asura** who managed to steal a drop of the **amṛta**, or elixir of **immortality**, when the

devas and asuras churned it from the cosmic ocean. Alerted to this fact by the sun and the **moon**, **Viṣṇu** beheaded Rāhu and placed his head in the sky. The rest of Rāhu's body became a separate entity, Ketu, also placed in the sky. The two of them periodically take their vengeance on the sun and the moon by swallowing them, causing solar and lunar eclipses. Ketu appears as a man with the head of a serpent. Both are considered inauspicious in Hindu **astrology**.

KHAJURAHO. **Temple** complex in north-central India located in the state of Madhya Pradesh; famous for the erotic imagery, modeled on the sexual positions described in the ***Kāma Sūtra***, that adorn the outer walls of many of the temples. The complex includes temples dedicated to **Śiva** and **Hanuman**, as well as several **Jain** temples.

KNOWLEDGE. *See* JÑĀNA.

KOLKATA. **Bengali** name for **Calcutta**.

KONĀRAK. Site in **Orissa** known for its **temple** to **Sūrya**, the sun **god**. The temple is designed in the shape of a massive 24-wheeled **chariot** representing the chariot in which Sūrya flies across the sky every day. This magnificent structure includes seven stone horses, supposed to be pulling the chariot, and three images of Sūrya positioned so as to receive direct sunlight at dawn, noon, and sunset.

KOŚA. "Layer, sheath." Five layers that surround the self (**ātman**). The outermost layer, the **anna-maya-kośa**, or "sheath made of food," is the gross, physical body. Next is the **prāṇa-maya-kośa**, or "sheath made of breath," which consists of the **prāṇa** or life force. Next is the **mano-maya-kośa**, or "sheath made of **mind**," which consists of a subtle organ of cognition (distinct from the human brain, which would be part of the anna-maya-kośa). Next is the **vijñāna-maya-kośa**, or "sheath made of consciousness." Finally, there is the **ānanda-maya-kośa**, or "sheath made of bliss."

KRISHNA. *See* KṚṢṆA.

KRISHNAMURTI, JIDDU (1895–1986). Philosopher and spiritual teacher. Born into a **Brahmin** family in Andhra Pradesh, in southern India, Krishnamurti was raised by members of the **Theosophical Society** who believed he was destined to be the "World Teacher"—the next **Buddha**, Maitreya—a messianic being whose coming is predicted in the **Buddhist** scriptures. In 1922, while staying in Ojai, California, Krishnamurti experienced a profound spiritual transformation to which he referred as "the process." In 1925, **An-**

nie Besant publicly announced Krishnamurti's messiahship. Krishnamurti himself did not endorse this idea, however, and famously left the Theosophical Society in 1927 in order to teach a radical questioning of all forms of authority.

Although Krishnamurti publicly rejected the Theosophical Society and its plans for him, and subsequently distanced himself from all organized religion, Besant and Krishnamurti remained on good terms until Besant's death in 1933.

In California, Krishnamurti became acquainted with literary figures like **Aldous Huxley** and **Christopher Isherwood** who were adherents of **Neo-Vedānta** and had an intense interest of expanding the boundaries of human consciousness. He was a hero of the countercultural movement of the 1960s. His lectures were heavily attended by young spiritual seekers of that era. In his later years, he returned to India where he set up a system of schools based on the idea of encouraging the curiosity of children in a spirit of free inquiry.

To the degree that it is possible to categorize Krishnamurti's teaching, it can be said to have affinities to both **Advaita Vedānta** and the thought of the second-century CE Mahāyāna Buddhist philosopher Nāgārjuna.

KṚṢṆA. "Dark one"; also "attractive one"; along with **Rāma**, one of the most popular incarnations or **avatāras** of **Viṣṇu** in Hindu devotional practice. For some **Vaiṣṇavas**, particularly the **Gauḍīya Vaiṣṇava** tradition, Kṛṣṇa is not merely an avatāra, but is **God** in a monotheistic sense—the "Supreme Personality of Godhead," to cite the terminology of the **Hare Krishna movement** (a subset of Gauḍīya Vaiṣṇavism). The textual sources on Kṛṣṇa's life consist mainly of the ***Mahābhārata***, the ***Harivaṃśa***, and the ***Bhāgavata Purāṇa***. There is also a very early, albeit brief, reference to Kṛṣṇa, son of **Devakī**, in the ***Bṛhadāraṇyaka Upaniṣad***. Though it is the earliest of these texts, the portions of the *Mahābhārata* dealing with Kṛṣṇa (including the famous ***Bhagavad Gītā***) relate the latter parts of this figure's life story, as king of **Dvāraka**. The ***Bhagavata Purāṇa***, composed later, deals with the earlier portions of Kṛṣṇa's life, including narratives of his infancy and adolescence. It is this text that is by far the most popular within Vaiṣṇava traditions. Kṛṣṇa's loving relations with the **gopīs**, or cowherd women of **Vṛndāvana**, in particular, are a very popular subject of **art**, song, **dance**, **poetry**, and philosophical and theological reflection. The ***Gītagovinda*** of **Jayadeva** (c. 1200), often likened to the biblical "Song of Songs," focuses on the love affair between Kṛṣṇa and **Rādhā**, a relationship that the tradition utilizes as an image for the relationship of the individual devotee to Kṛṣṇa—a saving bond known as **bhakti**, or devotion.

Major episodes from Kṛṣṇa's life include his peaceful youth in idyllic Vṛndāvan; his eventual slaying of his wicked uncle, **Kāṃsa**; his friendship

Kṛṣṇa and Rādhā

with **Arjuna** and the other **Pāṇḍava** brothers; and the tragic brawl among Kṛṣṇa's kinsmen, the **Yādavas**, which foreshadowed the fall of their kingdom, Dvārakā.

KṚṢṆA JANMĀṢṬAMI. Birthday of **Kṛṣṇa**; major Hindu holiday. Kṛṣṇa Janmāṣṭami occurs on the eighth day of the dark half (or **Kṛṣṇa Pakṣa**) of the month of **Śravaṇa**. Literally meaning, "Birthday of Kṛṣṇa, the Eighth," the number eight alludes to the fact that Kṛṣṇa was the eighth child of **Devakī**, his mother, and the eighth **avatāra** of **Viṣṇu** according to the list of 10 avatāras.

KṚṢṆA PAKṢA. The dark half of a Hindu month; the fortnight of a Hindu lunar month during which the **moon** is waning; the period between **Pūrṇima**, or full-moon day, and **Amavasya**, or new-moon day (which is also the last day of the Hindu month). The dark half of the month is generally considered a less auspicious time for undertaking any new ventures. *See also* CALENDAR, HINDU.

KṢATRIYA. Warrior; ruler; the second of the four **varṇas** or main **castes**. In terms of traditional occupation, this caste is responsible for maintaining **dharma** in the sense of law and order and the smooth running of society.

KUBERA. God of wealth; a very ancient deity associated with nature and assimilated into Hinduism, **Buddhism**, and **Jainism** as a **yakṣa**, or earth spirit. He was the lord of the yakṣas and **rākṣasas** until being overthrown by **Rāvaṇa**. For this reason, Kubera is an ally of **Rāma**. He is the guardian of the north and is usually depicted as a pot-bellied man with a large bag of coins and jewels.

KULĀRṆAVA TANTRA**.** Main **scripture** of the **Kaula Tantra** sect.

KUMĀRA. "Youth"; name for **Kārttikeya**, son of **Śiva** and **Pārvatī**.

KUMĀRILA BHAṬṬA (fl. 700 CE). Philosopher; prominent adherent of the **Pūrva Mīmāṃsā** or **Mīmāṃsā** system of Hindu **philosophy**. Kumārila spent much of his life in **Prayāga (Allahabad)**. Pūrva Mīmāṃsā, or "earlier exegesis," the philosophy on which Kumārila expounded, is a continuation of the ancient, orthodox system of Vedic **Brahmanism**, with a very strong emphasis on the correct performance of **Vedic** ritual and the correct pronunciation of the **Sanskrit** verses of the ***Vedas*** during a ritual performance. This emphasis on the correct Sanskrit usage led to the development of an elaborate linguistic philosophy by the Mīmāṃsakas. The term *Pūrva Mīmāṃsā* contrasts this school of thought with later, or **Uttara Mīmāṃsā**—more widely known as **Vedānta**. It emphasizes the earlier, ritualistic portion of the *Vedas*, while Vedānta emphasizes the later Vedic **literature**, the ***Upaniṣads***, and their teaching of **Brahman**.

Kumārila's contributions to Mīmāṃsā include his theory of language, which, in contrast to the holistic **sphoṭa** theory of **Bhartṛhari**, affirms that a sentence can only be understood when each of its words is comprehended correctly. Sharply critical of the **Buddhists** and **Jains**, Kumārila argues that the Buddhist and Jain **scriptures** cannot be true because they contain numerous grammatical errors and are not written in Sanskrit. In defense of the authority of the *Vedas*, he argued that they are *apauruṣeya*—that is, they have no author and are thus eternal. Kumārila's position on the *Vedas* is akin to *fideism*, the antifoundationalist notion of taking a particular tradition or set of claims on faith as axiomatically true. His critiques of Buddhism reveal a close acquaintance with Buddhist claims and arguments, and some accounts of his life claim that he studied at the famous Buddhist university at Nalanda.

KUMBHA MELĀ. "Festival of the Pot"; a massive pilgrimage and festival held on a rotating basis every three years at **Hardwar**, **Nāsik**, **Ujjain**, and **Prayāga**. It is said that at the time of the churning of the cosmic ocean of milk, four drops of **amṛta**—the elixir of **immortality**—fell to Earth at the locations of these holy cities. The pot to which the name of the festival refers is the one from which the drops of amṛta spilled. Pilgrims, including a massive number of renouncers, or **sannyāsins**, gather at each site every 12 years. The 144th Kumbha Melā of a cycle is known as the *Mahā* or "great" *Kumbha Melā*. The last Mahā Kumbha Melā, held in the year 2001, attracted 60,000,000 pilgrims, making this festival the largest gathering of human beings for a single purpose in history. The crowds at this gathering were visible to orbiting satellites.

The earliest written account of the Kumbha Melā is that of the Chinese **Buddhist** pilgrim Xuanzang, who traveled to India in the seventh century of the Common Era, during the reign of **Harṣa**. According to Xuanzang's account, Harṣa accompanied him to this gathering. It is likely, however, that the Kumbha Melā dates back many centuries before Xuanzang.

The Kumbha Melā begins on the **Pūrṇimā**, or full-moon day, of the month of **Pauṣa** (December–January) and ends on the Pūrṇimā of **Magha** (January–February).

KUṆḌALINĪ. "Coiled one"; serpent. According to **Tantric yoga**, in the space that corresponds to the base of the spine, a subtle energy or **śakti**, resides. While it is residing in this space, it is also referred to as the kuṇḍalini, or coiled energy, because it is said to resemble a coiled serpent in this state. One of the goals of Tantric yoga practice is to raise this energy from the base of the spine to the crown of the head, which are linked by a subtle nerve channel called the suṣumna nādī, and which occupies roughly the same space as the spinal cord. Along the suṣumna nādī are the seven **cakras**. These energy centers are activated as the śakti or kuṇḍalinī rises through the suṣumna nādī to the **sahāsrara cakra** or "thousand-petaled lotus," in the crown of the head, which, when energized by the rising śakti, produces a blissful state that, according to Tantra, advances one quickly toward **enlightenment**.

According to the tradition of **Siddha Yoga**, a contemporary **Śaiva** movement with a strongly Tantric dimension, an enlightened teacher, or **guru**, can raise one's śakti from the base of the spine to the crown of the head—activating all of the cakras in the process—with a thought, word, or touch. This experience is called **śaktipat**. *See also* KAULA TANTRA.

KUNTĪ. Character in the ***Mahābhārata***; wife of **Paṇḍu** and mother of **Karṇa** and three of the five **Pāṇḍava** brothers—**Yudhiṣṭhira**, **Bhīma**, and **Arjuna**. In her youth, **Durvāsa**, a sage, paid a visit to her father's palace. Impressed by the polite young woman, the sage gave her a secret **mantra** that she could use to summon any deity of her choosing for the purpose of bearing a child by that deity. Not fully comprehending the implications of the use of this mantra, the curious girl used it to call upon the sun **god**, **Sūrya**, who then impregnated her. Soon, Kuntī gave birth to a magnificent son from this union, Karṇa, who had the characteristics of his divine father.

But because she was unmarried and ashamed to have given birth, she hid the child, putting him in a basket and sending him down a river, from where he would later be rescued by a childless charioteer and his wife, who would take the boy in and lovingly raise him as their own.

Later in life, when she was married to the **Kaurava** king, **Paṇḍu**, Kuntī used her mantra again when the king was cursed to die if he approached either of his two wives for the purpose of lovemaking. Paṇḍu had not yet fathered an heir at this point, so Kuntī used her mantra to bear semidivine children who would legally be Paṇḍu's. This was the origin of the Pāṇḍava brothers, three of whom were Kuntī's sons and two of whom—the twins, **Nakula** and Sahadeva—were the sons of Paṇḍu's younger wife, **Mādrī**, with whom Kuntī shared her mantra.

When the Pāṇḍavas rejected Karṇa as unworthy to share the assembly of **kṣatriya** warriors, being (as they thought) the son of a humble charioteer, **Duryodhana**, seizing an opportunity to gain a powerful ally, made Karṇa a king, thus winning his enduring loyalty and ensuring that Karṇa would fight on Duryodhana's side against his brothers. On the eve of the climactic battle between the Pāṇḍavas and the Kauravas, Kuntī tells Karṇa the **truth** about his identity, hoping to win him over to the Pāṇḍavas' side. But Karṇa does not waver in his loyalty to Duryodhana. Karṇa later dies in the battle at Arjuna's hand, though Arjuna does not yet know at that point that Karṇa is really his eldest brother. *See also* WOMEN.

KŪRMA. The tortoise **avatāra** or incarnation of **Viṣṇu** and the second in the traditional list of 10 such avatāras. Viṣṇu assumes this form to act as the pivot for the churning of the ocean when the **devas** and **asuras** churn the cosmic ocean in their search for **amṛta**, the elixir of **immortality**.

KURU-PAÑCĀLA. Ancient **Vedic** polity located in northwestern India, roughly in the vicinity of the modern state of Haryana and **New Delhi**. The Kurus and Pañcālas were two distinct groups that formed a union. A historical kingdom (and later a republic), archaeologists believe the Kurus were a people who lived in the Delhi area between the 12th and ninth centuries before the Common Era and whose deeds and struggles formed the basis for the ***Mahābhārata***. The ***Ṛg Veda*** may reflect their ideology.

KURUKṢETRA. "Field of the Kurus." Field in northern India on which the climactic battle of the ***Mahābhārata*** takes place. This is the same battle that is the occasion for the dialogue between **Arjuna** and **Kṛṣṇa** that constitutes the ***Bhagavad Gītā***. In interpreting the *Bhagavad Gītā*, it is sometimes asserted (on the basis of *Bhagavad Gītā* 13:1) that the field of Kurukṣetra symbolizes the physical body as the location where the battle against spiritual enemies such as greed, hatred, and lust is waged—a battle symbolized, in turn, by the *Mahābhārata* war. **Mohandās K. Gāndhī** favored this interpretation as a way to negate Kṛṣṇa's apparent endorsement of violence in the first two chapters of this text, making it more compatible with Gāndhī's **philosophy** of nonviolence (**ahiṃsā**).

KUŚA. A type of sacred grass used in **Vedic** ceremonies.

KŪṬIYĀṬṬAM (KOODIYĀṬṬAM). "Acting together"; classical Indian **dance** style. Every year a series of eight dance dramas is performed at **Guruvayūr**, a town in **Kerala**, in the Kūṭiyāṭṭam style that depicts events from Kṛṣṇa's life. This is the one Indian style of classical dance that has continued to be performed without interruption since ancient times. Others fell into disuse at different points and have been revived in modern times.

L

LAKṢMAṆA. Character in the ***Rāmāyaṇa***; brother and close friend of **Rāma** who often takes on the role of Rāma's protector. Just as Rāma is regarded as an **avatāra** of **Viṣṇu**, and **Sītā**, Rāma's wife, as an incarnation of Viṣṇu's wife, **Lakṣmī**, Lakṣmaṇa is often seen as an incarnation of **Seśa**, the cosmic serpent on whom Viṣṇu reclines on the cosmic ocean, and who rears up his many heads to protect Viṣṇu. Lakṣmaṇa accompanies Rāma into exile and is his constant companion in his struggle with the demonic **Rāvaṇa**.

LAKSHMAN JOO, SWĀMĪ (1907–1991). Scholar, mystic, revered modern exponent of **Kaśmīr Śaivism**.

LAKṢMĪ. "Mark"; "sign"; **goddess** of good fortune and prosperity; wife of **Viṣṇu**. She emerged from the cosmic ocean when it was churned by the **devas** and **asuras** to retrieve the **amṛta**, or elixir of **immortality**. When **Viṣṇu** appears on the Earth as an **avatāra** he is accompanied by Lakṣmī, who manifests as **Rāma**'s wife, **Sītā**, and later as **Kṛṣṇa**'s wife, **Rukmiṇī**. In **Śrivaiṣṇava** theology, Lakṣmī and Viṣṇu, rather like **Śiva** and **Śakti**, are said to be two parts, aspects, or dimensions of one, undivided godhead. Analogously to the way in which Śakti is viewed as the power of Śiva, without which he can do nothing, it is said that Viṣṇu never does anything without Lakṣmī's approval and that he takes her advice. For this reason, Vaiṣṇava devotees sometimes approach Viṣṇu through Lakṣmī as a kind of intercessor. It is said that Lakṣmī represents the more gentle and benevolent aspect of Viṣṇu, who is sometimes represented as a rather stern and righteous deity. She is also a symbol of divine grace. In her origins, it is likely that she was first worshiped as a goddess of abundance and fertility. *See also* ŚRĪ.

LAKULĪŚA (fl. 2nd century CE). Yogi; founder of the **Paśupata** tradition of **Śaivism**.

Lakṣmī, goddess of wealth and prosperity, embodiment of divine grace and abundance.

LALLĀ (fl. 1300 CE). Female mystic, **bhakti poet**, and saint of the **Kaśmīr Śaiva** tradition, also known as Lalleśwarī. The collection of her poems is entitled the *Lalla Vākyāni* ("Sayings of Lallā"). *See also* WOMEN.

LALLEŚWARĪ. *See* LALLĀ.

LAMBODARA. "Pot belly"; epithet of **Gaṇeśa**.

LAṄKA. In the ***Rāmāyaṇa***, Laṅka is the island kingdom of **Rāvaṇa**, demonic lord of the **rākṣasas**. Subsequent tradition has come to identify this island with **Sri Lanka**, the large island off the southeastern coast of India, near **Tamil** Nadu.

LAW. *See* DHARMA.

LAWS OF MANU. *See MANUSMṚTI.*

LEFT-HANDED TANTRA. Tantric practices that include **actions** and items, such as the **Five M's**, which are normally regarded as impure, so called because the left hand is traditionally seen in Hindu culture as unclean. The purpose of such practices is to show that one has transcended the realm of duality—that if everything is one with the divine, the belief that certain actions, persons, or things can be impure is without foundation and is a part of the illusion to which those who are trapped in the cycle of **rebirth** have become enthralled. Such practices are traditionally shrouded in secrecy, both because they might be an occasion for scandal for the practitioner, but also because it is believed that such practices are only effective for those who truly are cultivating a nondual awareness. If pursued merely for pleasure or other unworthy purposes (like the cultivation of **siddhis**, or paranormal powers) they can be destructive and lead to rebirth in hell. Because of the perilous nature of such practices, the **Kaśmīr Śaiva** theologian **Abhinavagupta** (950–1020) recommended that one should practice them through contemplative visualization, rather than with literal, physical performance. The **Sanskrit** term for Left-Handed Tantra is Vāmācāra.

LEKHRĀJ, DĀDA (1876–1969). Founder of the **Brahmā Kumārī** movement; better known by his religious name of **Prajāpitar Brahmā**.

LIBERATION. Mokṣa; release from **saṃsāra**, the **karma**-fueled cycle of birth, **death**, and **rebirth**, and the ultimate goal of many systems of Hindu thought and practice.

LĪLĀ. "Play," the divine play. According to some theistic Hindu theologies, the world of time and space in which souls reside is a divine play, an exuberant and spontaneous burst of creativity in which **God** delights in infinite possibility. The concept of līlā is an attempt to answer the question of why God, who is self-sufficient and free from desire, engages in the act of **creation**, which implies a desire to create. According to the idea of līlā, creation is a spontaneous act pursued as an end in itself, rather than an **action** that is undertaken for some further, desired end.

LIṄGA (LIṄGAM). Symbolic form of **Śiva**; an abstract representation, in contrast to the more anthropomorphic **mūrtis** that represent Śiva as a human being, emphasizing his **nirguṇa**, or formless, nature.

Some, though not all, liṅgas have a phallic appearance, prompting speculation that the liṅga may originally have been a fertility symbol, and Śiva a deity connected with fertility. While this is certainly the case in some contexts—shrines or images; such as Gudimallam in Andhra Pradesh, where

A typical linga, symbol of Śiva.

the phallic nature of the liṅga is quite obvious—the preeminent view of the liṅga in general among contemporary Hindus is that it is an abstract, aniconic representation of a deity who is ultimately beyond form. The most commonly cited textual reference to the meaning and origin of the liṅga is not overtly phallic but refers to Śiva's appearance to **Brahmā** and **Viṣṇu** as an infinite pillar of fire whose full extent neither deity is able to comprehend (not unlike biblical apparitions of the divine as a pillar of fire). The liṅga, on this understanding, is an attempt to represent this pillar of fire in the form of a stone. *See also* YONI.

LIṄGĀYAT. **Śaiva** tradition based in **Karnataka** and established by the **bhakti poet** and social reformer **Basava** (1134–1196). Also known as the **Vīraśaivas**, the Liṅgāyats oppose **casteism** and teach the equality of all human beings as manifestations of **Śiva**. Believing in holding ritualism to a bare minimum, the only image the Liṅgāyats use is the abstract form of Śiva, the **liṅga** (hence the name *Liṅgāyat* for this tradition), which they traditionally wear on a necklace. The Liṅgāyats regard Śiva as **God** in the **monotheistic** sense—as the one supreme deity.

LITERATURE. Literature is a vital component of Hinduism, from the ancient **Vedic scriptures** to the writings of contemporary Hindu spiritual teachers (**gurus**). The range of Hindu literary genres is vast, encompassing very large epic narratives (the ***Mahābhārata*** and ***Rāmāyaṇa*** being the primary examples); the lyrical **poetry** of the **bhakti** saints; the terse didactic writings or **sūtras** of the various philosophical systems (or **darśanas**); the pragmatic "how-to" manuals of political science (***Artha Śāstra***), **law** (***Dharma Śāstra***), and sensory enjoyment (the ***Kāma Sūtra***); the dramas of playwrights such as **Kālidāsa**; and in the modern period, the novels of **Bankim Chandra Chatterjee** and the poems, plays, songs, and essays of **Rabindranath Tagore**.

The oldest extant Hindu literature is composed in **Sanskrit**. The ***Vedas***, the oldest and most sacred collection of Hindu scriptural literature, is regarded as **śrūti**, or divinely revealed. The Vedic literature includes both poetry and prose and was passed on orally for centuries by the community of **Brahmins** before being committed to writing in the modern period. Even larger (and more popularly known) than the *Vedas* is the collection of **smṛti**, or secondary scriptures, which includes the two main Sanskrit epics and many other sets of authoritative texts, such as the ***Purāṇas***, or ancient tales of the **gods**, and the sūtra and śāstra literature just mentioned.

In the first millennium of the Common Era, devotional poetry in the vernacular languages of India became increasingly popular. Some of this poetry, such as the **Tamil** works of the **Āḷvārs** and **Nāyanārs**, came to be regarded as scripture in its own right by the South Indian **Vaiṣṇava** and **Śaiva** traditions, respectively, that inherited it. As bhakti became a mass movement, translations of earlier Sanskrit works into spoken vernacular languages also increased in number, such as the **Hindi** rendering of the *Rāmāyaṇa*, the ***Rām Carit Mānas*** of **Tulsīdās** (1532–1623), which is better known among Hindus in the northern part of India today than the original *Rāmāyaṇa* of **Vālmīki**.

With the coming of the British to India and the institution of English education, many Hindu thinkers began to express themselves through the medium of English essays, including some of the major figures of the modern Hindu reform movement, like **Rām Mohan Roy**, **Swāmī Vivekānanda**, **Aurobindo Ghose**, and **Mohandās K. Gāndhī**, to name only a few. European genres, such as the novel, also became popular in the modern period, often being written in Indian vernacular languages, such as the **Bengali** novels of Bankim Chandra Chatterjee.

With the internationalization of Hinduism, the creation and adaptation of Hindu forms of literary expression continues today—including, for example, the science fiction adaptation of the *Rāmāyaṇa* in Ashok Banker's *Prince of Ayodhya* series of novels, and the American-produced graphic novel *Ramayana Reloaded*—as well as the maintaining of earlier literary forms, such as devotional songs, or **bhajanas**—the lyrics of all of which are bhakti poems—which have been incorporated into popular Indian cinema. And the Indian diaspora is producing a great variety of English novelists reflecting upon the relatively recent experience of being Hindu in predominantly non-Hindu cultures.

LOKA. World; realm; abode of a deity; also the human world; society.

LOKAPĀLA. The four leading **Vedic** deities, **Indra**, **Agni**, **Varuṇa**, and **Yama**. These deities are frequently invoked early in ritualistic worship, or **pūjā**, in order to ensure that the ritual will be completed without mishap.

LOKĀYATA. **Materialism**, doctrine of the **Cārvāka** system of philosophy, one of the heterodox or **nāstika** schools of Indian philosophy, or **darśana**. According to this view, the only valid **pramāṇa** or basis of **knowledge** is sensory perception. The adherents of this view reject such widely held doctrines of Indian philosophy as **karma** and **rebirth** or belief in anything that is not verifiable through sensory perception. This system was widely criticized by adherents of other schools of thought, both orthodox (the **Vedic** or **Brahmanical** systems) and heterodox (**Buddhism** and **Jainism**).

LOMAHARṢAṆA SŪTA. Disciple of **Vyāsa** who memorized the epics and ***Purāṇas***.

LOTUS. Flower frequently used in Hindu iconography to symbolize the state of spiritual **enlightenment**. The lotus typically grows in muddy water. The lotus blossom, sprouting from a stalk that rises out of the mud in which it is rooted to bloom above the surface of the water, represents spiritual enlightenment arising from the mud of worldly life, with its various forms of suffering and limitation. In recent decades, the lotus has also become a symbol of Hinduism, and is used as the logo of some **Hindu Nationalist** organizations such as the **Bharatīya Janata Party** (BJP).

LOTUS POSTURE. Padmāsana; **Haṭha Yoga** posture formed by placing the right foot on the left thigh and the left foot on the right thigh. This is the "full lotus." There is also a half-lotus posture (**ardhapadmāsana**), formed by placing the right foot on the left thigh and the left foot underneath the right leg. *See also* ĀSANA.

LOVE. Love has a wide range of meanings in Hinduism, some of which are denoted by distinct **Sanskrit** terms, including **bhakti** (absolute devotion to **God** in a personal form), **prema** (platonic love, affection, friendship), and **kāma** (erotic or romantic love, sexual desire). Love is theorized in Hindu thought as not a mere sentiment but rather as the felt experience of the interconnectedness of one being to another, and ultimately of all beings to one another and to God.

M

MĀ. Mother. Intimate form of address frequently used to call upon **Devī**, the **Mother Goddess**, especially popular in **Bengal**.

MADHVA (1238–1317). Vaiṣṇava ācārya; founder of the dualistic or **Dvaita** system of **Vedānta**. Born near **Udipi** in **Karnataka**, where he spent most of his life, Madhva is believed by his devotees to be the third incarnation or **avatāra** of **Vāyu**, the **Vedic god** of the wind (the first two incarnations being **Hanuman** and **Bhīma**). A devout **Vaiṣṇava**, Madhva was highly critical of the **Advaita Vedānta** of **Śaṅkara**, seeing it as diminishing the significance of **bhakti** and as relegating **God** to a role subordinate to an impersonal reality (**Nirguṇa Brahman**). Madhva sees Brahman as identical to **Viṣṇu**, the supreme deity, and the **jīva**, or individual soul of a living being, as an eternally existing reality distinct from Viṣṇu. **Liberation**, or **mokṣa**, therefore does not involve a real metaphysical union between the devotee and the divine (or, as in Advaita Vedānta, a realization that the distinction between the devotee and the divine is an illusion). The devotee and the divine are forever distinct. "Union" with the divine is a union of wills, of complete subordination of the will of the individual soul to the will of God (**Īśvara-praṇidhāna**). The individuality of one who attains liberation is not effaced. Liberation, rather, consists of residing for eternity in **Vaikuṇṭha**, or heaven, with God, a place of infinite bliss. Unusually for a Hindu tradition, Dvaita Vedānta teaches that it is possible that some souls may never reach liberation and remain eternally separated from God.

MADRAS. Also known as Chennai; fourth-largest city in India and capital of the state of **Tamil** Nadu, on the southeast coast of the Deccan peninsula. It was the first city to be established by the **British East India Company**, growing up around Fort Saint George, which was built in 1644. The city contains several major **temples** and also houses the world headquarters of the **Theosophical Society**, in a neighborhood known as Adyār. Its major temples include Kāpālīśvarar (a **Śiva** temple) and Śrī Parthasarathy (dedicated to **Kṛṣṇa**).

MĀDRĪ. Younger wife of **Paṇḍu** and mother of the twins **Nākula** and Sahadeva, the youngest of the **Pāṇḍava** brothers in the ***Mahābhārata***. When

Paṇḍu was cursed to die if he attempted to make love to either of his wives, his elder wife, **Kuntī**, utilized a secret **mantra** that gave her the power to summon any deity and bear a child by that deity. At Paṇḍu's request, Kuntī evoked the devas **Yama**, **Vāyu**, and **Indra** in order to give birth to **Yudhiṣṭhira**, **Bhīma**, and **Arjuna**, respectively. Mādrī, also desiring to bear divine children for Paṇḍu, asked Kuntī to share her mantra, which Mādrī then used to evoke the **Aśvins**, twin deities who then fathered Nākula and Sahadeva. *See also* WOMEN.

MADURAI. Site in **Tamil** Nadu, in southern India, which houses a major complex of **temples** dedicated to the **goddess Mīnākṣī** and **Śiva**; an important pilgrimage site. The annual festival celebrating the wedding of Mīnākṣī and Śiva (in his form as **Sundareśvara**, or "Lord of Beauty") is very popular and an occasion for great displays of **devotion**.

MAGHA. Month of the **Hindu calendar** that corresponds roughly to the period from mid-January to mid-February.

MAHĀBALIPURAM. *See* MĀMALLAPURAM.

MAHĀBHĀRATA. "Great Epic of the **Bharatas**"; along with the ***Rāmāyaṇa***, one of the two great epic poems of Hinduism. Together, these two texts make up the **Itihāsa** ("thus it was") or historical **literature** of Hinduism. In its current form, the *Mahābhārata* was probably composed over the course of several centuries, from about 300 BCE to 300 CE. According to Hindu tradition, the epic is the work of the sage **Vyāsa**, who is also credited with compiling the ***Vedas*** and the ***Purāṇas***. The events that make up the main narrative of the text may be based on a battle that took place among various **Āryan** tribes around 950 BCE. However, the text also refers to the sinking of the coastal city of **Dvārakā**, which took place around 1500 BCE, and at least one Hindu tradition locates the date of the battle as 3102 BCE—also regarded as the point at which the **Kali Yuga** began. In any case, the original narrative expanded substantially over the centuries, as a great variety of folk tales, philosophical writings, and even legal texts were incorporated into the epic through the process of telling and retelling. Consisting, in its finished form, of approximately 180,000 lines, the *Mahābhārata* is roughly four times the length of the Bible.

The basic narrative of the *Mahābhārata* is focused on the power struggle between two sets of cousins—the **Pāṇḍavas** and the **Kauravas**—who are competing for control of the kingdom of the Kurus. The succession to the throne has been rendered problematic by the vow of **Bhīṣma**, who renounces his claim to the throne at the request of his father, Śantanu, so Śantanu can marry a **woman** whose father wants her heirs to inherit the kingdom, and not

Bhīṣma. Subsequently, Śantanu's heirs by this woman die without any heirs. The **poet** Vyāsa, the queen's son from a previous relationship, is brought in to father children with the wives of the deceased heirs. One of these sons is blind and the other suffers from albinism, rendering neither fully fit to be king. Their sons, in turn—the Kauravas and the Pāṇḍavas—end up fighting for control of the kingdom.

Commentators frequently contrast the *Mahābhārata* with its companion epic, the *Rāmāyaṇa*, particularly in regard to its tragic tone. Whereas the *Rāmāyaṇa* is an uplifting classic rescue tale, in which the heroes and the villains are clearly delineated from one another, the *Mahābhārata* is far more ambiguous, with the putative heroes (the Pāṇḍavas) and their supporters not always behaving in an admirable, or even ethical, fashion, and the villains and their supporters (especially the tragic **Karṇa**) sometimes behaving with great nobility.

Religiously, the *Mahābhārata* has become especially significant to the **Vaiṣṇava** traditions of Hinduism because of the prominent role of **Kṛṣṇa** in the story—the eighth of the 10 **avatāras**, or incarnations, of **Viṣṇu**. Kṛṣṇa is a close friend and advisor to the Pāṇḍavas, especially the warrior **Arjuna**. Kṛṣṇa's counsel to Arjuna on the eve of the climactic battle of the epic is an especially beloved portion of this text and has become a sacred scripture in its own right: the famous "Song of the Blessed One," or ***Bhagavad Gītā***.

The *Mahābhārata* has been a major subject of Hindu **art** and literature throughout the centuries. Plays, such as the renowned poet **Kālīdāsa**'s *Abhijñānaśakuntala* ("The Recognition of **Śakuntalā**"), have been based upon it or upon select episodes within it. Depictions of scenes from the text adorn **temple** walls throughout India and **Southeast Asia**. In the modern period, it has become a popular **Hindi** television series and has been presented as an English stage play by Peter Brook.

MAHĀBHŪTAS. The five elements or states of being that constitute the physical world (mahābhūtas). The five elements are earth (**pṛthvi**), air (**vāyu**), fire (**agni**), water (**ap**), and space (**ākāśa**). Each element is the medium of a different type of experience on the subtle level (smell, touch, sight, taste, and sound, respectively).

MAHĀDEVA. Great **God**; epithet of **Śiva**.

MAHĀDEVĪ. Great **Goddess**; epithet of the **Mother Goddess**, who is known variously as **Umā**, **Devī**, **Śakti**, **Pārvatī**, **Durgā**, and **Kālī**, as well as other names.

MAHĀDEVIYAKKA (fl. 12th century CE). Female **Śaiva** saint and **bhakti** poet who gave up a royal marriage to wander as a naked renouncer, or **sannyāsinī**, devoted completely to **Śiva**, whom she regarded as her true husband. She refers to Śiva in her devotional **poetry** as her "Lord white as jasmine," saying, "O lord white as jasmine, if my head falls from my shoulders I shall think it your offering." The **Vīraśaivas** hold Mahādeviyakka in high esteem, revering her devotion. *See also* WOMEN.

MAHĀKĀLA. "Great time"; epithet of **Śiva** that refers to his role as time, the destroyer of all. *See also* NĀṬARĀJA.

MAHĀRĀJ JI, GURU (1957–). Born Prem Rawat; son of Sri Hāṃsā Mahārāj Ji. He succeeded his father as head of the **Divine Light Mission** in 1966, when was only nine years old. In 1974, he married an American woman against his mother's wishes. This led to a rift in the Divine Light Mission, which was renamed *Elán Vital* in 1983.

MAHARISHI MAHESH YOGI (MAHARṢI MAHEŚA YOGĪ) (1918–2008). Guru of the **Transcendental Meditation** tradition, which he began teaching in the Western world in 1958, his most famous students being the Beatles, who visited his **āśrama** in **Rishikesh** in 1968. Born **Mahesh Prasād Varma**, he first earned a degree in physics from **Allahabad** University in 1942 and then studied **meditation** under the tutelage of his guru, Swāmī Brahmānanda Sarasvatī (1869–1953), known to the Maharishi's disciples as "Guru Dev," or "Divine Teacher." Like the **Hare Krishna movement**, Transcendental Meditation was a popular component of the countercultural movement of the 1960s and early 1970s. Unlike the Hare Krishna movement, which (until fairly recently) reveled in its "Indianness," with followers dressed like medieval **bhakti** saints chanting **mantras** in public places, Transcendental Meditation has presented itself as a scientific and universal practice, promoted for health and peace of **mind**, rather than as a religious tradition with strong Hindu (specifically **Śaiva**) roots. In 1973, the Maharishi established the Maharishi University of Management in Fairfield, Iowa, to advance the study and promotion of his meditation practice. *See also* HARRISON, GEORGE.

MAHĀSABHĀ. "Great assembly"; epithet of the **Hindu Mahāsabhā**.

MAHĀŚIVARĀTRI. "Great night of Śiva"; a festival that is held in honor of **Śiva** on the 13th night and 14th day of the **dark half** of **Phalguna** (February–March). It is observed by devotees through fasting and staying up all night to engage in worship (**pūjā**) and listen to stories and sing songs relating to Śiva. Also known simply as **Śivarātri** ("Night of Śiva").

MAHĀTMA. "Great soul"; "one whose soul is great"; a saintly person.

MAHĀTMA GĀNDHĪ. *See* GĀNDHĪ, MOHANDĀS K. (1869–1948).

MAHĀVĪRA (c. 499–427 BCE). "Great Hero"; 24th **Tīrthaṅkara** of **Jainism**. According to Jain tradition, 24 "ford builders," or **enlightened** beings, appear in a cosmic epoch to build a *tīrtha*, or ford, across the waters of **rebirth** to the further shore of **mokṣa** or **liberation**. As the 24th Tīrthaṅkara of our current cosmic epoch, Mahāvīra is therefore the last such being to appear until the next cosmic epoch begins.

Mahāvīra is not, strictly speaking, the founder of Jainism, since, from a Jain point of view, he is the latest in a series of enlightened teachers. And there is at least some historical evidence for the existence of a couple of the previous Tīrthaṅkaras. Living at the same time as the **Buddha**, Mahāvīra's life story follows a similar pattern: the son of a king who renounces his kingship to pursue spiritual freedom.

According to Jain tradition, Mahāvīra practiced strict **asceticism** for 12 years prior to achieving **kaivalya**, a state in which he was able to separate his soul (**jīva**) from its entanglement with the material world of **karma**. He spent the rest of his life teaching the Jain path to others, establishing a fourfold community of monks, nuns, and male and female laypersons, and finally leaving his body at the age of 72. Jains celebrate **Dīwali** as Mahāvīra Nirvāṇa Divas in commemoration of Mahāvīra's final entry into the realm of enlightened beings.

MAHĀVĪRA. "Great Hero"; epithet of **Hanuman**.

MAHENDRA. "Great **Indra**"; epithet of Indra.

MAHENDRAVIKRAMA VARMAN (571–630 CE). A king of the **Pallava** dynasty of southern India, based in the capital city of **Kāñcipuram**. A scholar and playwright as well as a king, he authored a satirical play entitled the ***Mattavilāsa Prahasana*** ("Comedy of Drunken Play") that ridicules various religious sects of the period, including several **Śaiva** sects and **Buddhism**.

MAHEŚA. Great Lord; epithet of **Śiva**. *See also* MAHEŚVARA.

MAHEŚVARA. Great Lord; epithet of **Śiva**.

MAHIṢA, MAHIṢĀSURA. Buffalo Demon; creature slain by the **goddess Durgā**, an event commemorated in the 10-day festival of **Durgā Pūjā**.

MAJUMDAR, R. C. (1888–1980). Indologist and historian. His major scholarly work was the massive *History and Culture of the Indian People*.

MAKARA. Sea monster with a fairly strong resemblance to the Gangetic dolphin; also often compared to a crocodile; sometimes depicted as a fish with the head of an elephant. The makara is the **vahana** or animal vehicle of two Hindu deities related to water bodies: **Varuṇa**, the **Vedic god** of the ocean, and **Gaṅgā**, the **goddess** who personifies the River Ganges.

MAKARA SAṂKRĀNTI. A Hindu festival that marks the transition of the sun from Sagittarius to Capricorn. Being based on the position of the sun, the date of this festival is fixed as January 14th, unlike most Hindu holidays, whose dates are determined by the dominant lunar calendar of Hinduism. However, it does occur consistently during the lunar month of **Magha** (January–February) and corresponds to the **Tamil** harvest festival of **Pongal**. It is regarded as a highly auspicious day. *See also* CALENDAR, HINDU.

MAKKHALI GOSĀLA (fl. 5th century BCE). Sage; a contemporary of **Mahāvīra** and the **Buddha**; founder of the **Ājīvikas**, a **śramaṇa** sect that was a major rival of early **Jainism** and **Buddhism**. He is attributed with a doctrine of fatalism, which was likely a claim that, while one could avoid the accumulation of new **karma**, one could do nothing to speed up the fruition or "burning off" of already present karma.

MĀLA. Rosary; string of beads, usually 108 in number, which is used to keep track of the number of times one has recited one's **mantra**. *See also* JAPA.

MALHOTRA, RAJIV. Independent Hindu scholar who has engaged in a critique of the academic study of Hinduism, questioning many of the assumptions that underlie current scholarship as continuations of older colonial assumptions or as reflecting a **Christian** missionary agenda. A good deal of his work that has appeared on the Internet seems to be aimed at exposing **Hinduphobia**—a term he coined to refer to anti-Hindu bias. A controversial figure, reaction to his work among academic scholars has been mixed.

MĀMALLAPURAM. Site on the beach south of **Madras** in **Tamil** Nadu that houses a variety of **temples**, including one with a sculpture of **Kṛṣṇa** holding Mount **Govardhana** in his hand to shelter his devotees from a thunderstorm. One temple—the Shore Temple—has been declared a World Heritage protected site to help with its preservation. It is an unusual temple for its period in having similar shrines to both **Śiva** and **Viṣṇu**, rather than being devoted exclusively to one or the other deity. This site was built by the **Pallava** dynasty.

MAMMATA (fl. 12th century CE). Scholar from **Kashmir**; author of a work on **poetics** and aesthetics entitled the *Kāvya Prakāśa* ("Illumination of Poetry").

MAN-LION AVATĀRA. *See* NARASIṂHA.

MANAS. Mind. According to **Dvaita Vedānta, Sāṃkhya**, and **Buddhism**, mind is one of the sense organs, its objects being thoughts and emotional states. It is the intermediary between the realm of the senses and the self (**ātman**). All the various systems of Hindu **philosophy** agree that the mind is part of the material continuum and not intrinsic to the self, which is pure **consciousness**. The mind is the vehicle of consciousness, the organ by which it interacts with the sensory realm.

MANASĀ. A **goddess** of snakes and poisons worshiped in the northeastern part of India. Not unlike the snake-handlers of Appalachia, the devotees of this goddess honor her by handling cobras and allowing themselves to be bitten by them in order to show their faith and reliance on their deity. The word *manasā* also refers to contemplative reflection.

MĀNAVA DHARMA ŚĀSTRA. "Authoritative Text on the Duties of Human Beings"; alternative title for the ***Manusmṛti***.

MAṆḌALA. Literally, "circle"; a sacred diagram of the cosmos viewed from a spiritual perspective—as a series of concentric circles whose central point represents the state of **enlightenment**—which is used as an object of contemplative visualization. The maṇḍala is also a political theory of interstate relations that was first articulated in the ***Artha Śāstra*** of **Kauṭilya**, according to which a king should see himself as being in the middle of a series of concentric circles of alternating enemies and allies. It is possible that the political concept gave rise to the artistic one, in which a spiritual practitioner visualizes himself or herself passing through the circles of the maṇḍala, from the outermost to the innermost, symbolizing and facilitating the inner **meditative** journey to the divine core of one's being. *See also* TANTRA; YANTRA.

MANDARA, MOUNT. Mountain that **Kūrma**, the tortoise **avatāra** of **Viṣṇu**, allowed the **devas** and **asuras** to place on his back to use as the axis of a great churn—the rope of which was formed by the giant serpent **Vāsukī**, king of the **Nāgas**—in their joint effort to churn the cosmic ocean in search of the lost **amṛta**, or elixir of **immortality**.

MANDIRA. Literally "dwelling place"; a Hindu **temple**.

MĀṆḌUKYA UPANIṢAD. One of the principle ***Upaniṣads***, probably composed some time between 200 BCE and 200 CE. This brief text is a **meditation** on the meaning of the syllable **Oṃ**, which it analyzes in terms of a correlation between the four elements of that make up Oṃ—the sounds "A," "U," and "M"—and the four **states of consciousness**. One of the prominent commentaries or **bhāṣyas** on this *Upaniṣad* was written by **Gauḍapāda**, the **guru** of the guru of **Śaṅkara**.

MAÑGAL. The planet Mars. *See also* ASTROLOGY; NAVAGRAHAS.

MAÑGALVĀRA. Tuesday, the day of the week governed by the planet Mars. *See also* CALENDAR, HINDU.

MĀṆIKKAVĀCAKAR (fl. 9th century CE). One of the 63 **Nāyanārs**—saints and **bhakti** poets revered in the **Tamil Śaiva** tradition. Māṇikkavācakar was a **Brahmin**. He composed the *Tiruvācakam*, or "Blessed Utterance," a work of **poetry** that has conceptual similarities to the ***Bhagavad Gītā***, though it is a Śaiva, rather than a **Vaiṣṇava**, text.

MAṆIPŪRA CAKRA. Cakra aligned with the solar plexus. *See also* TANTRA.

MANIPURI. Style of classical Indian **dance** developed in Manipur, in the northeastern part of India.

MANO-MAYA-KOŚA. Mind layer; the third of the five **kośas**, or layers, surrounding the self (**ātman**) according to **Vedānta**.

MANOSAROVAR. Holy lake in the **Himālayas** at the base of Mount **Kailāsa**; sacred to **Śiva**. Manosarovar is located in Tibet.

MANTRA. A collection of sounds or words, sometimes in the form of a prayer, which is used to focus the **mind** in **meditation** or as part of a religious ritual. Some mantras have a literal meaning that is fairly easy to discern, such as *Oṃ Namaḥ Śivāya* ("I pay homage to **Śiva**."), whereas others—particularly **bīja** or "seed" mantras, which consist of only one syllable—are more evocative than denotative, connecting one with a deity or concept that the mantra symbolizes rather than communicating meaning in the fashion of sentences.

The oldest known mantras are those found in the **Vedic** hymns, or ***Saṃhitās***, such as the **Gāyatrī Mantra**. Some mantras are connected with particular Hindu traditions, being shared by all practitioners, whose use of them constitutes, among other things, a badge of sectarian identity. An example would be the just-cited *Oṃ Namaḥ Śivāya*, a mantra that is universal among the adherents of **Śaivism**. Another would be *Hare Kṛṣna Hare Kṛṣna, Kṛṣna Kṛṣna Hare Hare, Hare Rāma Hare Rāma, Rāma Rāma Hare Hare*, which consists of three names of **Viṣṇu** uttered in the order indicated in the vocative case, and which is used by the **Gauḍīya Vaiṣṇavas**. There are also secret mantras—mantras that one receives from one's **guru** upon receiving initiation, or **dīkṣā**, into a particular Hindu tradition. It is believed that the power of such mantras would be diluted were they to be shared publicly. The most powerful mantra of all is the primordial bīja mantra **Oṃ**.

In the ***Maṇḍukya Upaniṣad***, Oṃ is described as encompassing all of existence. Each of its parts (A, U, M, and the totality of these three) is associated with one of the four **states of consciousness**.

MANU. If one were to compare Manu to figures from biblical **literature**, he could well be described as combining the roles of Adam, Noah, Jonah, and Moses. Manu is, first of all, the progenitor of humanity—the first human being. When a deluge was threatening to flood the world, Manu and his family were saved from it by **Viṣṇu** in the form of a giant fish—the **Matsya** or fish **avatāra**, the first of the traditional 10 avatāras, or incarnations, of Viṣṇu. And he is attributing with writing an important legal text, or ***Dharma Śāstra***—the ***Manusmṛti***.

MANUSMṚTI. An important ***Dharma Śāstra***, or authoritative legal text, that was likely composed around 100 CE attributed to **Manu**, the father of humanity. The text has been controversial in the modern era, particularly for its affirmation of the **caste** system and its sanctioning of abuses against **women** and people of lower castes. Its more controversial aspects include the fact that it suggests a higher penalty for the killing of a person of a higher caste than for the killing of a person of a lower caste, as well as higher penalties against people of a lower caste for committing infractions for which people of a higher caste receive lesser penalties. **B. R. Ambedkar** famously burned a copy of the *Manusmṛti* in public as a protest against the mistreatment of **Dalits**.

The text was first translated into English by **Sir William Jones**, who sought to apply it to the administration of India on the understanding that the British Empire should govern its territories using local **laws** and customs as much as possible. Scholars have suggested that this application of texts like the *Manusmṛti* as legal reference works was not in keeping with their original intent, leading to a more rigid practice of caste than had actually been the case in ancient times.

MANVANTARA. *See* WORLD AGES.

MARĀṬHAS. A warrior people of Maharashtra, in central India (the current location of Bombay, or Mumbai), who successfully fought against the **Mughal Empire** in the late 17th century, during the period of Emperor Aurangzeb. Led by **Śivāji** (1627–1680), who even today remains a hero in

Maharashtra, the Marāṭhas utilized guerilla tactics against the numerically superior and better equipped Mughal army. Stunningly successful in their campaign, the Marāṭhas eventually controlled most of central India's Deccan plateau. After Śivāji's **death**, the Marāṭhas continued their expansion until being defeated in 1761 at the battle of Panipat.

MĀRGA. Road, path, way; a spiritual path; sometimes synonymous with one of the **four yogas** delineated by **Swāmī Vivekānanda**: the way of **action** (the **karma yoga** or karma mārga), **knowledge**, **devotion**, and **meditation**. *See also* YOGA.

MĀRĪCA. Character in the ***Rāmāyaṇa***; a **rākṣasa**, or demonic creature, and uncle of the main villain of the text, **Rāvaṇa**. Rāvaṇa persuaded Mārīca to assist him in his plot to abduct **Sītā**. He had Mārīca disguise himself as a beautiful golden deer. Sītā, on seeing the golden deer, asked **Rāma** and his brother, **Lakṣmaṇa**, to capture it for her. With Rāma and his brother thus lured away, Rāvaṇa was able to approach Sītā and abduct her.

MĀRKAṆḌEYA. A **Brahmin** sage of the **Bhārgava** clan to whom the ***Mārkaṇḍeya Purāṇa*** is attributed. Mārkaṇḍeya had a vision of the ongoing process of cosmic **creation** and dissolution in the form of an infant—**Viṣṇu**—who was constantly inhaling and exhaling the universe. *See also* WORLD AGES.

MĀRKAṆḌEYA PURĀṆA. One of the 18 major ***Purāṇas***, probably composed between 250 and 550 CE. The text includes the sage **Mārkaṇḍeya**'s vision of **creation** as a series of inhalations and exhalations by an infant **Viṣṇu** and a series of passages recounting the deeds of the **Mother Goddess**. *See also DEVĪ MAHĀTMYA*.

MARRIAGE. One of the Hindu sacraments, or **saṃskāras**; the ritual by which a person moves from the first **āśrama** or stage of life—the **brahmacarya**, or student stage—and into the **householder** stage. Traditional Hindu marriages are arranged by the families of the bride and groom based on considerations such as **caste** and **astrological** compatibility. In the modern period these traditions are being adapted to a more individualistic ethos. For example, at least in middle-class families, young men and **women** are allowed to reject a prospective spouse whom they find unacceptable; and in recent years some amount of (usually chaperoned) dating has become permissible to ensure personal compatibility. Increasingly, class and professional considerations outweigh such traditional concerns as caste. In rural areas, though, where caste traditions are much stronger, the older model remains the norm.

MARUTS. Vedic storm deities; sons of **Rudra**. The Maruts are depicted as a group of young warriors and are invoked to bring protection and timely rain. *See also* DEVAS.

MĀTĀ AMRITĀNANDAMAYĪ (1953–). *See* AMRITĀNANDAMAYĪ, MĀTĀ.

MATERIALISM. Doctrine of the **Cārvāka** or **Lokāyata** system of philosophy, one of the heterodox or **nāstika** schools of Indian philosophy, or **darśanas**. According to this view, the only valid **pramāṇa** or basis for **knowledge** is sensory perception. Adherents of this view reject such widely held doctrines of Indic thought as **karma** and **rebirth** or belief in anything that is not verifiable by sensory perception. This system is heavily criticized by adherents of other schools of thought, both orthodox (that is, the **Vedic** or **Brahmanical** systems) and heterodox (**Buddhism** and **Jainism**). The central critique is that the rejection of all pramāṇas other than sensory perception—including inference, or **anumāna**—would lead to a "solipsism of the present moment," in which one would not be able to make any judgments based on memory or past knowledge.

The materialist critique of the other systems alleges, much like modern critiques of religion, that unverifiable doctrines such as the existence of **God**, a **soul**, or karma and rebirth are propounded to deceive the ignorant into giving material support to the priests and monks who propound them. Only fragments of the original texts, or **sūtras**, of this system have survived since ancient times. According to tradition, this system was first developed by the sage **Bṛhaspati**—who is, ironically, the **guru** of the **gods**.

MAṬHA. Monastic institution, monastery. This term can refer to the community of **ascetics** who belong to such an institution, to an administrative unit, or to the building or complex of buildings where that unit is based. In this way it is analogous to the term *church*.

MATHURĀ. Ancient city in northern India, in what is now the state of Uttar Pradesh; birthplace of **Kṛṣṇa**; located in the **Vraja** region, near **Vṛndāvana**, where Kṛṣṇa spent his youth. Mathurā also has associations with **Buddhism** and **Jainism**. The **Buddha** is said to have visited this city during his lifetime (though this is doubtful, Mathurā being rather far west of the region where the Buddha lived). A Jain stūpa, or burial monument, was discovered in Mathurā, which suggests that there was a fairly large and thriving Jain community in this city at the beginning of the Common Era.

MATSYA. "Fish"; the fish **avatāra** of **Viṣṇu**; the first of the 10 avatāras or incarnations of Viṣṇu according to one popular list. The fish avatāra appeared to **Manu** to warn him of the coming of a great flood that would deluge the entire world. Manu caught the fish, who then spoke to Manu and promised that if Manu would release him, he would return to save Manu and his family from the flood. Manu agreed and released the fish. When the flood came, Manu had built a large boat, as the fish had instructed him. When the fish arrived, he was considerably larger than when Manu had first caught him and had also grown an enormous horn from his nose. Manu lashed his boat to the fish's horn with a rope and the fish carried Manu and his family to safety.

MATSYENDRANĀTH (fl. 11th century CE). Founder of the **Nāth Yogīs**, a **Tantric Śaiva ascetic** lineage. Matsyendranāth's successor, **Gorakhnāth**, invented **Haṭha Yoga**.

According to tradition, Matsyendranāth, whose name means "fish lord," was in the form of a fish when he overheard **Śiva** teaching his wife, the **goddess Pārvatī**. These teachings became the basis of the doctrines of the Nāth Yogīs.

***MATTAVILĀSA PRAHASANA*.** "Comedy of Drunken Play"; a satirical play written by **Mahendravikrama Varman** (571–630 CE), a king of the **Pallava** dynasty of southern India. The play ridicules various religious sects of the period, including several different **Śaiva** sects and **Buddhism**. Some have argued that the play may reflect a **Lokāyata** or **Cārvaka materialist** perspective, though it is also possible that its perspective is simply a more general cynicism regarding those who make a living off of the religious beliefs of others. It sheds an interesting light on how the various sects were perceived in ancient India, particularly by laypersons. *See also* LITERATURE.

MAURYA. First dynasty of ancient India to form an empire of considerable size. The dynasty lasted from approximately 320 to 184 BCE. It was founded by Candragupta Maurya shortly after Alexander of Macedon had weakened the polities of the northwest. Emerging from the northeastern Magadha region, Candragupta took advantage of the power vacuum left in the northwest after Alexander's campaign. The empire reached its height under the reign of Candragupta's grandson, Aśoka, which lasted from 268 to 233 BCE. After Aśoka's reign, the empire went into a period of gradual decline and was later succeeded by the Śuṅga dynasty in 184 BCE (which was founded by Puśyamitra Śuṅga, a rebel Maurya general who essentially staged a coup).

Religiously, the Mauryas practiced a policy of tolerance toward all sects, but gave preference to **śramaṇa** traditions. Candragupta himself is said to have had a leaning to **Jainism**, and his son, Bindusāra, supported the **Ājīvikas**. Most famously, Aśoka became a **Buddhist** after the final battle that led to the consolidation of his empire. Repenting of violence and warfare, he promoted a policy of **dharma**, which included respecting life and supporting Buddhist institutions. The emphasis on **ahiṃsā**, or nonviolence, in this policy led to a decline in the practice of **animal sacrifice** on the part of the **Brahmins**—a practice banned by Aśoka, at least on certain holy days. Brahmanical ascendancy only returned with the rise of the **Gupta** dynasty in 320 CE—albeit a transformed **Brahminism**, influenced by śramaṇic thought, which would become the basis of the Hinduism of the epics and ***Purāṇas***.

MĀYA. Asura architect credited with the building of the **Pāṇḍavas** fantastic palace of **Indraprastha**.

MĀYĀ. Illusion; magic; **creative** power; the power of a **god** to create. In the **philosophy** of **Vedānta**, māyā is the way the universe appears to us due to ignorance, or **avidyā**. In **Advaita Vedānta**, there is, in **truth**, no universe at all, the universe itself being an effect of ignorance, the reality being that **Brahman** alone is real. In theistic forms of Vedānta, māyā is the creative power of **God** that brings the world into being.

MĀYĀPUR. Town in **Bengal**; location of a major **temple** that is operated by the **International Society for Krishna Consciousness** (ISKCON). The town also houses an ISKCON-run school and press.

MĀYŪRĪ. The peacock; vehicle of **Kārttikeya**.

MEDITATION. Though in its Latin origins this word refers to reflective contemplation of a philosophical or religious topic, in regard to Hinduism, it typically refers to **dhyāna**, the seventh of the eight stages or "limbs" of **Patañjali**'s eight-limbed (**aṣṭāṅga**) system of **yoga**. The sixth limb, **dharaṇā**, is concentration on a single object. Dhyāna, the next step, is absorption in that object, with no awareness of any other phenomena. Meditation thus involves the stilling of the waking, conscious **mind** so deeper levels of consciousness can be experienced. The goal of meditation is **samādhi**—the eighth limb of Patañjali's system—which is complete absorption in the object of concentration, a state in which the distinction between subject and object vanishes.

In **Tantric** meditation, the imagination is actively utilized as a tool to bring about samādhi. Rather than suppressing the senses, as in Patañjali's system, they are actively engaged and channeled toward the goal of raising the **kuṇḍalinī** energy from the base of the spine to the crown of the head, bringing about a heightened state of consciousness.

The practice of meditation is shared by many Indic traditions, and is especially prominent in **Buddhism**. In early Buddhism, the term *dhyāna* also refers to the **states of consciousness** to which the practice of meditation can lead. When Buddhism was first transmitted to China, the term *dhyāna* was rendered as *ch'an*. When the tradition was transmitted to Japan, the term *ch'an* was transformed into *zen*.

MEHTA, NARSI (1414–1481). Vaiṣṇava bhakti poet and saint from Gujarat. Known for his universalist attitude toward religion, Mehta's most famous song is his *Vaiṣṇava Jana to tene kahiya*, which states that a true Vaiṣṇava is one "who feels for the suffering of another and forgets the good he does to another, taking no pride in it."

MELA. Festival; fair; celebration.

MERIT. The result of a good deed; "good **karma**." *See also* PUṆYA KARMA.

MERU, MOUNT. In traditional Hindu cosmology, the world is depicted as a series of ringed continents interspersed with oceans and extending over a vast region of space. At the center of these concentric circles of land and sea rests Mount Meru, the *axis mundi* and center of cosmic space. This conception of the universe is essentially a **maṇḍala**, or a spiritual representation of existence. In this sense, Mount Meru is not a literal mountain so much as a symbol of the highest spiritual attainment. When this model has been taken literally, though, Mount Meru has generally been understood to be located just beyond the **Himālayas**.

MĪMĀṂSĀ. Also known as **Pūrva Mīmāṃsā**, or "earlier exegesis," this **philosophy** is a continuation of the ancient, orthodox system of Vedic **Brahmanism**, with a very strong emphasis on the correct performance of **Vedic** ritual and the correct pronunciation of the **Sanskrit** verses of the ***Vedas*** during a ritual performance. This emphasis on the correct Sanskrit usage led to the development of an elaborate linguistic philosophy on the part of the Mīmāṃsakas. The term *Pūrva Mīmāṃsā* contrasts this school of thought with the later, or **Uttara Mīmāṃsā**—more widely known as **Vedānta**. Pūrva Mīmāṃsā focuses on the earlier, ritualistic portion of the *Vedas*, while Vedānta interprets the later Vedic texts—the ***Upaniṣads***—and their teaching of **Brahman**. *See also* JAIMINI; KUMĀRILA BHAṬṬA.

MĪNĀKṢĪ. "Fish-eyed **Goddess**"; the main goddess enshrined at the Mīnākṣī **temple** for which the town of **Madurai**, in **Tamil** Nadu, is famous. She is said to have been born with fish-shaped eyes, a fishy odor, and three breasts. Her father raised her as a son and she became a great warrior. According to a prophecy, she would lose her odor, her third breast, and her warlike nature when she met her true husband, **Śiva**, also enshrined at the temple complex at Madurai in his form as **Sundareśvara** ("Beautiful Lord"). Mīnākṣī's uncle is **Viṣṇu**, who showed up late to her wedding with Śiva. The wedding is re-enacted every year in the month of **Caitra** (March–April).

MIND. *See* MANAS.

MĪRĀ BAI (1498–1547). Female **Vaiṣṇava** saint and **bhakti poet** from Rajasthan. She was born a **Rajput** princess and married to a prince who was killed in battle while still a young man. Deeply devoted to **Kṛṣṇa** since her childhood, she became more immersed in devotion after her husband's **death**, declaring that Kṛṣṇa was her only true husband. Her in-laws disapproved of her deep piety, going so far as to make attempts upon her life. Renowned for her devotion, Mīrā Bai's life has been the subject of several **Hindi** movies. Her poetry, which remains popular today, proclaims the depth of her bhakti: "O Kṛṣṇa, charmer of hearts, lifter of mountains, I hear your flute calling me—Shall I come by the secret path through the tall grass? O Lord of Heavenly Blue, my heart cannot rest until we are together, until we walk along the banks of the **Yamunā** deep into the night." *See also* WOMEN.

MITRA. "Friend"; **Vedic** deity; one of the **Ādityas**; often paired with **Varuṇa**. His cult was popular in ancient Iran and spread to the Roman Empire as Mithraism.

MLECCHA. "Barbarian"; a person who does not know **Sanskrit** or who lacks cultural **knowledge** and etiquette; a derogatory term for non-Hindus. This term may be cognate originally with *Meluhha*, the name by which the people of the **Indus Valley civilization** possibly referred to themselves and their region. In its first uses, it does not seem to have a derogatory meaning but simply refers to persons from the region of the Indus Valley or to their customs. Over time, however, the view developed that the people of this region were uncouth and did not observe **Vedic** practices in the correct way (or at all). It later came to refer to anyone from outside the fold of mainstream **Brahmanical** culture, and in particular to foreigners (Greeks, Arabs, and so on).

MOHENJO-DARO. Largest city of the **Indus Valley civilization**.

MOHINĪ. Female form of **Viṣṇu**; Viṣṇu took the form of Mohinī so a deity could be born from the union of Viṣṇu and Śiva that would have their combined power in order to defeat the **asura** Princess Mahiṣī, sister of the **Mahiṣāsura** or Buffalo Demon. The deity born from this union of Viṣṇu and Śiva was **Ayyappan**.

MOKṢA. Liberation from the cycle of **rebirth**; the ultimate goal of most Hindu paths, though a good deal of religious activity is also devoted to penultimate goals, like a better rebirth, or more immediate this-worldly goods. Mokṣa is the fourth of the four goals of humanity or **puruṣārthas**. Different Hindu traditions present different strategies for the attainment of mokṣa, such as selfless work (**karma**), wisdom (**jñāna**), devotion (**bhakti**), **meditation** (**dhyāna**), or some combination of these.

MONK. A male renouncer; a man who has taken up the life of **sannyāsa**.

MONOTHEISM. Belief in one supreme **God**. Many Hindus see the many deities of the Hindu tradition as different aspects or manifestations of one Supreme Being. Others see a particular deity as preeminent (usually **Viṣṇu** or **Śiva**) and the others as subordinate, in the way that angels are subordinate to God in the Abrahamic religions. *See also* GODS.

MOON. One of the **Navagrahas**, the nine **planets** of Hindu **astrology** (**jyotiṣa**); often identified with the **Vedic** deity **Soma**, who also represents the hallucinogenic plant whose juice, mixed with milk, was used by ancient **Brahmins** to experience an altered **state of consciousness**. The phases of the moon represent this substance being consumed by the **devas** (during the **dark half** of the month, when the moon is waning) and replenished (during the **bright half**, when the moon is waxing).

MOTHER GODDESS. Devī, or **Mahādevī** (the Great Goddess) is identified in many Hindu traditions as the wife of **Śiva**. She has many forms, such as the docile wife and mother, **Pārvatī**; the warrior goddess, **Durgā**, who defeats **demonic** beings and drives away evil; and the fierce, demon-slaying **Kālī**. Also known as **Śakti**, the power of **creation**, the Goddess can also be identified with the many **goddesses** of the Hindu pantheon, who are seen as her various forms or manifestations. Goddesses such as **Lakṣmī** and Sarasvatī are therefore also called the *śaktis* or power centers of the deities that are their husbands—**Viṣṇu** and **Brahmā**, respectively. In this role, the Goddess and her various personae are seen as the energizing principle, in the absence of which their corresponding male gods would be incapable of effective activity. The divine pairing of Śiva and Śakti, in particular, is often presented, especially in Śākta texts, as a composite being, with the God and Goddess being ultimately inseparable from one another as parts of an internally differentiated, but finally unitary, godhead. In its affirmation of internal relations within the godhead, this concept is not unlike the **Christian** idea of the trinity.

Finally, the supreme Mother Goddess is identified, in **Tantric** traditions (and in **Neo-Vedānta**, which is strongly informed by the Tantric background and sensibility of **Ramakrishna**), with **Brahman**, the absolute, as it appears from the perspective of **māyā**, the universe of time and space. Ramakrishna states that "Kālī is verily Brahman, and Brahman is verily Kālī. It is one and the same Reality. When we think of It as inactive . . . then we call it Brahman. But when It engages in . . . activities, then we call It Kālī or Śakti." This statement implies a pantheistic or panentheistic understanding of the Goddess as being manifested within all beings. This understanding is also present in the ancient **Śākta** scripture, the ***Devī Mahātmya*** or ***Caṇḍī*** *Paṭh*, with its refrain of **mantras** that refer to "The Goddess who dwells within all beings."

MUDRĀ. Hand gesture that conveys a symbolic meaning. Hindu deities are depicted holding their hands in various positions, all of which communicate specific concepts to those who view their images. Human practitioners also utilize mudrās in certain types of worship and **meditative** practice. **Tantra**, in particular, makes extensive use of mudrās, often replicating the mudrās with which specific deities are depicted in order to facilitate a sense of identification with those deities.

Mudrā is also one of the **Five M's**, or traditionally impure substances of which practitioners of **Left-Handed Tantra** partake. It is said to refer, in that context, to puffed rice, although this is not generally seen as an impure substance (though it is forbidden in certain fasts where one abstains only from particular foods). This may be a confusion, with the mudrā in question actually referring to secret gestures only practiced in a ritual context. *See also* ABHAYA-MUDRĀ; DĀNA-MUDRĀ; IMAGES IN WORSHIP; MŪRTI.

MUGHAL EMPIRE. The last of the three major empires to encompass a substantial portion of the Indian subcontinent prior to British rule and independence, the first two being those of the **Maurya** and **Gupta** dynasties. The Mughals came from Central Asia and were related to the Mongols. Mughal rule in India lasted from 1526 until 1858, when control of India formally passed to Queen Victoria and direct British rule in the wake of the First War of Independence (or Sepoy Mutiny) of 1857. The religious affiliation of the Mughals was to **Islam**, though the religious attitudes and beliefs of the Mughal emperors varied a great deal, ranging from the tolerance and pluralism of **Akbar**, who displayed a good deal of appreciation for indigenous Indian traditions, to the nearly rabid persecution of non-Muslims by Aurangzeb, which led him into conflict with both the **Marāṭhas** and the **Sikhs**, among others. On the whole, the Mughal period was characterized by a good deal of creativity and interreligious innovation on the part of Hindus and Muslims. New architectural styles and forms of **art** and **music** that drew upon the traditional cultures of both Hinduism and Islam emerged, as well as direct religious interaction in the form of the **Sant** movement and the rise of Sikhism. *See also* GOBIND SINGH, GURU; KABĪR; NĀNAK, GURU; SUFISM.

MUHŪRTA. Unit of time; a **muhūrta** is approximately an hour and a half in length and each day is divided into 16 muhūrtas. The best time of day for **meditation** and worship is the **Brahmā-muhurtā**, from roughly 4:30 a.m. to 6 a.m.

MUKTĀNANDA, SWĀMĪ (1908–1982). Monk and spiritual teacher who brought the **Siddha Yoga** tradition to the Western world. Part of the broader phenomenon of Hindu teachers who began bringing their traditions to North America and Europe and tailoring them to a Western audience—starting with **Swāmī Vivekānanda** and continuing with the **Maharishi Mahesh Yogi** and **Bhaktivedānta Swamī Prabhupāda**, among others. The distinct emphasis of Muktānanda's tradition was **Tantric**, focused on the experience of the **Kuṇḍalinī Śakti**, or energy coiled at the base of the spine. In Siddha Yoga, it is said that this experience can be evoked by the grace of the **guru** through a thought, word, or gesture—a process known as **śaktipat**.

Muktānanda received śaktipat from his guru, **Swāmī Nityānanda** (1897–1961), a solitary monk who resided in a cave in **Gaṇeśapuri**, near Bombay. Before his death in 1982, Muktānanda designated his young female translator, **Malti Shetty**, and her brother to be his successors. After a falling out between the brother and sister team in 1985, the sister, Swāmī Chidvilāsānanda (more widely known as **Gurumayī**) became the leader of the lineage.

MUKTI. Liberation; freedom; synonym for **mokṣa**.

MŪLADHĀRA CAKRA. The bottommost of the seven **cakras**, located at the base of the spine. *See also* TANTRA.

MÜLLER, FRIEDRICH MAX (1823–1900). A giant in the field of **Indology**, Müller oversaw the translation of numerous **Sanskrit** texts through his *Sacred Books of the East* series, making many Hindu, **Buddhist**, and **Jain** writings available in English for the first time. He is also known for developing the **Āryan Invasion**—later modified to the **Āryan Migration**—theory of **Vedic** origins. Müller was the first Western scholar to be aware of **Ramakrishna**, writing one of the first works in a European language on the life and teachings of this Hindu saint in direct consultation with Ramakrishna's disciple, **Swāmī Vivekānanda**. Born in Germany, Müller studied Sanskrit at Leipzig and Berlin, and then in Paris. In 1847 the **British East India Company** hired him to edit and publish the ***Ṛg Veda***. In 1854 he began teaching at Oxford University where he remained until his **death** in 1900.

MUṆḌAKA UPANIṢAD. One of the principal ***Upaniṣads***; probably composed between 400 and 300 BCE. This *Upaniṣad* places a special emphasis on the value of **renunciation** and the transitory nature of the fruits of **Vedic** sacrifices, recommending that the spiritual aspirant live in the forest with an **enlightened** teacher, or **guru**.

MUNI. Literally, "one who has taken a vow of silence"; a sage or monk who practices **asceticism**.

MŪRTI. A physical image of a deity that enables a worshiper to interact with that deity as though it had a material body. *See also* IMAGES IN WORSHIP.

MŪRTI-PŪJĀ. Worship that utilizes a physical image of a deity in order to facilitate a concrete sense of interaction with that deity. *See also* IMAGES IN WORSHIP; PŪJĀ.

This mūrti, or image, is of the Goddess Lakṣmī.

MURUGAN (MURUKAN). Tamil name for **Kārttikeya**, son of **Śiva** and **Pārvatī** and brother of **Gaṇeśa**.

MŪŚAKA. The mouse; vehicle of **Gaṇeśa**.

MUSIC. Music has been an integral part of Hindu worship since ancient times. The ***Sāma Veda***, one of the original four **Vedic *Saṃhitās***, sets the Vedic **mantras** to music. The rhythmic chanting of mantras and the singing (kīrtana) of religiously themed songs (**bhajanas**) to evoke **bhakti**, or devotion, have been practiced continuously and have a widespread appeal that cuts across boundaries of gender, **caste**, and sect. The works of the bhakti poets were always intended to be sung, rather than read or recited as **poetry**. Classical Indian **dance**, which is also religiously themed, has always been accompanied by music as well. *See also* ART; LITERATURE.

N

NĀCIKETA. Character in the ***Kaṭha Upaniṣad***; a young **Brahmin** who journeys to the underworld in order to ask **Yama**, the **god** of **death**, the secret of **immortality**.

NĀGA. Serpent; in Hindu and **Buddhist literature**, they are often magical beings with a serpentine form. The dangerous nature of snakes, especially cobras, in India makes them creatures to be respected and feared, so a certain degree of awe surrounding snakes is not at all surprising. **Viṣṇu** is often depicted resting on the belly of **Śeṣa**, the cosmic serpent who is the deity's protector. **Śiva** is also depicted with snakes crawling on his body both to show his transcendent state of fearlessness and also to depict the coiled energy of the **Kuṇḍalinī śakti**, a manifestation of the **Mother Goddess**. The **Buddha** and Pārśvanāth, the 23rd **Tīrthaṅkara** of **Jainism**, are both depicted as being protected in their practice of **meditation** by the lord of the Nāgas. **Manasā**, a protector **goddess** revered in **Bengal**, has a serpentine form. It is said that the Nāgas reside in a portion of the underworld known as **Pātāla**, presided over by the giant serpent **Vāsuki**.

Nāga is also the name of an order of naked **Śaiva** warrior monks affiliated with the **Daśanāmi Order** charged with protecting **Brahmins** from physical attack, since the Brahmins are expected to practice **ahiṃsā** (nonviolence) and may not use weapons. The Nāgas have fought in battle both with Muslim forces and rival Hindu warrior monks.

Nāga is also the name of an **Ādivāsī**, or aboriginal, group of tribes based in the extreme northeast of India, in the state of Nagaland, on the border with Burma.

NAIMIṢA. Forest mentioned in Hindu **literature**, renowned as a place of pilgrimage for **ascetics**. It was in the Naimiṣa forest, or *Naimiṣāraṇya*, that a 12-year-long sacrifice (**yajña**) was held by the sage **Śaunaka** at which the ***Mahābhārata*** was first recited by a pupil of **Lomaharṣana Sūta**, who had in turn heard it from a direct pupil of **Vyāsa**, the author of the text.

NAKULA. Character in the ***Mahābhārata***; one of the **Pāṇḍava** brothers; twin brother of Sahadeva. These twins were the sons of the **Aśvins** and **Mādrī**.

NAMASTE. "I pay homage to the divine within you"; traditional Hindu greeting, often accompanied by the **añjali**, or gesture of respect with folded hands.

NAMBŪTIRI (NAMBOODIRI) BRAHMINS. Lineage of **Brahmins** based primarily in the state of **Kerala**, on the southwest coast of India. They are unusual in recognizing the validity of only the first three ***Vedas***, not the ***Atharva Veda***, and for the style of **Vedic** recitation they employ, which utilizes hand gestures (**mudrās**) and head movements as an aid to memorization. *See also* TRAYĪ VIDYĀ.

NĀMDEV (fl. 13th century CE). Vaiṣṇava bhakti poet and saint of Maharashtra. He was especially devoted to **Viṣṇu** in his form as **Viṭṭhala** (literally "standing on a brick"). He writes, "As a bee's heart might be set upon the fragrance of a flower, or as a fly might take resort to honey, similarly does my mind cling to **God**." Nāmdev was a disciple of **Jñāneśvara**.

NAMMĀḶVĀR (880–930). One of the **Āḷvārs**, 12 **Vaiṣṇava poets** of south India. Born a **Śūdra** or member of the servant **caste**, he composed numerous devotional poems in the **Tamil** language that were later collected in a volume called the ***Tiruvāymoḷi***. This text is revered in the **Śrivaiṣṇava** tradition as being no less sacred than the ***Vedas*** and continues to be used in **temple** rituals to the present day. Nammāḷvār's revered position as a person of low caste in this tradition is significant, being illustrative of the **philosophy** of **bhakti**, or devotion, according to which social categories like gender and caste are irrelevant to one's spiritual status or proximity to salvation.

NAMUCI. Demon slain by **Indra**. Namuci could be killed neither by day or night, nor by anything either wet or dry. Indra circumvented this difficulty by killing Namuci at dusk with sea foam. This story, mentioned in the ***Ṛg Veda***, is echoed in later **literature** by the story of the slaying of **Hiraṇyakaśipu** by the **Narasiṃha avatāra**.

NĀNAK, GURU (1469–1539). The founder of **Sikhism**; a contemporary of **Kabīr** and a fellow member of the **Sant** movement. Born a Hindu in the Punjab, Nānak claimed to have received a revelation from **God** while **meditating** in a forest. Nānak's message was: "There is no Muslim and there is no Hindu." Those who accepted his teaching of Hindu–Muslim unity came to be known as *Sikh*, a Punjabi word which means "disciple," and they took Nānak as their **guru**. Guru Nānak and his followers sought to harmonize the teachings of **Islam** and Hinduism, taking from Islam its strong emphasis on the unity of God. Guru Nānak called **the One** God, known by Hindus under many names and forms, *Sat Nām*, or the "True Name," or *Ek Onkar*, the One God. The One God is the **creator** of the entire universe, according to Sikhism, and humans are the highest of God's creations. From Hinduism, Nānak took the doctrines of **karma** and **rebirth** and the emphasis on the importance of the guru, or living teacher. **Liberation** from rebirth is given by God, much as in devotionally oriented forms of Hinduism. The community Guru Nānak established accepted all, regardless of religion, gender, or **caste**.

NANDA GOPA. The adoptive father of **Kṛṣṇa** who raised him after his wicked uncle, **Kāṃsa**, had imprisoned his parents and sought to have the infant Kṛṣṇa killed. Nanda Gopa was a cowherd, and it was for this reason that Kṛṣṇa spent his youth among the **gopīs** of **Vṛndāvana**.

NANDANAR (fl. 7th century CE). One of the 63 **Nāyanārs**—saints and **bhakti poets** revered in the **Tamil Śaiva** tradition. Nandanar was born in the **Śūdra** or servant **caste**. He was intensely devoted to **Śiva** and wanted to see the images of Śiva as **Nāṭarāja**, or "Lord of the Cosmic **Dance**," at the **temple** of **Cidambaram**, for the purpose of having **darśana**, or sacred visual communion. Because of his low caste, however, he was denied entry to the temple. Standing outside the temple, his view of the main image was blocked by an image of the bull, **Nandi**, who serves as Śiva's vehicle. It is said that in order to let Nandanar have his darśana, Śiva commanded Nandi to move aside, which he did. To this day, the image of Nandi outside the temple at Cidambaram is offset from the main door so as not to obstruct the view of the deity from outside. The name *Nandanar* comes from this incident, meaning the one whose devotion could make even Nandi move aside.

NANDI. The bull who serves as the vehicle of **Śiva**.

NARA. "Man"; the first man, the progenitor of mankind. *See also* NĀRĀYAṆA.

NĀRADA. One of the Seven Sages (**Saptarṣi**) presiding over the cosmos; a wandering minstrel and messenger of the **gods**, Nārada is frequently depicted in both the ***Vedas*** and the ***Purāṇas*** as a seeker of wisdom who goes to various deities and wise persons in order to receive instruction. From a literary perspective, he is often a stand-in for the reader or listener, who is also receiving instruction from the deity or wise person in question while Nārada is being instructed in the text. Nārada is also depicted as something of a troublemaker by passing on messages or news that may not be welcome or sharing information that should not be shared. He is a son of the sage **Kaśyapa** and some of the hymns of the ***Ṛg Veda*** are attributed to him. His first appearance as a literary character, though, is in the ***Chāndogya Upaniṣad***, where he is inquiring into the nature of the self (**ātman**). He is the lord of the **gandharvas**, or celestial musicians, and plays a **vīṇā**, or lute.

NARAKA. Hell. There are actually seven Hindu hells—layers or dimensions of existence that are highly unpleasant and in which beings are born who have extremely bad **karma (pāpa)**. The Hindu hells might better be described as purgatories; for unlike the hells of **Christianity** and **Islam**, the denizens of the Hindu hells do not reside there forever, but only as long as they have bad karma for which they need to atone. Once their bad karma has been exhausted, such beings are reborn, usually in human form. This can take a very long time, however—in some cases, until the end of a cosmic cycle (**kalpa**), which may be billions of years. In other cases, though, one's period of residence in one of the hells can be of a relatively short duration. Hell is also known as **Pātāla**. *See also* REBIRTH.

NARASIṂHA. "Man-lion." The Narasiṃha is the fourth on the traditional list of 10 **avatāras**, or incarnations, of **Viṣṇu**. The demonic **Hiraṇyakaśipu**, who is symbolic of ignorance, held a deep hatred for Viṣṇu. Annoyed by his son **Prahlāda**'s equally deep devotion to Viṣṇu, Hiraṇyakaśipu taunted Prahlāda. Once, asking Prahlāda where Viṣṇu could be found, Prahlāda replied that Viṣṇu (whose name means "all-pervasive") was everywhere, even within a nearby stone pillar. On hearing this, Hiraṇyakaśipu kicked the pillar. The pillar then broke asunder and Viṣṇu, in the form of the Narasiṃha, came forth. The man-lion grabbed Hiraṇyakaśipu, placed him on his lap, and slew him. This event occurred at dusk. The circumstances surrounding the **death** of Hiraṇyakaśipu were a result of the fact that he was magically protected from any attack by man or beast (the Narasiṃha was neither), on the ground or in the air (which is why Narasiṃha held him in his lap), and by day or night (making dusk and dawn times of vulnerability for him).

NĀRĀYAṆA. "Son of **Nara** (the primordial man)." Nara and Nārāyaṇa are associated with one another from the ***Ṛg Veda*** onward. These two are a pair of deities or sages who share a close bond of friendship. It is said in the ***Mahābhārata*** that **Arjuna** is Nara and **Kṛṣṇa** is Nārāyaṇa. Nārāyaṇa is identified with **Viṣṇu** from the ***Āraṇyakas*** onward. But in some sources, the names *Nara* and *Nārāyaṇa* are used interchangeably as dual epithets of Viṣṇu. *See also* SATYANĀRĀYAṆA.

NĀSATYA. "Helpful, kindly"; epithet of the **Aśvins**.

NĀSIK. One of the four cities where the **Kumbha Melā** is held every 12 years. It is in Maharashtra, on the bank of the Godāvarī River.

NĀSTIKA. Literally a "nay-sayer," one who says, "It is not." Traditionally, this term refers to those who deny the authority of the ***Vedas***—specifically, the followers of the **Cārvāka** or **Lokāyata materialist philosophy**, the **Jains**, and the **Buddhists**. In modern Hinduism this term is also used to refer to an atheist—though again, this is not the ancient understanding, and some schools of thought regarded as **āstika**, or orthodox, affirmed the authority of the *Vedas* while being nontheistic, such as the early **Sāṃkhya** system and the **Pūrva Mīmāṃsā** system.

NĀṬARĀJA. "Lord of the **Dance**"; epithet of **Śiva** in his role as creator, destroyer, and re-creator of the world as it passes through its ongoing cosmic cycle. The image of Śiva as lord of the cosmic dance, particularly as it is captured in the **artistic** style of the **Coḷa** dynasty, has become emblematic of Hinduism. The image depicts the ascetic Śiva, with his matted hair flying behind him, in an ecstatic dance. One of his four hands holds the drum with which he keeps the beat of his dance. One holds a flame, which he is spinning rapidly around, an **action** depicted with a ring of fire that frames the entire image, like a stop-action photo of someone swirling a lit torch, creating a ring of light. One hand is held up in the **abhaya-mudrā**, and the fourth hand points toward his upraised foot.

The symbolism of the image is profound. The rapid movement that it depicts, if juxtaposed with the stillness of the image itself, represents a coming together of time and eternity—the realm of change over which the deity presides and the deity himself, who is beyond time and change. The abhaya-mudrā means "do not be afraid," advising devotees not to fear the awe-inspiring power of **creation** and destruction that the deity embodies. The flame represents the power of both creation and destruction, having both capacities. The deity dances upon a dwarf, representing the ego, which must be overcome in order for one to realize one's inner divinity.

The overall message is that creation and destruction are part of the same process and that one need not fear change, knowing that everything is finally one with the divine.

NĀTH YOGĪS. Tantric Śaiva sect of **ascetics** established by **Matsyendranāth** (fl. 11th century CE) and his successor, **Gorakhnāth** (fl. 12th century CE). Gorakhnāth is credited with the invention of **Haṭha Yoga**, the system of yogic postures designed to prepare the body for the rigors of **meditation**. Membership in the Nāth Yogī tradition is open to members of all **castes** and has been especially prominent in northern India.

NĀTHDWĀRA. Site in Rajasthan that houses a black stone image of **Kṛṣṇa** known as Śrī Nāthji. It is a popular pilgrimage site, with large crowds gathering for the opening of the **garbha-gṛha**, or inner sanctum, to have **darśana**, or sacred visual communion with the image.

NĀṬYA ŚĀSTRA. "Authoritative Text on Drama"; ascribed to the sage **Bharata**. This **Sanskrit** text from the first millennium of the Common Era is the authoritative guide to Indian classical theater and **dance**. A lengthy and detailed work, the *Nāṭya Śāstra* gives a thorough account of not only the practicalities of staging a play or dance drama but also the religious dimensions of such performances, plus a theory of aesthetics. *See also* LITERATURE; POETRY; RASA.

NAVAGRAHAS. The nine planets. These do not refer to the nine planets of the solar system of modern astronomy (now eight, with the recent demotion of Pluto), but to the five planets that are visible to the naked eye (Mercury, Venus, Mars, Jupiter, and Saturn), the **moon**, the sun, and **Rāhu** and **Ketu**, the latter two being postulated to account for the phenomena of solar and lunar eclipses, respectively. **Pūjā**, or ritualistic worship of deities, often includes the paying of respects to the nine planets to maximize the benefits and to minimize the inauspicious effects of their various astrological influences. The planet Mercury is called **Buḍha**. Venus is **Śukra**. Mars is **Mañgal**, Jupiter **Bṛhaspati**, and Saturn **Śāni**. Each of the planets—except for Rāhu and Ketu—presides over a day of the week in the **Hindu calendar**. The sun presides over Sunday (**Ravivāra**), the moon over Monday (**Somavāra**), Mars over Tuesday (**Mañgalvāra**), Mercury over Wednesday (**Buḍhavāra**), Jupiter over Thursday (**Guruvāra**), Venus over Friday (**Śukravāra**), and Saturn over Saturday (**Śānivāra**). *See also* ASTROLOGY.

NAVARĀTRĪ PŪJĀ. "Nine-Night Worship"; festival of devotion to **Durgā** and **Rāma**. The nine nights of the worship correspond to the 10 days of the festival of **Daśahrā**. This festival is celebrated in the **bright half** of the month of **Āśvina**. In northern India, this festival celebrates **Rāma**'s victory over **Rāvaṇa** and it culminates in **Dīpāvali** (or Dīwali), the festival of lights in honor of the **goddess Lakṣmī**. In Gujarat, the **Garbha** dance is frequently used to celebrate this festival. In **Bengal** and southern India, this festival celebrates **Durgā**'s victory over the Buffalo Demon (**Mahiṣāsura**). In Bengal, it culminates in **Kālī pūjā**.

NAVYA NYĀYA. "New logic"; system of philosophy (**darśana**) that is in continuity with the older **Nyāya** system of logic, but with important revisions and clarifications that were the result of centuries of reflection and debate among Indian logicians; established in the 13th century by the philosopher Gaṅgeśa Upādhyāya and incorporating some concepts from earlier philosophers, like **Vācaspati Miśra** and **Udayana** (both of whom lived in the 10th century of the Common Era). Navya Nyāya is largely a response to the criticisms of the **Advaita Vedānta** tradition of the Naiyāyikas' realist ontology. Advaita Vedānta teaches that the universe is ultimately a delusory appearance, or **māyā**, the only true reality being **Nirguṇa Brahman**, or Brahman without differentiating **qualities**. The Nyāya system, on the other hand, teaches that the world is both real and knowable. The Navya Nyāya system appealed not only to Hindus but also to Jain thinkers, who also hold a realist ontology. One of the most revered of Jain philosophers, Yaśovijaya (1624–1688), was a student of Navya Nyāya and incorporated its categories and arguments into his defense of **Jainism**.

NAVYA ŚĀSTRA. "New **Scripture**"; Hindu organization dedicated to the eradication of **casteism** and, ideally, of the **caste** system itself from Hinduism. Navya Śāstra, unlike some **Dalit** organizations, is avowedly Hindu and argues that the caste prejudice is not intrinsic to Hinduism and is contradicted by important currents of Hindu **philosophy**, such as **Vedānta**. The organization has offered a public apology on behalf of the Hindu tradition to Dalits for the centuries of abuse they have experienced.

NĀYANĀRS. A group of 63 saints and **bhakti poets** revered in the **Tamil** Śaiva tradition. Their life stories are contained in a text called the *Periya Purāṇa*, a scriptural text of the **Śaiva Siddhānta** tradition of **Śaivism**. According to the **philosophy** of bhakti, **caste** and gender are irrelevant to the level of devotion of which one is capable—and thus to the attainment of **mokṣa**. This is in clear contrast with the more conservative tradition of **Brahmanism**, according to which **rebirth** as a male **Brahmin** is a prerequisite for the attainment of mokṣa. The Nāyanārs illustrate this spiritual egalitarianism, coming from a wide range of backgrounds, including members of the humblest strata of Indian society.

NEHRU, JAWAHARLAL (1889–1964). First prime minister of India. Though a close confidant of **Mohandās K. Gāndhī**, Nehru did not share Gāndhī's radical vision of returning India to its ancient traditions, preferring a model of rapid industrialization and modernization. Under Nehru's leadership, independent India embraced secularism and a "mixed economy," consisting of aspects of both capitalism and socialism. He also helped to start the movement of nonaligned countries and sought a position of neutrality between the Soviet Union and the United States during the Cold War.

NEO-VEDĀNTA. Modern **Vedānta**. It is distinguished from traditional Vedānta by its commitment to the authority of direct experience (**anubhāva**) over that of **scripture** and its universalism. That is, Neo-Vedāntins see Vedānta not so much as an interpretation of the ***Vedas***—the traditional preserve of the **Brahmins**—but as a universal **knowledge** that is available, in principle, to all—a **perennial philosophy**. In the words of one of its leading exponents, **Sarvepalli Radhakrishnan**, Vedānta is "not a religion, but religion itself in its most universal and deepest significance." All religions, according to Neo-Vedānta, are paths to **God-realization**, if properly understood.

The historical origins of Neo-Vedānta can be found in the **Bengal** Renaissance of the 19th century, when **Rām Mohan Roy** and other Hindu reformers began to rethink Hinduism in modern, rationalist terms. Roy's **Brahmo Samāj** sought to purge the Hindu tradition of all elements that it regarded as irrational, such as the use of **images in worship**, **satī**, and **casteism**. **Swāmī Dayānanda Sarasvatī**'s **Ārya Samāj** had a very similar agenda, and both reform movements saw in the *Vedas* a primordial **monotheism**. The two differed, however, inasmuch as Roy saw the culmination of **Vedic** wisdom being in the ***Upaniṣads***, whereas Dayānanda emphasized the early Vedic ***Saṃhitās***. The Ārya Samāj therefore defined itself as distinct from Neo-Vedānta.

Neo-Vedānta, however, did not capture the imaginations of many Hindus beyond the relatively small circle of middle- and upper-class, English-educated Indians until the coming of **Ramakrishna** and **Swāmī Vivekānanda**. Ramakrishna, who was in many ways a thoroughly traditional figure—a passionate devotee in the mold of the **bhakti** movement—adhered to practices and beliefs antithetical to those of the Brahmo Samāj and rooted his teachings in his direct experiences rather than scriptural study. In this way, he was thoroughly traditional and thoroughly modern. Partaking of both of these worlds, Ramakrishna embodied an approach that could be appreciated by the rationalists and the traditionalists alike.

Ramakrishna's disciple, Vivekānanda, went on to become an articulate voice for this movement and transformed it into an international phenomenon by traveling to the West and initiating non-Indians into Vedāntic practice, and even into the **Ramakrishna Order** of **renouncers**. Inspiring many Hindus with the idea that their ancient traditions had universal significance, he helped to fuel national pride and the movement for Indian independence (although he was himself steadfastly apolitical).

NEPAL. Largely Hindu country located between India and Tibet. Until 2006, when its parliament declared it to be a secular state, Nepal was the only officially Hindu nation in the world. Nepal also has the highest percentage of Hindus in its population of any other country. The other major religion of Nepal is **Buddhism**, and the **Buddha** is believed to have been born and to have grown up within what are now the borders of Nepal. Hindu traditions in Nepal have blended in many ways with those of Buddhism. Both religions have a strong **Tantric** orientation in Nepal. Nepali Hinduism has also preserved many traditions that have largely been superseded in India, including **animal sacrifice** and a variety of rituals associated with having a Hindu monarchy.

NETI NETI. "Not this, not that"; an approach to **Brahman** recommended in some parts of the ***Upaniṣads*** that consists of realizing that Brahman is unlimited. It therefore cannot be identified with any one thing that can be grasped by the senses or the mind. Akin to a **Buddhist** approach to **enlightenment**—which consists of realizing that no one thing is the **self**—the path of distinguishing Brahman from any limiting **quality** is a form of the **jñāna yoga**, or yoga of wisdom, whereby one realizes that Brahman alone is real, that all things are limited and transitory, and therefore not Brahman, and not fully real. Brahman is thus "Not this, not that." *See also* VEDĀNTA.

NEW DELHI. *See* DELHI.

NIMBĀRKA (c. 12th–14th centuries CE). Ācārya of the *Bhedābheda* system of **Vedānta**. In this system, both difference (*bheda*) and nondifference (*abheda*) are affirmed. In other words, if one thinks of the various systems of Vedānta as existing on a continuum, with **Advaita** at one extreme end (affirming the unreality of genuine difference and the reality of **Brahman** alone) and **Dvaita** at the other end (affirming the reality of difference and denying an underlying unity), then Nimbārka's system can be seen as a "middle path" that tries to bring these two ideas together, affirming that both difference and unity are real.

In some ways an anticipation of the **Neo-Vedānta** of **Ramakrishna**, Nimbārka's teaching sees difference and nondifference simply as different approaches to an ultimate reality that cannot finally be categorized or conceptualized. Religiously, Nimbārka's tradition is a **bhakti**-oriented **Vaiṣṇava** path focused on **Rādhā** and **Kṛṣṇa**.

The dates of Nimbārka's life are highly uncertain, although most scholars locate him somewhere between the early 12th and 14th centuries. He was from Andhra Pradesh, in southern India.

NIRGUṆA BRAHMAN. "Brahman without **qualities**"; Brahman, the ultimate reality, free from limiting qualities; infinite being (**sat**), consciousness (**cit**), and bliss (**ānanda**); the eternal and unchanging absolute. According to **Advaita Vedānta**, Nirguṇa Brahman alone is real. All other entities that can be perceived are in various ways limited, and so deficiently real. The universe of limited entities is a mere appearance, or **māyā**. Māyā is projected onto the true reality of Brahman by the **mind** as an effect of ignorance (**avidyā**).

NIRṚTI. Vedic goddess of misfortunate and destruction. A portion of the **sacrifice** (or **yajña**) is offered to Nirṛti to ensure that she stays away from the ritual and does not cause problems.

NIRVĀṆA. "Absorption"; term used primarily by **Buddhists** (but by **Jains** and Hindus as well) for the highest state of spiritual attainment in which one is free from bondage to the cycle of **death** and **rebirth**. Buddhist traditions tend to describe this state in negative terms, as not characterized by suffering, rebirth, or limitation of any kind. Hindu texts, such as the ***Bhagavad Gītā***, speak of *brahma-nirvāṇa*, or absorption in **God**. *See also* MOKṢA.

NIRVIKALPA SAMĀDHI. State of meditative absorption that is completely free from any sense of the duality of subject and object; a state without dichotomizing conceptual constructions. **Samādhi**—absorption in the object of one's **meditation**—is the eighth and final "limb" of **Patañjali**'s eight-limbed (**āṣṭāṅga**) system of **yoga**. Later traditions that utilize Patañjali's system distinguish between samādhi in which there remains a sense of subjectivity (**savikalpa samādhi**) and samādhi with no subject–object duality (nirvikalpa samādhi). This distinction is most prominent in **Buddhism**, **Kaśmīr Śaivism**, and the **Neo-Vedānta** tradition of **Ramakrishna**.

NITYĀNANDA, SWĀMĪ (1897–1961). Guru of **Swāmī Muktānanda**; founder of the **Siddha Yoga** lineage. Nityānanda, a mysterious figure, spent much of his life in a cave in **Gaṇeśapuri**, near Bombay, where the Siddha Yoga tradition's main **āśrama** is located today. Speaking little, he communicated mainly through gestures and inarticulate sounds, though he was capable of speech, and sometimes spoke in great depth. An interview with one of his disciples that contains his teachings was published as the *Cidākāśa Gītā*. Born in **Kerala**, he is said to have lived in a state of constant bliss throughout his childhood and is believed by his devotees to have been born **enlightened**. He became a **sannyāsin**, or renouncer, before the age of 20, eventually wandering to Gaṇeśapuri.

NIVEDITĀ, SISTER (1867–1911). Born in Ireland as Margaret Elizabeth Noble, the first Westerner to take monastic vows in a Hindu religious order, becoming a **sannyāsinī** or nun in the **Ramakrishna Order**. Noble's **guru** was **Swāmī Vivekānanda**, the first Hindu spiritual teacher to bring his tradition successfully to the West. Moving to **Bengal**, she established a school for girls in 1898, open to people of all **castes**. She befriended a number of prominent Bengali Hindus of the period, including **Rabindranāth Tagore** and **Aurobindo Ghose**. She was also very close to **Saradā Devī**, the wife of **Ramakrishna**—known to his followers as the **Holy Mother**—who referred to Noble as "Baby." Wanting to work for the cause of Indian independence, Noble formally left the Ramakrishna Order so it would experience no negative repercussions from her political activities.

NIVṚTTI MĀRGA. "Path of negation"; "path of turning away from activity." If one is interested in attaining **mokṣa**, or release from the cycle of **rebirth**, some Hindu traditions claim that it is necessary to renounce life in society and practice **asceticism**. This is the path of negation, of turning away from activity. The basic idea is that a worldly life, in which one does one's duty (**dharma**) and pursues pleasure (**kāma**) and wealth (**artha**) is not compatible with the attainment of mokṣa. In terms of the four goals of humanity or **puruṣārthas** of classical Hindu thought, the pursuit of kāma, artha, and dharma make up the **pravṛtti mārga**—the path of activity, of turning toward the world. Pursuit of the goal of mokṣa, the fourth of the puruṣārthas, requires one to follow the path of nivṛtti. And in terms of the four stages of life, or **āśramas**, the first three stages—the stages of student, householder, and retiree—make up the pravṛtti mārga and the fourth stage—renunciation, or **sannyāsa**—makes up the nivṛttii mārga.

NIYAMA. "Observance"; "discipline"; the second "limb" of **Patañjali**'s eight-limbed (**aṣṭāṅga**) system of **yoga**. The niyamas consist of five virtues: *śauca* (purity), *santoṣa* (contentment), *tapas* (**asceticism**), *svādhyāya* (study), and surrender to the Lord (***Īśvara-praṇidhāna***).

NOBLE, MARGARET ELIZABETH (1867–1911). *See* NIVEDITĀ, SISTER.

NONDUALITY, PRINCIPLE OF. *See* TANTRA.

NYĀYA. Logic; one of the six systems of Hindu philosophy, or **darśanas**; often paired with the **Vaiśeṣika** system, with which it shares a basic worldview and a realist ontology. The chief concern of Nyāya is epistemology, or the theory of **knowledge**. According to the Naiyāyikas (adherents of Nyāya), there are four **pramāṇas**, or valid foundations of knowledge: **pratyakṣa**, or sensory perception; **anumāna**, or inference; **upamāna**, or verbal comparison—in other words, recognizing a perceived entity to be a member of an already known category; and śabda, the verbal testimony of a knowledgeable person. Nyāya, as an **āstika** or "orthodox" system of philosophy, identifies the Vedic **scriptures** as the preeminent example of the śabda pramāṇa.

The root text of this system of thought—the *Nyāya Sūtra*—is attributed to a sage by the name of **Gautama** (not the **Buddha** or the **Vedic** sage of the same name). This text was probably composed around 300 BCE. The

Naiyāyikas debated extensively with the **Buddhists** until Buddhism had largely vanished from India (by 1300 CE) and with other systems of Indian philosophy, particularly **Advaita Vedānta**. Major figures of the Nyāya tradition include **Vācaspati Miśra** (900–980 CE)—who was also an adherent of Advaita—and **Udayana** (fl. 10th century CE). In the 13th century, largely in response to Advaitic critiques, a Naiyāyika philosopher named Gaṅgeśa established the **Navya Nyāya**, or New Nyāya system, a refined version of the older system of Nyāya.

O

OLCOTT, HENRY STEELE (1832–1907). Cofounder—along with the Russian heiress **Helena Petrovna Blavatsky**—and first president of the **Theosophical Society**. Formally established in 1875, the objectives of the Theosophical Society were (and remain) "to form a nucleus of the universal brotherhood of humanity without distinction of race, creed, sex, **caste**, or color," "to encourage the study of comparative religion, **philosophy**, and science," and "to investigate the unexplained **laws** of nature and the powers latent in man." Influenced deeply by Hinduism and **Buddhism**, Olcott and Blavatsky moved to India in 1879, where the global headquarters of the society are located today (in Adyār, **Madras**). Members of the Theosophical Society began to play prominent roles in the movement for Indian political independence, arousing the suspicion of the British government.

Theosophists promoted pride and interest among Hindus and Buddhists in their religious and cultural heritage, acting as "reverse missionaries," and articulating the idea that Hinduism and Buddhism preserve an ancient global wisdom tradition, or **perennial philosophy**. At one point, a strategic alliance began to form between the Theosophical Society and the **Ārya Samāj**. But **Swāmī Dayānanda Sarasvatī** fell out with Blavatsky and Olcott in 1880, when they announced their conversions to Buddhism in **Sri Lanka**. Olcott remained in Sri Lanka for a number of years, promoting Buddhism and writing a Buddhist catechism that continues to be in use among Theravāda Buddhists in Sri Lanka today.

OṂ. Also spelled AUM, the most sacred sound and **bīja mantra** of Hinduism. In the ***Maṇḍukya Upaniṣad***, Oṃ is described as encompassing all of existence. Each of its parts (A, U, M, and the totality of these three) is associated with one of the four **states of consciousness**. It figures prominently in Hindu prayer and **meditation** and is frequently incorporated into more lengthy **mantras** as their first syllable, such as *Oṃ namaḥ Śivāya*, or *Oṃ namo bhagavate Vasudevāya*.

OṂ JAYA JAGADĪŚA HARE. Devotional song popularized in the 20th century by the Hindi singer Lata Mangeshkar (1929–). Frequently sung during **āratī** in modern Hindu **temples** in North America and Europe.

ONAM. Harvest festival that is celebrated in the state of **Kerala**, on the southwest coast of India. It occurs in the month of **Bhadra** (August–September).

ONE, THE. The supreme reality or absolute that underlies all existence. In the ***Ṛg Veda*** it is said that the One is the reality behind the appearance of diversity that gives rise to the world of phenomena. It is also said that the many **devas** or deities are all names for the One (***Ṛg Veda*** 1.164.46)—"Reality is one, but the wise speak of it in many ways." In the ***Upaniṣads***, the ultimate reality—**Brahman**—is frequently said to be "One alone, without a second." Such **Vedic** references to the One are the basis for the view that an ancient thread of **monotheism** underlies the Hindu practice of **polytheism**, the idea being that what appear to be many deities are forms, aspects, or manifestations of the One. Though this view is certainly ancient in Hindu traditions, it has been reemphasized in the modern period in response to the criticisms of **Christian** and **Islamic** missionaries.

ORISSA. State on the eastern coast of India, between **West Bengal** in the northeast and Andhra Pradesh in the south; location of several prominent Hindu **temples**, including the **Vaiṣṇava** temple of **Jagannātha** in the city of **Puri**, where the Vaiṣṇava **bhakti** saint and **ācārya**, **Caitanya**, resided for much of his life. Orissa is also home to **Bhuvaneśvara**, with its prominent temples to **Śiva** and **Kālī**, and **Konārak**, with its massive temple in the shape of a **chariot** to **Sūrya**, the sun **god**. One of the four **maṭhas**, or monasteries that were established by **Śaṅkara** in the four corners of India, is also located in Puri.

OSHO. *See* RAJNEESH, BHAGWAN.

OUT OF INDIA THEORY. Alternative theory of **Vedic** origins, presented as a critique of the more widely accepted **Āryan Migration Theory**. According to this theory (which has many subvarieties that differ on a number of issues), **Indo-European** languages and cultures originated in India, rather than being brought to India through migration or trade. Mainstream scholarship regards this scenario as unlikely, given the existence of older, non-Indo-European substrate elements in **Sanskrit**. Concern is also raised by the **Hindu Nationalist** assumptions and agenda that clearly fuel at least some versions of this theory. Much of the evidence presented in its favor consists of mathematical calculations based on references to **astrological** phenomena mentioned in Vedic texts (which suggest a much greater age for these texts than the dominant model proposes) and on the absence of any explicit reference to a major migration from Central Asia in Indic textual sources.

While mainstream scholars have not ultimately found it persuasive, advocates of this theory have raised important critical questions about the dominant model—especially its older variant, the **Āryan Invasion Theory**, which was used in the 20th century to advance an agenda of European superiority. The debate remains very politically charged.

Among scholars with less obviously political motivations, the debate over Āryan migration tends to pit archaeology against linguistics. The linguistic evidence suggests that some kind of migration has to have occurred, while the archaeological evidence is more ambiguous (and does not support the older idea of a massive invasion).

OUTCASTE. One who has no **caste**; an **Untouchable**. *See also* DALIT; HARIJAN.

P

PADMA. Lotus flower, often used to symbolize spiritual attainment. The growth of the beautiful lotus flower out of mud and muck represents the process of **enlightenment**, in which the spiritual aspirant starts out in the "mud and muck" of mundane existence, with all of its various worries and forms of suffering, and progresses to a state of higher awareness. Hindu deities are often depicted as being seated upon large lotus flowers, and the **cakras** of **Tantric yoga** are also depicted as lotus flowers with varying numbers of petals that symbolically blossom when activated by the rising **kuṇḍalinī śakti**, the latent energy at the base of the spine. As a prominent Hindu symbol, it is also used as a symbol of the **Hindu Nationalist Bharatīya Janatā Party** (BJP).

PADMANĀBHI. "Lotus-navel"; image of **Viṣṇu** reclining on the cosmic serpent, **Śeṣa**, with a lotus stalk emerging from his navel. At the end of the stalk is a **lotus** blossom on which **Brahmā**, the creator deity, sits. Viṣṇu's feet are lovingly massaged by his wife, the **goddess Lakṣmī**. This image captures the moment of Brahmā's emergence from the body of Viṣṇu, just before Brahmā begins the process of **creating** a new universe. A large version of this image is housed at Padmanābhaswāmi **temple** in **Kerala**.

PADMĀSANA. Lotus posture; **Haṭha Yoga** posture formed by placing the right foot on the left thigh and the left foot on the right thigh. This is the "full lotus." There is also a half-lotus posture (**ardhapadmāsana**), formed by placing the right foot on the left thigh and the left foot underneath the right leg.

The **goddess Lakṣmī** is also sometimes referred to as *Padmāsanā* because she is seated upon a lotus flower. Other deities are also sometimes represented as *padmāsana* in this sense. *See also* ĀSANA.

PAILA. One of the five **Brahmin** students of **Vyāsa**, also known as **Veda Vyāsa**, who is attributed not only with authoring the ***Mahābhārata*** but also with organizing the ***Vedas*** into their current distribution of four texts: the ***Ṛg Veda***, ***Yajur Veda***, ***Sāma Veda***, and ***Atharva Veda***. According to the ***Purāṇas***, each of Vyāsa's students was responsible for memorizing and passing on a separate **Vedic** text—one for each of the four *Vedas* and one for the *Mahābhārata*. Paila was the student responsible for transmitting the *Ṛg Veda*.

PALLAVA. Dynasty that ruled southern India from **Kāñcīpuram** from the sixth to the eighth centuries of the Common Era. Its first king was **Mahendravikrama Varman** (571–630), who, in addition to being the successful founder of a powerful dynasty, was a scholar and a playwright, authoring the ***Mattavilāsa Prahasana*** ("Comedy of Drunken Play"), which ridicules various religious sects of the period. The Pallavas were overthrown in the eighth century by the **Coḷa** dynasty.

PAÑCA-MAKĀRA. The **Five M's**. Pañca ("five") "ma-kāra" (the letter "m," or "ma").

PAÑCARĀTRA, PĀÑCARĀTRA. "Five nights"; early **Vaiṣṇava** sect, whose name may be derived from a five-night **yajña**, or sacrifice, performed by **Nārāyaṇa (Viṣṇu)** in the *Śatapatha* ***Brāhmaṇa***. The ***Āgamas***, or **scriptures** of this tradition, are largely "how to" manuals concerned with correct ritual performance, **yoga** practice, the construction of **temples**, and the consecration of sacred images (**mūrtis**). By the 10th century of the Common Era, other devotional, **bhakti**-oriented sects had largely absorbed the Pañcarātra tradition, continuing to utilize its **mantras** and ritual manuals.

PAÑCAYĀTANA PŪJĀ. "Worship of Five Objects"; system of worship developed by **Śaṅkara** (788–820) according to which one could cultivate **bhakti**, or devotion, toward one of five possible chosen deities or **iṣṭadevatās** as a practice of purifying the **mind** to prepare it for the liberating knowledge (**jñāna**) of the unity of the self (**ātman**) and the supreme reality (**Brahman**).

The five deities that Śaṅkara recommends for this devotional practice are **Gaṇeśa**, **Śiva**, **Śakti**, **Viṣṇu**, and **Sūrya**. This practice may be the source of the **Neo-Vedāntic** practice of seeing any sacred figure as a potential iṣṭadevatā and way to **God-realization**, including figures from outside the Hindu tradition, such as Jesus Christ, the **Buddha**, the Prophet Muhammad, and various **Christian** and Muslim saints.

PĀṆḌAVA. Son of **Paṇḍu**. The five Pāṇḍava brothers—**Yudhiṣṭhira**, **Bhīma**, **Arjuna**, **Nakula**, and Sahadeva—are the heroes and main characters of the ***Mahābhārata***.

PAṆḌIT. Wise person; scholar; usually, though not necessarily, a **Brahmin**.

PAṆḌU. "Pale"; character in the ***Mahābhārata***, so named because of his extremely pale complexion (possibly referring to albinism); father of the **Pāṇḍavas**, the main heroes of the epic; husband of **Kuntī** and **Mādrī**; brother of the blind **Dhṛtarāṣṭra**.

PĀṆINI (c. 5th–4th centuries BCE). Sanskrit grammarian; author of an authoritative work on grammar called the *Aṣṭadhyāyi*, which defines the rules of classical Sanskrit usage.

PĀPA. Evil; sin; a wicked deed; also demerit, the negative aftereffects of an evil deed upon the **soul**—that is, "bad **karma**." Some Hindu traditions claim that pāpa can be expiated through **prāyaścitta**, thus eliminating the need to experience a negative result at some point in the future, which would be the normal result of evil **action**.

PARAMAHĀṂSA. "Great swan"; literally, "great goose." However, the word *goose* has connotations of silliness not culturally appropriate to the **Sanskrit** term *hāṃsa*, which conveys a sense of gracefulness and transcendence better matched by the English *swan*. The actual animal, *hāṃsa*, though, is a type of goose. *Paramahāṃsa* is a title given to a Hindu saint held to be especially holy, having achieved a state transcending mundane consciousness even while still alive, in the physical body.

PARAMAHĀṂSA YOGĀNANDA (1893–1952). *See* YOGĀNANDA, PARAMAHĀṂSA.

PARAMĀṆU. "Supremely small"; an atom, not in the sense in which this term is used in contemporary physics, but the smallest possible unit into which any material substance can be broken down. *See also* VAIŚEṢIKA.

PARAMĀTMAN. "Supreme self"; supreme **ātman**; **God**, understood as an indwelling presence that resides in every individual soul (**jīvātman**); the world-soul; the **soul** of the universe.

PARAṂPARĀ. "From one to another"; teaching lineage or tradition that is passed from teacher (**guru**) to disciple (**śiṣya**) through the ritual of initiation (**dīkṣā**). The student, or disciple, in time becomes the teacher to another group of students to whom the lineage is then passed. Those students themselves become teachers to other students, and so on. A possible analogy from **Christianity** would be the apostolic succession traced through the popes back to Peter and ultimately to Christ. *See also* GURU-ŚIṢYA-PARAṂPARĀ.

PARĀŚARA. **Vedic** sage attributed with the composition of several hymns of the ***Ṛg Veda*** in praise of **Agni**. Parāśara is also a character in the ***Mahābhārata***, where he is the father of **Vyāsa** by the daughter of the fisher-king, Satyavatī. Vyāsa is both the author of the *Mahābhārata* and the biological father of the kings **Dhṛtarāṣṭra** and **Paṇḍu**, making Parāśara an ancestor of the **Pāṇḍavas**' royal lineage.

PARAŚURĀMA. Sixth out of the traditional list of 10 **avatāras**, or incarnations, of the deity **Viṣṇu**; a wrathful avatāra who is said to have slain the entire **kṣatriya** (or warrior) **caste** in vengeance for his father, **Jamadagni**, having been killed by a kṣatriya, Arjuna Kārtavīrya (not the **Pāṇḍava** hero **Arjuna** of the ***Mahābhārata***). Paraśurāma was a **Brahmin** of the **Bhārgava** clan. After all the kṣatriyas had been slain by Paraśurāma, they had to be replaced by Brahmins. It is therefore believed that all living kṣatriyas are actually descended from Brahmins.

PARIKṢIT. Character in the ***Mahābhārata***; son of **Abhimanyu**, grandson of **Arjuna**. After **Yudhiṣṭhira** and the other **Pāṇḍava** brothers stepped down from the rule of their kingdom, it was Parikṣit who inherited the throne and continued the family lineage.

PARIVRĀJAKA. "Wanderer"; a Hindu **ascetic** who has renounced home life and does not normally remain in the same place for more than one day at a time; a **sannyāsī**.

PĀRVATĪ. "Daughter of the Mountain"; the **Mother Goddess**; the wife of **Śiva** in her most gentle, domestic form (in contrast with her fierce, warrior forms, such as **Durgā** and **Kālī**); mother of **Gaṇeśa** and **Kārttikeya**. Her father is the **god** of the **Himālayas**, hence her name. Pārvatī dwells with Śiva in the Himālayas, on Mount **Kailāsa**.

PAŚUPATA. A **Tantric** **Śaiva** lineage of **ascetics** known for their antinomian behavior, seeking to break down traditional distinctions between the pure and the impure as rooted in deluded, dualistic thinking, the reality being that all is **Śiva** (**Brahman**).

PAŚUPATI. "Lord of the animals"; epithet of **Śiva** that, in **Śaiva** theology, represents the relationship of Śiva to the **jīvas**, or souls of living beings, who are analogized with the animals for which Śiva cares. A similar image in **Christianity** is of Jesus as the "Good Shepherd."

PĀTĀLA. Hell. There are actually seven Hindu hells—layers or dimensions of existence that are highly unpleasant and in which beings are born who have extremely bad **karma** (**pāpa**). The Hindu hells might better be described as purgatories; unlike the hells of **Christianity** and **Islam**, the denizens of the Hindu hells do not reside there forever but only as long as they have bad karma for which they need to atone. Once their bad karma has been exhausted, such beings are reborn, usually in human form. This can take a very long time, however—in some cases, until the end of a cosmic cycle (**kalpa**), which may be billions of years. In other cases, though, one's period of residence in one of the hells can be of a relatively short duration.

Pātāla is also the realm of the **Nāgas**, presided over by the giant serpent, **Vāsuki**. *See also* REBIRTH.

PĀṬALIPUTRA. Ancient capital of the **Maurya** dynasty; located on the site of what is now the city of Patna, capital of the modern Indian state of Bihar.

PATAÑJALI. Author to whom the ***Yoga Sūtra*** is attributed (the root text of the **Yoga darśana**, or philosophical system); the inventor of the eight-limbed (**aṣṭāṅga**) system of yoga that the *Yoga Sūtra* describes. Patañjali probably lived between 100 BCE and 500 CE. Someone named Patañjali is also attributed with a work on **Sanskrit** grammar—the *Mahābhāṣya*, a commentary on the *Aṣṭadhyāyi* of **Pāṇini**—though it is not clear that these two Patañjalis are the same person.

PATH OF ACTION. *See* FOUR YOGAS; KARMA-MĀRGA, KARMA-YOGA; YOGA.

PATH OF DEVOTION. *See* BHAKTI; FOUR YOGAS; YOGA.

PATH OF KNOWLEDGE. *See* FOUR YOGAS; JÑĀNA; JÑĀNA-MĀRGA, JÑĀNA-YOGA; YOGA.

PATH OF MEDITATION. *See* AṢṬĀṄGA YOGA; DHYĀNA; FOUR YOGAS; **RĀJA-YOGA**; YOGA.

PAṬṬADAKAL. Site in **Karnataka** that houses several **temples** built by the **Cālukya** dynasty between the sixth and 12th centuries of the Common Era, including a temple with statues depicting **Kṛṣṇa** instructing **Arjuna** in the ***Bhagavad Gītā*** and another with sculptures depicting episodes from the ***Mahābhārata*** and the ***Rāmāyaṇa***.

PAUṢA. Month of the **Hindu calendar** that corresponds roughly to the period from mid-December to mid-January.

PERENNIAL PHILOSOPHY. The idea of a common thread of **truth** shared by all (or most) of the world's religions; in the words of **Aldous Huxley**, "the metaphysic that recognizes a divine Reality substantial to the world of things and lives and **minds**; the psychology that finds in the **soul** something similar to, or even identical with, divine Reality; the ethic that places man's final end in the **knowledge** of the immanent and transcendent Ground of all being." Modern Hindu thinkers, especially **Neo-Vedāntins**, endorse this idea, identifying this underlying truth with **Vedānta philosophy**, such as when **Sarvepalli Radhakrishnan** writes that Vedānta is "not a religion, but religion itself in its most universal and deepest significance." If they are properly understood, all religions, according to Neo-Vedānta, are paths to **God-realization**.

PHALGUNA. Month of the **Hindu calendar** that corresponds roughly to the period from mid-February to mid-March.

PHILOSOPHICAL SCHOOLS. *See* DARŚANA.

PHILOSOPHY. *See* DARŚANA.

PILGRIMAGE. A journey to a sacred place. Such a journey is a form of meritorious **action**, or **puṇya karma**. *See* YATRA.

PIṆḌA. A ball of rice offered to one's ancestors as part of the **śrāddha** ritual. *See also* ANCESTRAL RITES.

PITṚ. Literally "father," but also refers to one's ancestors in general.

PITṚLOKA. Realm of the ancestors; one of the possible afterlife destinations in **Vedic** thought, the other being the **Devaloka**, or realm of the **gods**.

PLANETS. *See* NAVAGRAHAS.

POETRY. Popular genre for conveying Hindu religious themes. **Kālīdāsa** (fl. 400 CE) is the most renowned **Sanskrit** poet, whose elegant verse is frequently analogized with the work of Shakespeare as a major contribution to world **literature**. Many of the saints of the **bhakti** or devotional traditions of Hinduism have communicated their devotion in the form of poems and songs. The study of Sanskrit poetics, or *kāvya*, is connected with the **philosophy** of **rasa**, or the aesthetic sensibility, which many Hindu theologians tie to the spiritual path, seeing the beauty of poetry and of poetic imagery as a way to evoke the experience of devotion and draw the devotee ever nearer to the divine. *See also* ABHINAVAGUPTA; ĀḶVĀRS; ĀṆḌĀL; BASAVA; BAULS;

BHARTṚHARI; CAṆḌĪDĀS; CHATTERJEE, BANKIM CHANDRA; CIVAVĀKKIYAR; DAṆḌIN; GOSVĀMINS; JAYADEVA; JÑĀNEŚVARA; KABĪR; KĀLIDĀSA; KANNAPPA; LALLĀ; MAHĀDEVIYAKKA; MAMMATA; MĀṆIKKAVĀCAKAR; MEHTA, NARSI; MĪRA BAI; NĀMDEV; NAMMĀḶVĀR; NANDANAR; NĀYANĀRS; RĀMPRASĀD; RAVIDĀS; SURDĀS; TAGORE, RABINDRANĀTH; *TIRUVĀYMOḶI*; TUKĀRĀM; TULSĪDĀS.

POLYTHEISM. Affirmation of the existence of and reverence for multiple deities, or **gods**. Most, though not all, Hindu traditions are polytheistic in practice. Many of these systems, however, affirm a deeper **monotheism** that underlies their polytheistic practices, according to which the **One God** manifests in many forms that correspond to the many gods of Hinduism—and even to the deities of other religions. The issue of polytheism and monotheism in Hinduism is further complicated by the fact that there are many **Sanskrit** terms that can be translated as "**God**," some of which have polytheistic connotations and some of which have monotheistic, or even pantheistic or panentheistic, connotations. Not all Hindu traditions agree, furthermore, in regard to which understanding is correct.

Devas are many in number and correspond closely to a polytheistic conception of divinity—many divine beings personifying natural phenomena, like **Agni**, the deva of fire; **Sūrya**, the deva of the sun; **Vāyu**, the deva of the wind; and so on. **Īśvara** or **Bhagavān** correspond to God in more of a monotheistic sense—the Supreme Being or overlord of the cosmos. **Brahman**, the eternal and absolute reality that is ultimately one with all things, conveys a pantheistic or panentheistic sense of the divine as present in all beings.

PONGAL. Four-day harvest festival that is celebrated in the state of **Tamil** Nadu, on the southern tip and southeastern coast of India. It occurs on the last day of the lunar month of **Pauṣa** (December–January) and the first three days of the month of **Magha** (January–February).

POONA (PUNE). *See* PUNE.

POONJAJI (POONJA, HARILAL W.) (1910–1997). Punjab-based **guru** who had a number of Western followers. Poonjaji is said to have attained **samādhi** at the young age of nine. He met **Ramaṇa Maharṣi** in 1944, becoming his disciple and teaching a form of **Advaita Vedānta** mixed with **bhakti** for the rest of his life. His most famous disciple was the Catholic monk Swāmī Abhiṣiktānanda (Henri Le Saux), who delved very deeply into the experience of Hinduism, seeking common ground between Advaita Vedānta and **Christianity**.

POTANA (1400–1470). Vaiṣṇava scholar and saint; translated the ***Bhāgavata Purāṇa*** into Telugu to make this text more widely available to the common people. Though born a **Śaiva**, Potana took initiation from a Vaiṣṇava **guru**. He is said to have seen both Śaiva and Vaiṣṇava traditions as equally valid.

PRABHAVĀNANDA, SWĀMĪ (1893–1976). Scholar and monk of the **Ramakrishna Order** who did a good deal to promote **Neo-Vedānta** in North America. Prabhavānanda founded the **Vedānta Society** of Southern California in 1930 and ran it until his death in 1976. Under his leadership, this organization became the largest Vedānta Society in the Western world. Prominent disciples of Prabhavānanda include **Christopher Isherwood** and **Aldous Huxley**. Isherwood's relationship with Prabhavānanda is chronicled in his autobiography, *My Guru and His Disciple*. The two of them collaborated on a number of scholarly projects, including popular translations of the ***Bhagavad Gītā*** and **Patañjali**'s ***Yoga Sūtra***. Prabhavānanda also wrote a Vedāntic commentary on **Christianity** entitled *The Sermon on the Mount According to Vedanta.*

PRADAKṢINA. Circumambulation; to walk in a circle around a sacred image (**mūrti**) in a clockwise direction, keeping the image to one's right side, as a way of paying respect to the deity that the image represents. *See also* IMAGES IN WORSHIP.

PRAHLĀDA. Son of the demonic **Hiraṇyakaśipu** and ardent devotee of **Viṣṇu**; often held up in **Vaiṣṇava** traditions as a model of **bhakti**. Hiraṇyakaśipu held deep hatred for **Viṣṇu**. Annoyed by Prahlāda's equally deep devotion for his archenemy, Hiraṇyakaśipu taunted Prahlāda. Once, asking Prahlāda where Viṣṇu could be found, Prahlāda replied that Viṣṇu (whose name means "all-pervasive") was everywhere, even within a nearby stone pillar. On hearing this, Hiraṇyakaśipu kicked the pillar. The pillar then broke open and Viṣṇu, in the form of the **Narasiṃha** or man-lion **avatāra**, came forth. The man-lion grabbed Hiraṇyakaśipu, placed him on his lap, and slew him. This event occurred at dusk. The circumstances surrounding the **death** of Hiraṇyakaśipu were a result of the fact that he was magically protected from any attack by man or beast (the Narasiṃha was neither), on the ground or in the air (which is why Narasiṃha held him in his lap), and by day or night (making dusk and dawn times of vulnerability for him).

PRAJĀPATI. "Father of Offspring"; "progenitor"; **Vedic** creator deity, often identified with **Brahmā**. *See also* CREATION.

PRAJĀPITAR BRAHMĀ (1876–1969). Founder of the **Brahmā Kumārī** movement; born **Dāda Lekhrāj**.

PRAKRIT (PRĀKṚTA). "Natural"; the natural languages of northern India in ancient times, in contrast with the "artificial" or "cultured" **Sanskrit** language. This term refers to the Middle **Indo-Āryan** languages spoken across northern India from ancient times up to the medieval and modern periods, when these languages evolved into the contemporary north Indian languages, such as **Hindi, Bengali,** Gujarati, and Marathi. There are many Prakrits, including Pāli (the language of the earliest extant canonical texts of **Buddhism**) and Ardha-Māgadhi (the language of the canonical texts of **Jainism**).

PRAKṚTI. "Nature"; "matter." In **Sāṃkhya philosophy**, one of two main categories into which reality is divided, the other being **puruṣa**, or pure spirit. Whereas puruṣa is pure consciousness, both **mind** and matter—all phenomena—are manifestations of prakṛti. Prakṛti manifests as three **guṇas**, or qualities—**sattva** (clarity, luminosity), **rajas** (**action** or dynamism), and **tamas** (inertia). The universe of changing phenomena is an effect of the constant interplay of these three guṇas. The goal of Sāṃkhya and the related system of **Yoga** is for puruṣa to realize its nature as pure spirit and disentangle itself from prakṛti, with which it has become falsely identified.

PRALAYA. Dissolution. The end of a cosmic cycle or century of **Brahmā**. At the end of a cycle, the forces of chaos and entropy overcome the forces of order, or **dharma**, and the universe dissolves, returning to a potential state. There follows the great sleep, or *mahāpralaya*, after which a new **creation** will emerge and a new century of Brahmā, lasting for trillions of years, will begin. The karmic states of the beings in the universe at the time of the pralaya will determine their character in the new cycle. *See also* WORLD AGES.

PRAMĀṆA. In Indian philosophy, a valid basis for making a judgment. The most basic pramāṇa, accepted by all **darśanas**, or systems of Indian philosophy, is **pratyakṣa**, or sensory perception. After pratyakṣa are **anumāna**, or inference, and **upamāna**, or verbal comparison—in other words, recognizing a perceived entity to be a member of an already known category. Finally, there is śabda, or the verbal testimony of a trustworthy and knowledgeable person. The **āstika** or "orthodox" Hindu systems of philosophy identify the **Vedic scriptures** as the preeminent example of the śabda pramāṇa. The **materialist Cārvāka** or **Lokāyata** system accepts only pratyakṣa as valid. **Buddhism** accepts only pratyakṣa and anumāna. The orthodox Hindu systems generally accept all four pramāṇas.

PRĀṆA. Breath. Vital energy. The second most "gross" or physical of the five sheaths or **kośas** surrounding the **ātman**—the **prāṇa-maya-kośa**. In some ***Upaniṣads*** it is speculated that the prāṇa might be the ātman—that the ātman is the primal life force that manifests as the power of breath in the physical body.

PRĀṆA-MAYA-KOŚA. Breath layer; vital energy layer; the second of the five **kośas**, or layers, surrounding the self (**ātman**) according to **Vedānta**. This kośa is "between" the physical or "food" layer (**anna-maya-kośa**) and the **mind** layer (**mano-maya-kośa**).

PRĀṆĀYĀMA. Breath control, fourth of the eight stages or "limbs" of **Patañjali**'s eight-limbed (**aṣṭāṅga**) **yoga**, as outlined in the ***Yoga Sūtras***. Such control helps to bring the **mind** under control.

PRĀRABDHA KARMA. The effects of past **actions**, or **karma**, which have gone into the **creation** of one's current physical body and which cannot be eliminated. It is due to prārabdha karma that even an **enlightened** being—one who has attained **liberation** from the cycle of **rebirth**, or **mokṣa**, in this lifetime (a **jīvanmukta**)—continues to stay alive and is subject to bodily experiences such as injury, sickness, old age, and **death**. Even while the **soul** is free, the body experiences the effects of this ripening past karma.

PRASĀDAM. Divine grace, gift from **God**. In its most common usage, this term refers to food offerings made during **pūjā** and then distributed back to the worshiper and, often, to other members of the community as well. The basic concept operating is transactional in nature. The worshiper makes an offering of **devotion** to God (in a specific form, such as one of the personal deities of Hinduism), which is symbolized by food items, and the deity, in turn, bestows blessings upon the devotee, which are symbolized by the devotee's consumption of the food. Any food that has been thus offered is prasādam, even if the one who eventually consumes it was not present at the pūjā but has been given the prasādam later by a friend or family member. It is widely regarded as bad luck to refuse prasādam that has been offered in this way, as fortunate to receive it, and as good act—an act of **puṇya karma**—to offer it.

PRASTHĀNA TRAYA**.** "Threefold foundation," three textual sources foundational to all of the systems of **Vedānta** philosophy: the ***Upaniṣads***, the ***Brahmā Sūtras***, and the ***Bhagavad Gītā***. Every Vedāntic **ācārya**, or founder of a formal system of Vedānta, has written commentaries upon the three texts of the *Prasthāna Traya*. It is largely through the medium of these commentaries, or **bhāṣyas**, that the various ācāryas have established the point of view of their particular school of thought—with **Śaṅkara**, for example, providing an interpretation of these texts supportive of **Advaita Vedānta**, **Rāmāṇuja** providing an interpretation supportive of **Viśiṣṭādvaita Vedānta**, and so on. The internal diversity of the *Upaniṣads* and the terseness of the *Brahmā Sūtras*, in particular, have lent themselves to these varying interpretations.

PRATYAKṢA. Perception; sensory perception; one of the valid sources of **knowledge**, or **pramāṇas**, of Indian philosophy; the only pramāṇa that all of the systems of Indian philosophy (**darśanas**) accept as valid.

PRAVṚTTI MĀRGA. "Path of inclination toward **action**"; way of life of a **householder** who has not renounced **action**; the way of life of persons in the first three of the **āśramas** or four stages of life. These persons are dedicated to pursuing **kāma** (sensory pleasure), **artha** (wealth), and **dharma** (moral virtue) by following the Pravṛtti Mārga. This is in contrast with the **Nivṛtti Mārga**, the path of the renouncer (**sannyāsin**), who pursues the fourth goal of life: **mokṣa**, or **liberation** from the cycle of **rebirth**.

PRAYĀGA (ALLAHABAD). Holy city at the confluence of the rivers **Yamunā** and **Gaṅgā**.

PRĀYAŚCITTA. Atonement for bad past acts—**pāpa** or "bad **karma**"—through **actions** prescribed by a priest or by one's **guru**. These can include practicing special **asceticism**, performing a special **pūjā**, or giving charity (**dāna**) to worthy persons or institutions.

PREMA. Love; affection; close friendship.

PRETA. Ghost; one of the types of creature against which one prays for protection; an unquiet spirit, often because the proper funeral rites were not performed. *See also* ANCESTRAL RITES; ANTYEṢṬI.

PṚTHVĪ. Earth; the medium of smell (**gandha**); one of the five elements or states of being that constitute the physical world (**mahābhūtas**). The five elements are earth (pṛthvi), air (**vāyu**), fire (**agni**), water (**ap**), and space (**ākāśa**).

PŪJĀ. Worship; chief ritual by which deities are honored. The basic structure of pūjā is modeled on the favors that one would bestow upon an honored guest, such as offerings of food, a bath, and clean clothing.

PUNARJANMA. Rebirth, reincarnation.

Priest performing puja to the Goddess Kālī.
The photograph to the priest's left is of Sri Ramakrishna.

PUNDIT. A wise or **knowledgeable** person; a common English spelling of **paṇḍit**. This word has entered English usage to refer to an expert or a commentator in any discipline.

PUNE (POONA). City in Maharashtra, in central India; birthplace of **Śivāji**, renowned leader of the **Marāṭhas** in the 17th century. Pune is also home to many universities and a major center of **Indology** and **Sanskrit** scholarship. The **āśrama** or commune of **Osho** (**Bhagwan Rajneesh**) is located here as well.

PUṆYA. Merit, good **karma**.

PURĀṆAS. Ancient lore; a collection of 18 texts dedicated to the deeds of deities such as **Viṣṇu**, **Śiva**, and **Devī**. These texts were composed in their current form during the first millennium of the Common Era (although they likely contain material from an earlier period). Along with the ***Mahābhārata*** and ***Rāmāyaṇa***, these texts largely define the worldview and mythology of contemporary Hinduism. The material contained within them is much better known to the average Hindu than the contents of the ***Vedas***. Rituals such as **pūjā** and the representations of deities in the forms in which they are depicted in **mūrtis** are based on accounts given in these texts. Whereas the deities of the *Vedas* are not as prominent in contemporary Hinduism as they were in ancient times, the deities that are the focus of the *Purāṇas* have been central to Hindu traditions for over 2,000 years. The 18 major *Purāṇas* are divided into three collections that are made up of six texts each. Each collection is dedicated primarily to one of the three main deities at the basis of the three main theistic traditions—Viṣṇu, Śiva, and Devī, or **Śakti**. There are a variety of minor *Purāṇas* in addition to the major ones. The *Purāṇas* include many genealogical lists that connect royal families and **Brahmanical** lineages to heroes and sages of the ancient past. The *Purāṇas* form a substantial part of the **smṛti literature**, the category of Hindu **scripture** whose sanctity is derivative from that of the **śrūti**—the *Vedas*.

PURI. City on the coast of the eastern Indian state of **Orissa**. Location of the **Vaiṣṇava temple** of **Jagannātha**.

PUROHITA. Priest; traditionally a **Brahmin**; the main officiating priest of any Hindu ritual.

PURŪRAVAS. Ancient king; character of a story, first mentioned in the ***Ṛg Veda*** and later elaborated upon in the ***Brāhmaṇas*** and the ***Mahābhārata***, and finally in a famous play by the renowned **Sanskrit poet** and playwright **Kālīdāsa** (the *Vikramorvaśī*). In the story, Purūravas falls in love with a celestial maiden (**apsaras**) named **Urvaśī** and asks to marry her. She agrees, on the condition that he protect her rams from being stolen and he never lets her see him naked. They live together happily for many years until a group of mischievous **gandharvas** steals one of Urvaśī's rams in the middle of the night. Hearing the commotion, Purūravas leaps naked out of bed to save the ram. The gandharvas flash a bright light on him, revealing his naked form to Urvaśī, and make off with the ram. At this, Urvaśī returns to the heavens.

PURUṢA. "The person"; "the man"; the primordial being whose body is dismembered in a famous chapter of the ***Ṛg Veda***—the ***Puruṣa Sūkta***, or "Hymn of the Cosmic Man"—in order to form the universe. The various parts of this being's body become the various phenomena that make up the cosmos—his eye becoming the sun, his **mind** becoming the **moon**, and so on. The **varṇas**, or four main **castes**, are also formed from various parts of his body. He is identified in later **Vedic literature** with **Nārāyaṇa**, who is subsequently identified with **Viṣṇu**, whose body is identified with the cosmos in the **Viśiṣṭādvaita Vedānta** of **Rāmāṇuja**. In fact, the idea of the universe as coming from the body of a single cosmic being anticipates the later Vedāntic themes of the unity of all existence and of **God** dwelling within all beings.

Also, in **Sāṃkhya philosophy**, puruṣa is the term used for the **soul**, understood as pure consciousness, and contrasted with the realm of matter, or **prakṛti**. The goal of Sāṃkhya and the related system of **Yoga** is for puruṣa to realize its nature as pure spirit and disentangle itself from prakṛti, with which it has become falsely identified.

PURUṢA SŪKTA. Chapter of the ***Ṛg Veda*** that depicts the **creation** of the universe by means of the primordial self-sacrifice of a being—the **puruṣa**, or cosmic man—whose body becomes the basis of all that exists. According to this text, only one fourth of the body of the cosmic man become the visible, physical universe. The other three fourths become the spiritual world. The text establishes a set of correspondences between various parts of the body of the cosmic man and elements of the physical world. This text is probably best known for drawing correspondences between parts of the cosmic man and the four main **varṇas** or **castes**: the **Brahmin** caste corresponds to the head of the cosmic man, the **Kṣatriya** or warrior caste to the cosmic man's arms, the **Vaiśyas** or common people to his stomach, and the **Śūdra** or servant caste to his feet. This is the earliest reference to the varṇa system in the **Vedic literature**.

PURUṢĀRTHA. The four goals of humanity; physical or sensory pleasure (**kāma**), wealth (**artha**), virtue (**dharma**), and **liberation** from the cycle of rebirth (**mokṣa**). Each successive goal is regarded as superior to (because it is more enduring than) the one prior to it. The first three are regarded as "worldly" (*laukika*) goals and mokṣa is regarded as a transcendental or "otherworldly" (*alaukika*) goal. The worldly goals are appropriate to people in the first three of the four stages of life or **āśramas**—that is, the celibate student (**brahmacarya**), the householder (**gārhasthya**), and the retired, "forest-dwelling" (**vanaprastha**) stage. The fourth goal is pursued by renouncers (**sannyāsins**). This, at least, is the classical Hindu model of society, as found in the legal texts, or ***Dharma Śāstras***. In **Tantric** and **bhakti**-oriented Hindu traditions, a householder can also aspire to mokṣa by performing the correct rituals and **meditations** (the Tantric path) or cultivating devotion to **God** (bhakti).

PURUṢOTTAMA. Supreme person; **God**; the Supreme Being; an epithet of **Kṛṣṇa** in the ***Bhagavad Gītā*** and in subsequent **Vaiṣṇava** traditions; God, or **Īśvara**, in the ***Yoga Sūtra*** of **Patañjali**, not identified with any specific Hindu deity.

PŪRVA MĪMĀṂSĀ. The "earlier exegesis." The term *Pūrva Mīmāṃsā* contrasts this system of thought with the later, or **Uttara Mīmāṃsā**—more widely known as **Vedānta**. Pūrva Mīmāṃsā focuses upon the earlier, ritualistic portion of the ***Vedas***, while Vedānta interprets the later **Vedic** texts—the ***Upaniṣads***—and their teaching of **Brahman**. *See also* MĪMĀṂSĀ.

PŪRVAMĪMĀṂSĀ SŪTRA. Root text of the **Mīmāṃsā** or **Uttara Mīmāṃsā darśana**, or system of philosophy; attributed to **Jaimini** and likely composed around 300 BCE.

PŪRVAPAKṢA. "Prior view," the point of view of the opponent in classical Indian philosophical texts. After this view is refuted, the final or "perfected view" (**siddhānta**) of the author is presented.

PŪṢAN. "Nourisher"; **Vedic** deity; one of the 12 **Ādityas**; guardian of animals and human beings and ensurer of prosperity; identified in some sources as an earth **god**.

PUṢKARA. "Blue Lotus"; site in **Rajasthan** of one of the handful of **temples** in India devoted to **Brahmā**; believed to be a highly meritorious site of **pilgrimage**.

Q

QUALIFIED NONDUALISM. Metaphysical teaching of the **Viśiṣṭādvaita** system of **Vedānta** developed by the Vedāntic **ācārya Rāmāṇuja**. According to this view, all of reality is, as **Advaita Vedānta** teaches, one with **Brahman**. But unlike in the Advaitic concept of Brahman, Brahman is here conceived as having internal differences. The idea of Brahman with which this system operates is one of organic unity, rather than the pure, undifferentiated unity taught by Advaita Vedānta. Brahman, in this system, is the totality of being, including within itself differentiated beings such as **God**, souls (**jīvas**), and the world (**jagat**).

QUALITIES. *See* GUṆAS.

R

RĀDHĀ. Foremost of the **gopīs**, or cowherdesses with whom **Kṛṣṇa** spent his youth, as recounted in the ***Bhāgavata Purāṇa***. The intense love between Kṛṣṇa and Rādhā is the ideal of **bhakti**, or devotion. The fact that Rādhā, who was married to another man, still loves Kṛṣṇa against all social conventions and norms, rather than being condemned in the **Vaiṣṇava** traditions, is upheld as a model of devotion to **God**—a love that is spontaneous and dismissive of all other concerns. The longing of Rādhā for Kṛṣṇa during his absence is also a model for the longing of the soul for God until the dawning of **God-realization** and God-consciousness. In Hindu iconography, Rādhā and Kṛṣṇa are frequently paired as a divine couple, symbolizing the loving bond between God and the **soul**. The story of the love affair of Rādhā and Kṛṣṇa is narrated in the vivid, erotically charged **poetry** of **Jayadeva** in his ***Gītagovinda***, or "Song of the Cowherd."

RADHAKRISHNAN, SIR SARVEPALLI (1888–1975). Indian philosopher; diplomat; vice president of India from 1952 to 1962 and president from 1962 to 1967; translator of many **Sanskrit** texts and major exponent of **Neo-Vedānta**.

RĀDHĀSOĀMĪ SATSANG. "Holy Fellowship of Rādhā's Master"; Hindu movement started in 1861 by **Swāmī Shiv Dayal Singh** (1818–1878). This movement currently has both Indian and Western adherents. Having a close continuity with the teachings of the **Sant** movement and **Sikhism**, the central emphasis is the relationship between disciple and **guru**, who is the intermediary of the liberating love of **God**. There is also a strong emphasis on morality, **vegetarianism**, and the practice of **meditation**.

RAGHAVAN, V. (1908–1990). Indologist; born in **Tamil** Nadu and professor for many years of **Sanskrit** at **Madras** University; author of many works on Sanskrit **literature** and drama.

RĀHU. One of the **navagrahas**; companion of **Ketu**. Rāhu was an **asura** who managed to steal a drop of the **amṛta**, or elixir of **immortality**, when the **devas** and asuras churned it from the cosmic ocean. Alerted to this fact by the sun and the **moon, Viṣṇu** beheaded Rāhu and placed his head in the sky. The rest of Rāhu's body became a separate entity, Ketu, also placed in the sky. The two of them periodically take their vengeance on the sun and the moon by swallowing them, causing solar and lunar eclipses. Rāhu appears as a demonic, decapitated head floating in the sky. Both are considered inauspicious in Hindu **astrology**.

RAI, LALA LAJPAT (1865–1928). Martyr of the Indian independence movement; born in the Punjab. Rai founded the pro-independence journal *Young India* in 1915 and was its editor and its publisher until 1919, when **Mohandās K. Gāndhī** assumed these roles. Rai died in 1928 due to injuries suffered during a protest march in Lahore.

RĀJ. "Reign"; popular term for the period of British rule of India, which began around the middle of the 18th century, with the increasing ascendancy of the **British East India Company**, and ended with the official independence of India and Pakistan on the 15 August 1947. The British presence in India began as early as 1600, initially for the purpose of trade. This presence was gradually expanded until, by the mid-1800s, the British controlled most of India's coasts. After the Sepoy Mutiny of 1857, known in India as the First War of Independence, the British crown assumed direct control of the British East India Company's holdings and most of India came under the rule of Queen Victoria. At this time, opposition to British domination of India began to spread among English-educated, middle-class Indians, encouraged by Western members of the **Theosophical Society**. This led to the founding of the Indian National Congress in 1885. In the early 20th century, the independence movement greatly expanded in popularity under the leadership of **Mohandās K. Gāndhī**, finally achieving its goal in 1947. Gāndhī's strategy of nonviolent noncooperation made it possible for ordinary Indians to participate in a movement that had been limited to political leaders or those willing to take up arms. The movement was not able to prevent the partition of India and Pakistan along religious lines when British rule ended.

RAJAS. Dynamism; the second of the three **guṇas** or qualities of phenomenal existence as delineated in the **philosophies** of **Sāṃkhya** and **Yoga** as well as in the ***Bhagavad Gītā***.

RAJASTHAN. Largely desert state in northwestern India; home to such famous Hindu pilgrimage sites as **Nāthdwāra**, which is dedicated to **Kṛṣṇa**, and **Puṣkara**, dedicated to **Brahmā**; also the location of many Jain **temples** and home to a relatively large number of Jains. One of the most prominent **Jain**

temples is located in this state, on Mount Abu. Mount Abu is also home to the world headquarters of the **Brahmā Kumārīs**. Known for its martial culture, Rajasthan is probably most famous as the home of the **Rajputs**. The 16th-century **Vaiṣṇava** saint and **bhakti poet Mīrā Bai** hailed from Rajasthan.

RĀJASŪYA. Vedic sacrifice or **yajña** that ensures the future success of a king. The rājasūya of **Yudhiṣṭhira** is depicted in the second book of the ***Mahābhārata***, the *Sabhā Parvan* ("Book of the Meeting Hall").

RAJNEESH, BHAGWAN (RĀJANĪṢA, BHAGAVĀN) (1931–1990). Guru who led a modern Hindu movement with a mainly Western following. His eclectic teachings drew upon a variety of traditions, Hindu and non-Hindu, particularly **Tantra**. Having a strong emphasis on sexual freedom as a way to spiritual **liberation**, the movement's practices are quite close to the Vāmācāra or **Left-Handed** Tantric practice, which seeks to embody the ideal of nondualism (**advaita**) by overcoming traditional taboos regarding impurity and purity on the understanding that all is **One**. Such taboos are therefore arbitrary. In the early 1980s, Rajneesh and many of his disciples settled in the United States near the town of Antelope, Oregon. But in 1985, Rajneesh was deported back to India for immigration fraud. Returning to his home in **Pune**, Rajneesh reestablished his community there. In 1989, he changed his name to **Osho**, a Japanese term for a high-ranking **Buddhist** priest. Rajneesh was born Candra Mohan **Jain**.

RAJPUTS. Large community of **kṣatriya** or warrior clans based in **Rajasthan**. Arising around the sixth century of the Common Era, Rajput kingdoms were prominent in many parts of northwestern India, but primarily in the region now known as Rajasthan. Their name—*Rajput*—is derived from the **Sanskrit** *rājaputra*, or "sons of kings." Many Rajput clans fought quite ferociously against Turkish and **Mughal** invaders in the early medieval period, but some allied with the Mughal Empire. It is likely that the practice of **satī**, in which a widow immolates herself on the funeral pyre of her deceased husband, began in this community. According to the Rajputs' own lore, on hearing that their husbands had fallen in battle against invaders, many of the Rajput women immolated themselves rather than be captured or raped by the enemy. Eventually, this became an expected display of **devotion** in Rajput families. The practice was transmitted to **Bengal** when a number of Rajput clans transplanted themselves to that region. It was banned by the British in 1829 due to the efforts of the Bengali Hindu reformer **Rām Mohan Roy** and soon ceased to be practiced on a large scale (and had, in any case, been largely confined to the upper **castes** in Bengal and Rajasthan). But occasional exceptions have occurred in subsequent history, the last satī having taken place at Deorala, in Rajasthan, in 1987. This event was protested by many Hindus, including **Swāmī Agniveśa**.

RAKHI, RAKṢABANDHAN. Hindu and **Sikh** festival held on the **Pūrṇimā** (or full-**moon** day) of the month of **Śravaṇa** (July–August). Celebrated mainly in northern India, the observance of the festival involves **women** tying a **sacred thread** on the right wrists of their brothers. A woman can also perform this ritual on a man who is not her relative in order to make him her brother in a formal sense. This ritual can thus sanctify the platonic friendship between a man and a woman.

RĀKṢASA. Monster; demonic creature, often depicted as having a semi-human, semi-bestial form and as being of great size and strength. Rākṣasas can also change their shape for a limited period of time in order to deceive human beings. They are represented in Hindu texts as creatures of chaos, delighting in disrupting the **yajñas**, or sacrifices, of the sages who have withdrawn to the forest. They also have a taste for human flesh. They are the primary enemies of **Rāma** in the ***Rāmāyaṇa***. Their king, **Rāvaṇa**, abducts **Sītā**, Rāma's wife, whom Rāma must then rescue. There are also, however, "good" rākṣasas, such as Rāvaṇa's cousin **Vibhīṣana**, who is a devotee of **Viṣṇu** and betrays Rāvaṇa after failing to persuade him to release Sītā, joining Rāma's army as a military advisor against his fellow rākṣasas. In the ***Mahābhārata***, **Bhīma** has an affair with a female rākṣasa and fathers the massive human-rākṣasa hybrid Ghaṭotkaca, who assists the **Pāṇḍavas** in their battle with the **Kauravas**.

RAKTABĪJA. "Blood seed"; demon slain by **Kālī**. Each drop of Raktabīja's blood that spilled on the ground would transform into a completely new Raktabīja. Spilling this demon's blood in battle therefore served only to create an entire army of Raktabījas. It is for this reason that Kālī used her tongue to catch or lick up every drop of blood of this demon that was spilled in the course of her battle with him. This is why this **goddess** is depicted with a long, bloody tongue sticking out of her mouth.

RĀM. Hindi pronunciation of **Rāma**. *See* RĀMA.

RĀM CARIT MĀNAS. "Lake of the Deeds of Rāma"; highly popular rendering of the ***Rāmāyaṇa*** in medieval **Hindi**; composed by the **Vaiṣṇava** devotee and **bhakti poet Tulsīdās** (1532–1623). The text is so popular, even being frequently quoted by ordinary devotees, that it is safe to say that it is this version of the text, rather than the **Sanskrit** original, that is better known by most Hindus, particularly in northern India. The popular Hindi television serialization of the *Rāmāyaṇa* ("*Rāmāyaṇ*") is based upon the *Rām Carit Mānas*.

During the festival of **Rāmnavamī**, it is not uncommon for 24-hour nonstop readings of this text to be held in Hindu **temples**, with devotees taking turns reciting the verses in a call-and-response fashion.

RĀMA. Along with **Kṛṣṇa**, one of the most popular of the **avatāras**, or incarnations, of **Viṣṇu**; the seventh such incarnation, according to the traditional list of 10; prince of the kingdom of **Ayodhyā** and son of its king, Daśaratha. Rāma's biography forms the central narrative of one of the two Hindu epics, or **itihāsas**—the ***Rāmāyaṇa*** (the other epic being the ***Mahābhārata***). At the beginning of the *Rāmāyaṇa*, the **gods** approach Viṣṇu for help because the Earth has fallen under the oppression of **Rāvaṇa**, the powerful lord of the **rākṣasas**. Due to a boon that he has received, Rāvaṇa cannot be harmed by any type of creature except one: a human being. Viṣṇu therefore takes the form of Rāma in order to bring about Rāvaṇa's destruction. In his human form as Rāma, however, Viṣṇu remains unaware of his true divine nature and mission. Both of these are only gradually revealed in the course of the narrative. Rāma is trained in the arts of combat against rākṣasas by the sage **Viśvamitra**. He also wins the hand in marriage of Princess **Sītā**, daughter of the wise sage King **Janaka**. Prepared to inherit his father's throne, Rāma is abruptly sent into exile by his father at the instigation of Kaikeyī. Kaikeyī, one of the three wives of Daśaratha (and not Rāma's mother), fearing that her own son, **Bharata**, will be in danger as a potential rival under Rāma's rule, forces Daśaratha to order Rāma's exile and her own son's installation as king by invoking a promise of any two boons that Daśaratha had made to her in the past, when she had saved his life on the field of battle. Rāma accepts his father's command and willingly goes into exile, accompanied by Sītā (who is really an incarnation of the **goddess Lakṣmī**) and his brother **Lakṣmaṇa** (an incarnation of the cosmic serpent, **Śeṣa**). Daśaratha dies of sorrow at having to exile his beloved son to the forest, and Bharata, Rāma's half-brother, curses his mother for causing so much distress in the family (there actually being no rivalry between Bharata and Rāma). While in exile, Rāma, Sītā, and Lakṣmaṇa live as **ascetics** in the forest. During this period, Rāvaṇa takes Sītā captive and imprisons her in his island kingdom of **Laṅka**. Rāma and Lakṣmaṇa, with the assistance of **Hanuman** and a great army of monkeys, eagles, and other assorted animals, build a bridge to Laṅka and successfully rescue Sītā, slaying Rāvaṇa and many other rākṣasas in the process. Rāma rules Ayodhyā for many years afterward, a period of peace and prosperity known as the *Rāma Rājya*, or kingship of Rāma. The ideal of the Rāma Rājya is invoked even today by many Hindus—particularly **Hindu Nationalists**—as an image of the ideal society.

In December 1992, Ayodhyā—which is an actual town in northern India—became a center of controversy when a group of Hindu Nationalists demolished a mosque called the **Babrī Masjīd** (Babur's Mosque), which they believed had been built from the remains of a **temple** on the location marking the exact spot of Rāma's birth (*Rāma-janma-bhūmī*)—a claim contested by some historians and archaeologists. This demolition sparked riots in India, Pakistan, and Bangladesh between Hindus and Muslims, in which many members of both communities were killed, and a number of Hindu temples destroyed in retaliation. In September 2010, an Indian high court ruled that the property should be divided among Hindu and Muslim organizations, a compromise that appears to have defused the issue, at least for the time being.

Politics aside, Rāma is one of the most popular of Hindu deities, and was in fact the **iṣṭadevatā**, or favorite deity, of **Mohandās K. Gāndhī**, who invoked the name of Rāma at the moment of his **death** at the hands of an assassin. According to traditional **Vaiṣṇava** belief, one who calls upon Viṣṇu at the time of death is guaranteed salvation.

RAMAKRISHNA (RĀMAKṚṢṆA) (1836–1886). Bengali spiritual teacher and chief inspiration behind the **Ramakrishna Mission** and **Ramakrishna Order**, as well as the **Neo-Vedānta** interpretation of Hinduism. Born Gangadhar Chattopadhyay, Ramakrishna would very likely, in an earlier period of Hindu history, have been regarded as a **bhakti** saint in the tradition of the **Mother Goddess**. His spiritual eclecticism, however, which coincided with the intellectual crisis and subsequent reforms of Hinduism in 19th-century Bengal, became the catalyst for a radical reinterpretation and reinvigoration of Hindu thought and practice, particularly through the activities of his prominent disciple **Swāmī Vivekānanda** (1863–1902).

Ramakrishna was born and raised in a poor **Brahmin** family in Kamarpukur, a village in rural Bengal. From an early age, he was prone to ecstatic visions and states of trance, which he identified with the experience of **samādhi**, or **meditative** absorption. At times, these states were induced by songs or spiritual conversation. But sometimes they would be brought on by natural phenomena, such as his first recorded samādhi when, as a small boy, he saw a flight of white geese against the background of a dark storm cloud, the beauty of which overwhelmed him.

When Ramakrishna was 19 years old, his older brother, Rāmkumar, became the priest at a **temple** to the **goddess Kālī** in Dakṣineśwar, near **Calcutta**. Ramakrishna replaced Rāmkumar in this role the following year, due to Rāmkumar's premature **death**. Soon, Ramakrishna became deeply immersed in devotion to Kālī, claiming to have had a powerful vision of this goddess in the process of performing her worship. Subsequently, he similarly immersed himself in worship of various deities, such as **Śiva**, **Rāma**, and **Kṛṣṇa**, eventually reaching a state of complete absorption in each deity in succession.

Having experienced the height of spiritual attainment in the various theistic forms of Hinduism, he devoted himself with the same intensity to the realization of impersonal, or formless (**Nirguṇa**) **Brahman**, having this experience under the guidance of a monk of the **Daśanāmī Order** named Toṭapuri. He then practiced both **Islam** and **Christianity**, devoting himself to each practice until it culminated in samādhi. Because of all of these experiences, Ramakrishna concluded that all the religions are paths to **God-realization**, a view that has become a cornerstone of **Neo-Vedānta** philosophy.

At the age of 23, Ramakrishna married Saradamaṇi Mukhopadhyāya, later known as **Saradā Devī** and the **Holy Mother** to Ramakrishna's disciples. Ramakrishna believed his wife to be a manifestation of the **Mother Goddess**. After his death, she became the informal leader of the movement based on his teachings.

In his later years, Ramakrishna attracted the attention of the middle-class, English-educated intelligentsia of Calcutta, including prominent members of the **Brahmo Samāj**, such as **Keshub Chunder Sen** (1838–1884). Many young men were also drawn to his teaching and personality, becoming **sannyāsins** in the Daśanāmī Order after his death in 1886 and establishing the **Ramakrishna Order**.

A part of the fascination that Ramakrishna held for educated Bengalis was his insistence on direct experience as the foundation of all spiritual teaching—a teaching very much in keeping with the modern focus upon experience and reason over blind faith in **scripture**. This experimental approach to religion was combined, paradoxically, with his endorsement, on the basis of his experience, of very traditional Hindu beliefs and styles of worship, a good deal of which had been condemned by the Brahmo Samāj as anti-rational and idolatrous. He thus allowed English-educated Hindus to reappropriate their older traditions, but with a new rationale.

RAMAKRISHNA MISSION. Organization devoted primarily to education and charity; known outside of India as the **Vedānta Society**; the religious institution built upon the teachings of **Ramakrishna** by his disciples—including his wife, **Saradā Devī**, and their successors. The Ramakrishna Mission was established by **Swāmī Vivekānanda** in 1897. *See also* NEO-VEDĀNTA; VEDĀNTA.

RAMAKRISHNA ORDER. Order of monks established by **Swāmī Vivekānanda** after the **death** of **Ramakrishna** in 1886. The first generation of monks was made up of immediate disciples of Ramakrishna. Vivekānanda and his fellow monks took their monastic vows within the **Daśanāmī Order**, established by **Śaṅkara** in the ninth century of the Common Era. The monks of the new order quickly differentiated themselves from more traditional

Hindu **sannyāsins**, or renouncers, by engaging in relief work among the poor—an activity which, along with education, constitutes a large portion of the activity of the order. Derided by traditionalists as "scavenger monks," the monks persisted in their work, following Vivekānanda's philosophy that the **yoga** of good works (**karma yoga**) is as valid a part of the path to **God-realization** as the more traditional paths (for monks) of study (**jñāna yoga**) and **meditation** (**dhyāna yoga**). This order was also the first Hindu monastic order to accept Western members when Swāmī Vivekānanda initiated an Irish **woman**, Margaret E. Noble (**Sister Niveditā**) as a nun. There are now many Westerners in the Ramakrishna Order, though the order remains predominantly Indian. *See also* NEO-VEDĀNTA; VEDĀNTA.

RAMAKRISHNA VEDĀNTA. That branch of the otherwise unstructured and informal **Neo-Vedānta** movement that explicitly sees itself to be in continuity with the teachings and **Ramakrishna, Swāmī Vivekānanda, Holy Mother Saradā Devī**, and the monks of the **Ramakrishna Order**.

RAMAṆA MAHARṢI (1879–1950). Modern Hindu spiritual teacher. He was born near **Madurai** in **Tamil** Nadu. His father died when he was 12 years old, after which his family moved to Madurai and enrolled him in an English-medium missionary school. At the age of 17, he had a powerful spiritual experience that prompted him to adopt the life of a **sannyāsin**. He eventually settled at the mountain **temple** of Aruṇācala, in the northern part of Tamil Nadu, where he remained until his **death** in 1950. His reputation for holiness and profound wisdom spread rapidly and many pilgrims visited him at his Aruṇācala retreat, which continues to be regarded as a holy site, due to his presence there. He is best known for asking many of his visitors, "Who are you?" thereby directing them to a process of self-enquiry intended to lead to the realization of the true nature of the self or **ātman**. Though not **Advaita Vedānta** in a formal sense, Ramaṇa's teaching can well be characterized as a modern form of Advaita, based not so much on **scriptural** enquiry (like the classical Advaita of **Śaṅkara**) as on direct enquiry into the self. It is therefore akin to **Neo-Vedānta** in taking direct experience as its basis. There are also affinities between Ramaṇa's method and that of **Jiddu Krishnamurti**.

RĀMĀNANDA (fl. c. 14th–15th centuries CE). Vaiṣṇava saint and **ascetic**; born in **Prayāga** (**Allahabad**). Rāmānanda was first affiliated to the **Śrīvaiṣṇava** tradition, holding a high position in its institutional hierarchy, but left this tradition in protest against its concern for **caste**-related practices and restrictions. He established the **Rāmānandi saṃpradāya**, which teaches that all are equal before **God**. Winning a large following among common people of his time, he is believed to have influenced such major figures of the

bhakti and **Sant** movements as **Mīrā Bai** (who claimed to be his disciple), **Kabīr**, and **Guru Nānak**.

RĀMĀNANDI SAṂPRADĀYA. The "sect or denomination of those whose bliss is Rāma." **Vaiṣṇava** tradition focused on **bhakti**, or devotion, to **Rāma** and established by **Rāmānanda** for the common person, as a protest against the **casteism** practiced in his time by the **Śrīvaiṣṇava** tradition from which he came. Rāmānanda deliberately taught in **Hindi**, the vernacular language of northern India, rather than the more elite **Sanskrit**, developing a large following in the process and influencing many other figures, such as **Mīrā Bai**, **Kabīr**, and **Guru Nānak** with his spiritual egalitarianism. Membership in the Rāmānandi saṃpradāya is open to all, regardless of caste. The primary **scripture** of this movement is the ***Rām Carit Manas*** of **Tulsīdās**—a popular version of the ***Rāmāyaṇa*** that is better known among the masses than the original Sanskrit version by **Vālmīki**.

RĀMĀṆUJA (1077–1157). Vedāntic **ācārya** and theologian of the **Śrīvaiṣṇava** system of **Vaiṣṇavism**; from **Tamil** Nadu. The dominant form of **Vedānta** in southern India at the time of Rāmāṇuja was the **Advaita Vedānta** of **Śaṅkara**, which affirms that the true nature of **Brahman** is ultimately impersonal and formless (**nirguṇa**). **Bhakti**—devotion to a personal form of divinity—while commended as a purifying practice that diminishes the hold of the ego through the process of worship, is seen as a preparatory discipline that readies one for **jñāna**, the liberating knowledge that the self (**ātman**) and Brahman are **One**. The personal deity (**Īśvara**) is ultimately an illusion, a product of the same **māyā** that creates the differentiation between the self and the absolute.

Troubled by this teaching in part due to the undermining of devotion and spiritual arrogance that he felt it could evoke if not understood properly, Rāmāṇuja dedicated his life to the reinstatement of bhakti as the central mode of relating to the divine. He took the informal **Vaiṣṇava** devotional tradition of the **Āḷvārs** and organized it into a system of worship and theological reflection. This system—the Śrīvaiṣṇava system—continues to be highly popular among Hindus today, particularly in the southern part of India, where Vaiṣṇava **temples** and their images (**mūrtis**) are constructed, consecrated, and utilized by Rāmāṇuja's precise specifications. It is a system that integrates "high" **Sanskrit** culture with the popular devotionalism of the bhakti **poets**, with the vernacular songs and prayers of the Āḷvārs regarded as a "fifth **Veda**" and recited in Śrīvaiṣṇava temples and services.

Śrīvaiṣṇava theology places high importance on **Śrī**, or **Lakṣmī**, the consort of **Viṣṇu**, who is regarded as his **śakti** and a personification of his divine grace. The divine pair of Viṣṇu and Lakṣmī is regarded as one deity, similar to **Śiva** and Śakti.

In terms of Vedānta, Rāmāṇuja characterizes his philosophy as **Viśiṣṭādvaita**, or **Qualified Nondualism**. According to this view, all of reality is, as the Advaita Vedānta of Śaṅkara teaches, one with **Brahman**. But unlike in the Advaitic concept of Brahman, Brahman is conceived as having internal differences. The idea of Brahman with which this system operates is one of organic unity, rather than the pure, undifferentiated unity taught by Advaita Vedānta. Brahman, in this system, is the totality of being, including within itself differentiated beings such as God, souls (**jīvas**), and the world (**jagat**), and bhakti is seen as the one true path to **God-realization**.

RAMANUJAN, A. K. (1929–1993). Scholar and author; born in **Karnataka**, in the city of Mysore. Ramanujan was a person of many talents—a **poet**, playwright, translator, and collector of folklore. Among his better-known works in the field of **Indology** are his translations of the **bhakti** poetry of **Basava** (entitled *Speaking of Śiva*) and **Nammāḷvār** (entitled *Hymns for the Drowning*) and his collection of Indian folk tales (*Folk Tales of India*). Ramanujan taught at the University of Chicago from 1983 until his **death** in 1993.

RĀMĀYAṆA*.** "Life of **Rāma**"; along with the ***Mahābhārata, one of the two main epics or **itihāsas** (historical tales) of Hinduism; attributed to the sage **Vālmīki** but very likely a result of many centuries of compilation and refinement by many different hands. In its current form, the text can be traced to the period between 200 BCE and 200 CE. Though the events in the text precede those of the *Mahābhārata* in Hindu tradition, most scholars suspect that the *Mahābhārata* is the older of the two texts, at least in their current forms.

At the beginning of the *Rāmāyaṇa*, the **gods** approach **Viṣṇu** for help because the Earth has fallen under the oppression of **Rāvaṇa**, the powerful lord of the **rākṣasas**. Due to a boon that he has received, Rāvaṇa cannot be harmed by any type of creature except one: a human being. Viṣṇu therefore takes the form of Rāma—prince of **Ayodhyā** and son of the king, **Daśaratha**—to bring about Rāvaṇa's destruction. While in his human form as Rāma, however, Viṣṇu remains unaware of his true divine nature and mission. Both of these are only gradually revealed in the course of the narrative. Later interpretations suggest that this is a metaphor for the gradual process by which all beings realize the presence of the divine within them.

In his youth—and over his father's objections—Rāma is trained in the art of combat against rākṣasas by the sage **Viśvamitra**. At the end of a lengthy stay in the wilderness with his **guru**, Rāma wins the hand in marriage of Princess **Sītā**, daughter of the wise sage King **Janaka**. He does this through a contest of arms in which the challenge is to string the bow of **Śiva**—a nearly impossible task that only Rāma can complete.

Later, having returned to Ayodhyā prepared to inherit his father's throne, Rāma is abruptly sent into exile by his father at the instigation of Kaikeyī. Kaikeyī, one of the three wives of Daśaratha (and not Rāma's mother)—fearing that her own son, **Bharata**, will be in danger as a potential rival under Rāma's rule—forces Daśaratha to order Rāma's exile and her own son's installation as king by invoking a promise of any two boons that Daśaratha had made to her in the past, when she had saved his life on the field of battle by taking his unconscious body to safety.

Rāma dutifully accepts his father's order and goes into exile, accompanied by Sītā (who is really an incarnation of the **goddess Lakṣmī**) and his brother **Lakṣmaṇa** (an incarnation of the cosmic serpent, **Śeṣa**). Daśaratha dies of sorrow at having to exile his beloved son to the forest, and Bharata, Rāma's half-brother, curses his mother for causing so much distress in the family (there actually being no rivalry between Bharata and Rāma).

While in exile, Rāma, Sītā, and Lakṣmaṇa live as **ascetics** in the forest. During this period, Rāvaṇa takes Sītā captive and imprisons her in his island kingdom of **Laṅka**. Rāma and Lakṣmaṇa, with the assistance of **Hanuman** and an army of monkeys, eagles, and other assorted animals, build a bridge to Laṅka and successfully rescue Sītā, slaying Rāvaṇa and many other rākṣasas in the process. In one of the more controversial scenes in the epic, Rāma does not immediately accept Sītā back as his wife, insisting that she first prove that she did not betray him with Rāvaṇa by forcing her to undergo a test of fire (which she passes). (The justification given for this is that, as king, Rāma must maintain an appearance of propriety for his subjects.) Rāma rules Ayodhyā for many years, in a period of peace and prosperity known as the *Rāma Rājya*, or kingship of Rāma.

Religiously, the *Rāmāyaṇa* has become especially significant to the **Vaiṣṇava** traditions of Hinduism, particularly in its popular **Hindi** rendition, the ***Rām Carit Manas***, by the medieval **bhakti poet Tulsīdās** (1532–1623).

Like the *Mahābhārata*, the *Rāmāyaṇa* has been a major subject of Hindu **art** and **literature** throughout the centuries. Plays are based on it, or on select episodes within it. Depictions of the scenes from the text adorn **temple** walls throughout India and Southeast Asia. In the modern period, it has become a popular Hindi television series.

RAMEŚVARAM (RAMESHWARAM). Site in **Tamil** Nadu where Rāmanāthaswāmy **temple** is housed. The temple is sacred to both **Vaiṣṇavas** and **Śaivas**, marking the spot where **Rāma** worshiped **Śiva** in gratitude after defeating **Rāvaṇa** and rescuing **Sītā**. *See also RĀMĀYAṆA*.

RĀMLĪLĀ. "Play of **Rāma**"; a northern Indian tradition of reenacting the ***Rāmāyaṇa*** during the 10-day festival of **Daśahrā** (or Dussehra), which is celebrated in the **bright half** of the month of **Āśvina**. In northern India, this festival celebrates **Rāma**'s victory over **Rāvaṇa** and it culminates in **Dīpāvali** (or Dīwali), the festival of lights in honor of the **goddess Lakṣmī**. The Rāmlīlā is an extremely popular part of the observance of this festival. Enactments range from purely local productions, put together by neighborhood associations, to massive, lavish programs with sophisticated lighting and special effects. The climactic moment is the defeat of Rāvaṇa, which is often accompanied by fireworks and other pyrotechnics.

RĀMNĀMI SAMĀJ. Vaiṣṇava devotional tradition based in the rural central Indian state of Chattisgarh and made up almost entirely of persons from lower **castes** (**Harijans** or **Dalits**). The group's scripture is the ***Rām Carit Manas*** of **Tulsīdās**.

RĀM NAVAMĪ. Festival of **Rāma**'s birth; held on the ninth day of the **bright half** of the month of **Chaitra** (March–April). During this festival, it is not uncommon for 24-hour nonstop readings of the ***Rām Carit Manas*** of **Tulsīdās** to be held in Hindu **temples**, with devotees taking turns reciting the verses in a call-and-response fashion. To have **darśana** of a **mūrti** (a sight of an image, usually in a temple) of Rāma is particularly auspicious on this day.

RĀMPRASĀD (1718–1775). "Grace of **Rāma**." Despite his name, Rāmprasād was a **bhakti poet** devoted completely to the **Divine Mother** or **Mother Goddess**. He is best known for composing many passionate hymns in her honor in which he presents himself as her ungrateful and petulant child. These deeply personal hymns were particularly dear to **Ramakrishna**, another famous devotee of the Divine Mother, who popularized them. *See also* ŚĀKTA.

RASA. Taste, flavor, the sense of taste; also, aesthetic experience of any kind. Rasa has been theorized extensively by Hindu philosophers, most prominently in the ***Nāṭya Śāstra*** of **Bharata**—the authoritative manual of classical Hindu drama and **dance**—as well as by the 10th-century **Kaśmīr Śaiva** philosopher **Abhinavagupta** and the medieval **Vaiṣṇava Gosvāmins**. Abhinavagupta, reflecting a **Tantric** sensibility, likens aesthetic experience to the experience of **God-realization**, seeing it as a foretaste of the bliss of realizing unity with **Śiva**. The Gosvāmins—the Vaiṣṇava theologians established by **Caitanya** in the 16th century—take this a step further, claiming that the rasa experienced specifically when one is enjoying the stories of **Kṛṣṇa** and his love for the **gopīs** of **Vṛndāvana** as narrated in the ***Bhāgavata Purāṇa*** could evoke the saving experience of **bhakti**.

RĀṢṬRĪYA SVAYAMSEVAK SAṄGH (RSS). "National Volunteer Association"; a **Hindu Nationalist** organization that was started in 1925, during the Indian independence movement, by K. V. Hedgewar (1890–1940). A controversial organization due to its anti-Muslim rhetoric, the RSS violently opposed the partition of India and Pakistan, blaming **Mohandās K. Gāndhī** for allowing it to occur. Gāndhī's assassin, Nathuram Godse, was a member of this organization. The RSS has advocated transforming India into a Hindu state and denying Indian citizenship to Muslims, **Christians**, and communists. As one of the more radical Hindu Nationalist organizations, its ties to the **BJP** or **Bharatīya Janata Party** have drawn criticism to that political party.

RĀVAṆA. Chief villain of the ***Rāmāyaṇa***; lord of the chaotic evil **rākṣasas** and king of **Laṅka**. Rāvaṇa achieved, through **ascetic** practice, the boon of not being harmed by any kind of creature except one: a human being. Achieving total dominance over the Earth, Rāvaṇa oppresses many beings, including the **gods**, who go to **Viṣṇu** for assistance. In order to vanquish Rāvaṇa, Viṣṇu takes human form as **Rāma**, prince of **Ayodhyā**. In the course of the *Rāmāyaṇa*, Rāvaṇa abducts Rāma's beautiful wife, **Sītā** (who is an **avatāra** of the **goddess Lakṣmī**). Rāma rescues Sītā, killing Rāvaṇa in battle in the process. It is said that Rāvaṇa is exceedingly strong and has 10 heads.

RAVI. Alternative name for **Sūrya**, the sun.

RAVIVĀRA. Sunday, day of the week governed by the sun. *See also* CALENDAR, HINDU.

RAVIDĀS (fl. 15th century CE). Mystic and **bhakti poet** of the medieval period; born in a cobbler **caste** (a low caste or **Dalit** community) in **Banaras**. Part of the **Sant** movement, Ravidās had no regard for caste distinctions, nor for formal differences between religions, such as Hinduism and **Islam**. Many of his poems are included in the **Sikh scripture**—the *Ādi Granth* or *Guru Granth Sahib*. His teachings have close affinities to those of **Kabīr** and **Guru Nānak**. Starting in the 19th century, a new tradition emerged based on his teachings and devoting itself to him as Guru Ravidās.

REBIRTH. One thread that ties together the highly internally diversified traditions that make up Hinduism is the widespread—indeed, nearly universal—affirmation of the concept of rebirth, or reincarnation, that these traditions share. Among the various philosophical systems (**darśanas**) and religious denominations (**saṃpradāyas**) of Hinduism, only the **materialist Cārvāka** or **Lokāyata** darśana explicitly rejects the concept of rebirth. The **Pūrva**

Mīmāṃsā darśana, whose focus is the exegesis of the earliest **Vedic** texts—where the concept of rebirth is either implicit or altogether absent—does not emphasize rebirth but also does not explicitly reject it. For the remainder of Hindu systems, reincarnation is affirmed and release from the cycle of reincarnation—**mokṣa**—is the ultimate aspiration, each tradition presenting itself as a different set of strategies for achieving this goal.

The concept of rebirth is a corollary of the concept of **karma**, the universal **law** of **action** that draws morally appropriate effects to the agent who commits an act in thought, word, or deed. The fact of physical **death** does not necessarily imply that one has already exhausted one's karma, and the unequal circumstances of the births of the entities in the world also have to be accounted for in terms of karma. This requires the idea of rebirth, in order to explain how the effects of unaccounted-for good and bad deeds are going to be experienced after one dies, and why beings are born in unequal circumstances. One also meets with the claims of those who say they can remember past lives—a phenomenon that is consistent with the deduction that rebirth must occur if there is such a thing as karma.

The **Sanskrit** term for rebirth is punarjanma (literally, rebirth). The term for the entire cycle of birth, death, and rebirth from which one aspires to escape is **saṃsāra**. The desire to achieve **liberation** from rebirth—which, at first glance, can be an appealing idea, implying virtual **immortality**—is a function of the fact that the karmically produced goods experienced within saṃsāra are, at best, impermanent. The desire for such goods and the actions that yield them are the fuel that drives the rebirth cycle. The pursuit of ephemeral goods is ultimately a source of suffering. The soul, or **jīva**, can be likened to a hamster running on a wheel and never getting anywhere. The soul eventually desires permanent peace and bliss without limitation, which can only be achieved through the realization of **Brahman**, understood as a purely impersonal being, consciousness, and bliss at the basis of one's self (**ātman**), or theistically, as a loving **God** with whom one attains a mystical union.

REINCARNATION. *See* REBIRTH.

RENOUNCER. *See* SANNYĀSA.

RENUNCIATION. *See* SANNYĀSA.

ṚG VEDA. The most ancient extant **Vedic** text and the earliest extant Hindu **scripture**. Conventional dating of the text, based on both linguistic evidence and the technological references within the text that can be correlated with archaeology, places it somewhere between 1700 and 1200 BCE. Critics of the **Āryan Migration Theory** have argued that the text is much older, based on **astrological** references within the text and references to the **Sarasvatī** River, which had dried up or gone underground by 1900 BCE. Although these arguments have not been persuasive to mainstream scholarship, they do suggest that at least some elements of the text—which all agree is a compilation undertaken over many generations—may predate the conventional dating, which could be taken as the dating of the text in its present form.

Rather than a continuous narrative, the text consists of 1,028 hymns—or **mantras**—which are organized thematically into 10 books, called **maṇḍalas**. Most of these hymns are in praise of deities called **devas** (literally, "shining ones"), the most popular of whom are **Indra**, Lord of the Devas, and **Agni**, the deity of fire, which is the central element of the Vedic ritual of sacrifice (**yajña**). The Vedic devas are usually associated with natural phenomena, such as **Sūrya** the sun god, **Uśā** the goddess of the dawn, **Soma** the god of the **moon** and of the hallucinogenic plant of the same name, **Vāyu** the god of the wind, **Yama** the god of **death**, and so on. The lord of the Vedic devas, Indra, who is associated with thunder, is analogous to the Greek Zeus and the Norse Thor. Also of considerable importance is **Prajāpati**, whose name literally means the "father of offspring," and who is regarded as the creator of the universe—later known as **Brahmā**. The two chief deities of later Hinduism, **Viṣṇu** and **Śiva**, receive relatively little mention in the *Ṛg Veda* (the latter typically under the name **Rudra**).

The *Ṛg Veda* also contains references to kings and battles and alludes to stories that are presented more fully in later **literature**, such as the ***Brāhmaṇas*** and the ***Purāṇas***. Some of the references remain mysterious today, having already been forgotten by the period of the 14th-century Vedic scholar **Sāyaṇa**. Some of the later Vedic hymns contain philosophical reflections that anticipate many elements of **Vedānta**. *See also PURUṢA SŪKTA.*

RIGHT-HAND TANTRA. Tantric practice that does not make use of the antinomian practices that characterize **Left-Handed** or Vāmācāra Tantra. Right-Hand Tantra either does not utilize these practices or projects them into a realm of symbolic visualization, on the assumption that their actual practice is perilous, leading to **rebirth** in hell if performed out of an impure motive and not for the cultivation of a nondualistic consciousness. The vast majority of Tantric practice is of the Right-Handed variety, not violating social norms regarding purity and impurity. A major innovator in the development of this system was the 10th–11th-century **Kaśmīr Śaiva** theologian **Abhinavagupta**.

RISHIKESH (ṚṢIKEŚA, HṚṢĪKEŚA). Popular place of pilgrimage in the foothills of the **Himālayas**. The **Gaṅgā** or Ganges River flows through Rishikesh and many places of spiritual retreat, or **āśramas**, are located upon its banks here. One was once that of the **Maharishi Mahesh Yogi**, with whom the Beatles studied **Transcendental Meditation** in Rishikesh in the summer of 1968.

ROY, RĀM MOHAN (1772–1833). First major Hindu reformer of the modern period; often called the "Father of Modern Hinduism." Roy established the **Brahmo Samāj** in **Calcutta** in 1828. The Brahmo Samāj was mainly popular among middle-class **Bengali** intellectuals who had received significant exposure to European culture and education, often through the efforts of Christian missionaries, but who also had a strong sense of identification with Hinduism and Indian culture. Led by Roy, these intellectuals sought to reform Hinduism, opposing practices such as **satī** and the use of images (**mūrtis**) in worship, which they held to be later additions to an originally **monotheistic** Hinduism taught in the ***Upaniṣads***. Roy, a prolific author and energetic activist, translated some of the *Upaniṣads* into Bengali and wrote a good many pamphlets as well, decrying what he perceived to be the evils of certain Hindu practices, and of **Christianity** as well. Brahmo Samāj worship was modeled upon Protestant worship services, with hymns and sermons drawing upon the *Upaniṣads*, rather than the Bible. Roy successfully campaigned to get the practice of satī—the immolation of **widows**—banned in Bengal in 1829.

Theologically, the teachings of the Brahmo Samāj display a strong leaning toward Unitarianism, and a number of Brahmo Samāj members traveled to England in the 19th century to study at the Unitarian seminary at Harris-Manchester College in Oxford. With its emphasis on an original, "pure" **Vedic** monotheism later corrupted into popular Hindu **polytheism**, Brahmo Samāj teaching in many ways anticipates that of the **Ārya Samāj** of **Swāmī Dayānanda Sarasvatī**.

ROYAL ASIATIC SOCIETY. The first scholarly society wholly devoted to the study of **Indology**; established by **Sir William Jones** in **Calcutta** in 1784.

ṚṢABHA. Literally "the bull"; the best or foremost; epithet of **Śiva** (whose **vahana**, or animal vehicle, is also a bull named **Nandi**); also the first **Tīrthaṅkara** of **Jainism**, who is sometimes listed as an **avatāra** of **Viṣṇu**. A Ṛṣabha is mentioned in the ***Ṛg Veda***. The large number of representations of bulls in the artifacts of the **Indus Valley civilization** suggests that the bull was sacred from an early period of Indian cultural history. It has also been suggested that there is a link between the figure of Śiva and the **Jain** Ṛṣabha, who is sometimes depicted, like Śiva, as a naked **ascetic** with long, matted hair.

ṚṢI. Sage; seer; wise person; one of the sages who composed or transmitted the ***Vedas***; one of the Seven Sages (**Saptarṣi**) who preside over the cosmos.

ṚTA. Sacred order; **truth**. In the ***Vedas***, *ṛta* refers to the cosmic order upheld by the act of sacrifice (**yajña**). In later Hindu **literature**, the term *ṛta* is gradually superseded by the term **dharma** and takes on an explicitly moral, less ritually oriented tone.

RUDRA. "Roarer"; awe-inspiring and fearsome **Vedic** deity better known in later Hindu traditions as **Śiva**; a **god** of the wilderness, whose offerings are traditionally placed on the outside of the sacrificial arena so he will not enter and disrupt the sacrifice (**yajña**). In the ***Ṛg Veda***, Rudra is associated with the fearsome power of the thunderstorm. Rudra has 11 forms. *See also* ADITI; ĀDITYAS; DEVAS.

RUDRĀKṢA. "Eye of **Rudra**"; seeds used as beads in **mālas** or rosaries used in **japa**, the practice of repeating a **mantra**—either aloud or mentally and silently—while keeping track of the number of repetitions on a string of beads. Especially sacred to the devotees of **Śiva**, the use of rudrākṣa mālas is now prevalent in all forms of Hinduism, not only the **Śaiva** traditions.

RUKMIṆĪ. Wife of **Kṛṣṇa**; **avatāra**, or incarnation, of **Lakṣmī**. *See also* VIṢṆU.

S

ŚABARA. Author of a major commentary, or **bhāṣya**, on the root text of the **Mīmāṃsā** system of philosophy (**darśana**)—the ***Pūrvamīmāṃsā Sūtra*** of **Jaimini**. Simply entitled "Śabara's Commentary" (*Śabara-bhāṣya*), the text was likely composed during the first century before the Common Era.

ŚABARĪ. Character in the ***Rāmāyaṇa***; a woman who was deeply devoted to **Rāma**. She tested the fruits she offered to Rāma by taking a bite of them first, which is technically a taboo act. But because she did it out of **bhakti**, Rāma found no fault with her. It is said that her devotion was so great that she was reborn as **Rādhā**.

SABARIMALAI. Hill in **Kerala** sacred to **Ayyappan**'s sect.

SACRED THREAD. Thread given to a young person, usually a **Brahmin** male, at his **upanayana**, the ceremony marking the passage from childhood into the student stage of life, an initiation into adulthood that is comparable to the Bar Mitzvah of Judaism or the sacrament of Confirmation in **Christianity**. *See also* ĀŚRAMA.

SACRIFICE. *See* YAJÑA.

SĀDHANA. Spiritual practice or discipline. The term refers primarily to ritual worship and **meditation**. Roughly equivalent, in general usage, to **yoga**.

SĀDHU. Literally, "excellent, wonderful, well done"; exclamation of praise at a thing well done, especially in a religious context; also, a holy man, usually a **sannyāsī**. For a holy woman, the feminine version of the word is **sādhvī**.

SĀDHVĪ. A Hindu or **Jain** nun. *See also* SĀDHU; SANNYĀSINĪ; WOMEN.

SAGUṆA BRAHMAN. Brahman with **qualities**, in contrast with **Nirguṇa Brahman**, or Brahman without qualities or attributes. In **Advaita Vedānta**, the distinction between the two is the distinction between Brahman perceived as it truly is—without limiting qualities or attributes—and Brahman as perceived through the veil of **māyā**, or delusory ignorance, as having qualities. As such, Saguṇa Brahman is coextensive with the entire universe of phenomena, including the personal **God (Īśvara)**. In the more theistic forms of **Vedānta**, in which the realm of phenomena is not illusory, Saguṇa Brahman refers specifically to God as the abode of all *good* qualities (*guṇāśraya*).

SAHAJA. "Born with"; innate; natural; spontaneous; **Tantric** term for human impulses that are generally regarded as being in need of restraint in most Hindu spiritual traditions but that are seen as potential sources of divine realization in Tantra. These tendencies are the special focus of the **Sahajīya** tradition of Tantra.

SAHAJIYĀ. Tantric movement particularly prevalent in **Bengal**. The original Sahajīya movement, which probably emerged around the eighth century of the Common Era, crossed a number of sectarian boundaries, having **Śākta**, **Vaiṣṇava**, and **Buddhist** forms. Sahajīya Tantra emphasizes **sahaja**, or innate, human tendencies, such as the sex drive, which it regards as an expression or manifestation of ultimate reality. Rather than suppressing the innate tendencies, as most classical **yoga** traditions seek to do, Sahajīya Tantra cultivates spontaneity in the belief that this will lead to **mokṣa**—**liberation** from **rebirth**. Elements of Sahajīya Tantra can be found in the beliefs and practices of the **Bauls**.

SAHĀSRARA CAKRA. "Thousand-petaled lotus"; **cakra** at the crown of the head that, when energized by the rising **Kuṇḍalinī Śakti**, produces a blissful state that, according to **Tantra**, advances one quickly toward **enlightenment**.

SAI BABA. *See* SATHYA SAI BABA; SHIRDI SAI BABA.

ŚAIVA. Devotee of **Śiva**; adherent of **Śaivism**.

ŚAIVA SIDDHĀNTA. "Final, perfect **truth** about **Śiva**"; **Śaiva** tradition predominant in **Tamil** Nadu, in southern India, though drawing upon Śaiva traditions of other regions as well, such as **Kaśmīr Śaivism**. Inspired largely by the **Nāyanār bhakti poets**, of whose thought this tradition is a systematization, Śaiva Siddhānta emerged as a widespread form of Śaiva thought and practice around the 13th century of the Common Era, superseding and absorbing the earlier **Paśupata** tradition. This tradition has experienced a recent revival due to the efforts of **Satguru Śivāya Subramuniyaswāmī**, an American convert who has promoted it extensively.

ŚAIVISM. In terms of adherents, the second largest (after **Vaiṣṇavism**) of the four main sectarian subdivisions that make up Hinduism. The various subtraditions that constitute Śaivism share the common trait of being oriented toward **Śiva** as the supreme deity—**God** in something like a **monotheistic** sense. Like Vaiṣṇavism, most forms of Śaivism focus on **bhakti**, or devotion to the supreme deity, as the preeminent—or even exclusive—path to **mokṣa**, or **liberation** from the cycle of **rebirth**. Although there is internal theological diversity among Śaiva denominations (**saṃpradāyas**), it can broadly be said that Śaivas are less inclined than Vaiṣṇavas to insist upon a strong metaphysical distinction between God and the individual soul (**jīva**). **Kaśmīr Śaivism**, for example, tends to affirm, in a fashion closely akin to **Advaita Vedānta**, the ultimate unity of existence, claiming that at the highest level of awareness, "All is Śiva." **Śaṅkara** is believed to have been Śaiva (as his name indicates) and is attributed with a devotional poem in which he proclaims, at the height of his **meditation**, "I am Śiva! I am Śiva!" (*Śivo 'ham! Śivo 'ham!*). The **Śaiva Siddhānta** tradition, on the other hand, does insist on the metaphysical distinctness of the soul and God as a precondition of bhakti, and is in this way much closer to Vaiṣṇavism.

Śakti, the **Mother Goddess** and wife of Śiva, plays a prominent role in much of Śaiva thought and practice, with some texts affirming that these two are inseparable, even forming a single, composite deity. **Gaṇeśa** and **Karttikeya**, the sons of Śiva and Śakti, are also popular objects of devotion in these traditions. Both Śaiva and **Śākta** traditions tend to have a **Tantric** orientation. *See also* NĀYANĀRS; PAŚUPATA; RUDRA.

ŚĀKTA. Devotee of **Śakti**; adherent of **Śāktism**.

ŚAKTI. Power; creative energy; name of the **Mother Goddess** that emphasizes her role as the creative power of the universe. Śakti is also identified with the many goddesses of the Hindu pantheon, who are seen as her various forms or manifestations. **Goddesses** such as **Lakṣmī** and Sarasvatī are therefore also called the *śaktis* or power centers of the deities that are their husbands—**Viṣṇu** and **Brahmā**, respectively. In this role, the Mother Goddess and her various personae are seen as the energizing principle, in the absence of which their corresponding male gods would be incapable of effective activity. The divine pairing of Śiva and Śakti, in particular, is often presented, especially in Śākta texts, as a composite being, with the God and Goddess being ultimately inseparable from each other as parts of an internally differentiated, but finally unitary, godhead. In **Tantric yoga**, the

kuṇḍalinī energy at the base of the spine is also called śakti and is regarded as a form of this Goddess. *See also* DEVĪ; DURGĀ; KĀLĪ; MAHĀDEVĪ; PĀRVATĪ; UMĀ.

ŚĀKTISM. In terms of adherents, the third largest (after **Vaiṣṇavism** and **Śaivism**) of the four main sectarian subdivisions that make up Hinduism. The various subtraditions constituting Śāktism share the common trait of being oriented toward **Śakti**, the **Mother Goddess** as the supreme deity—**God** in something like a **monotheistic** sense. As husband of Śakti, **Śiva** plays a prominent role in Śākta thought and practice, which, like Śaivism, tends to have a strong **Tantric** orientation. Śāktism is especially prominent in **Bengal**.

Theologically, Śāktism tends to have a more **syncretistic** and pluralistic tendency than either Vaiṣṇavism or Śaivism, frequently affirming that the various deities of other traditions are forms or manifestations of Śakti. This tradition is thus one possible source for the emphasis on religious pluralism in **Neo-Vedānta**, given that **Ramakrishna**, one of the major figures for this modern interpretation of Hinduism, was a priest and ardent devotee of **Kālī**, one form of the Mother Goddess.

ŚAKTIPAT. Practice in **Siddha Yoga** whereby the **guru** raises the **śakti** or **kuṇḍalinī** energy from the base of the spine to the crown of the head. This can be done through the medium of a touch, a word, or even a thought. The guru can be physically present for the process or—in the case of śaktipat performed through thought—not. Śaktipat is the ritual of initiation, or **dīkṣā**, of the Siddha Yoga tradition.

ŚAKUNI. Character in the ***Mahābhārata***; wicked maternal uncle of **Duryodhana** who devises a scheme by which Duryodhana is able to rob the **Pāṇḍavas** of their wealth, their kingdom, and their personal freedom through an unfair gambling match. Śakuni is also the brother of **Gāndhārī**. *See also* YUDHIṢṬHIRA.

ŚAKUNTALĀ. Character in a minor episode of the ***Mahābhārata*** later adapted into the most famous play in **Sanskrit literature**—the *Abhijñānaśakuntala*, or "Recognition of Śakuntalā," by **Kālidāsa**, the "Shakespeare of Sanskrit." In the story and the play, the sage **Durvāsa**, angered by her inattentiveness, curses Śakuntalā to be forgotten by her beloved, a king named Duśyanta, until Duśyanta sees his ring (which he once gave to her as a token of their love). Eventually, Duśyanta does see the ring and remembers his love for Śakuntalā. The two marry and become the parents of **Bharata**, first emperor of all India according to Hindu literature.

SĀMA VEDA*.** One of the four ***Saṃhitās or collections of **Vedic** hymns; a compilation of hymns of the ***Ṛg Veda*** set to **music**, with instructions for chanting in particular ritual settings. It is one of the foundations of Indian classical music.

SAMĀDHI. Contemplative absorption in the object of one's **meditation**; the eighth and final stage or "limb" of the "eight-limbed" (**aṣṭāṅga**) **yoga** system of **Patañjali**, outlined in his ***Yoga Sūtra*** and believed to lead to **mokṣa**, or **liberation** from the cycle of **rebirth**. As later traditions elaborate, samādhi is of two kinds—**savikalpa samādhi**, in which there is a faint trace of the distinction of subject and object, and **nirvikalpa samādhi**, in which this distinction vanishes completely.

SĀMAGRĪ. "Complete collection"; an assemblage of the items needed for a religious ritual.

SAṂHITĀ*.** A collection of **Vedic** hymns, or **mantras**. There are four Vedic saṃhitās: the ***Ṛg Veda, ***Yajur Veda***, ***Sāma Veda***, and ***Atharva Veda***. These saṃhitās constitute the first historical "layer" of the Vedic literary corpus, the others being, in order, the "priestly texts," or ***Brāhmaṇas***, the "forest texts," or ***Āraṇyakas***, and the "secret teaching," or the ***Upaniṣads***.

SAṂKALPA. Resolve, resolution. Most Hindu rituals, such as **pūjās** and **saṃskāras**, begin with a *saṃkalpa*, in which one announces oneself, the purpose for which one seeks to perform the ritual, and the precise date and time in terms of the traditional Hindu time measurement system of **muhūrtas** and the **Hindu calendar**.

SĀṂKHYA. "Enumeration"; one of the six **āstika** or "orthodox" **darśanas**, or systems of **Vedic** philosophy; frequently paired with the **Yoga** darśana of **Patañjali** and attributed to the sage **Kāpila**. Sāṃkhya philosophy posits a strong dualism between the **soul**, called the **puruṣa**, and matter, or nature, which is known as **prakṛti**. The goal of Sāṃkhya and the related system of **Yoga** is for puruṣa to realize its nature as pure spirit and disentangle itself from prakṛti, with which it has become falsely identified. Whereas puruṣa consists of pure consciousness alone, all phenomena, or contents of consciousness—including both **mind** and matter—are manifestations of prakṛti. Prakṛti manifests as the three **guṇas**, or qualities—**sattva** (clarity, luminosity), **rajas** (**action** or dynamism), and **tamas** (inertia). The universe of changing phenomena is an effect of the constant interplay of these three guṇas.

SAṂPRADĀYA. Sect, denomination, teaching lineage. The four major divisions of Hinduism—**Smārta**, **Vaiṣṇava**, **Śaiva**, and **Śākta**—are themselves further subdivided into saṃpradāyas. It is often noted that Hinduism is not an "organized religion," in the sense of having a central institution or creed, but rather a loose collection or family consisting of many overlapping and criss-crossing traditions. The saṃpradāyas are more cohesive, individually, than is Hinduism as a whole. They are closer to a conventional idea of what constitutes a religion, having specific founders, doctrines, distinct rites of initiation, and so forth.

SAṂSĀRA. Literally "wandering about," the cycle of birth, **death**, and **rebirth**. This term also refers to the realm of karmically determined spatio-temporal phenomena in which the rebirth process occurs. It is therefore also equivalent to "the world." Finally, it also refers to human society—that which the renouncer (**sannyāsin**) abandons in order to seek **liberation** (**mokṣa**). Saṃsāra refers to the sphere in which death and rebirth occur, or to the entire process. The term for rebirth itself, though, is punarjanma.

SAṂSKĀRA. This term has two related meanings. First, it is an impression made upon the **soul** (technically, on one of its **subtle bodies** or **sukṣma śarīra**) through repeated acts of the same kind. A saṃskāra, in other words, is a habit. Collectively, one's saṃskāras constitute one's character, thereby determining, among other things, the kind of form one will take in one's next **rebirth**. On the spiritual path, one wishes to cultivate wholesome saṃskāras—saṃskāras conducive to good **karma**, and ultimately to **liberation**—and get rid of unwholesome ones.

Saṃskāra is also the term for a Hindu sacramental ritual, such as giving a name to a newborn baby (the *nāmakaraṇa-saṃskāra*), the investiture with the **sacred thread** of an adolescent (the ***upanayana***-*saṃskāra*), or the rites of **marriage** (***vivāha***-*saṃskāra*).

The two meanings are related because a sacramental ritual is supposed to make a deep impression upon one's soul, transforming one on a spiritual level.

SANĀTANA DHARMA. "Eternal religion"; a Hindu term for Hinduism, typically used to distinguish the ancient **Vedic** mainstream of the tradition from the particular sectarian movements that have proliferated within it, especially modern reform movements such as the **Ārya Samāj**.

SANDALWOOD. An aromatic wood that is often ground into a paste and utilized in Hindu rituals; believed to be a purifying and cooling substance. The **Sanskrit** term for it is *candana*.

SAṄGH PARIVĀR. "Family of Associations"; a loose collection of **Hindu Nationalist** organizations that share the agenda of advancing the cause of either a Hindu or a Hindu-dominated nation of India. The particular aims of these organizations and the degree to which each might be characterized as "extreme" or "moderate" vary a great deal. But they tend to be regarded as constituting the "Hindu right" in the Indian political spectrum. The Saṅgh Parivār includes many organizations, the most prominent being the **Rāṣṭrīya Svayamsevak Saṅgh** (RSS), **Viśva Hindu Pariṣad** (VHP), and the **Bharatīya Janatā Party** (BJP).

ŚĀNI. The deity who personifies the planet Saturn. His gaze is said to be unfortunate and his presence in one's **astrological** chart is generally inauspicious. According to one version of the story of **Gaṇeśa**, it is Śāni's gaze that causes the infant deity's head to fall off, requiring it to be replaced with the head of an elephant.

ŚĀNIVĀRA. Saturday, the day of the week that is governed by the planet Saturn. *See also* CALENDAR, HINDU.

SAÑJAYA. Character in the ***Mahābhārata***; clairvoyant minister of King **Dhṛtarāṣṭra**. When Dhṛtarāṣṭra asks Sañjaya to describe for him the events of the battle of **Kurukṣetra**, Sañjaya narrates the dialogue of **Kṛṣṇa** and **Arjuna** that becomes the ***Bhagavad Gītā***.

ŚAṄKARA (788–820). Philosopher and religious leader; the **ācārya** and founder of four **maṭhas**, or monastic institutions, located at the four corners of India; the founder of the **Daśanāmī Order** of Hindu ascetics; systematizer and renowned exponent of the **Advaita** system of **Vedānta**. Śaṅkara has been one of the most influential intellectual figures in all of Hinduism. A child prodigy, Śaṅkara is said to have bested major intellectual rivals in debate at an early age. His commentaries on the ***Brahma Sūtra***, ***Bhagavad Gītā***, and the principle ***Upaniṣads*** established Advaita Vedānta as a major philosophical system to be reckoned with in classical Hindu thought—a status it retains even today. Born in what is now the state of **Kerala**, on the southwest coast of India, into the **Nambūtiri Brahmin** community, Śaṅkara undertook **sannyāsa**, or renunciation, at a young age and moved to the city of **Banaras**. He spent much of the rest of his short life in Banaras, but traveled extensively throughout the rest of India as well. He established the Daśanāmī Order and the four maṭhas of **Puri**, **Badrīnāth**, **Dvārakā**, and **Śṛṅgerī**, as well as organizing Hindu worship into the system of five objects of worship (**pañcayātana pūjā**) in part as a way of combating the highly successful and well-organized tradition of **Buddhism**. His later critics, however, from the more theistically and devotionally oriented systems of Vedānta, found his system too much like Buddhism.

ŚAṄKARĀCĀRYA. The head monk, or **ācārya**, of one of the four **maṭhas** or monastic institutions started by **Śaṅkara**—**Puri**, **Badrīnāth**, **Dvārakā**, and **Śṛṅgerī**. The original Śaṅkara is often called the "First Śaṅkarācārya"—*Ādi Śaṅkarācārya*—to distinguish him from the subsequent heads of the four monasteries that he established.

ŚAṄKHA. A conch shell; item often used in Hindu rituals. The conch shell is hollowed out and blown like a horn. The sound of the śaṅkha is believed to be auspicious and to dispel negative forces from the area of the ritual. Hollowed out conch shells have been found in India dating back to the **Indus Valley civilization**, where it is possible that they had a similar ritual purpose (though this is not known with any certainty).

ṢAṆMUKHA. "Having six faces"; epithet of **Kārttikeya**, so called because of his six heads and 12 arms.

SANNYĀSA. Renunciation; the fourth of the four stages of life, or **āśramas**, outlined in the ***Dharma Śāstras***; the **nivṛtti mārga**, or "path of negation" of the person seeking **mokṣa**, or **liberation** from the cycle of **rebirth**. This path is in contrast with the **pravṛtti mārga**, or "path of inclination toward **action**," which characterizes the first three stages of life, which are focused on worldly attainments (including a better rebirth). Sannyāsa is an **ascetic** way of life chosen on the basis of the idea that engagement with the affairs of this world is incompatible with the quest for liberation. A male renouncer is referred to as a monk, and a female renouncer as a nun. A renouncer, or **sannyāsin**, thus abandons his or her former identity—including **caste**—in order to be free from obligations that can bind one to the cycle of rebirth. All action, even good action, produces **karmic** results. The idea of renunciation is to withdraw from action in order to become free from the effects of karma. According to the ***Bhagavad Gītā*** and the later texts of the **bhakti** movement, total freedom from action is impossible and undesirable. These texts instead recommend an inner attitude of renunciation called "renunciation of the fruits of action"—engaging in virtuous—or dharmic—action, but with detachment from the results. But the ancient practice of actually withdrawing from society and joining an ascetic order is still quite common in Hindu traditions.

Many Hindu ascetic orders are peripatetic—having no fixed abode and traveling from place to place as a form of ascetic practice, in order to avoid developing attachment for one particular place. This trait is shared by both Hindu and **Jain** ascetics, and is one of the reasons these traditions survived the invasions of the early medieval period and the mass destruction of settled monastic institutions that led to the demise of **Buddhism**. At the same time, many Hindu ascetic orders do dwell in monasteries, or **maṭhas**, in many ways similar to the **Christian** monasteries of medieval Europe. *See also* ĀCĀRYA.

SANNYĀSIN. A Hindu monk; a male renouncer; a man who has taken up the life of **sannyāsa**.

SANNYĀSINĪ. A Hindu nun; a female renouncer; a **woman** who has taken up the life of **sannyāsa**.

SANSKRIT. Literally, "cultured"; the actual word being *saṃskṛta*. The language of the ***Vedas*** and the majority of "classical" Hindu **literature**, in contrast with more localized, vernacular Hindu literatures (which are highly important and central to those Hindus who utilize them—sometimes more so than Sanskrit texts, which relatively few persons can read). Sanskrit is the language of **Brahmanism**, the **Vedic** tradition that, in conjunction with a host of other Indic traditions, forms Hinduism.

Sanskrit is sometimes referred to as an "artificial language." There probably was a spoken Sanskrit at one point in time that was the language of daily use of a people in the Punjab region of northern India. The Sanskrit of the *Vedas* may be an approximation of this language. Classical Sanskrit—utilized in all post-Vedic Sanskrit literature—is not in every respect identical to Vedic Sanskrit, but differs from it in a number of ways. In the fifth or fourth century BCE, a Sanskrit grammarian—a **Brahmin** named **Pāṇini**—authored the *Aṣṭadhyāyi*, an authoritative work on grammar that has defined the rules of classical Sanskrit usage ever since. Because of the influence of Pāṇini's grammar, Sanskrit has, in effect, become frozen in the form in which it was spoken in the fifth and fourth centuries BCE. It has not continued to develop in the way that natural languages typically do as a result of frequent use. This is why it is called an "artificial language." A highly formal language, it has traditionally been used primarily for writing authoritative texts on a wide variety of subject and in liturgical settings, performing a role in Indian culture analogous to that which Latin has played in the intellectual and religious history of Europe.

In linguistic terms, Sanskrit is identified with Early **Indo-Āryan**. The languages of daily use in ancient India were the **Prakrits**, or "natural" languages (in contrast with the "cultured" and artificial Sanskrit). The Prakrits are sometimes thought of as dialects of Sanskrit, but it is more accurate to refer to them as Middle Indo-Āryan. They evolved into the Late Indo-Āryan modern languages of northern India, such as **Hindi**, **Bengali**, Gujarati, Marathi, and so on. *See also* SANSKRITIZATION.

SANSKRITIZATION. The **Sanskrit** language has long been identified with the "high" culture of India—specifically, the **Vedic** culture of **Brahmanism**—

which has dominated a Hindu self-understanding for millennia. This is in contrast with the popular local cultures that are more often expressed in vernacular languages. Within the **caste** system, when a particular group has decided to raise its status in the larger caste hierarchy, this has often been accomplished through a process of adopting certain high-caste cultural and religious practices, modes of speech, and so on. This process is known as "Sanskritization," a term coined by sociologist M. N. Srinivas (1916–1999). It can include such practices as the wearing of the **sacred thread**—traditionally a practice reserved for **Brahmins** or members of the three **twice-born** castes. Sanskritization can also include the incorporation into the Brahmanical or Vedic tradition of practices, ideas, and even deities that are of non-Vedic origins. It is likely that this process can be traced back even to the period of the ***Vedas***, in which certain indigenous deities and practices came to be incorporated into the originally **Indo-European** Vedic worldview. This practice still continues today, with many of the concepts and practices of **Islam**, **Christianity**, and modern science being assimilated to a Hindu worldview and self-understanding.

SANT. Saint; holy person; a movement among prominent religious figures in northern India in the 15th and 16th centuries who were disdainful of sectarian boundaries, teaching that personal devotion, or **bhakti**, is of greater significance than ritual, **caste**, or sectarian affiliation. Including **Rāmānanda**, **Kabīr**, and **Nānak**, the Sants typically saw the divine as personal but formless. In this way, their teaching reflects the influence of **Islam**.

ŚĀNTI. Peace; especially peace of **mind**; a sense of calm equanimity; a mental state that is widely associated with **meditation**.

SANTOSHI (SAṂTOŚĪ) MĀ. "Mother who brings satisfaction or contentment"; recent **goddess** whose worship emerged in the 1970s; daughter of **Gaṇeśa** who was created to relieve the sufferings of human beings. Santoshi Mā is particularly popular among Hindu **women**. Her devotees perform a **vrata**, or sacred vow, on Fridays that consists of fasting and offering a very simple **pūjā** to the goddess. The story of this goddess was the subject of a popular **Hindi** film in 1975 entitled *Jai Santoshi Mā* ("Victory to Santoshi Ma"). In appearance, she is depicted in a way that is evocative of the goddess **Durgā**—youthful and beautiful but also holding weapons for destroying evil and worldly obstacles. Prayers to Santoshi Mā are traditionally for this-worldly goals and wishes rather than transcendence.

SAPTARṢI. "Seven Sages"; seven wise beings who preside over the cosmos; born from the mind of **Brahmā**; founders of the **gotras**, or **Brahmanical** lineages. **Astrologically**, they are identified with the seven stars of the Great

Bear (or "Big Dipper"). A different set of seven sages appears from the **mind** of Brahmā in every cosmic cycle—which is a way of explaining the fact that there are different lists of these sages in different textual sources. According to most texts, the seven sages of the current cosmic cycle are **Atri**, **Bharadvāja**, **Gautama**, **Jamadagni**, **Kaśyapa**, **Vasiṣṭha**, and **Viśvamitra**.

SARADĀ DEVĪ (1853–1920). Born Saradamaṇi Mukhopadhyāya, the wife and spiritual companion of **Ramakrishna**, one of the founding figures of the **Neo-Vedānta** movement and the revival of modern Hinduism. During Ramakrishna's lifetime, although greatly revered by his disciples, she was largely a behind-the-scenes figure. After Ramakrishna's **death**, in 1886, she began to play a more prominent role in the movement that he began, advising his disciples in their organizing of the **Ramakrishna Order** and **Ramakrishna Mission**, as well as initiating many disciples of her own. Even at this point, though, she remained relatively secluded and did not seek out a large public role for herself.

Born in the village of Jayrambati, in **West Bengal**, she was formally betrothed to Ramakrishna at the age of five, going to live with him in Dakṣineśwar, where he was the priest at a **temple** of the **goddess Kālī**, only in her late teens. (Such arrangements were not unusual among rural Hindus at that time, and their abandonment was championed by many Hindu social reformers of the 19th century.) Ramakrishna is said to have worshiped her as an incarnation of the **Mother Goddess**. She continues to be regarded as such by many devotees in the **Ramakrishna Vedānta** tradition today.

SARASVATĪ. Goddess of wisdom; sometimes depicted as the wife of **Brahmā** and the daughter of **Śiva**. Her vehicle (**vahana**) is a white swan. Iconographically, she usually has four arms. In two of her hands she holds a stringed **musical** instrument called a **vīṇā**. In one of her right hands she holds a **māla**, or string of prayer beads, and in one of her left hands she holds a book. All of the items in her hands represent different aspects of wisdom: the vīṇā symbolizing the **arts**, the māla symbolizing spirituality, and the book representing **knowledge** derived from study. She was originally a river goddess presiding over the Sarasvatī River, which is believed to have disappeared around 1900 BCE. Her festival, Sarasvatī Pūjā, is held on the fifth day of the bright half (**Śukla Pakṣa**) of the Hindu month of **Magha** (January–February). As the goddess of wisdom, she is especially popular with students, who often celebrate her pūjā by placing their books at the feet of her **mūrti**, or image, for the duration of the holiday. She is also especially popular in **Bengal**.

SARASVATĪ, DAYĀNANDA. *See* DAYĀNANDA SARASVATĪ.

Sarasvatī, goddess of wisdom.

ŚARĪRA. Body. This term can refer to the gross, physical body (**sthūla śarīra**) or one of several "subtle" bodies (**sukṣma śarīra**). These bodies correspond to the **kośas**, or "layers," that cover the self or **ātman**. The physical body corresponds to the "food layer" (**anna-maya-kośa**) and the other layers being nonmaterial or "subtle" bodies.

SARVODAYA. "Uplifting of all"; movement for empowerment of the poor based on **Mohandās K. Gāndhī**'s **philosophy** of **satyāgraha** and promoted by his close associate and disciple **Vinobha Bhave**.

ŚĀSTRA. **Scripture**; science; authoritative text on a particular topic; authoritative body of **knowledge**.

SAT. Being, existence. Along with pure consciousness (**cit**) and infinite bliss (**ānanda**), sat is one of the three inherent attributes of **Brahman** according to **Vedānta**. The word for truth (**satya**) is derived from sat, as referring "that which is the case."

SATGURU. True **guru**; spiritual teacher of particularly high authority; a teacher who presides over an entire tradition; roughly equivalent to an **ācārya**.

SATHYA SAI BABA (1926–). Contemporary **guru** based in Andhra Pradesh, southern India; believed by his devotees to be a reincarnation of **Shirdi Sai Baba**; famous for the miracles he is believed to have performed, including spontaneous appearances of sacred ash from his hands. In 1940, when he was 14 years old, it is said that he was bitten by a scorpion. The poison sent him into a delirium from which it is said he awoke with a realization of his true, **enlightened** nature as a great Hindu sage. He began to develop a following that today is global in extent. His teachings emphasize **bhakti**, the study of **scripture**, personal self-discipline, and **vegetarianism**.

SATĪ. Good **woman**; virtuous woman; name of the **Mother Goddess**, **Pārvatī**, in her previous incarnation as a daughter of the deity **Dakṣa**. Satī was deeply in love with **Śiva** and married him, but Dakṣa never fully approved of Śiva. Dakṣa insulted Śiva by failing to invite him to a massive sacrifice to which he had invited all the other sages and deities. Feeling deeply hurt by this insult to her husband, Satī immolated herself in the sacrificial fire. It was this, and not the previous snub, that enraged Śiva, who destroyed Dakṣa's sacrifice and beheaded him. (Later repenting of this act, Śiva resurrected Dakṣa and gave him the head of a ram.) Śiva was inconsolable in Satī's absence. Satī's love for Śiva, though, caused her to be reborn as Pārvatī, and the couple was reunited.

The name of this **goddess** was later applied to **widows** who immolated themselves on the funeral pyres of their husbands. According to **Rajput** lore, upon hearing that their husbands had fallen in battle against foreign invaders, many Rajput women immolated themselves rather than be captured or raped by the enemy. Eventually, this became an expected display of **devotion** in Rajput families. The practice was transmitted to **Bengal** when a number of Rajput clans transplanted themselves to that region. It was banned by the British in 1829 due to the efforts of the Bengali Hindu reformer **Rām Mohan Roy** and soon ceased to occur on a large scale (and had, in any case, been largely confined to the upper **castes** in Bengal and Rajasthan). But occasional exceptions have occurred in subsequent history, the last known satī having taken place at Deorala, in **Rajasthan**, in 1987. This event was protested by many Hindus, including **Swāmī Agniveśa**.

SATTVA. Clarity, luminosity; the first of the three **guṇas** or qualities of phenomenal existence as delineated in the **philosophies** of **Sāṃkhya** and **Yoga** and in the ***Bhagavad Gītā***.

SATYA. Truth. The motto of the modern Republic of India is the **Sanskrit** phrase "Truth alone triumphs" (*Satyam eva jayate*). **Mohandās K. Gāndhī** viewed the pursuit of truth and the practice of nonviolence (**ahiṃsā**) as inseparable, seeing truth and nonviolence as different sides of the same coin, the truth being the interconnected and ultimately unified nature of all beings (his interpretation of **Advaita Vedānta**) and nonviolence being the implication of this truth in practice. Gāndhī also underwent a shift in his thinking over the course of his lifetime from the idea that "**God** is truth" to the idea that "Truth is God." The significance of this shift is that, whereas by holding that "God is truth" one might identify one's own idea of God with the truth, by holding that "Truth is God" one is committed to pursuing the truth wherever it may lead. The motto of the **Theosophical Society** is also "There is no religion higher than truth" (*Satyam paramo dharmaḥ*).

SATYĀGRAHA. Holding fast to truth, **soul** force. Satyāgraha, or "soul force," is **Mohandās K. Gāndhī**'s term for his method of nonviolent resistance to evil. Having some resonance with the epic concept of the vow of truth, the idea behind satyāgraha is that the truth always prevails, and that one who is faithful to the truth will also prevail, despite adversity and opposition. The nonviolent activist who adheres to methods that are in harmony with the ends that he pursues is behaving in a manner consistent with truth. The inherent power of truth will ensure the ultimate success of the activist's cause. *See also* SATYA.

SATYAKĀMA. "One who desires **truth**"; **Vedic** sage whose early career is presented in the ***Chāndogya Upaniṣad***. Satyakāma's **guru** was the sage Haridrumata **Gautama**. As a boy, Satyakāma was keenly interested in studying the ***Vedas***. To do this, it was necessary to approach a qualified teacher and recite one's lineage in order to prove that one was a **Brahmin** and thus worthy of being taught. Satyakāma did not know his father, so asked his mother, Jabāla, a servant woman, his lineage. She told him that she was not sure who his father was, since she had been with many men (possibly having been sexually abused as a servant woman in many homes, although the text does not say this explicitly). She tells her son to refer to himself by her name, calling himself Satyakāma Jabalā, because his paternal lineage is unknown. When he approaches Haridrumata Gautama, Satyakāma is asked to recite his lineage, according to Brahmanical custom. Satyakāma repeats to the teacher what his mother told him. Rather than reject Satyakāma—the illegitimate son of a servant woman—as unworthy of being taught, Haridrumata Gautama exclaims, "Who but a Brahmin could speak thus!" and promptly initiates Satyakāma as his student. The idea of the story seems to be that personal characteristics such as truthfulness are of greater importance than birth status. *See also* ADHIKĀRA; CASTE.

SATYANĀRĀYAṆA. "True Lord," an epithet and form of **Viṣṇu**, typically depicted as Viṣṇu in his conventional four-armed form, holding a conch shell, discus, **lotus**, and club, but surrounded by a group of worshipers who are performing **Satyanārāyaṇa Pūjā**.

SATYANĀRĀYAṆA PŪJĀ. A **pūjā** that is devoted to **Viṣṇu** in his manifestation as **Satyanārāyaṇa**. This pūjā is traditionally held on a full-moon day (**pūrṇimā**), but can also be held by a **householder** in order to celebrate and give thanks for any major event or to invoke blessings for a major undertaking, such as the building of a new house, the starting of a new business, the marriage of a son or daughter, and so on. Like most pūjās, the Satyanārāyaṇa pūjā involves the offering of fruits, flowers, rice, and a mixture of milk, **ghee**, honey, wheat flour, and yogurt, to the deity, and its distribution afterward as **prasād**. It also involves the worshipers listening to, and sometimes participating in, a recitation of the Satyanārāyaṇa **Vrata Kathā**, or Story of the Satyanārāyaṇa Vow. The kathā narrates the stories of devotees who have enjoyed good fortune or have averted misfortune through the performance of the Satyanārāyaṇa pūjā, or who have brought misfortune upon themselves by failing to perform the pūjā after having vowed to do so, or by failing to take the prasād after having participated in the pūjā.

ŚAUNAKA (fl. 5th century BCE). Sage and scholar attributed with authoring the ***Bṛhad-devatā***, or the "Great Text on Deities"—a systematic presentation of the attributes and the deeds of the **Vedic** deities (**devas**)—and a work on correct pronunciation of the verses of the ***Ṛg Veda*** called the *Ṛg Veda Prātiśākhya*. Both texts were likely composed between 500 and 400 BCE.

SAVARKAR, VINAYAK DAMODHAR ("VEER") (1883–1966). Hindu Nationalist leader and author of the essay ***Hindutva*** ("Hinduness"). Hindutva is a concept of Hindu identity that conflates it with Indian identity. According to Savarkar, a Hindu is one who is of Indian descent, who claims India as his or her "fatherland," and who adheres to a religion of Indian origin. Indians who do not practice a religion of Indian origin are, on this understanding, less "Indian" than are self-identified Hindus. Similarly, non-Indians who practice a Hindu religion are not, according to this understanding, truly Hindu.

Savarkar participated in the Indian independence movement, being jailed by the British from 1910 to 1937 for his revolutionary activities. It was during the period of his imprisonment that he authored *Hindutva*, as well as other essays and **poems**. After being released from prison, he resumed his political activities, opposing **Mohandās K. Gāndhī**'s strictly nonviolent strategy and joining the **Hindu Mahāsabhā**, of which he served as president from 1937 to 1943. Savarkar was strongly opposed to the partition of India. Greatly revered by Hindu Nationalists, Savarkar is seen by many as the founding father of the Hindu Nationalist movement.

SAVIKALPA SAMĀDHI. State of meditative absorption with a residual sense of the duality of subject and object. **Samādhi**—absorption in the object of one's **meditation**—is the eighth and final "limb" of **Patañjali**'s eight-limbed (**āṣṭāṅga**) system of **yoga**. Later traditions that utilize Patañjali's system distinguish between that samādhi in which there remains a sense of subjectivity (savikalpa samādhi) and a samādhi with no subject–object duality (**nirvikalpa samādhi**).

SAVITṚ. "Giver of life"; **Vedic** solar deity; one of the 12 **Ādityas**. The **Gāyatrī mantra** is dedicated to this deity. It is not always clear if Savitṛ is identical to **Sūrya**, the more commonly invoked Vedic sun **god**. According to the authoritative commentator, **Sāyaṇa**, the name *Savitṛ* refers to the sun before and just as it rises and *Sūrya* is the name of the sun once it has risen fully.

SĀVITRĪ. An alternative name for the **Gāyatrī mantra**. As a **goddess**, Sāvitrī is the daughter of **Savitṛ** and wife of **Brahmā**.

SĀYAṆA (fl. 14th century CE). Highly respected and authoritative commentator upon the ***Vedas***; author of the *Vedārtha Prakāśa*, or "Illumination of the Meaning of the *Vedas*," as well as numerous other works on **Vedic** ritual. Sāyaṇa lived within the **Vijayanāgara** Empire.

SCHEDULED CASTES. Official Indian government term for the lower **castes**—that is, the **Dalits**, **Harijans**, or **Untouchables**, as these communities are variously known. This term refers to the fact that these castes have been included in an official list or *schedule* indicating that they are eligible for specific government benefits and privileges due to their traditionally oppressed status.

SCRIPT. Writing system; "alphabet." Writing has existed in India since the period of the **Indus Valley civilization**, which was at its height from roughly 2600 to 1900 BCE. The script of this civilization, however, remains undecipherable today. The next script to emerge, called *Brāhmī*, can be found on inscriptions from as early as the seventh century BCE. The famous edicts of the **Maurya** emperor Aśoka are carved in Brāhmī script and date from the third century BCE. Around the fifth century BCE, the *Kharoṣṭhī* script also comes into use. Early versions of *Devanāgarī*, the script used today in **Sanskrit**, **Hindi**, Marathi, and some other northern Indian languages, come into use by the fourth century of the Common Era, and are clearly based on the earlier Kharoṣṭhī and Brāhmī scripts.

SCRIPTURES. Hindu sacred **literature** consists of a vast collection of texts. There is no single authoritative work that all Hindus regard as divinely inspired, equivalent to the Bible for **Christianity** or the Qur'an for **Islam**. There are, instead, many such works, whose relations to one another are quite complex and that are regarded in a variety of ways by different groups of Hindus. The most basic division of Hindu scripture is that between **śrūti** and **smṛti**. These terms refer, respectively, to "that which is heard" and "that which is remembered." The "heard" texts—the śrūti—are believed to be direct, divine revelations perceived by the ancient **Vedic** sages, or **ṛṣis**. They are *apauruṣeya* or "non-man-made." The "remembered" texts—or smṛti—are not directly revealed but are made up of traditional **knowledge** passed down from the ancient past. Their authority is derivative from that of the śrūti, whose basic teachings they communicate through popular narrative. The śrūti is the Vedic literature, while the smṛti consists of all subsequent Hindu texts.

SELF. *See* ĀTMAN.

SELF-REALIZATION FELLOWSHIP (SRF). Religious organization established by **Paramahāṃsā Yogānanda** in 1920 to disseminate the practice of *Kriya* ***Yoga***, into which he had been initiated by his **guru**, **Sri Yukteśwar Giri**. In 1952, after Yogānanda's death, Swāmī Janakānanda (formerly James Lynn) took over the leadership of the organization. He was succeeded in 1955 by Śrī Dayā Mātā, who continues to head the organization. Among the distinctive aspects of the Self-Realization Fellowship (or SRF, as it is widely known) is its emphasis on devotion to Jesus as an enlightened master and its teaching of the unity of science and religion. Its membership consists primarily of Westerners. It resembles the **Vedānta Society** and **Siddha Yoga** in its inclusion of Western initiates as monks and nuns. Its main headquarters are located in Los Angeles, California.

SEN, KESHUB CHUNDER (KEŚAVA CANDRA) (1838–1884). Nineteenth-century **Bengali** Hindu reformer; member of the **Brahmo Samāj**; known for his open admiration of **Christianity** and his concept of a "New Dispensation" that would involve a synthesis of Christian and Hindu elements, and ultimately elements of all religions. Sen's ideas led him to split with the Brahmo Samāj, starting a new organization called the Brahmo Samāj of India in 1866. As Sen's thought continued to evolve, he began to take his organization in a more traditionally Hindu direction—very likely under the influence of **Ramakrishna**, whom he met in 1876. A number of his followers, unhappy with his perceived deviations from the original ideals of the Brahmo Samāj, split away from the Brahmo Samāj of India to form the Sadharan Brahmo Samāj in 1878. Sen played an important role in bringing Ramakrishna to the attention of a wider audience of Bengali intellectuals.

ŚEṢA. The cosmic serpent on whose belly **Viṣṇu** rests. When Viṣṇu becomes incarnate as an **avatāra**, Śeṣa frequently becomes incarnate as well, to act as Viṣṇu's protector. So when Viṣṇu was born as **Rāma**, Śeṣa became his brother **Lakṣmaṇa**. Similarly, when Viṣṇu was born as **Kṛṣṇa**, Śeṣa, according to some accounts, was born as **Bālarāma**, his brother.

SEVEN SAGES. *See* SAPTARṢI.

SHANKAR, RAVI (1920–). Indian classical musician instrumental in popularizing the **musical** traditions of India—especially the sitar—to the attention of the Western world. In his youth, he traveled frequently to North America and Europe as part of a **dance** troupe run by his brother, Uday Shankar. In 1938, he gave up dancing to learn the sitar, which is the instrument for which he is best known. Though Indian **music** had long been enjoyed by a small segment of the Western public, Shankar's association with **George Harrison** of the Beatles, starting in 1966, brought him, and Indian classical music more generally, to a much wider audience.

SHARMA, ARVIND. Prolific scholar of Hinduism and professor of religious studies at McGill University, in Montreal, Canada. Though not referring to himself explicitly as a Hindu theologian, much of Sharma's work has a constructive theological character that seeks to reinterpret Hindu thought in an effort to show its relevance to the contemporary world. His notable efforts in this regard include his work on Hinduism and human rights and his reinterpretation of the **caste** system, which argues that all Hindus have a duty to study their **scriptures** and **philosophies** (the traditional work of a **Brahmin**), to stand up for what is right (the traditional work of a **Kṣatriya**), to be economically productive (the traditional work of a **Vaiśya**), and to serve humanity (the traditional work of a **Śūdra**).

SHETTY, MALTI (1955–). *See* GURUMAYĪ.

SHIRDI SAI BABA (?–1918). Also known as Sai Baba of Shirdi, Shirdi Sai Baba was a spiritual teacher of the 19th and early 20th centuries with a large following of both Hindus and Muslims. His teaching is evocative of that of the **Sant** movement, with elements of both **Advaita Vedānta** and **Sufism**. The contemporary teacher, **Sathya Sai Baba**, claims to be a reincarnation of Shirdi Sai Baba—a claim not accepted by all Shirdi Sai Baba devotees.

SIDDHA. Perfected being; one who has attained perfection; a person who has achieved **liberation** from **rebirth** (**mokṣa**) in this lifetime; a **jīvanmukta**.

Though used in many Indic traditions, this term is associated most prominently with **Tantra** and **Jainism**.

SIDDHA YOGA. Contemporary **Tantric** tradition with roots in **Kaśmīr Śaivism**. The practice of Siddha Yoga focuses primarily upon **meditation** and the relationship between the **guru** and the disciple. Initiation (**dīkṣā**) into Siddha Yoga occurs through the process of **śaktipat**, whereby the guru raises the **śakti** or **kuṇḍalinī** energy residing at the base of the spine of the aspirant through the various **cakras** to the **sahāsrara cakra** at the top of the head. It is believed that the guru can do this through a touch, word, or thought. In the Siddha Yoga tradition, it is believed that śaktipat can accelerate the aspirant's journey to **mokṣa**, or **liberation** from the cycle of **rebirth**.

Though having more ancient roots, the modern Siddha Yoga tradition begins with the figure of **Swāmī Nityānanda** (1897–1961), the guru of **Swāmī Muktānanda** (1908–1982), who brought the tradition to the West, where it continues to have a large following today. The current head of the lineage, **Swāmī Chidvilāsānanda**, more popularly known as **Gurumayī**, is notable for being one of only a handful of female gurus who head large Hindu-inspired global organizations. Siddha Yoga is based at **Gaṇeśapuri Āśrama**, near Bombay (Mumbai), the site of Nityānanda's spiritual retreat in his later years. There is a large Siddha Yoga **āśrama** near South Fallsburg, New York, as well.

SIDDHĀNTA. Perfect teaching; final goal; settled opinion; term by which most systems of Indian philosophy (**darśana**) refer to themselves in the context of debate.

SIDDHI. "Perfection," "success," "accomplishment"; paranormal power cultivated as a result of spiritual practice such as **asceticism** and **meditation**. Hindu traditions are, on the whole, ambivalent toward such powers, with some texts and teachers explicitly endorsing specific practices aimed at producing particular siddhis and others dissuading practitioners from being distracted by such powers from the ultimate goal of **mokṣa**.

Also, along with **Buddhi** ("Intellect"), Siddhi ("Success") is the name of one of the two wives of **Ganeśa**. *See also* TANTRA; YOGA.

SIKHISM. Highly egalitarian religious tradition that emerged from the **Sant** movement and the interplay between Hinduism and **Islam** during the **Mughal** period; founded by **Nānak** (1469–1539), better known by his disciples as Guru Nānak. Born a Hindu in the Punjab, Nānak claimed to have received a revelation from **God** while **meditating** in a forest. Nānak's message was: "There is no Muslim and there is no Hindu." Those who accepted his teaching of Hindu–Muslim unity came to be known as *Sikh*, a Punjabi word that means "disciple," and they took Nānak as their **guru**.

Guru Nānak and his followers sought to harmonize the teachings of Islam and Hinduism, taking from Islam its strong emphasis on the unity of God. Guru Nānak called **the One** God, known by Hindus under many names and forms, *Sat Nām*, or the "True Name," or *Ek Onkar*, the One God. The One God is the creator of the entire universe, according to Sikhism, and humans are the highest of God's creations. From Hinduism, Nānak took the doctrines of **karma** and **rebirth** and the emphasis on the importance of the guru, or living teacher. **Liberation** from rebirth is given by God, much as in **bhakti**-based, devotional forms of Hinduism. The community Guru Nānak established accepted all, regardless of religion, gender, or **caste**, a teaching that is illustrated in the Sikh practice of the *langar*, a meal in which all participate and dine together (inter-dining being prohibited in Nānak's time between members of the various castes and religious communities).

Nānak was succeeded by a series of nine gurus. Under each guru, suspicion of the new movement grew within the Mughal state, culminating in fierce persecution by the Mughal emperor Aurangzeb. The 10th and final Sikh guru, **Gobind Singh** (1666–1708), responded to this persecution by militarizing the Sikh community, establishing the *khalsa*, or order of Sikh warriors, marked by the "Five K's," or five items whose names, in Punjabi, start with the letter K: *keś*, or long hair; *kangha*, a special comb with which the hair is tied on top of the head; *kara*, a circular steel bracelet; *kacha*, an undergarment ensuring preparedness for battle; and the *kirpan*, a sword or dagger. Gobind Singh's father, Guru Tegh Bahadur, had been beheaded by Aurangzeb, and Gobind Singh himself had to spend much of his time in hiding. Knowing that he might not survive in the ongoing conflict, he designated the sacred text of the Sikhs, the *Ādi Granth*, the perpetual guru of the community after his **death**.

In the post-independence period, some Sikhs began to agitate for a Sikh state that would be known as *Khalistan*. This agitation escalated into violence throughout the late 1970s, culminating in an Indian army attack in 1984 on the Golden Temple of Amritsar, where the original *Ādi Granth* is housed. This, in turn, provoked the assassination of Prime Minister Indira Gāndhī by her Sikh bodyguards, which provoked anti-Sikh riots.

Since 1984, relations between Sikhs and the Hindu majority of India have been improving, with Manmohan Singh—a Sikh—being elected to the office of prime minister of India in 2004.

Worldwide, there are approximately 23,000,000 Sikhs today. Roughly 80 percent of Sikhs live in India—and specifically, in the Punjab. The other 20 percent live both in other parts of India and throughout the rest of the world, with relatively large populations in the United States, Great Britain, and Canada.

SINDHU. **Sanskrit** name of the **Indus** River that flows through what is now Pakistan, and around which the **Indus Valley civilization** flourished from approximately 2600 to 1900 BCE. The Persian pronunciation of this word is the source of the term *Hindu.*

SINGH, SWĀMĪ SHIV DAYAL (1818–1878). Founder of the **Rādhāsoāmī Satsang.**

ŚIṢYA. Student; disciple or follower of a **guru**, or spiritual teacher.

SĪTĀ. Character in the ***Rāmāyaṇa***; wife of **Rāma** and human incarnation, or **avatāra**, of the **goddess Lakṣmī**; daughter of the sage King **Janaka**. Rāma wins the right to marry Sītā by completing a nearly impossible task set by her father—the stringing of **Śiva**'s bow, which Rāma not only strings successfully but actually breaks. Happily marrying Rāma and returning with him to **Ayodhyā**, she later suffers exile with him when he is sent into the wilderness at the command of his father, **Daśaratha**, who is forced into sending his son away by one of his wives, Kaikeyī, who fears that her own son—Rāma's half-brother, **Bharata**—will be marginalized if Rāma becomes king. While in exile with Rāma and his brother **Lakṣmaṇa**, Sītā is abducted by the **rākṣasa** lord, **Rāvaṇa**, who takes her to his capital on the island of **Laṅka**. During her imprisonment, Rāvaṇa seeks to woo her, but she remains steadfastly loyal to Rāma. When Rāma and his allies finally free her, Rāma does not immediately embrace her but forces her to pass a test of fire in order to prove that she did not betray him while in captivity. This distressing episode is explained by the fact that Rāma is concerned that, as king, he and his family must be above reproach in the eyes of the public. At a later point in the story—after the family has returned and ruled in Ayodhyā for many years—members of the public begin to question her fidelity and Sītā again has to pass through the fire test. At this point, she leaves the city and goes to the wilderness, raising her two sons, Lava and **Kuśa**, in seclusion.

The ill treatment of Sītā after her **liberation** from Rāvaṇa has been a source of a good deal of controversy within the Hindu tradition. On the one hand, Sītā is held up as a model Hindu wife, ever faithful and obedient to her husband even in the worst of times. At the same time, the repeated demands that she prove her fidelity are clearly demeaning. Alternative versions of the *Rāmāyaṇa* vary a good deal in their approaches to this issue. The most popular variant—the **Hindi *Rām Carit Mānas*** of **Tulsīdās**—claims that the scene never really occurred: that the real Sītā was never captured by Rāvaṇa and that only an etheric double appeared to undergo the fire test. *See also* WOMEN.

ŚĪTALA. "Cold **goddess**"; goddess associated with smallpox; sometimes believed to be a form of **Kālī**; especially popular in **Bengal**.

ŚIVA. "Good, benevolent"; alongside **Viṣṇu** and **Śakti**, one of the most popular deities of Hinduism; regarded by many of his devotees, known as **Śaivas**, as **God** in something like a **monotheistic** sense—the supreme deity. Śiva is an ancient deity whom some argue was worshiped, alongside the **Mother Goddess**, in the **Indus Valley civilization**. This argument is based on the resemblance of a deity depicted in some Indus Valley carvings to Śiva in his forms as **Paśupati**, or Lord of the Animals, and **Yogeśvara**, Lord of **Yoga**. This identification cannot be verified, however, until the **script** of the Indus Valley is deciphered. Śiva is also identified with the **Vedic** storm deity, **Rudra**. Rudra, a fierce deity of the wilderness, shares with Śiva the attribute of living far from society. Rudra is also depicted as a hunter, and another epithet of Śiva is—as just mentioned—the Lord of the Animals. And Śiva, like Rudra, can have a fierce temper when roused to anger. Many of the prayers in the ***Ṛg Veda*** devoted to Rudra entreat him to keep his temper in check and to keep his destructive activities far from the area of human activity. *Śiva* likely became an epithet of Rudra due to prayers that refer to him in this way—"good, gentle, kind"—in an effort to pacify the deity and keep him in a calm and gentle mood.

By the time of the ***Purāṇas***, in the first millennium of the Common Era, Śiva is generally depicted in a way that lives up to his name—as a gentle, kind, and generally "laid back" deity. But he can still be roused to fierce anger, such as when he destroys the sacrifice of **Dakṣa** or when he burns **Kāmadeva** to a crisp with a blast of energy from his **third eye**. He is typically remorseful after such outbursts, however, such as when he gives Dakṣa the head of a ram after beheading him in anger, and when he gives his son **Gaṇeśa** the head of the elephant **Airāvata** after beheading him. As these last two examples indicate, Śiva is a destroyer and a creator—destroying old forms to make way for new ones. This process, and Śiva's role as both destroyer and re-creator of the universe in an ongoing cycle, is illustrated in the popular image of Śiva dancing the cosmic **dance** of **creation** and destruction—Śiva as "Lord of the Dance" (**Nāṭarāja**).

Śiva and his wife, Śakti, the Mother Goddess, form a composite deity, with Śakti being the power of creation and Śiva the pure consciousness that underlies it. Their two children, Gaṇeśa and **Karttikeya**, are popular deities in their own right but are also often worshiped in conjunction with their parents. Both Śaiva and Śākta worship often have a **Tantric** character.

ŚIVĀJĪ (1627–1680). Leader of the **Marāṭhas**, a warrior people of Maharashtra, in central India (the current location of Bombay, or Mumbai), who success-

Śiva, Lord of Yoga and of the cosmic dance of creation and destruction.

fully fought against the **Mughal Empire** in the late 17th century, during the period of Emperor Aurangzeb. Led by Śivāji, who even today remains a folk hero in Maharashtra, the Marāṭhas utilized guerilla tactics against the numerically superior and better equipped Mughals. Stunningly successful in their campaign, the Marāṭhas eventually controlled most of central India's Deccan plateau.

ŚIVARĀTRI. "**Śiva**'s night"; the 13th night and 14th day of each month of the **Hindu calendar** is sacred to the deity Śiva and is therefore known as "Śiva's night," observed by devotees through fasting. The Śivarātri of the month of **Phalguna** is especially sacred and is also known as "Śiva's great night" (**Mahāśivarātri**).

SKANDA. Alternative name for **Kārttikeya**, the son of **Śiva** and **Pārvatī** and brother of **Gaṇeśa**.

SMĀRTA. Along with the **Vaiṣṇava**, **Śaiva**, and **Śākta** traditions, one of the four major streams of tradition that make up Hinduism. The Smārta tradition, whose name means "derived from the **smṛti**," is a continuation of the ancient tradition of **Brahmanism**. It sees itself as nonsectarian, in contrast with the often exclusive adherence of other Hindu traditions to a single deity, such as **Viṣṇu**, **Śiva**, or **Śakti**. The Smārta **Brahmins** follow the directives of **Śaṅkara**, worshiping by means of the **Pañcayātana Pūjā**, or "fivefold worship" dedicated to **Gaṇeśa**, Śiva, Śakti, Viṣṇu, and **Sūrya**, the sun **god**. Otherwise, they adhere closely to **Vedic** customs as understood by the **Pūrva Mīmāṃsā** system of philosophy (**darśana**). They are orthodox Brahmins, whose lifestyle follows the Hindu **śāstras** quite closely, but whose nonsectarian outlook has also been a major influence on **Neo-Vedānta**, with its emphasis on religious pluralism and many effective paths to **God-realization**.

SMṚTI. "Remembered"; along with **śrūti** ("that which is heard"), one of the two main categories of Hindu **scripture**. Smṛti is sacred tradition. Although not directly revealed by **God** or heard by the **ṛṣis** or sages of the distant past while deep in **meditation**, it has a derivative authority, being based upon such authoritative sources and attempting to make their **knowledge** available to the wider Hindu society. The smṛti **literature** consists of a vast collection of texts—essentially, all authoritative Hindu literature other than the **Vedic** corpus, which constitutes the śrūti. As such, the smṛti includes the historical epics—that is, the ***Rāmāyaṇa*** and ***Mahābhārata***—the ***Purāṇas***, the various **sūtras** of the **darśanas**, or philosophical systems, the ***Dharma Śāstras***, and the whole range of śāstra literature on a whole host of topics, such as medicine, **astrology**, economics, political science, grammar, aesthetics, sexuality, the construction of **temples** and sacred images, and so on. Most of this literature is composed in **Sanskrit**, but some of it, such as the devotional **poetry** of the **bhakti** movement, is in vernacular languages.

SOMA. **Vedic** deity of the **moon**, who also represents the hallucinogenic plant whose juice, mixed with milk, was used by ancient **Brahmins** to evoke an experience of the divine. The phases of the moon represent this substance being consumed by the **devas** (during the **dark half** of the month, when the moon is waning) and replenished (during the **bright half**, when the moon is waxing). There has been a great deal of speculation on the actual plant that was pressed and whose juice was used to produce the soma drink. It has been suggested by some that it was a mushroom grown in what is now Afghanistan. Others suggest a leafy plant that has either become extinct or whose properties have been forgotten. **Indra** is depicted as being particularly fond of consuming this drink. Many hymns in the ***Ṛg Veda*** are devoted to this deity.

SOMAVĀRA. Monday, the day of the week that is governed by the **moon**. *See also* CALENDAR, HINDU.

SOMNĀTH (SOMANĀTHA). Lord of the **Moon**; epithet of **Śiva**, so called in part due to the fact that he is often depicted wearing a crescent moon on his forehead. A large and exceedingly wealthy **temple** dedicated to Śiva in this form was located in Gujarat in the first millennium of the Common Era. It was destroyed by the invading army of Mahmud of Ghazni in 1026, who made its seven-foot stone **Liṅga**, or abstract image of Śiva, part of the threshold of a mosque, to be stepped upon by Muslim worshipers, in a gesture of contempt for Hinduism. For this reason, the temple has become a symbol to Hindus—and especially to **Hindu Nationalists**—of insults suffered under medieval **Islamic** rule. The temple was repeatedly rebuilt and destroyed by Muslim rulers throughout its history—in 1297, 1394, and 1706. Its most recent rebuilding was in 1950.

SOUL. *See* JĪVA; ĀTMAN.

SOUTHEAST ASIA. The region today made up of such nation states as Thailand, Laos, Cambodia, Vietnam, Burma, Malaysia, Singapore, and Indonesia. This area was heavily influenced by both Hinduism and **Buddhism** during the first millennium of the Common Era. The influence was largely peaceful, with Indian culture being viewed as prestigious and therefore consciously imitated by the royal families of the region. Examples of this influence include the popularity of the ***Rāmāyaṇa*** and ***Mahābhārata*** in this region, the adoption of **Sanskrit** names and royal titles, Hindu and Buddhist **temples** (which often take the form of composite Hindu–Buddhist temples) like **Angkor Wat** in Cambodia, the continuing practice of Hinduism as the predominant religious tradition of **Bali**, Indonesia, today, and the heavy influence of **Sanskrit** and Pāli on the languages of these countries. The Indic cultural influence on this region has been so great that some scholars refer to it as "Greater India."

SPANDA. Vibration. According to **Śaiva** thought, vibration is the means by which the cosmos emerges from **Śiva**'s pure consciousness. The various elements that make up the physical universe (**mahābhūtas**), such as **earth**, **water**, **air**, **fire**, and the etheric element, **ākāśa**, can all be seen as different "wavelengths" of the primordial vibration. *See also* OṂ.

SPHOṬA. A theory of **Sanskrit** grammar developed by **Bhartṛhari** (6th–7th century CE). According to this theory, the letters or sounds that make up a word have a special power to manifest the meaning of that word. This power to make meaning is the true essence of a word. The letters and sounds that make up the word are merely the means by which this true essence is revealed.

ŚRADDHĀ. Faith; according to the ***Bhagavad Gītā***, śraddhā is a basic commitment that could be said to constitute a person.

ŚRĀDDHA. Periodic **ancestral rite** that consists of offering food and water to the dead. If one does not offer śrāddha to one's ancestors—typically in the form of balls of rice called **piṇḍa**—one may run the risk that they will wander through the world as **pretas**, or hungry ghosts. The food offered in the śrāddha is also said to become the food of one's ancestors in their next **rebirth**.

ŚRAMAṆA. Striver; member of a **renouncer** movement that distinguishes itself from the **Brahmins** by its belief that one's spiritual status is a function of one's personal effort, to which birth **caste**, or **jāti**, is irrelevant. The śramaṇa movement likely emerged during the first millennium BCE, but may be even older than this, or based on older antecedents. This movement consisted of many distinct groups, each of which was centered on a spiritual teacher believed to have attained **enlightenment** and **liberation** from the cycle of **rebirth**. The only two śramaṇa traditions to survive to the present day are **Buddhism** and **Jainism**, though other śramaṇa groups, such as the **Ājīvikas**, existed in the ancient period. Though initially antagonistic to **Brahmanism** and to aspects of **Vedic** thought and practice—particularly **animal sacrifice** and the belief that birth caste is a measure of spiritual evolution—the śramaṇa traditions exerted considerable influence upon Hinduism, especially in regard to the practice of **vegetarianism** and later critiques of birth caste.

ŚRAUTA SŪTRAS. **Sanskrit** texts, likely composed around 500 BCE, that describe in detail the correct way to perform a **Vedic** ritual of sacrifice (**yajña**).

ŚRAVAṆA. Month of the **Hindu calendar** that corresponds roughly to the period from mid-July to mid-August. The word *śravaṇa* also refers to "listening" or "hearing."

Also the name of the son of a **Brahmin** in the ***Rāmāyaṇa*** who is accidentally shot and killed by **Rāma**'s father, King **Daśaratha**. Daśaratha, hunting in the forest, mistakes Śravaṇa for a deer. The boy's father, enraged, curses Daśaratha to suffer the loss of his son as well—a curse brought to fulfillment when Daśaratha is forced to disinherit Rāma and banish him to 14 years of exile. Daśaratha dies from sorrow as a result of this event—and ultimately, as a result of the angry Brahmin's curse.

ŚRĪ. Prosperity; that which is auspicious. Name of an ancient **Vedic goddess** mentioned once in the ***Ṛg Veda*** and many times in the ***Atharva Veda*** and the ***Brāhmaṇas***. She is the embodiment of success of any kind. By the time of the ***Purāṇas*** (the first millennium of the Common Era), she is identified with **Lakṣmī**, wife of **Viṣṇu**, though some sources suggest these two were, at one point, two distinct goddesses.

SRI AUROBINDO. *See* GHOSE, AUROBINDO.

SRI CHINMOY (1831–2007). Modern **Bengali** Hindu spiritual teacher with a following in the West. In 1964, he immigrated to New York City, where he remained based for the rest of his life. His teaching is very much in line with **Neo-Vedānta**, emphasizing social service, the practice of **meditation**, and respect for all religions as "essentially divine." Sri Chinmoy was deeply influenced by the teaching of **Aurobindo Ghose**, whom he cited frequently in his own teaching.

SRI LANKA. Island country off the southeast coast of India, near **Tamil** Nadu; widely identified with the **Laṅka** of **Rāvaṇa** in the ***Rāmāyaṇa***; home to what is likely the most ancient continuously existing **Buddhist** community in the world. The Buddhist majority of Sri Lanka speaks Siṅhala, or Sinhalese. From 1983 to 2009, a fierce civil war raged between the Sinhalese majority and the Tamil-speaking Hindu minority, which sought to have an independent state in the northern part of the island. This tragic and destructive conflict, often cast in religious terms, appears to have been more of an ethnic struggle.

SRI RAMAKRISHNA. *See* RAMAKRISHNA.

ŚRĪRAṄGAM. Massive **temple** complex in **Tamil** Nadu and center of the **Śrīvaiṣṇava** tradition.

ŚRĪVAIṢṆAVA. Of or pertaining to **Śrīvaiṣṇavism**.

ŚRĪVAIṢṆAVISM. Highly popular **Vaiṣṇava** tradition found mainly in southern India and traced to the devotional **poetry** of the **Āḷvārs**, or **Tamil**-speaking **bhakti** poets of the period from approximately 600 to 900 CE. A **Brahmin** scholar named Nāthamuni introduced the poetry of the Āḷvārs into the ritual of formal **temple** worship in the 10th century. His grandson, **Yāmuna**, translated many of the poems into **Sanskrit** and continued the process of formalizing and systematizing the tradition. This process was completed by Yāmuna's student **Rāmāṇuja** (1077–1157). The name of the tradition is an expression of the fact that the **goddess Śrī**, or **Lakṣmī**, is regarded in this tradition as inseparable from **Viṣṇu**, with whom she forms a composite deity (not unlike **Śiva** and **Śakti** in **Śaivism** and **Śāktism**).

After Rāmāṇuja, this tradition experienced a division over an issue analogous to the issue of the relationship of faith and works in **Christianity**. The Vaṭakalai school holds that some human effort is involved in the process of achieving **mokṣa**, or **liberation** from the cycle of **rebirth**. This school likens the human aspirant for mokṣa in relation to **God** as similar to a baby monkey in relation to its mother. The mother carries the baby, but the baby must also exert effort by clinging to its mother. The Teṅkalai school, on the other hand, likens the human aspirant to a baby kitten, whose mother carries it without any effort being made by the kitten. (Theologically, then, the Vaṭakalai school could be likened to Roman Catholicism and the Teṅkalai school to Protestantism.)

ŚRĪVIDYĀ TANTRA. System of Tantric worship focused on the **Mother Goddess**. It was systematized by **Bhāskararāya Makhin** (1690–1785), a **Śākta** theologian from the region of Maharashtra, in central India. Unlike other Śākta systems of Tantric worship, Śrīvidyā Tantra focuses on the Goddess's benign and beautiful aspects, rather than on her terrifying ones. It is predominantly a **Right-Handed** system of **Tantra**.

ŚṚṄGERĪ. Site of one of the four **maṭhas**, or monasteries established by **Śaṅkara** (788–820) at the four corners of India. Śṛṅgerī, in **Tamil** Nadu, is in the southern part of the country.

ŚRŪTI. "That which is heard"; along with **smṛti** ("that which is remembered"), one of the two main categories of Hindu **scripture**. Śrūti is believed to be directly revealed by **God** (in theistic systems of Hinduism), or to simply be the sound of the cosmos heard by the **ṛṣis** or sages of the distant past while deep in **meditation**. It is *apauruṣeya* (non-man-made) and consists of the **Vedic** literary corpus.

STATES OF CONSCIOUSNESS. *See* CONCIOUSNESS, STATES OF.

STAGES OF LIFE. *See* ĀŚRAMA.

STHŪLA ŚARĪRA. Gross body; the physical body. *See also* ANNA-MAYA-KOŚA; ŚARĪRA.

SUBRAMAṆYA. An alternative name for **Kārttikeya**, the son of **Śiva** and **Pārvatī** and brother of **Gaṇeśa**.

SUBRAMUNIYASWĀMĪ, SATGURU ŚIVĀYA (1927–2001). Born Robert Hansen in California, Subramuniyaswāmī is one of a handful of Western initiates into Hindu **ascetic** orders to have attained a high level of authority and respect in the broader community of Hindus. Trained in both Western and Indian **dance**, Subramuniyaswāmī was drawn to Hindu thought at an early age. He was particularly inspired by the writings of **Swāmī Vivekānanda**. In 1947 he traveled to **Sri Lanka** where he met his **guru**, a Hindu monk named Yogaswāmī, who initiated him into his **Śaiva Siddhānta** lineage. He returned to the United

States to spread Hindu teachings and established a **temple** in San Francisco 1957. In 1970, he relocated to the island of Kauai, in Hawaii, where he established an **āśrama** and later a monastery and temple. He began to publish a journal in 1979 called *Hinduism Today*, which continues to be a highly regarded source of information on Hinduism in the increasingly global Hindu community. By the time of his **death**, Subramuniyaswāmī had initiated several monks into his order. He has been succeeded by Satguru Bodhinātha Veylanswāmī.

SUBTLE BODY. *See* SUKṢMA ŚARĪRA.

SUDĀMĀ. Boyhood friend of **Kṛṣṇa**. When Kṛṣṇa leaves his boyhood home to become king of **Dvārakā**, the two lose contact. When Sudāmā, a poor man, falls upon especially hard economic times, his wife reminds him of his friendship with Kṛṣṇa and suggests he go to Kṛṣṇa for help. Traveling to Dvārakā, Kṛṣṇa immediately recognizes him and treats him with great kindness, letting him stay in his palace. Sudāmā is so overwhelmed by all of this that he forgets the purpose of his journey. Kṛṣṇa, however, understands Sudāmā's situation. By the grace of his wife, **Rukmiṇī**, who is an incarnation of **Lakṣmī**, **goddess** of wealth and good fortune, Kṛṣṇa is able to save Sudāmā miraculously from his poverty. Returning home, he unexpectedly finds that his house has been transformed into a palace and his family is dressed in the finest clothes and has abundant food.

ŚŪDRA. The fourth of the four **varṇas** or **castes**. In terms of traditional occupation, this caste is made up of trades that involve menial labor and servitude. In the ***Puruṣa Sukta*** of the ***Ṛg Veda***, this caste is said to have been formed from the feet of the cosmic person (**puruṣa**). The practice of **Untouchability** arose from the fact that some of the duties of this caste are regarded as polluting, particularly those involved with the cremation of the dead or the cleaning of human waste. On some interpretations, the **Untouchables** (also called **Dalits** or **Harijans**) are even beneath the **Śūdras** in the caste hierarchy.

SUFI, SUFISM. Mystical movement within **Islam**. The Sufi traditions often interpret the Qur'an allegorically, and sometimes skirt (or even violate) the boundaries of Islamic orthodoxy, particularly in regard to the question of mystical union with **God**. An ecstatic tradition of devotion, there are many affinities between the sensibilities of Sufism and the **bhakti** movement of Hinduism. Both find expression in songs and **poetry**. Both focus on a sense of exquisite longing for God as an essential religious emotion. And both tend to see the cultivation and presence of such longing as being of vastly greater importance than the niceties of either correct ritual practice or orthodoxy. As a consequence of these shared sensibilities—and in the process, reinforcing them—Sufis and practitioners of bhakti in medieval India frequently interacted quite closely, crossing religious boundaries with relative ease, with Sufi practitioners taking Hindus as their spiritual teachers, and Hindus also taking Sufi masters as their **gurus**. The interaction between Sufism and bhakti was a major catalyst in the gradual synthesis of Hindu and Islamic cultures during the **Mughal** period. This synthesis produced the **Sant** movement and **Sikhism**. *See also* KABĪR; NĀNAK, GURU.

ŚUKA. Son of the sage **Vyāsa**. Śuka was a great **ascetic** who attained **mokṣa** (**liberation** form the cycle of **rebirth**) quite quickly, vanishing into the sun. (The path of the sun is presented in some sources as the route to liberation after **death**, with the alternative path, the path of the **moon**, leading to rebirth.) Vyāsa missed his son greatly and was consoled by **Śiva** with the gift of an etheric double of his son to keep him company.

ŚUKLA PAKṢA. The **bright half** of a Hindu month; the fortnight of a Hindu lunar month during which the **moon** is waxing; the period between **Amavasya**, or new-moon day (which is also the last day of the Hindu month) and **Pūrṇima**, or full-moon day. The bright half of the month is generally considered a more auspicious time to undertake new ventures. *See also* CALENDAR, HINDU.

ŚUKRA. The planet Venus. *See also* ASTROLOGY; NAVAGRAHAS.

ŚUKRAVĀRA. Friday, the day of the week that is governed by the planet Venus. *See also* CALENDAR, HINDU.

SUKṢMA ŚARĪRA. Subtle body. Subtle bodies occupy roughly the same space as the "gross" or physical body, but at a different energetic or spiritual wavelength. The subtle bodies correspond approximately to the **kośas** (layers or "sheaths") that cover the **ātman**, or self: the **ānanda-maya-kośa** (the layer of bliss), the **vijñāna-maya-kośa** (the layer of consciousness), the **mano-maya-kośa** (the layer of mind), and the **prāṇa-maya-kośa** (the layer of "breath," or vital energy).

SUKTHANKAR, V. S. (1887–1943). Indologist; he served as the general editor of the Bhandarkar Oriental Research Institute's critical edition of the ***Mahābhārata***, which has been the authoritative version for scholars ever since.

SUMANTU. One of the five **Brahmin** students of **Vyāsa**, also known as **Veda Vyāsa**, who is attributed not only with authoring the ***Mahābhārata*** but also with organizing the ***Vedas*** into their current distribution of four texts: the ***Ṛg Veda***, ***Yajur Veda***, ***Sāma Veda***, and ***Atharva Veda***. According to the ***Purāṇas***, each of

Vyāsa's students was responsible for memorizing and passing on a separate **Vedic** text—one for each of the four *Vedas* and one for the *Mahābhārata*. Sumantu was the student who was responsible for transmitting the *Atharva Veda*.

SUN. *See* SŪRYA.

SUNDAREŚVARA. "Beautiful Lord"; form of **Śiva** enshrined at the **temple** complex in **Madurai**. In this form, Śiva is the husband of **Mīnākṣī**, the "fish-eyed **goddess**."

SURABHĪ. "Good flavor"; an epithet of **Kāmadhenu**, the wish-fulfilling cow.

SURDĀS (c. 1479–1584). Blind **bhakti poet** of the **Mughal** period; a devotee of **Kṛṣṇa** and **Rādhā**. His songs reflect the **Vaiṣṇava** teachings of **Vallabha** (1479–1531), which emphasize complete surrender to the grace of Kṛṣṇa. *See also* POETRY.

SŪRYA. Vedic deity or **deva** who is the personification of the sun. As in other **Indo-European** religious systems, the Vedic sun god rides a flying **chariot** through the sky, representing the sun's daily passage from east to west. In the ***Mahābhārata***, Sūrya is the father of the character **Karṇa**. He is the object of prayer in the **Gāyatrī mantra**. A massive **temple** to Sūrya is located at **Konarak**, in the eastern Indian state of **Orissa**. Sūrya is also one of five deities recommended by **Śaṅkara** as an **iṣṭadevatā**, or chosen deity, in his system of **Pañcayātana Pūjā**, or "five objects of worship" (the other four deities being **Gaṇeśa**, **Śiva**, **Śakti**, and **Viṣṇu**).

SŪTA. Charioteer; also a bard. Charioteers in ancient India also recited **poetry**, passing on stories such as those making up the epics.

SŪTRA. Literally, "thread" (and cognate with the English word "suture"); the root text of a system of Indian philosophy (**darśana**). Traditionally, a sūtra is written in a style so terse as to require a commentary (or **bhāṣya**) in order to be comprehensible. It is likely that sūtras originated as mnemonic devices developed to preserve the oral teachings of the founding figure who established the system of thought to which a sūtra belonged. The intent would have been for students to memorize the sūtra and then have it explained by their teacher, who would "unpack" its meaning through a process of question and answer that became more formal and ritualized through the centuries. *See also* LITERATURE.

SUTTEE. Alternative spelling of **Satī** generally used by the British in the 19th century.

SVĀDHIṢṬHĀNA CAKRA. Cakra aligned with the navel. *See also* TANTRA.

SVARGA. Heaven; heavenly realm. Svarga is not an eternal everlasting paradise—as in the Abrahamic religions, or the **Vaikuṇṭha** of the **Vaiṣṇava** traditions of Hinduism. It is a temporary abode (though one in which a **soul** may reside for many eons) into which one is reborn as a consequence of meritorious **action** (**puṇya karma**). One eventually dies in this realm and is reborn as a human being. *See also* DEVALOKA.

SVAYAṂVARA. "Own choice," ancient ceremony in which a **kṣatriya** woman would choose her husband based on athletic prowess as demonstrated in a contest of arms. This ceremony figures prominently in the ***Rāmāyaṇa*** and the ***Mahābhārata***, whose respective heroes win their brides by performing extremely difficult feats of strength and skill that no other warrior can master. *See also* ARJUNA; DRAUPADI; RĀMA; SĪTĀ.

ŚVETĀŚVATĀRA UPANIṢAD. One of the principal ***Upaniṣads***; probably composed in the fourth century before the Common Era. The **philosophy** expressed in this text is close to that of the ***Bhagavad Gītā***. But unlike the *Gītā*, this text displays a **Śaiva** rather than a **Vaiṣṇava** orientation. More than most of the other principal *Upaniṣads*, the *Śvetāśvatāra Upaniṣad* promotes devotion (**bhakti**) and reliance on the grace of **God** (**Īśvara**, **Rudra**, or **Śiva**, in this text) as the path to **liberation** from the cycle of **rebirth**. The name of the text comes from its purported author, whose name means, "the man with a white mule."

SWADHYAYA PARIVAR. Contemporary Hindu movement based mainly in Gujarat and Maharashtra. The movement was established in 1954 by Pandurang Shastri Athavale (1920–2003), popularly known as "Dadaji," or "elder brother" within the movement. The primary focus of the movement is social service, study, and self-empowerment, based on Athavale's interpretation of the ***Bhagavad Gītā***.

SWĀMĪ (SVĀMĪ, SVĀMIN). "Master"; traditional title of a monk or **sannyāsin**. *See also* SANNYĀSA.

SWĀMĪNĀRĀYAṆ (1781–1830). An early modern Hindu teacher, also known as Śrī Sahajānand Swāmī. After undertaking **sannyāsa** or renunciation as a small boy, it is said that he traveled to the **Himālayas** where he practiced **meditation** and **yoga**. He traveled extensively throughout India, eventually settling in Gujarat, where the movement based on his teachings continues to be most popular. This teaching is close to the **Viśiṣṭādvaita** or **Qualified Non-Dualism** of **Rāmāṇuja**, combined with a strong emphasis on **ahiṃsā**, or nonviolence. Swāmīnarayan's devotees believe him to be an **avatāra** of **Kṛṣṇa**. *See also* SWĀMĪNĀRĀYAṆ MOVEMENT.

SWĀMĪNĀRĀYAṆ MOVEMENT. Movement based on **devotion** to and the practice of the teachings of **Swāmīnārāyaṇ** (1781–1830). The movement is especially popular in Gujarat, but has become global due to extensive emigration of Gujaratis out of India to various parts of the world. The movement, broadly speaking, is not a formally organized one. But an organization does exist, internal to the movement—the Bocāsanvāsī Akṣar Puruṣottam Swāmīnārāyaṇ Sansthā (BAPS).

SWASTIKA (SVASTIKA). "That which is auspicious"; auspicious four-armed symbol of the **goddess Lakṣmī**, also sacred in both **Jainism** and **Buddhism** as a symbol of the fourfold communities of monks, nuns, laymen, and laywomen in those two traditions. In the popular imagination of the West, this symbol is associated with Nazism. This is due to the misappropriation by the Nazis and other white supremacist movements of the early 20th century of the **Āryan Invasion Theory**, with its assumption of a correlation of culture and ethnicity. The **Indo-European** roots of **Vedic** culture were assumed to be

Traditional Hindu swastika, an auspicious symbol of wealth and abundance associated with the goddess Lakṣmī.

the product of a "pure" white race from Central Asia or Eastern Europe, and Vedic culture, as the most ancient living Indo-European culture, to represent an early form of that race's culture. The Nazis therefore appropriated Vedic symbols such as the swastika based on the belief that their occult power could grant the Nazis victory in battle, connecting them with their ancient "Aryan" ancestors. *See also* ĀRYAN.

SYNCRETISM. The tendency to combine elements of several different religions. It has often been remarked that syncretism is widespread among Hindus. Such syncretism can be intra-Hindu, consisting of combining elements from distinct Hindu traditions, such as **Vaiṣṇavism**, **Śaivism**, and **Śāktism**, or it can draw from traditions other than Hinduism, such as when Hindus include images of Christ or **Christian** saints in their home altars, or pray at the tombs of **Sufi** saints. Syncretism can be practiced as a matter of principle, as an expression of a belief that all or many traditions are divinely revealed and can lead to salvation, or it can be more "accidental," a function of ignorance of the original meaning of particular symbols or practices in the traditions from which they emerge historically, combined with a vague sense that these symbols or practices are holy and good. Both types of syncretism can be observed in Hindu practice.

T

TAGORE, DEBENDRANĀTH (1817–1905). Leader of the **Brahmo Samāj** starting in 1843. Technically Tagore was the founder of this organization, on the basis of the earlier *Brahmo Sabhā* of **Rām Mohan Roy**, though Roy is widely credited with being the father of the Brahmo movement as a whole and with defining its basically Unitarian orientation. Tagore was deeply devout and put considerable energy into promoting his organization and its ideals. Under his leadership, the Brahmo Samāj widened its following and began to influence other, similar movements across India. His youngest son, **Rabindranāth**, is widely revered, particularly in **Bengal**, for his considerable literary and **musical** talents.

TAGORE, RABINDRANĀTH (1861–1941). Nobel laureate; son of **Brahmo Samāj** leader **Debendranāth Tagore**. The multitalented Rabindranāth distinguished himself as a **poet**, novelist, songwriter, dramatist, essayist, and philosopher. He won the Nobel Prize for **literature** in 1913, making him the first non-European to win a Nobel Prize. He was knighted in 1915, but returned his knighthood in 1919 after British soldiers massacred hundreds of Indian independence activists—including dozens of **women** and children—at Amritsar in the Punjab. In 1916 and 1917 he undertook a world tour, visiting Japan and the United States. Controversially, he denounced nationalism of all kinds as inherently violent. He taught what he called the **philosophy** of "universal man," arguing for the inherent unity of all beings—an ancient Hindu theme. On this basis, he also wrote many plays and musical works that questioned the **caste** system, such as the opera *Caṇḍālikā*, which tells the story of a low-caste woman who becomes a **Buddhist** nun to escape the cruelty of caste. In the area of religion, he was long a skeptic, but adopted a view akin to **Neo-Vedānta** after he had a number of mystical experiences. He was drawn to religious figures like the **Bauls** and the **bhakti** poets who rebelled against social conventions. The **music** of these groups was highly influential upon his songwriting.

In 1901 Tagore established an **āśrama** at a town called Śantiniketan. This āśrama would later develop into a famous school. Tagore was deeply dedicated to the education and self-empowerment of the poor. He met **Mohandās K. Gāndhī**—with the two being captured together in a famous photograph.

Their relationship was cordial, but Tagore was critical of what he saw as the narrowness of Gāndhī's vision versus the universality to which he himself aspired. Today, Tagore is a universally beloved cultural hero in his native **Bengal**, as well as a globally respected literary figure.

TAMAS. Inertia; the third of the three **guṇas** or qualities of phenomenal existence as delineated in the **philosophies** of **Sāṃkhya** and **Yoga** as well as in the ***Bhagavad Gītā***.

TAMIL. Southern Indian language of the **Dravidian** family; a particularly rich language in regard to Hinduism. Tamil is the language of the **bhakti poetry** of both the **Vaiṣṇava Āḷvārs** and the **Śaiva Nāyanārs** and of such wisdom **literature** as the ***Tirukkuṟaḷ***. The region where the Tamil language is predominant—the modern Indian state of Tamil Nadu—is the site of numerous elaborate Hindu **temples** and was home to such major dynasties as the **Pallava** and **Coḷa**—both significant patrons of Hinduism.

TANJORE. *See* THAṄJAVŪR.

TANMĀTRAS. In **Sāṃkhya philosophy** and **Vedānta**, the subtle elements that give rise to the gross elements (**mahābhūtas**) that make up physical phenomena. Each tanmātra is equivalent to a mental state or sensation—smell, touch, sight, taste, and sound. Each one of the tanmātras corresponds to a specific mahābhūta: smell to earth (**pṛthvi**), touch to air (**vāyu**), sight to fire (**agni**), taste to water (**ap**), and sound to space (**ākāśa**).

TANTRA. System of spiritual practice based on the principle that the senses, rather than being restrained, as in other forms of **yoga**, can be used to transcend themselves. Many forms of Tantra exist. Tantric practice became a prominent feature of Hindu practice in the eighth century of the Common Era, though its roots may be much more ancient than this date would indicate. Tantric forms of **Buddhism** also became prominent at this time.

There are two basic types of Tantric practice: **Right-Handed** and **Left-Handed**, or Vāmācāra. Right-Handed Tantra is relatively uncontroversial, its practices consisting of **meditation** and visualization exercises, the use of geometric diagrams such as **maṇḍalas** and **yantras**, the chanting of **mantras**, and **pūjā**. Left-Handed Tantra, on the other hand (pun intended), is widely regarded as perilous and tends to be viewed negatively in the mainstream Hindu traditions. In an effort to embody the realization of non-duality, Left-Handed Tantric practitioners perform rituals that consciously violate the traditional norms of purity and impurity, such as partaking of the **Five M's**—substances like wine, meat, and fish, and activities such as sexual intercourse with someone other than one's spouse, the terms for all of which start with the letter "m" in **Sanskrit**. Some Tantric sects, like the **Śaiva Aghorīs**, meditate at night in cremation grounds and use human skulls as begging bowls.

Some scholars have argued that Right-Handed Tantra was developed to make the spiritual powers that Left-Handed Tantra is believed to yield available to a wider group of adherents, but without the attendant peril—the danger of Left-Handed Tantra being that a practitioner who engages in it out of the wrong motive, in the absence of a non-dualistic awareness, will experience the bad **karma** normally associated with the activities that it involves, including possible **rebirth** in one of the hells. Right-Handed Tantra transforms the more antinomian practices of Left-Handed Tantra into visualization exercises that are performed not literally but mentally. Well-known theologians who developed the Right-Handed practice of Tantra include the **Abhinavagupta** (950–1020), who systematized the **Kaśmīr Śaiva Kaula Tantra**, and **Bhāskararāya Makhin** (1690–1785), who similarly systematized the **Śākta Śrīvidyā** school of Tantra. Most Hindu systems of Tantra either have a **Śaiva** or **Śākta** orientation. The relationship between **guru** and disciple is of great importance in Tantra. Both Left-Handed and Right-Handed practices are passed on with a good deal of secrecy, due to the power that they are believed to evoke. Only one who has received initiation (**dīkṣā**) from a Tantric guru is eligible to utilize a Tantric practice.

A shared goal of all Tantric systems is the arousal of the **kuṇḍalinī** energy at the base of the spine and its elevation through the various **cakras** to the **sahasrāra cakra** at the crown of the head. This experience is believed to give the practitioner great spiritual power that can be channeled toward the attainment of **mokṣa**, or **liberation** from the cycle of rebirth. **Gorakhnāth**, the second guru of the Tantric Śaiva **Nāth Yoga** tradition, is credited with inventing **Haṭha Yoga** as a way to prepare the Tantric practitioner for the kuṇḍalinī forces and their movement throughout the body.

TAPAS. *See* ASCETICISM.

TAPASYA. **Asceticism**, either in general or in reference to particular ascetic practices.

TĀRA. Literally "star"; mother of Buḍha (the planet Mercury), whose father is **Soma**. A **goddess** widely revered in **Tantric Buddhism**.

TEJAS. Splendor, brilliance, glory; one of the qualities of a **deva**, or deity.

TEMPLE. Though communal worship is not mandated in Hinduism as it is in many other religions, such as **Christianity** or **Islam**, temple worship is believed to facilitate the inner journey to communion with the divine. The experience of **darśana**, for example—seeing and being seen by an image of a deity—is an occasion for forming a direct connection with divinity.

Temples traditionally have an outer chamber, where a variety of different **mūrtis**, or images, may be housed, and an inner sanctum, or **garbhagṛha**, where an image of the central deity of the temple is housed. The images in the temple are treated as respected persons, and the temple is their house. Following this metaphor, the priests of the temple are the servants of the **gods**. The images are regularly bathed, clothed, and offered food. The food is later distributed to the community as **prasādam**. *See also* AIHOLE; AJANTA; ANGKOR WAT; ĀRATĪ; AYODHYĀ; BĀDĀMĪ; BANARAS; BELUR; BHAJANA; BHUVANEŚVARA (BHUBANESHWAR); CIDAMBARAM; ELEPHANTA; ELLORA (ELŪRĀ); GURUVAYŪR; HALEBID; JAGANNĀTHA; KĀLĪBĀRĪ; KĀLĪGHĀṬ; KĀÑCĪPURAM; KANYĀKUMĀRĪ (CAPE COMORIN); KHAJURAHO; KONĀRAK; MADURAI; MĀMALLAPURAM; MĀYĀPUR; PADMANĀBHI; PAṬṬADAKAL; PŪJĀ; RAMEŚVARAM (RAMESHWARAM); SOMNĀTH (SOMANĀTHA); ŚRĪRAṄGAM; THAṄJAVŪR (TANJORE); THIRUVANANTHAPURAM (TRIVANDRUM); THRISSUR (TRICHUR); TIRUPATHI; UDAIGIRI; *VASTU ŚĀSTRA*; VIṢṆUPUR (BISHNUPUR); VIŚVANĀTHA MANDIR.

TEṄKALAI. Subdivision of **Śrīvaiṣṇavism**.

ṬHAGS. A 19th-century criminal sect that offered human sacrifices to the **goddess Kālī**. Their victims were usually unwitting travelers who would hire the Ṭhags as tour guides. The Ṭhags would then take them to an isolated place and strangle them. Although the basis of the film *Indiana Jones and the Temple of Doom*, the actual Ṭhag cult consisted of a small group of men, not the elaborate and well-organized **temple** community depicted in the sensationalist film. Human sacrifice is not condoned in mainstream Hinduism, nor even in mainstream **Tantric** or **Śākta** thought. The Ṭhag cult could perhaps be seen as a particularly extreme example of **Left-Handed** or Vāmācāra Tantra, which advocates the performance of traditionally impure acts as a way to affirm the non-duality of being. The Ṭhag cult was eliminated by the British in the 1830s, with the last known Ṭhag being hanged in 1882. *Ṭhag* is the origin of the English word "thug." It was during filming of the Beatles' movie *Help!*—a parody of the Ṭhag cult—that **George Harrison** first heard the sitar and became interested in Hinduism.

THAṄJAVŪR (TANJORE). Site in **Tamil** Nadu, in southern India, which is home to a massive **Śiva temple**, with a 63-meter-high tower and a sculpture of **Nandi** the bull that is one of the largest in India. Thañjavūr was the capital of the **Coḷa** Empire.

THAPAR, ROMILA (1931–). Historian and **Indologist**; student of **A. L. Basham** and author of *Early India: From the Origins to AD 1300*. She is currently professor emerita from Jawaharlal Nehru University, in **New Delhi**, where she taught for most of her career in the Centre for Historical Studies. Thapar has been outspoken on the topic of **Ayodhyā** and the **Babrī Masjīd** controversy, arguing there is insufficient evidence to support the claims of **Hindu Nationalists** that a **temple** to **Rāma** existed in ancient times on the site of the demolished mosque.

THEOSOPHICAL SOCIETY. Organization established in 1875 by **Helena Petrovna Blavatsky** and **Henry Steele Olcott**. The stated objectives of the society are "to form a nucleus of the universal brotherhood of humanity without distinction of race, creed, sex, **caste**, or color," "to encourage the study of comparative religion, **philosophy**, and science," and "to investigate the unexplained **laws** of nature and the powers latent in man." Holding very positive views of Hinduism and **Buddhism** and believing that both traditions preserve a primordial universal wisdom religion, or **perennial philosophy**, Blavatsky, Olcott, and other Theosophists promoted pride and interest among Hindus and Buddhists in their religious and cultural heritage, acting as "reverse missionaries," and also played prominent roles in the movement for Indian independence.

At one point a strategic alliance began to form between the Theosophical Society and the **Ārya Samāj**. But **Swāmī Dayānanda Sarasvatī** fell out with Blavatsky and Olcott in 1880, when they announced their conversions to Buddhism in **Sri Lanka**. Under the leadership of **Annie Besant**, the society contributed to the founding of **Banaras Hindu University**, as well as promoting **Jiddu Krishnamurti** as "Maitreya," a long-awaited messianic figure. Today, the society continues to promote education and an esoteric interpretation of the world's religions.

THIRD EYE. *See* AJÑĀ CAKRA.

THIRUVANANTHAPURAM (TRIVANDRUM). Capital of **Kerala**, on the southwest coast of India, and site of Śrī Padmanābhaswāmy **temple**, which houses a massive image of **Viṣṇu** as **Padmanābhī** (having a **lotus**, on which the creator deity **Brahmā** is seated, emerging from his navel).

THOREAU, HENRY DAVID (1817–1862). American **Transcendentalist**; associate of **Ralph Waldo Emerson**; author of *Walden* and *Civil Disobedience*.

Thoreau was deeply inspired by Hindu thought, particularly the ***Bhagavad Gītā***, from which he read regularly during his experiment of living as an American **sannyāsin** in a cabin at Walden Pond. A pacifist, Thoreau was jailed for his opposition to the Mexican–American War and slavery, which he expressed by refusing to pay taxes. His essay, *Civil Disobedience*, influenced **Mohandās K. Gāndhī**.

THRISSUR (TRICHUR). City in **Kerala**; site of Vaḍakkunāthan, a large **Śiva temple**. The **Kūṭiyāṭṭam** classical Indian **dance** style is performed at this **temple**, as well as in the nearby town of **Guruvayūr**. This is the one Indian style of classical dance that has continued to be performed without interruption since ancient times. Other styles fell into disuse at different points and have been revived in modern times.

THUGS. *See* ṬHAGS.

TILAK. A mark, usually made of a mix of vermillion and **sandalwood** paste, placed on the forehead as a symbol of divine blessing, often at the end of a **pūjā**. A simple tilak is typically in the shape of a small circle or vertical line in the center of the forehead in the location of the "third eye" or **ajñā cakra**. More complex tilaks are an indicator of one's sectarian affiliation. A **Vaiṣṇava** tilak, in its simplest form, consists of two vertical lines down the middle of the forehead. A simple **Śaiva** tilak, on the other hand, is made up of three horizontal lines across the forehead. Further detail indicates the particular Vaiṣṇava or Śaiva **saṃpradāya**, or denomination, of which one is a member.

TILAK, BAL GANGADHAR (1856–1920). Major leader in the movement for Indian political independence and early inspiration to the **Hindu Nationalist** movement. Tilak advocated violent revolution against the British in a commentary on the ***Bhagavad Gītā***. He encouraged the public performance of **Gaṇeśa Pūjā** in his native Maharashtra as a way of promoting Hindu pride and raising political consciousness.

TĪRTHA. "Ford"; a shallow point in a river allowing one to cross over. Metaphorically, a tīrtha refers to any sacred place of pilgrimage (**yatra**) that provides the devotee with an opportunity to advance across the "river" of **rebirth** to the further shore of **mokṣa**, or **liberation**. In **Jainism**, a tīrtha refers to the fourfold community of Jain monks, nuns, laymen, and laywomen who preserve and perpetuate the teachings of **enlightened** beings. *See also* TĪRTHAṄKARA.

TĪRTHAṄKARA. "Ford maker"; in **Jainism**, an **enlightened** being who creates a **tīrtha** or ford across the river of **rebirth** for others to cross to the further shore of **mokṣa** (**liberation** from the rebirth cycle). In Jain traditions, this tīrtha consists of the fourfold community of Jain monks, nuns, laymen, and laywomen who preserve and perpetuate the teachings of the Tīrthaṅkara. Twenty-four Tīrthaṅkaras appear on the Earth in the course of a single cosmic cycle. The 24th Tīrthaṅkara of our current cosmic cycle, **Mahāvīra**, appeared around the fifth century BCE and established the contemporary Jain community.

TIRUKKUṚAḶ. **Tamil** book of wise sayings, greatly revered in Tamil cultural tradition, attributed to **Tiruvalluvar** and likely composed between 100 BCE and 100 CE.

TIRUMANKAI (fl. 9th century CE). Last of the **Āḷvārs**—12 early medieval devotees of **Viṣṇu**, and exponents of **bhakti**, or devotion, as the supreme path to **mokṣa**. The teachings of the Āḷvārs are expressed in the form of **poetry** in **Tamil**.

TIRUPATHI. An enormous and wealthy **temple** in Andhra Pradesh, in southern India, dedicated to **Viṣṇu** in his form as **Veṅkaṭeśvara**.

TIRUVALLUVAR (c. 1st century BCE/1st century CE). Tamil author (or perhaps compiler) of the ***Tirukkuṛaḷ***, a book of wise sayings greatly revered in the Tamil cultural tradition. **Buddhists**, **Jains**, **Vaiṣṇavas**, and **Śaivas** all claim him as one of their own.

TIRUVĀYMOḶI. The collected **Tamil bhakti poems** of **Nammāḷvār** (880–930), one of the **Āḷvārs**, 12 **Vaiṣṇava** poets of southern India. Nammāḷvār was born a **Śūdra**, or a member of the servant **caste**. His text is revered in the **Śrivaiṣṇava** tradition as being no less sacred than the ***Vedas***, and it continues to be used in **temple** rituals up to the present. Nammāḷvār's revered position as a person of low caste in this tradition is significant, being illustrative of the **philosophy** of **bhakti**, or devotion, according to which social categories such as gender and caste are irrelevant to one's spiritual status or proximity to salvation. *See also* POETRY.

TORAṆA. Arched gateway of a Hindu **temple**; also used in Indian **Buddhist** temples. The design was transmitted by Buddhists to East Asia, becoming the model for the *torii*, or gate of a Shinto shrine in Japan. The toraṇa marks the boundary between the mundane realm and the sacred space of the temple.

TRAILANGA SWĀMĪ (1607?–1887?). Hindu holy man of **Banaras** who is claimed to have lived to the incredibly old age of 280—and according to some accounts, 358. Stories of his paranormal abilities and unusual qualities abound. He is said to have eaten little and yet to have weighed approximately 300 pounds. He did not wear clothing. He is attributed with great psychic powers, being able to read the minds of others easily. His disciples worshiped him as a living incarnation or **avatāra** of **Śiva**. He is believed to have been born in Andhra Pradesh and was a member of the **Daśanāmī Order** of Hindu monks. Both **Ramakrishna** and **Swāmī Vivekānanda** met him in Banaras, where he resided on the banks of the **Gaṅgā**, or Ganges River. He is in many ways the prototype of the image of the mysterious Indian holy man with miraculous powers.

TRANSCENDENTAL MEDITATION (TM). Mantra-based practice of **meditation** taught and promoted globally by **Maharishi Mahesh Yogi**; popularly known as "TM." One of the main centers for the teaching and promotion of this practice is Maharishi University of Management (formerly Maharishi International University) in Fairfield, Iowa. Though it has strong **Tantric Śaiva** roots, the practice is presented in a nonsectarian fashion as a scientifically based, holistic path to a state of complete well-being: spiritual, emotional, and physical. It is maintained by some adherents that practice of TM by a sufficient number of persons in a given geographic region leads to what is known as the "Maharishi Effect," resulting in a drop in violent crime and an increased sense of peace and happiness. The movement has put considerable effort into validating these claims statistically. To promote its program for world peace through meditation, some members of the movement started a political party in the 1990s called the "Natural **Law** Party," fielding candidates in both the United States and Great Britain.

TRANSCENDENTALISTS. Nineteenth-century group of American authors, **poets**, and activists inspired to varying degrees by Indic traditions as presented in the very early translations of such texts as the ***Upaniṣads*** and the ***Bhagavad Gītā*** into English and other European languages. The transcendentalist ethos both draws from Hindu sources and, in turn, inspires modern Hindu thinkers of the nascent **Neo-Vedānta** movement in India. Its prominent members include **Ralph Waldo Emerson**, **Henry David Thoreau**, and Walt Whitman. They emphasize self-reliance and the immanence of the divine within nature.

TRAYĪ VIDYĀ. "Threefold knowledge"; term for the ***Vedas*** in very ancient sources as well as in the tradition of the **Nambūtiri Brahmins** of **Kerala**. This term is one piece of evidence for the view that the fourth Vedic **Saṃhitā**, the ***Atharva Veda***, is later than the other three *Vedas*, and was not immediately accepted as authoritative by all Brahmins.

TRILOKA. "Three worlds." In early **Vedic** thought, the universe is divided into three levels—the Earth, the lower atmosphere, and the upper atmosphere, or celestial realm. In the ***Purāṇas***, this threefold cosmology is modified into a division into the heavens, the Earth, and the hells. In some sources, the three worlds are also said to refer to the three divisions of time—the past, present, and future. In **Vaiṣṇava** texts, **Kṛṣṇa** is often referred to as "Lord of the Three Worlds."

TRIMŪRTI. "Three forms"; sometimes referred to as the Hindu Trinity; a model of the godhead as consisting of three personae defined by their roles in the creative process of the cosmos: **Brahmā** the Creator, **Viṣṇu** the Preserver, and **Śiva** the Destroyer. This idea seems to emerge from the nonsectarian **Smārta** tradition. In the **literature** of the sects that take one or other of the deities to be supreme—**God** in a **monotheistic** sense—the deity in question performs all three roles—**creation**, preservation, and destruction—and not just one. Though sharing with the Trinity of **Christianity** the basic structure of three persons in one deity, attempts to correlate the roles of the three persons of each model fail to yield a perfect correspondence. A closer set of correspondences is possible between the Trinity of Christianity and the actual trinity of popular Hindu **devotion**: Viṣṇu, Śiva, and **Śakti**, the **Mother Goddess**.

TRINITY. *See* TRIMŪRTI.

TRIŚULA. Trident; divine weapon, often depicted as being carried by **Śiva** and **Durgā**. Many Hindu **ascetics**, especially **Śaiva** ascetics, often carry a triśula as a symbol of their religious allegiance.

TRIVANDRUM. *See* THIRUVANANTHAPURAM.

TRUTH. *See* SATYA.

TUKĀRĀM (1608–1649). Vaiṣṇava bhakti poet and saint of Maharashtra. Tukārām claimed to have been given initiation **(dīkṣā)** by **Caitanya** in a dream and the **Gauḍīya Vaiṣṇava** tradition claims him on this basis. Many of his writings can also be found in the *Ādi Granth*, the sacred **scripture** of **Sikhism**. Like many bhakti saints, Tukārām was more concerned with doing good in the world than with sectarian divisions and ritualism. Tukārām is regarded as part of the **Sant** movement.

TULSĪ. Basil plant sacred to **Vaiṣṇavas**, who regard it as an embodiment of **Viṣṇu**.

TULSĪDĀS (1532–1623). Vaiṣṇava bhakti poet and saint greatly revered for his ***Rām Carit Mānas***, a retelling in medieval **Hindi** of the **Sanskrit *Rāmāyaṇa*** of **Vālmīki**, of whom he is regarded by some as a **reincarnation**. Like many bhakti saints and **Sants** of his time, Tulsīdās had little regard for the **caste** system and specifically chose to translate the *Rāmāyaṇa* in order to make its saving message available to the common people. It is said that he was opposed by his fellow **Brahmins** in his native **Banaras** for undertaking this project. The project was, in any case, an enormous success. The *Rām Carit Mānas* is better known among most north Indian Hindus than is the original *Rāmāyaṇa*. *See also* LITERATURE.

TURĪYA. "The Fourth"; the fourth of the four basic **states of consciousness**. The first is the waking state, or conventional consciousness. It consists of a subject experiencing external objects of awareness. The second is the dream state, which consists of a subject experiencing internally generated objects of awareness. The third is the state of dreamless sleep, in which there is no distinction of subject and object, but also no awareness. In turīya, the fourth state, there is no distinction of subject and object, but there is awareness. This is a state that is identified by the **Advaita Vedānta** tradition with **jñāna**, or direct awareness of the unity of the experiencing subject (**ātman**) and the universal reality (**Brahman**). It is the experience of **mokṣa**, or **liberation** from the cycle of **rebirth**.

TVAṢṬṚ. Vedic deity; one of the 12 **Ādityas**; divine artisan; also called "maker of all"; credited with fashioning **Indra**'s thunderbolt weapon. *See also* VIŚVAKARMAN.

TWICE-BORN. A person who has received the **sacred thread** through the **upanayana** ritual, thus entering the first of the four stages of life, or **āśramas**.

TYĀGARĀJA (1767–1847). A composer of south Indian classical **music** (also known as *Carnatic* music); native of Andhra Pradesh, where he is a cultural hero. His deeply devotional songs continue to be performed in Hindu **temples** today.

U

UDAIGIRI. Site in Madhya Pradesh, in central India; location of numerous **temples** and carven caves utilized by both Hindus and **Jains** and dating from the **Gupta** period (320 to 550 CE).

UDAYANA (fl. 10th century CE). Philosopher in the **Nyāya** system, or **darśana**; renowned for his arguments for the existence of **God**. Udayana's chief philosophical interlocutors were **Buddhists** who sought to refute the traditional Hindu notion of a creator deity. He argued that the universe is an effect that requires a cause, and also that the atomic units or **paramāṇus** that make up material substances could not organize themselves in this way without an outside agency.

UDDHAVA GĪTĀ. Section of the ***Bhāgavata Purāṇa*** that consists of **Kṛṣṇa**'s teaching to his disciple Uddhava. Often circulated as a standalone text, the *Uddhava Gītā* has a special significance to **Vaiṣṇavas** as Kṛṣṇa's final teaching—for it is presented just before he retires to the forest where he knows he will die, being shot by a hunter.

UDGĀTṚ. Brahmin priest whose traditional duty is to sing hymns from the ***Sāma Veda*** at **Vedic** rituals of sacrifice (**yajña**).

UDIPI. Town in **Karnataka**; birthplace of **Madhva** (1238–1317), a **Vaiṣṇava ācārya** and founder of the dualistic or **Dvaita** system of **Vedānta**. Madhva spent most of his life in Udipi.

UJJAIN (UJJAYINĪ). City in Madhya Pradesh, in central India; one of the traditional locations of the **Kumbha Melā**. It is located on the Śiprā River.

UMĀ. Alternative name for **Pārvatī**, the **Mother Goddess** and wife of **Śiva**. Umā first appears in the *Kena* ***Upaniṣad***, where she teaches **Indra** about **Brahman**, thus making him foremost among the **devas**, or **gods**.

UNTOUCHABILITY. The **caste**-based practice of viewing certain occupations as so polluting as to render those who practice them inherently and permanently impure, and so a source of pollution to members of higher groups in the caste hierarchy. The lowest—and so most impure—group in most versions of the caste system is the **Caṇḍālas**, responsible for burning corpses in cremation grounds. Other such groups include those responsible for cleaning human toilets and sweeping streets. These Untouchable castes today are known as **Dalits**—"the oppressed"—or **Harijans**—"children of **God**." The term *Dalit* is a reference to the suffering such groups have experienced due to caste prejudice (**casteism**) and the term *Harijan* was coined by **Mohandās K. Gāndhī** to indicate that God is on the side of those who suffer most due to social injustice. Different low-caste communities prefer different terms depending upon their political orientation toward Hinduism, with Dalits tending to see Hinduism in a negative light, as warranting their oppression, and Harijans tending to see Hinduism in a positive light, seeing caste prejudice as a perversion of the tradition. All such groups are officially termed **Scheduled Castes** by the government of India, because they are on a list, or "schedule," of groups that warrant special benefits on the basis of the discrimination from which they have traditionally suffered.

UNTOUCHABLE. *See* UNTOUCHABILITY.

UPACĀRA. "Approach"; offerings made to a deity in **pūjā**. They traditionally include such items as water, flowers, food, incense, light (in the form of the lit flame of a lamp [**dīyā**] or candle), and a **tilak** of **sandalwood** paste, and **actions** such as prayer.

UPANAYANA. The **sacred thread** ceremony, or "second birth"; the **Vedic** ritual of investiture with the sacred thread marks the transition from childhood to **brahmacarya**, the first of the four stages of life, or **āśramas**. The thread is traditionally worn over the left shoulder, from where it hangs diagonally across the chest and back. As a coming-of-age ritual, the upanayana is analogous to the Bar Mitzvah of Judaism, or the **Christian** sacrament of Confirmation. It is a ritual traditionally reserved for **Brahmin** males. In the modern period, though, this ritual has been opened to girls as well. The process of **Sanskritization**, by which some lower-**caste** communities elevate themselves in the caste hierarchy, includes performing rituals of this kind. The idea of this ritual as a "second birth" is why higher castes—especially Brahmins—are often called **twice born**.

UPANIṢADS. "Secret doctrine"; the final portion of the **Vedic literature**, which is also known, for this reason, as the **Vedānta**, or "end of the ***Vedas***." The *Upaniṣads* are seen as the "end" of the *Vedas* in both a literal sense (as the last part of the Vedic literature to be composed), but also, in the traditions of Vedānta **philosophy**, in a more extended sense as conveying the ultimate meaning to which the Vedic literature points. The *Upaniṣads* were composed, at least in their current form, primarily between the fifth century BCE and the first two centuries of the Common Era. They consist largely of dialogues on the nature of **Brahman**, the ultimate reality.

UPĀSANA KANDA. "Contemplative portion"; the section of the **Vedic literature** that comes, historically, between the early **Karma Kanda**, or "**action** portion" of the ***Vedas***, and the later **Jñāna Kanda**, or "wisdom portion." The Karma Kanda consists of the early Vedic hymns, or ***Saṃhitās*** and the "priestly texts," or ***Brāhmaṇas***. The Jñāna Kanda consists of the ***Upaniṣads***. The Upāsana Kanda, however, is made up of the "Forest Texts," or ***Āraṇyakas***.

URVAŚĪ. Character of a story, first mentioned in the ***Ṛg Veda*** and later elaborated upon in the ***Brāhmaṇas*** and the ***Mahābhārata***, and finally in a famous play by the renowned **Sanskrit poet** and playwright **Kālīdāsa** (the *Vikramorvaśī*). In the story, a mortal king, **Purūravas**, falls in love with **Urvaśī**, who is a celestial maiden (**apsaras**), and asks to marry her. She agrees, on the condition that he protect her rams from being stolen and he never lets her see him naked. They live together happily for many years until a group of mischievous **gandharvas** steals one of Urvaśī's rams in the middle of the night. Hearing the commotion, Purūravas leaps naked out of bed to save the ram. The gandharvas flash a bright light on him, revealing his naked form to Urvaśī, and make off with the ram. At this, Urvaśī returns to the heavens.

In another story in the *Mahābhārata*, Urvaśī becomes enamored of **Arjuna** during his sojourn in the heavens during the period of the **Paṇḍavas**' exile. In response to her overtures—and knowing the story of his distant ancestor, Purūravas—Arjuna responds that he sees Urvaśī as his mother. Angry at being thus spurned, Urvaśī curses Arjuna to live for a year as a **woman**. This turns out to be fortuitous, however; the year following the Pāṇḍavas' exile, during which they are to live incognito, Arjuna uses this curse to disguise himself as a woman, his identity remaining hidden. *See also* LITERATURE.

UṢAS. Vedic goddess of the dawn.

UTTARA MĪMĀṂSĀ. Later exegesis; another term for **Vedānta**, which contrasts this system of thought with **Pūrva Mīmāṃsā**, or "earlier exegesis," which focuses upon the interpretation of the earlier, ritualistic portion (or **Karma Kanda**) of the **Vedic literature**. Uttara Mīmāṃsā, in contrast, focuses upon the later Vedic literature, the ***Upaniṣads*** (also known as the **knowledge** portion, or **Jñāna Kanda** of the *Vedas*). *See also* MĪMĀṂSĀ.

V

VĀC. "Speech"; **Vedic goddess** who is later identified with **Sarasvatī** and embodies the powers of speech and thought. It is through the power of speech that **Prajāpati** is able to create the world.

VĀCASPATI MIŚRA (900–980 CE). Prolific philosopher; author of commentaries on all of the **āstika** ("orthodox") systems of Hindu philosophy (**darśanas**). Although he was an adherent of **Advaita Vedānta**, his thought was influential on the later **Navya Nyāya** school established by the 13th-century philosopher Gaṅgeśa Upādhyāya.

VAHANA. "Vehicle"; the animal that accompanies each deity and serves as that deity's vehicle. Examples include **Śiva**'s bull, **Nandi**; **Viṣṇu**'s eagle, **Garuḍa**; and **Gaṇeśa**'s mouse, **Mūśaka**.

VAIKHĀNASA. Community of south Indian **Brahmins** whose traditional job is to serve as priests in **Vaiṣṇava temples**.

VAIKUṆṬHA. Heavenly abode of **Viṣṇu**. In many of the **Vaiṣṇava** traditions, **mokṣa**, or **liberation** from the cycle of **rebirth**, is conceived as dwelling for eternity in Vaikuṇṭha with Viṣṇu, or **Kṛṣṇa**, who is conceived as **God** in a **monotheistic** sense, as the supreme deity.

VAIŚAKHA. Month of the **Hindu calendar** that corresponds roughly to the period from mid-April to mid-May.

VAIŚAṂPAYANA. One of the five **Brahmin** students of **Vyāsa**, also known as **Veda Vyāsa**, who is attributed not only with authoring the ***Mahābhārata*** but also with organizing the ***Vedas*** into their current distribution of four texts: the ***Ṛg Veda***, ***Yajur Veda***, ***Sāma Veda***, and ***Atharva Veda***. According to the ***Purāṇas***, each of Vyāsa's students was responsible for memorizing and passing on a separate Vedic text—one for each of the four *Vedas* and one for the *Mahābhārata*. Vaiśaṃpayana was the student responsible for transmitting the *Yajur Veda*. In the *Mahābhārata*, he recites the text to King Janamejaya, great-grandson of **Arjuna**, at the former's snake sacrifice.

VAIŚEṢIKA. "Differentiation"; one of six "orthodox" (**āstika**) systems of philosophy (**darśanas**); attributed to the sage Kaṇāda, who most probably lived in the fourth century before the Common Era. Later aligned closely with the **Nyāya** system of logic, with which it is often paired and with which it had effectively merged by the medieval period, Vaiśeṣika is focused primarily upon the analysis of the material world, positing a theory of atoms (**paramāṇu**) and of compound and noncompound substances.

VAIṢṆAVA. Devotee of **Viṣṇu**; adherent of **Vaiṣṇavism**; of or referring to Vaiṣṇavism. Vaiṣṇavas form the largest subdivision of Hinduism, with roughly 60 percent of Hindus identifying themselves as Vaiṣṇava.

VAIṢṆAVISM. In terms of the numbers of its adherents, Vaiṣṇavism is the largest of the four main sectarian subdivisions that make up Hinduism. The various subtraditions that constitute Vaiṣṇavism share the trait of being oriented devotionally toward **Viṣṇu** as the supreme deity, regarding him as **God** in a **monotheistic** sense. Vaiṣṇava traditions have a strong focus on **bhakti**, or devotion to the supreme deity, as the preeminent—or even exclusive—path to **mokṣa**, or **liberation** from the cycle of **rebirth**. Though there is internal theological diversity among the many Vaiṣṇava denominations (**saṃpradāyas**), it can broadly be said that the Vaiṣṇavas are more inclined than the adherents of other Hindu traditions to insist upon a strong metaphysical distinction between God and the individual soul (**jīva**). The sharpest arguments for this view are presented by **Madhva**, the **ācārya** of the **Dvaita**, or dualistic form of **Vedānta**.

The other Vaiṣṇava systems of Vedānta, such as the **Viśiṣṭādvaita** or **Qualified Nondualism** of **Rāmāṇuja**, the *Bhedābheda* ("Difference-and-Non-Difference") taught by **Nimbārka**, and the *Acintya Bhedābheda* teaching ("Inconceivable Difference-and-Non-Difference") of **Caitanya**, affirm, in varying degrees and senses, an organic unity of God and the world, while maintaining the real distinction between God and the soul that all of these schools of thought see as a precondition for bhakti. They uniformly reject the **Advaita Vedānta** system's subordination of the personal deity to an impersonal absolute (**Nirguṇa Brahman**) and its claims that the personal God is part of the realm of illusion (**māyā**) and that bhakti is a merely preparatory discipline for **jñāna**, or knowledge, which **Śaṅkara** claims to be constitutive of mokṣa.

In practice, the most popular object of devotion for most Vaiṣṇavas is actually not Viṣṇu in his celestial form, but the **avatāras**, or incarnations, **Kṛṣṇa** and **Rāma**. Indeed, the **Gauḍīya Vaiṣṇava** tradition claims that Kṛṣṇa is not merely an incarnation, but is in fact the supreme deity, from whom the celestial form of Viṣṇu is a projection. And there is, indeed, support for this view in such early Vaiṣṇava texts as the ***Bhagavad Gītā***.

Lakṣmī, or **Śrī**, the **goddess** of prosperity and wife of Viṣṇu, plays a prominent role in many Vaiṣṇava traditions—particularly **Śrīvaiṣṇavism**, which claims that Lakṣmī and Viṣṇu are inseparable, forming a single, composite deity.

VAIŚYA. The third of the four **varṇas** or **castes**. In terms of traditional occupation, this caste is made up of trades that involve economically productive activity, such as **arts** and crafts and farming, as well as trade. In the ***Puruṣa Sukta*** of the ***Ṛg Veda***, this caste is said to have been formed from the stomach of the cosmic person (**puruṣa**). The word *vaiśya*, or "commoner," for this caste also suggests that its membership was relatively large in ancient India.

VĀJAPEYA. "Drink of strength"; a royal **Soma** sacrifice offered by a king who aspires to victory in battle. *See also* AŚVAMEDHA; RĀJASŪYA; YAJÑA.

VAJRA. Thunderbolt; favored weapon of **Indra**; fashioned by **Tvaṣṭṛ**; a symbol of the sudden flash of **enlightenment** in **Tantric** forms of **Buddhism**.

VĀK. *See* VĀC.

VALLABHA (1479–1531). Ācārya of the **Vallabha Saṃpradāya**, a **Vaiṣṇava** tradition also known as the Puṣṭi Mārg ("Way of Prosperity"), largely popular among the Gujarati **Vaiśya** communities. His teaching, known as *Śuddhādvaita*, or "Pure **Nondualism**," is that all souls (**jīvas**) are ultimately one with **Kṛṣṇa**. Strong emphasis is placed on **bhakti** and cultivating a personal relationship with Kṛṣṇa as his servant, friend, parent, or lover—a theme of many Vaiṣṇava traditions. Vallabha, a south Indian **Brahmin** who relocated to Gujarat and made many pilgrimages to **Vṛndāvana**, where Kṛṣṇa spent his youth, is held by adherents of his tradition to be an incarnation of Kṛṣṇa. Not an **ascetic** tradition, the **gurus** of the Vallabha Saṃpradāya are direct male descendants of Vallabha.

VĀLMĪKI. Sage attributed with authorship of the ***Rāmāyaṇa***. It is said that although Vālmīki was born a **Śūdra**, or member of the servant **caste**, he achieved the status of a **Brahmin** through his great learning—an indication, similar to the story of **Satyakāma** in the ***Chāndogya Upaniṣad***—of voices within the **Vedic** tradition that regard one's personal **qualities** rather than one's parentage as determinative of one's role in society. Although the *Rāmāyaṇa*, in its present form, is regarded by scholars as the work of many authors working over the course of several centuries (from roughly 200 BCE to 200 CE by most estimates), it is possible that a historical Vālmīki existed at an early period whose initial composition formed the basis for the current **Sanskrit** text. *See also* LITERATURE.

VĀMĀCĀRA. *See* LEFT-HANDED TANTRA.

VĀMADEVA. Major **Vedic ṛṣi**, or sage, to whom much of the fourth **maṇḍala** or book of the ***Ṛg Veda*** is attributed; patriarch of a **Brahmin** family charged with transmitting the *Ṛg Veda* to future generations.

VĀMANA. The dwarf **avatāra**, or incarnation, of **Viṣṇu**; the fifth of the 10 avatāras in the most popular traditional list of incarnations of Viṣṇu. **Bali**—the grandson of **Prahlāda** and great-grandson of **Hiraṇyakaśipu**, who was destroyed by the **Narasiṃha** or man-lion avatāra of Viṣṇu—was a mighty **asura** who achieved dominance over the Earth. In order to defeat Bali, Viṣṇu approached his court as a dwarf and asked to be given the land that he could cover in three steps. Seeing the tiny creature, Bali laughed arrogantly and granted the dwarf's request. At that, the dwarf rapidly grew until he filled the universe and took three steps, encompassing the "three worlds" (**triloka**), or all of existence. Bali was humbled and allowed the dwarf to put his foot on his head, pressing him down to the underworld. This story could be seen as an explanation for references in the ***Ṛg Veda*** to Viṣṇu's "three steps" by which he creates the world.

VANAPRASTHA. Literally, "forest-dwelling"; retirement; withdrawal; the third of the four stages of life or **āśramas** that map out the life of an orthodox Hindu according to the ***Dharma Śāstras***. The name of this stage and descriptions in the *Dharma Śāstras* suggest that at one time **householders** actually did withdraw with their wives to a forest to practice **asceticism**. Today, however, this stage refers simply to a life of retirement and withdrawal from daily responsibilities to focus upon religious duties and prepare for the end of one's life, typically spent residing in the home of one of one's children as part of an extended family. It is said that one should enter this stage when one's hair begins to turn gray and one's children give birth to children of their own.

VARĀHA. The boar **avatāra**, or incarnation, of **Viṣṇu**; the third of the 10 avatāras in the most popular traditional list of incarnations of Viṣṇu. The **asura Hiraṇyakṣa** is said to have cast the Earth into the cosmic ocean, from which the boar avatāra rescued it. He then slew Hiraṇyakṣa. Varāha is traditionally depicted iconographically as a warrior with the head of a boar holding the sphere of the Earth in his tusks and standing on the body of the demonic Hiraṇyakṣa.

VĀRĀṆASĪ. Alternative name for **Banaras**.

VARMA, MAHESH PRASĀD (1918–2008). *See* MAHARISHI MAHESH YOGI (MAHĀRṢI MAHEŚA YOGĪ).

VARṆA. Literally, "color"; principal unit of division of the **caste** system. It is probably due to the literal meaning of this term that the term *caste* was coined to refer to the Indian traditional division of social labor—*casta* being the Portuguese word for "color" that was later Anglicized to *caste*. The use of this term, combined with 19th-century racial assumptions, led early **Indologists** to speculate that caste originated as a system of racial segregation imposed by light-skinned **Āryan** invaders upon the dark-skinned indigenous peoples of ancient India, an interpretation that fit well with the **Āryan Invasion Theory**.

An alternative theory, however, based on the ***Dharma Śāstras***, is that the "colors" of the varṇas are symbolic of the **guṇas**, or qualities, that persons in these varṇas are believed to embody. The three guṇas, or qualities, that make up all phenomena according to **Sāṃkhya philosophy** are each assigned colors—the **sattva** guṇa being white, the **rajas** guṇa being red, and the **tamas** guṇa being black. The colors traditionally assigned to the varṇas are white for the **Brahmins**, red for **Kṣatriyas**, yellow for **Vaiśyas**, and black for **Śūdras**. **Untouchables** or **Outcastes**—persons whose duties are regarded as so polluting as to be beyond the pale of the caste system—are called *avarṇa*, or "without color." This does not fit well with an interpretation of the varṇas as skin tones—nor does the variation of skin tones that one actually finds internally to all of the varṇas in India.

In terms of actual social status and practice, varṇa is of far less consequence in the caste system than **jāti**—literally "birth"—the subgroups or "subcastes" into which each of the four varṇas is divided. The relative locations of the jātis within the varṇa hierarchy vary a good deal regionally, due in part to **Sanskritization**.

VARṆĀŚRAMA-DHARMA. "The ordering of **castes** and stages of life"; the duties of a person as mapped out according to one's location within the caste, or **varṇa**, system and within the system of four stages of life or **āśramas**; the classical Hindu way of life as it is outlined in the ***Dharma Śāstras***.

VARUṆA. Vedic deity of the **ocean**; one of the **Ādityas**; along with **Indra**, **Agni**, and **Yama**, one of the **Lokapālas** or "World Guardians"; close associate of the deity **Mitra**. Some hymns of the ***Ṛg Veda*** suggest that Varuṇa was, at one point, the supreme deity of the Vedic religion. Varuṇa is associated with judgment and the forgiveness of sins. He is sometimes depicted as holding a noose with which he ensnares the **souls** of the wicked. In some verses he is referred to as an **asura**, not in the later sense that this word has as a reference to the demonic, but in its more ancient sense as meaning "powerful."

He may be related to **Ahura Mazda**, the supreme deity of **Zoroastrianism**. In the ***Rāmāyaṇa***, Varuṇa assists **Rāma** and his armies by keeping the oceans calm as they build a bridge to **Laṅka** to rescue **Sītā** from **Rāvaṇa**.

VASIṢṬHA. One of the Seven Sages (**Saptarṣi**) born from the mind of **Brahmā** who is said to preside over the cosmos during our current **world age**. Vasiṣṭha is a significant figure in the ***Ṛg Veda***, attributed with authoring much of the seventh **maṇḍala** or book of this text. In the ***Rāmāyaṇa***, he is a priest to the royal family in which **Rāma** is raised. A major **Advaita Vedānta** text, the ***Yoga-Vāsiṣṭha***, is presented as the teaching of Vasiṣṭha to the young Rāma. In the ***Mahābhārata***, a set of eight deities called the **Vasus** conspire to steal Vasiṣṭha's cows. Upon discovering that they had stolen his cows, Vasiṣṭha curses the Vasus to be born as human beings. They then ask the **goddess Gaṅgā** to give birth to them and immediately drown them in her waters so they can return to the heavens. Only one of the Vasus—the original conspirator who hatched the cow-stealing plot—cannot get out of his situation so easily. He is not drowned and grows up to become **Bhīṣma**, the grandsire of the **Pāṇḍavas** and a major character of the *Mahābhārata* who lives to a very great age.

VASTU ŚĀSTRA. "Science of objects"; a Hindu analogue of *feng shui*. *Vastu Śāstra* encompasses architecture, the construction and consecration of **temples** and **mūrtis**, or images of Hindu deities, and the placement of objects in a room in order to maximize the positive flow of subtle energies.

VASU. "Good, prosperous"; category of **Vedic** deities frequently invoked for material benefits. There are eight Vasus altogether. In the ***Mahābhārata***, the Vasus conspire to steal the cows of the sage **Vasiṣṭha**.

VASUDEVA. Father of **Kṛṣṇa** and **Bālarāma**; husband of **Devakī**; chief minister of the wicked King **Kāṃsa**, of whom it was prophesied that a son of Vasudeva would slay him. Kāṃsa therefore imprisons Vasudeva and Devakī and conspires to kill their children. But Kṛṣṇa and Bālarāma are rescued and the prophecy is eventually fulfilled.

VĀSUDEVA. "Of **Vasudeva**"; epithet of **Kṛṣṇa** that refers to the fact that he is the son of Vasudeva.

VĀSUKĪ. Gigantic celestial serpent; king of the **Nāgas**. The Nāgas reside in a portion of the underworld known as **Pātāla**, over which Vāsukī presides. Vāsukī permitted the **devas** and **asuras** to use his body as the rope for a massive churn when they churned the cosmic ocean together in search of the elixir of life, or **amṛta**.

VAṬAKALAI. Subdivision of **Śrīvaiṣṇavism**.

VĀTSYĀYANA (c. 4th–6th centuries CE). Brahmin; author of the ***Kāma Sūtra***.

VĀYU. Vedic deity or **deva**, personification of the wind. Known for his great power, Vāyu is the father of **Hanuman** in the ***Rāmāyaṇa*** and of **Bhīma** in the ***Mahābhārata***. **Madhva**, founder and **ācārya** of the **Dvaita**, or dualistic school of **Vedānta** is believed to be the third incarnation, or **avatāra**, of Vāyu. *See also* GODS.

VEDA, VEDAS. "Wisdom"; the most revered, ancient, and authoritative collection of Hindu **scripture**; the **śrūti**, or "that which is heard"; the direct, divinely revealed word of **God**, or the original sound of the universe heard in the distant past by the **ṛṣis** or sages; non-man-made (*apauruṣeya*), in contrast with **smṛti** ("that which is remembered"), the sacred tradition that takes as its foundation the more ancient and fundamental *Vedas*; the primordial knowledge that underlies **creation**. The *Vedas* are a collection of texts written over a period spanning more than a thousand years, with the earliest Vedic texts being composed around 1500 BCE (according to mainstream scholarship) and the latest **Vedic** texts—the later ***Upaniṣads***—being composed in the first couple of centuries of the Common Era.

The *Vedas* are organized into four collections, each of which can be subdivided into a further four historical "layers" or "strata" of texts composed during different periods, and each of which serves as a commentary upon or elaboration of the texts that precede it. The four basic collections are the ***Ṛg Veda***, ***Yajur Veda***, ***Sāma Veda***, and ***Atharva Veda***. The first historical "layer" of each is a **Saṃhitā** or collection of **mantras**, or hymns. The largest and the oldest is the ***Ṛg Veda,*** whose Saṃhitā consists of 1,028 hymns to various **devas** or deities and philosophical reflections on the nature of creation. Next come the *Yajur Veda* and the *Sāma Veda*. The former is concerned with the correct performance of ritual and the latter sets hymns from the *Ṛg Veda* to **music**, forming the basis of Indian classical music. The *Atharva Veda* is a later text that includes hymns, magical spells, and philosophical reflections. The second historical layer consists of the ***Brāhmaṇas***, or "priestly texts," that focus on the meaning of the ritual of sacrifice (**yajña**) and include a good deal of narrative **literature**. The third layer consists of the ***Āraṇyakas***, or "forest texts," and the fourth is the ***Upaniṣads***, each of which is progressively more esoteric.

These four layers of text are also divided in a threefold fashion based on subject matter. The *Saṃhitās* and *Brāhmaṇas*, being concerned mainly with ritual **action**, form the **Karma Kanda**, or "action portion." The *Āraṇyakas* are called the **Upāsana Kanda**, or "contemplative portion," as they begin to reflect upon mystical correspondences between the elements making up the Vedic ritual and broader realities both within the cosmos and interior to the individual person. Finally, the *Upaniṣads* are called the **Jñāna Kanda**, or "wisdom portion," which reveals the ultimate meaning of the Vedic corpus as a whole in the form of dialogues on **Vedānta** philosophy. And the *Upaniṣads* themselves are also known as *Vedānta*, or "end of the *Veda*," a term with a double meaning, referring both to the fact that these texts form the final section of the Vedic corpus and to their content as the ultimate "end" or purpose toward which all Vedic wisdom and practice is directed.

VEDA VYĀSA. Epithet of **Vyāsa** that refers to his role in organizing the **Vedic** literary corpus into its current form.

VEDĀNTA. "Ultimate end or purpose of wisdom"; "end of the ***Veda***"; the philosophy of the ***Upaniṣads***, which are also called *Vedānta*. The term has a double meaning, referring both to the fact that the *Upaniṣads* form the final section of the **Vedic** corpus and to their content as the ultimate "end" or purpose to which Vedic wisdom is directed. Because the *Upaniṣads* do not present a single consistent **philosophy** in a linear fashion but convey their concepts through dialogues, **poetry**, and riddles, one must interpret these texts utilizing some hermeneutical principles as a basis. Differences of approach in this regard have led to the emergence of several different schools or systems of Vedānta over the centuries. One of the oldest of these systems is the **non-dualistic** or **Advaita** Vedānta associated prominently with **Śaṅkara** (788–820), which affirms that **Brahman**—infinite being, consciousness, and bliss—is the sole reality and that all phenomena are merely an appearance, or **māyā**—an effect of ignorance (**avidyā**) that gives rise to the process of **rebirth** and **liberation** from rebirth (**mokṣa**), which arises only when one has knowledge (**jñāna**) of the true nature of reality as Brahman.

Subsequent systems of Vedānta, of which there are many, express discomfort with Śaṅkara's insistence on the final unreality of phenomena, including the personal **God**, devotion (**bhakti**) toward whom Śaṅkara does commend as a purifying discipline preparatory to the arising of true knowledge but which other systems see as the preeminent path to liberation, which is seen as a salvation given by the grace of a loving God. Because of the centrality of bhakti in their understanding of the spiritual path, these thinkers insist, to varying degrees, on a real metaphysical distinction between the individual soul (**jīva**) and God as a necessary condition for the relationship of bhakti. The most radical in this regard is **Madhva** (1238–1317), whose dualistic **Dvaita** Vedānta draws a sharp distinction between God (**Viṣṇu**) and the world of souls. Most, such as the **Viśiṣṭādvaita** or **Qualified Non-Dualism** of **Rāmāṇuja** (1077–1157), seek to affirm both unity and duality, in different ways and in different senses. All of these approaches to the nature of Brahman can find justification in the *Upaniṣads*. In addition to the traditional or classical systems of Vedānta, which are concerned primarily with the correct interpretation of **scripture**, there is the **Neo-Vedānta** of the modern period, which is associated with **Ramakrishna** and **Swāmī Vivekānanda**, but is also expressed by such major figures of modern Hindu thought as **Aurobindo Ghose** and **Ramaṇa Maharṣi**, as well as many others. Adherents of Neo-Vedānta see Vedānta as universal knowledge available preeminently, but not exclusively, through the Vedic texts, which are seen as the records of the insights and experiences of the Vedic seers, or **ṛṣis**. It is the experience (**anubhāva**) of Brahman rather than the texts that speak of it that is regarded as primary in Neo-Vedānta, which sees itself less as a system of Hindu thought and more as a **perennial philosophy**, present in all cultures and religions to varying degrees but expressed with particular clarity in the Vedic tradition.

VEDĀNTA SOCIETY. Organization devoted to teaching and promoting the **Vedānta** of **Ramakrishna** and **Swāmī Vivekānanda**; established by Swāmī Vivekānanda in New York in 1894. Its Indian companion organization is the **Ramakrishna Mission**. It is closely tied to the **Ramakrishna Order**, which provides the monks and nuns who run the various centers that the society runs around the world.

VEDĀNTA SŪTRAS. Root text of the **Vedānta** systems of **philosophy**; alternative name for the ***Brahma Sūtras***.

VEDI (VEDĪ). Area within the sacred space of a **Vedic** ritual where implements such as ladles and spoons (for pouring **ghee** and other substances onto the sacred fire) are kept. It is also the space where the **gods** are invited to sit during the ritual. *See also* YAJÑA.

VEDIC. Of or referring to the ***Vedas***; adjective often used to refer to Brahmanical culture in general; also the archaic form of **Sanskrit** in which the ***Vedas*** are written. *See also* BRAHMANISM.

VEGETARIANISM. Dietary practice of avoiding foods that involve harm to animals, primarily meat, but also eggs and, in some cases, milk products (a practice more widely known as *veganism*). Vegetarianism is practiced to varying degrees in Indic traditions, ranging from the very strict dietary rules of **Jainism** to the relatively loose vegetarianism of many **Brahmins** in **Bengal** who eat fish but abstain from land animals. Most Hindu vegetarians eat no meat or eggs, but do partake of milk products. Jains are traditionally in this category as well, but avoid root vegetables that involve the killing of the entire plant. Some have recently become vegan, avoiding even milk due to the cruelty that is involved in modern milk-gathering techniques. Vegetarianism is a practice of **ahiṃsā**, or nonviolence, though it is also promoted as a healthy diet, conducive to spiritual practices such as **meditation**. Vegetarian food is held to contain more of the **sattva guṇa** that is a quality conducive to clarity of mind. About one third of Hindus are actually vegetarian.

VEṄKAṬEŚVARA. "Lord who destroys sins"; form of **Viṣṇu** that is highly popular in southern India. Veṅkaṭeśvara's main shrine is in **Tirupathi**, in Andhra Pradesh, on the sacred hill of Tirumāla. His gaze is believed to be so powerful that his eyes are covered. Indeed, he is also popularly known as "Bālaji," or "powerful one."

VIBHĪṢANA. Character in the ***Rāmāyaṇa***; a "good" **rākṣasa** who is devoted to **Rāma**, perceiving Rāma's true, divine nature as an **avatāra** of **Viṣṇu**. Vibhīṣana first advises his cousin, **Rāvaṇa**, not to abduct **Sītā** and then to return her to Rāma when she is being held as a prisoner in **Laṅka**, warning that this act will bring destruction upon the rākṣasas. In the end, he betrays Rāvaṇa, joining Rāma's army and advising him on how best to defeat Rāvaṇa. After the battle, when Sītā has been rescued and Rāvaṇa defeated, Rāma gives Vibhīṣana the kingship of Laṅka.

VIDYĀ. Wisdom; liberating **knowledge**; direct knowledge that **Brahman**, the universal reality, and **ātman**, the self, are one and the same.

VIJAYANĀGARA. "City of Victory"; highly successful kingdom that ruled the entire southern portion of the Indian continent from 1336 to 1646. Its capital, a city of the same name, was located in **Karnataka**, near the border with Andhra Pradesh. The city was sacked after the battle of Talikota in 1565, beginning a long period of decline and gradual disintegration of the kingdom. The city remains in ruins today but still contains a great many architectural and **artistic** wonders. The kings of Vijayanāgara practiced religious tolerance, supporting **Vaiṣṇavism**, **Śaivism**, **Śāktism**, and **Jainism**.

VIJÑĀNABHIKṢU (fl. 1550–1600). Philosopher who wrote commentaries on three of the **āstika**, or "orthodox," systems of Indian philosophy—**Vedānta**, **Sāṃkhya**, and **Yoga**. He sought to synthesize these three systems, paving the way for future Hindu thinkers who have increasingly seen these systems as forming a unitary whole. It has been argued that some of his interpretations of these systems involved some distortion carried out in the name of his agenda of unification—particularly his claim that Sāṃkhya is theistic. He was critical of the **Advaita Vedānta** doctrine of the illusory nature of phenomena (**māyā**) and adhered to the *Bhedābheda* interpretation of Vedānta associated with **Nimbārka** that seeks to accommodate both the **Upaniṣadic** teaching that all is one in **Brahman** and the realist understanding that difference is not a mere appearance, but that real metaphysical differences obtain, particularly between individual souls (**jīvas**) and **God**. His approach to unifying diverse systems of thought anticipates **Neo-Vedānta**.

VIJÑĀNA-MAYA-KOŚA. "Layer made up of consciousness." One of the five layers or "sheaths" (**kośas**) that surround the self (**ātman**). The vijñāna-maya-kośa is between the **mano-maya-kośa**, or "layer made up of **mind**," and the **ānanda-maya-kośa**, which is the inmost layer, closest to the self.

VIKRAMĀDITYA. "Sun of heroism"; title held by several ancient Hindu kings. The first, whose ascent to power is marked by one of the most popular Hindu dating systems (the *Vikrama Saṃvat*, which begins in 58–57 BCE), is believed to have lived in the first century before the Common Era and ruled from the city of **Ujjain**, which is today located in the state of Madhya Pradesh, in central India. The second major ruler to carry this title is Candragupta II, a king of the **Gupta** dynasty who successfully expanded his empire to its height, encompassing all of northern India from the **Indus** River to the **Ganges** delta.

VIMĀNA. Flying **chariot**; preferred method of locomotion among many of the **gods**; the inspiration for such works (many would say pseudo-scientific works) as Erich Von Daniken's *Chariots of the Gods*, which speculate that extraterrestrial astronauts visited the Earth in ancient times, providing a basis for such concepts of traditional mythology as the vimāna.

VĪṆĀ. Indian lute; stringed **musical** instrument. **Sarasvatī**, the **goddess** of wisdom, and the sage **Nārada** are both depicted carrying this instrument.

VĪRABHADRA. Fierce form of **Śiva**, created by him to avenge the **death** of his wife, **Satī**, by destroying the sacrifice performed by her father, **Dakṣa**, and beheading Dakṣa in the process.

VĪRAŚAIVA. "Follower of the heroic **Śiva**"; **Śaiva** tradition based in **Karnataka** and established by the **bhakti poet** and social reformer **Basava** (1134–1196). Also known as the **Liṅgāyats**, the Vīraśaivas oppose **casteism** and teach the equality of all human beings as manifestations of Śiva. Believing in holding ritualism to a bare minimum, the only image the

Vīraśaivas use is the abstract form of Śiva, the **liṅga** (hence the alternate name *Liṅgāyat* for this tradition), which they traditionally wear on a necklace. The Vīraśaivas regard Śiva as **God** in the **monotheistic** sense—as the one supreme deity.

VIŚIṢṬĀDVAITA VEDĀNTA. The metaphysical teaching developed by the Vedāntic **ācārya Rāmāṇuja**. According to this view, all of reality is, as **Advaita Vedānta** teaches, one with **Brahman**. But unlike in the Advaitic concept of Brahman, Brahman is here conceived as having internal differences. *See* QUALIFIED NON-DUALISM.

VIṢṆU. "The all-pervasive one"; the single most popular Hindu deity. He is regarded by many of his devotees, who are called **Vaiṣṇavas**, as **God** in a **monotheistic** sense. He is seen in the broader Hindu tradition as that aspect of the divine that preserves the world from chaos during the vast interval of time between its periodic **creation** and destruction. He carries out this act of preservation, as stated in the ***Bhagavad Gītā*** (4:7), by projecting himself into the world in the form of an **avatāra**, or incarnation, to protect **dharma** and destroy the demonic forces of chaos (usually represented as demonic beings—**asuras** and **rākṣasas**). A benevolent deity, he is a popular savior and object of **bhakti**, or devotion.

In his origins, Viṣṇu appears to be a solar deity, closely associated with imagery of sunlight. He is mentioned infrequently in the ***Vedas***—though in one of these references he is attributed with creating the entire universe by taking three steps, which gives rise to the "three worlds" (**triloka**)—the Earth, the atmosphere, and the celestial realm. He is far more prominent in the later epic **literature**—the ***Rāmāyaṇa*** and ***Mahābhārata***—and in the ***Purāṇas***. Several, perhaps originally distinct, deities seem to have gone into his classical form (such as **Nārāyaṇa**). Viṣṇu is worshiped most frequently not in his celestial form—as Viṣṇu per se—but in the form of his two most popular avatāras—**Kṛṣṇa** and **Rāma**. His wife, **Lakṣmī**, is also a highly popular **goddess**. She is viewed by some traditions, such as **Śrīvaiṣṇavism**, as essentially one with Viṣṇu, with the two forming a composite deity.

Viṣṇu is most frequently represented as a celestial monarch, holding in his four hands a conch shell (**śaṅkha**), a discus (**cakra**), a club, and a **lotus**. His skin is the blue color of the infinite sky and his clothing is yellow, which is symbolic of the Earth. These colors of sky and Earth represent his all-pervasive nature (which is also the meaning of his name).

VIṢṆUPUR (BISHNUPUR). City in **West Bengal** renowned for its artisans and brick **temples** with terracotta tiles that depict events from the ***Rāmāyaṇa*** and ***Mahābhārata***.

VIŚUDDHA CAKRA. Cakra that is located in the throat. *See also* TANTRA.

VIŚVA HINDU PARIṢAD (VHP). "World Hindu Council." This **Hindu Nationalist** organization was established in 1964. Also known as the VHP, it defines Hinduism broadly (and in keeping with **Savarkar**'s definition) as encompassing all Indic religions, and so as incorporating **Buddhism**, **Jainism**, and **Sikhism**. Of course, some Buddhists, Jains, and Sikhs do not approve of their traditions being incorporated into Hinduism by definitional fiat. But others do not object, as evidenced by the fact that some Buddhist, Jain, and Sikh religious leaders—including the Dalai Lama—are members of the VHP and were present at its founding.

The controversial stands that the VHP has taken include its demand that a **temple** to **Rāma** be built at the site of the demolished **Babrī Masjīd** in **Ayodhyā** (a site recently divided among Hindu and Muslim organizations by an Indian high court) and its stated desire to transform India formally into a Hindu, rather than a secular, state. Its ties to the **Bharatīya Janata Party** (BJP) have proven controversial for this party. The VHP shares with the BJP the agenda of developing a "Uniform Civil Code" for India to replace the system of multiple civil codes for different religious communities that exists at present. The VHP is also an outspoken critic of proselytizing activities by **Christian** and **Islamic** groups directed at Hindus in India.

VIŚVAKARMAN. "Maker of all"; the supreme architect of the universe; an epithet of **Tvaṣṭṛ**, the divine artisan of the ***Vedas***; one of the **Ādityas**. He represents creative power and **knowledge** and is attributed with creating the science of architecture (***Vastu Śāstra***).

VIŚVAMITRA. One of the Seven Sages (**Saptarṣi**) born from the **mind** of **Brahmā** that preside over the cosmos; an important seer or **ṛṣi** of the ***Ṛg Veda***, to whom many of the hymns of the third **maṇḍala** of this work are attributed. In the ***Rāmāyaṇa***, he is depicted as **Rāma**'s and **Lakṣmaṇa**'s **guru**, taking them to the wilderness during their youth and teaching them to slay demonic beings. He is also the father of **Śakuntalā**.

VIŚVANĀTHA MANDIR. Major **temple** in **Banaras** that is dedicated to **Śiva**. It is controversial for not permitting entry to non-Hindus.

VIŚVEDEVAS. "All **gods**"; a term sometimes used in the ***Ṛg Veda*** to refer to a specific group of deities, but also used (in the same text) to refer to all gods in general. It may be that the Viśvedevas are invoked to ensure that no deity has been forgotten in the course of a ritual performance. *See also* DEVAS.

VIṬṬHALA. "Standing on a brick"; an image of **Viṣṇu** that is popular in Maharashtra.

VIVĀHA. The Hindu sacrament of **marriage**; the Hindu wedding ceremony. *See also* SAṂSKĀRA; WOMEN.

VIVASVAT. Name for **Sūrya**, **god** of the sun.

VIVEKA. Discernment; discrimination. An important intellectual virtue in **Vedānta**.

VIVEKĀNANDA, SWĀMĪ (1863–1902). Born Narendranāth Datta; chief disciple of **Ramakrishna** and the first of many Hindu spiritual teachers to successfully spread their traditions in the West. A member of the **Brahmo Samāj** early in his life, and with a tendency to view religion from a skeptical perspective, Datta was quite powerfully drawn to the teaching and personality of Ramakrishna. After Ramakrishna's **death** in 1886, he joined the **Daśanāmī Order** of monks, becoming Swāmī Vivekānanda, and leading other young disciples of Ramakrishna to do the same, thus starting the **Ramakrishna Order**.

In 1893, Vivekānanda accepted an invitation to speak at the first Parliament of the World's Religions. His address to the parliament was a success and led to a speaking tour that took him across the United States—where he established the first **Vedānta Society** in New York City in 1894—and to Great Britain. In 1897, he initiated Margaret E. Noble as the first known Westerner to join a Hindu monastic order (from which point she came to be known as **Sister Niveditā**). That same year, he returned to India and established the **Ramakrishna Mission**.

Vivekānanda's teachings in many ways reflect and in many ways go beyond the teachings of his master, Ramakrishna. His primary innovation was to direct the monks of the Ramakrishna Order to engage in work for the uplift of the poor—a break with tradition inasmuch as **sannyāsins** have generally been expected to pursue study, **meditation**, and **ascetic** practice exclusively. He was also the first to explicitly articulate the concept of **four yogas**, or paths to **mokṣa** (**liberation** from **rebirth**) and to see these paths as equally valid and effective.

VRAJA. Region of northern India in which **Kṛṣṇa** is believed to have spent much of his life on Earth, and therefore particularly holy to **Vaiṣṇava** devotees. It includes **Mathurā**, the city where he was born and later slew the wicked King **Kāṃsa**, and **Vṛndāvana**, the town where he lived amongst the **gopīs**, or cowherdesses, during his adolescence.

VRATA. Vow. A *vrata* generally refers to a period of fasting undertaken for a set time either as a way to ask for a particular divine favor or as a more general act of spiritual and mental purification. Some vratas are regarded as being especially auspicious if carried out on particular holy days or at particular points on the **Hindu calendar**. A vrata may involve abstaining from particular foods (or from all food) for a set period of time, doing a particular **pūjā**, abstaining from sexual activity, giving gifts to the poor or to religious institutions, or going on a pilgrimage (**yatra**). Such vows are a form of lay **asceticism**, which is especially popular among **women**.

VRĀTYA. "One who has taken a vow"; an ancient type of **ascetic** mentioned in both the ***Ṛg Veda*** and the ***Atharva Veda***. The descriptions of their activities in these texts suggest they were early practitioners of what would later be known as **Yoga** and **Tantra**. They may have been warrior monks. It is possible that they were precursors of the **śramaṇa** movement, which would include **Jainism** and **Buddhism**.

VṚNDĀVANA. Town where **Kṛṣṇa** resided during his adolescence, after being taken into hiding to protect him from the evil King **Kāṃsa**. It is where Kṛṣṇa played with the **gopīs** and met his beloved **Rādhā**, as described in the ***Bhāgavata Purāṇa*** and in greater detail in the ***Gītagovinda*** of **Jayadeva**. It is highly sacred to the devotees of Kṛṣṇa and a very popular site for pilgrimage (**yatra**).

VṚTRA. "Obstructor, restrainer"; serpentine monster defeated by **Indra**. Vṛtra captured the world's cattle and its water—both important symbols of prosperity—keeping them in a mountain cave that he then surrounded with his enormous body, coiling it around the mountain. Indra slew Vṛtra with his thunderbolt weapon (**vajra**) and freed the cattle and the waters, both of which could then flow freely across the Earth.

In terms of **Indo-European** mythology, Indra's struggle with Vṛtra is comparable to Thor's battle, in Norse mythology, with the Midgard Serpent. *See also VEDAS.*

VYĀSA. Sage who is attributed with compiling the ***Vedas*** into their current form, a feat for which he is known as **Veda Vyāsa**, and with authoring the ***Mahābhārata***, which he is said to have dictated to the deity **Gaṇeśa**. Vyāsa is also a character in the *Mahābhārata*, where he is said to be the son of Satyavatī, the daughter of the king of the fishermen, and the sage **Parāśara**. He is the father of **Dhṛtarāṣṭra** and **Paṇḍu**, the kings whose sons' rivalry is the main topic of the epic. *See also BRAHMA SŪTRAS.*

VYŪHA. "Manifestation"; appearance of **Viṣṇu** in his full power; similar to an **avatāra**, though not all avatāras are vyūhas. Some of the avatāras are **aṃśas**, or manifestations of merely a portion of Viṣṇu's total being.

W

WAKING CONSCIOUSNESS. One of the four **states of consciousness** described in the ***Upaniṣads***. The other three levels are the dream state, dreamless sleep, and the fourth state, or **turīya**, associated with spiritual transcendence and **enlightenment**.

WARRIOR. Kṣatriya, the second of the four **varṇas** or "castes," the first being the **Brahmin** priesthood, and the third and fourth, respectively, being the **Vaiṣya** or common people and the **Śūdra** or servant caste.

WEST BENGAL. Portion of **Bengal** that became part of the Republic of India after the 1947 partition of India and Pakistan. East Bengal first became East Pakistan and, after breaking away from Pakistan in a revolution in 1971, Bangladesh. East and West Bengal were first partitioned under the British **Rāj** in 1905.

WIDOW IMMOLATION. *See* SATĪ; WOMEN.

WIDOW REMARRIAGE. *See* WIDOWS; WOMEN.

WIDOWS. Because Hindu **marriage** is traditionally seen as being for life—and on some interpretations, as extending over many lifetimes—the remarriage of widows is frowned upon in the ***Dharma Śāstras***. It is not clear, however, to what extent such prohibitions were observed in practice in ancient times, or if the very point of such prohibitions is to put an end to a widespread practice of which the **Brahmanical** authors of these texts do not approve. In the traditional Brahmanical schema of a human lifetime, measured out in terms of social location (**varṇa**) and stages of life (**āśrama**), the only roles assigned to a **woman** are to be a daughter to her father, wife to her husband, and mother to her children. The single adult woman, without a husband, therefore does not fit neatly into this scheme.

It has often been the case that widows have entered the **vanaprastha āśrama**—the retirement or withdrawal stage of life—upon the deaths of their husbands, being cared for by their adult children. But in the case of women who are not elderly, or even young and childless—not an uncommon occurrence at an earlier time when marriages were often arranged in which a young girl was betrothed to a much older man—it is often expected that they will enter a state of **sannyāsa** (renunciation), becoming a Hindu nun. There are many communities of such women, particularly in the city of **Banaras**, who dedicate themselves to religious activity. Such women have often suffered exploitation of various kinds, leading the Hindu reformers of the 19th century to advocate for widow remarriage and against childhood betrothals. As a result of their efforts, widow remarriage is now more common than it used to be. But it is still regarded as a grave infraction by orthodox Hindus.

WILSON, HORACE HAYMAN (1786–1860). British **Indologist**; translator of the ***Ṛg Veda***; first Boden Professor of **Sanskrit** at Oxford University.

WIND. *See* VĀYU.

WOMEN. The roles of women in Hinduism have been far too complex throughout the centuries for any generalization to be adequate. And prior to the modern period, so many of our sources consist of prescriptive texts—such as the ***Dharma Śāstras***—that reflect what their **Brahmin** authors regarded as an ideal situation that it is nearly impossible to deduce from them what the ground realities were at any given time. Were the injunctions of the Brahmins followed closely by most people? Or was the entire point of these injunctions to seek to change a ground reality that was radically different from what their authors felt should be the case? It is likely that both situations—as well as a mix of both—occurred at different times and in different locations. When alternative voices are available, such as in the folk tales and vernacular **literatures** of the local non-**Sanskrit** traditions, or in the inscriptions left by kings or wealthy patrons of religious institutions, they suggest a more mixed picture than do the Brahmanical texts. And such voices also intrude into the texts of the Brahmins from time to time—just as, with regard to the issue of **caste**, one can find a **Satyakāma** or a **Vālmīki**, as well as an **Ekalavya**. If the reader will bear all of this in mind, what follows can be understood for what it is—a very broad set of generalizations based on the sources that are available in abundance (Brahmanical Sanskrit texts) that can sometimes reflect and can sometimes be in radical discontinuity with the social realities of actual Hindu women.

The overall orientation of the Brahmanical tradition is decidedly patriarchal. The system of **varṇas** ("castes") and **āśramas** (stages of life) defines the ideal life trajectory of a male. It is males who traditionally receive the **sacred thread (upanayana)** and who take up an occupation appropriate to their caste after **marriage** and entering the stage of the **householder**. They then retire, entering the **vanaprastha** stage. Alternatively, they may, at any point, renounce the life of a layperson, undertaking **sannyāsa**.

The **dharma** of a woman, however, is to be a daughter to her father, a wife to her husband, and a mother to her children. A woman may enter the retirement phase along with her husband, or have it forced upon her by **widowhood**. Her social role is entirely defined in terms of her relationships with men—her father in childhood, her husband as a married woman, and her sons, first as their caretaker, and then, perhaps, as the recipient of their care in her old age. Her daughters, if she has any, will join the families of their husbands and their first duty will be to their husbands and their husbands' parents.

Again, the degree to which this Brahmanical ideal has been observed in practice is open to question. Certainly in the modern period it has been observed quite rigorously in many settings—particularly rural settings—but also set aside quite decisively, particularly among the wealthy and well educated. Premodern exceptions—independently wealthy women who were patrons of particular religious communities, and who were more often than not courtesans by trade—did exist.

On the classical model, the only route for a woman to live independently—and for which a good deal of evidence exists—is the religious life. In the religious arena, women could attain not only a degree of independence from male domination but could even rise to a considerable level of social authority, wielding power—even over men—as **gurus** and as highly revered saints. Figures such as **Āṇḍāl**, **Mahādeviyakka**, and **Mīra Bai** could transgress their traditional social roles because they did so out of love for **God**.

This model continues into the modern period, with such figures as **Ānandamāyī Mā**, **Mātā Amritānandamayī**, and **Gurumayī** being highly revered and independent. It may be argued that the price of such independence is the total religious commitment that these women's lives display. But we would also be erring if we presumed that the sole motive of these women has been personal independence, and has not included a spiritual aspiration of a fairly traditional sort—a desire for **mokṣa** or to be nearer to God.

Like the discourses of democracy and human rights, however, feminist discourse has also made inroads into Hinduism. Though it is in many ways a deeply conservative tradition, it has also proven to be highly adaptive through the centuries. In recent years, on the basis of the same doctrine of the unity of all beings that has served to undercut the caste system, women have increasingly made inroads into former bastions of orthodoxy, engaging in public reading of the ***Vedas***, for example, receiving the sacred thread, and, as more women in urban areas have taken up jobs outside of the home—either out of desire or necessity—being seen as co-householders with their husbands.

At the same time, the heavy hand of patriarchy is still very much in evidence. A traditional preference for sons over daughters has led to a widespread practice of aborting female fetuses. And the ongoing practice of dowry—in which the family of a new bride is expected to pay a considerable fee to the family of her husband—fuels the preference for sons, because sons will bring money into the family when they marry, whereas daughters will cost money. Dowry **death**, too, is a result of this practice—in which families conspire to marry their sons to women, extract a dowry from the woman's family, and then murder the woman, sometimes doing this serially.

The practice of **satī**, or widow immolation—which many non-Hindus wrongly take to be a widespread and current practice—is nearly unheard-of. The last such event, at least to receive publicity, occurred in 1987, and received widespread condemnation from the wider Hindu community. The practice was banned in 1829, due largely to the activism of the Hindu reformer **Rām Mohan Roy**.

The presence of a vigorous **Goddess** tradition, and a wide range of assertive and powerful **goddesses**, might suggest a broader feminist streak in Hinduism than is actually the case. But the worship of goddesses and the roles of actual women have largely been independent variables.

The range of options available for traditional Hindu women is often discussed in terms of the contrast between the heroines of the ***Rāmāyaṇa*** and ***Mahābhārata***—**Sītā** and **Draupadī**, respectively. Sītā is obedient to every wish of her husband, even to the point of suffering the indignity of the fire test, when she has all along been perfectly faithful to him. She suffers both through her husband's troubles and through the indignity society imposes upon her without complaint. Draupadī is also a faithful wife who suffers with her husbands. But when her rights are violated, when her husband does not protect her honor but, quite literally, gambles it away as though it were a possession, she speaks up for her rights, not only questioning the rightness of her husband's choices but also displaying a considerable **knowledge** of dharma. Of the two, Sītā has generally been upheld as the model Hindu woman. But the model of Draupadī suggests another way, from within the Hindu tradition, for a woman to live—with dignity and equality.

WORK. *See* KARMA; KARMA YOGA.

WORLD AGES. Hindu traditions conceive of time as flowing on a vast, cosmic scale. Strictly speaking, on a mainstream Hindu understanding—as shaped by the ***Purāṇas***—there is no precise beginning (or end) of time. In terms of **Advaita Vedānta**, time itself is an illusion, the only reality being the eternal, timeless, and formless **Brahman**. But within the realm of **māyā**, of the appearance of time and space, the universe is continuously and repeatedly created, endures, is destroyed, and is re-created. In the ***Purāṇas*** and ***Dharma Śāstras***, these vast cycles are conceived as days and nights of **Brahmā**, the creator **god**. Each day of Brahmā—a **kalpa** or cosmic epoch—is divided into 14 "ages of **Manu**" or Manvantaras, each of which is presided over by a Manu, or being born from the **mind** of Brahmā. It is also divided into 1,000 *Mahāyugas*, or "great eons." Each Mahāyuga is made up of four **yugas**, or eons. Each yuga within a Mahāyuga is somewhat worse (but also, mercifully, shorter) than the one before it. The Kṛta or **Satya** yuga is equal to 4,000 divine years (which equals 518,400,000 terrestrial years). The Tretā yuga lasts 3,000 divine years (388,800,000 terrestrial years). The Dvāpara yuga lasts 2,000 divine years (259,200,000 terrestrial years). The Kali yuga (which we currently inhabit) lasts 1,000 divine years (129,600,000 terrestrial years). Between the yugas are intermediate periods that last 800, 600, 400, and 200 divine years. An entire Mahāyuga is therefore equal to 12,000 divine years, or 1,555,200,000 terrestrial years, and an entire kalpa or day of Brahmā is equal to 12,000,000 divine years, or 1,555,200,000,000 terrestrial years. After 100 years of Brahmā—that is, 36,500 days of Brahmā, which equals a cosmic cycle—a **pralaya**, or dissolution, occurs. At the end of a cosmic cycle, the forces of chaos and entropy overcome the forces of order, or dharma, and the universe dissolves, returning to a potential state. There follows the great sleep, or *mahāpralaya*, which also lasts for 100 years of Brahmā, after which a new **creation** will emerge and a new age of Brahmā will begin.

WORLD COUNCIL OF THE ĀRYA SAMĀJ. Organization distinct from the **Ārya Samāj**, based on the ideals and teachings of **Swāmī Dayānanda Sarasvatī**, and founded by **Swāmī Agniveśa**, who became president of the organization in 2004.

WORLD GUARDIANS. *See* LOKAPĀLAS.

Y

YADAVA. "Descendent of Yadu"; the family lineage of **Kṛṣṇa**, of which his father, **Vasudeva** and his aunt, **Kunti**, were both members. The city of the Yadavas, **Dvārakā**, tragically sank into the ocean at the end of the ***Mahābhārata***.

YAJÑA. Sacrifice; the central **Vedic** ritual. The most ancient Vedic sacrifices consisted of offerings to the **gods**, or **devas**, in return for which they hoped to attain specific goods, usually of a material sort—health, wealth, long life, security, good weather, and so on. In the ***Brāhmaṇas***, one begins to see a more sophisticated theory of sacrifice develop. No longer a mere transaction, the sacrifice comes to be seen as something that the gods *need*, making the human performance of sacrifice an essential element in the smooth running of the cosmos. Sacrifice becomes vital to the upholding of **ṛta**, the cosmic order—a concept later denoted with the term **dharma**. In the ***Upaniṣads***, there is a divergence from this ritual concept. The ritual is internalized. It becomes a metaphor for all of life. Breath is a kind of sacrifice. Speech is a kind of sacrifice. Sexual activity is a kind of sacrifice. **Actions** of all kinds—**karma**—are seen as yielding definite effects in the world, and not only the ritual action of the sacrificial arena. This leads to a gradual devaluation of the ritual of sacrifice and its replacement with practices such as **meditation** and worship (**pūjā**).

It is probably not a coincidence that the offering of **animal sacrifice** is viewed with increasing disfavor over the course of this development, with **vegetarian** substitutes eventually becoming far more prevalent than the ritual offering of slain animals. By the time of the ***Bhagavad Gītā***, sacrifice is seen in at least some Hindu traditions as a matter of mentally offering all of one's actions to **God** as a form of devotion (**bhakti**), or as an act of purification in preparation for the knowledge (**jñāna**) that everything is **Brahman**.

YĀJÑAVALKYA. **Brahmin** sage greatly revered for his wisdom; a major character in the ***Bṛhadāraṇyaka Upaniṣad***. The first explicit articulation of the doctrines of **karma** and **rebirth** in a Hindu text is placed in the mouth of Yājñavalkya, in a conversation with the sage King **Janaka**.

YAJUR VEDA. The second **Saṃhitā** of the ***Vedas***, likely composed between 1200 and 1000 BCE, according to mainstream scholarship. The main concern of this text is correct performance of the ritual of sacrifice (**yajña**). It exists in two distinct recensions called the "Black" or *Kṛṣṇa Yajur Veda* and the "White" or *Śukla Yajur Veda*.

YAMA. Vedic deity of **death** and the underworld. It is said that Yama attained this distinction by being the first human being to die, and therefore the first inhabitant of the underworld. Yama is one of the **Lokapālas**, or "World Guardians." *See also* DEVAS.

YAMAS. Restraints; five moral principles set forth in the ***Yoga Sūtras*** of **Patañjali** that together make up the first stage or "limb" of his eight-limbed (**aṣṭāṅga**) system of **yoga**. The five yamas are **ahiṃsā** (nonviolence), **satya** (truthfulness), **asteya** (nonstealing), **brahmacarya** (control of sexual desires and activities), and **aparigraha** (detachment).

The yamas provide evidence that the yoga system of Patañjali shares a common cultural milieu with the **ascetically** oriented **śramaṇa** traditions, **Jainism** and **Buddhism**. The content and order of the yamas are identical with those of the **vratas** (moral vows) of Jainism and with four of the Five Precepts of Buddhism.

YĀMUNA (fl. 11th century CE). Śrīvaiṣṇava theologian; grandson of Nāthamuni, a scholar who introduced the **poetry** of the **Āḷvārs** into formal **temple** worship in the 10th century. Yāmuna translated many of the poems into **Sanskrit**, contributing to the process begun by his grandfather of formalizing the systematization of the Śrīvaiṣṇava tradition, a process completed by **Rāmāṇuja** (1077–1157). *See also* VAIṢṆAVISM.

YAMUNĀ RIVER. River that flows from the **Himālayas**, past **New Delhi**, and through the **Vraja** region associated with **Kṛṣṇa**. It joins the **Gaṅgā** at **Prayāga (Allahabad)**.

YANTRA. Abstract, diagrammatic representation of a Hindu deity, often used as a focus of **meditation**, particularly in **Tantric** practice. *See also* MAṆḌALA.

YATRA. Pilgrimage; travel to a sacred place. Making such a journey, particularly if it involves some hardship, is a form of meritorious **action**.

YOGA. Literally, "yoke"; spiritual discipline; path to **mokṣa** (**liberation** from **rebirth**). There is speculation that yoga may have originated as a form of military training among **Kṣatriya** warriors. It includes, but is far from limited to, the physical exercises of **Haṭha Yoga** that come to the minds of most Westerners who hear or use this term. In classical Indian texts, the term often refers to a total way of life, and is akin, in its semantic range, to the term *religion*. It also refers to a specific system of spiritual practice—the **Aṣṭāṅga**, or "eight-limbed" system of **Patañjali**, outlined in his ***Yoga Sūtra***. In the modern period, **Swāmī Vivekānanda** identifies this system with the Rāja Yoga of the ***Bhagavad Gītā***. In Vivekānanda's usage—based, again, on the *Gītā*—yoga encompasses such activities as working for the good of humanity, devotional activity (**bhakti**), and study for cultivation of wisdom (**jñāna**). *See also* FOUR YOGAS; YOGĪ; YOGINĪ.

YOGA DARŚANA. System of philosophy based on the **Aṣṭāṅga** or "eight-limbed" type of **yoga** outlined in **Patañjali**'s ***Yoga Sūtra***. Within the system of six orthodox or **Vedic** (**āstika**) systems of philosophy or **darśanas**, the Yoga darśana is traditionally paired with the **Sāṃkhya** system, with which it is almost identical, being related to Sāṃkhya in the way that a practice is related to the theory that underlies it. The chief difference between the Sāṃkhya and Yoga worldviews is the incorporation into the Yoga system of the idea of **God** or **Īśvara**. Contemporary scholars debate the degree to which this incorporation of Īśvara into the Yoga system reflects a serious commitment to theism on the part of Patañjali (such as that found in the **Vaiṣṇava** traditions), or is more of an afterthought. The role of Īśvara in the *Yoga Sūtra* is not to act as creator or savior of the world. He is solely an object of contemplation (**Īśvara-praṇidhāna**), which is one of the five **niyamas** or observances that form the second stage or "limb" of Patañjali's system.

YOGA SŪTRA. Root text of the **Yoga darśana**, or system of philosophy. Attributed to **Patañjali**, the text was composed some time between 100 BCE and 500 CE. It outlines the eight stages or "limbs" of the "eight-limbed" (**Aṣṭāṅga**) system of yoga.

YOGĀNANDA, PARAMAHĀṂSA (1893–1952). Bengali spiritual teacher and founder of the **Self-Realization Fellowship** (SRF); author of the classic *Autobiography of a Yogi*, a popular work among Westerners drawn to Indic traditions; after **Swāmī Vivekānanda**, the second in a series of Hindu **gurus** who have found a following in the West. Coming to the United States in 1920 for a conference of religious liberals, Yogānanda remained in the country and established the Self-Realization Fellowship that same year to disseminate the practice of *Kriya* ***Yoga***, into which he had been initiated by his guru, **Sri Yukteśwar Giri**. Among the distinctive aspects of the Self-Realization Fellowship is its emphasis on devotion to Jesus as an **enlightened** master.

As chronicled in his famous autobiography, Yogānanda met a number of important figures of modern Hinduism in his lifetime, such as **Mohandās K. Gāndhī**, **Rabindranāth Tagore**, and **Ānandamāyī Mā**.

***YOGA-VĀSIṢṬHA-RĀMĀYAṆA*.** Also known simply as the *Yoga-Vāsiṣṭha*, this text is a presentation of **Advaita Vedānta** in the form of the teaching of the sage **Vasiṣṭha** to a young **Rāma**.

YOGEŚVARA. Lord of **Yoga**; an epithet of both **Śiva** and **Kṛṣṇa**; in the ***Yoga Sūtra*** of **Patañjali**, **God** as an object of **meditation**. It is not clear from the text if Patañjali has in mind any specific sectarian conception of divinity (like Śiva or Kṛṣṇa) or a more generic conception into which any deity preferred by the practitioner (**iṣṭadevatā**) could fit.

YOGĪ. A male practitioner of **yoga**.

YOGINĪ. A female practitioner of **yoga**; a female **yogī**.

YONI. Womb; the female reproductive organ; often depicted in an abstract iconographic form, and frequently in conjunction with the **liṅga**. The joining of the yoni, a symbol of female fertility and of the **Mother Goddess** (**Śakti**) with the liṅga (often interpreted as a phallic symbol of **Śiva**) symbolizes both fertility and creativity in general, with the union of Śiva and Śakti representing the conjoining of pure consciousness and creative principle (symbolized in **Sāṃkhya** philosophy by **puruṣa** and **prakṛti**, respectively).

YUGA. *See* WORLD AGES.

YUKTEŚWAR GIRI, SRI (1855–1936). A spiritual teacher from **Bengal**. Although he has his own following, Yukteśwar is best known for being the **guru** of **Paramahāṃsa Yogānanda**.

Z

ZAEHNER, ROBERT CHARLES (1913–1974). Indologist; known for his translation of the ***Bhagavad Gītā***.

ZARATHUSTRA (fl. 1100 BCE). Founder of **Zoroastrianism**.

ZED, RAJAN. Nevada-based Hindu priest. On 12 July 2007, Zed made history as the first chaplain to recite a Hindu prayer for the opening ceremonies of the U.S. Senate. Prior to this, Zed had opened the Alaska state legislative session. Zed's prayer for the U.S. Senate was met with some protest from fundamentalist **Christians**. The prayer consisted of the recitation of an English translation of the **Gāyatrī mantra**.

ZOROASTRIANISM. One of the world's oldest religions, Zoroastrianism is practiced today by a small community (approximately 150,000 adherents) in India. The official religion of the Persian Empire for over a thousand years, Zoroastrianism had a profound impact upon the Abrahamic religions—Judaism, **Christianity**, and **Islam**. It also shares historical roots with Hinduism and is known to have influenced Mahāyāna **Buddhism**. The founder of Zoroastrianism, **Zarathustra**, was a priest in Iran during what, in India, was the **Vedic** period. The religion of Iran at the time was a close relative of the Vedic religion, with its hymns and its rituals of sacrifice (**yajña**). This is because the culture of ancient Iran was, like that of the Vedic tradition, **Indo-European**. The pre-Zoroastrian Iranians worshiped deities called *daevas* with names such as *Intar* (cognate with **Indra**), *Uruwana* (**Varuṇa**), *Haoma* (**Soma**), and *Mithra* (**Mitra**). Supreme over all of these deities was the "Wise Lord"—**Ahura Mazda** (whose name is cognate with the **Sanskrit** term **asura**, which did not yet have demonic connotations at this early period).

According to the Zoroastrian **scriptures**, Zarathustra received divine revelations from Ahura Mazda, who was revealed to be the **One**, supreme **God** and creator of the universe. Zarathustra's teachings also included the idea of linear time—with a beginning and an end—a single lifetime for each human being followed by a judgment, an afterlife of reward or punishment until the end of time for good or bad behavior, and a resurrection and restoration of all beings to an everlasting earthly paradise at the end of time. When **Islam** became the dominant religion of Iran in the seventh century of the Common Era, many Zoroastrians fled to India, where they are known as *Parsis*.

Bibliography

CONTENTS

INTRODUCTION

To compile a comprehensive bibliography of Hinduism is a daunting—and arguably an impossible—task. In terms of primary sources, Hinduism is a tradition—or rather, a family of traditions—that has been producing texts for over 3,000 years. The "classical" or premodern sources that survive are largely composed in Sanskrit. However, there are also a variety of vernacular literatures, such as the popular devotional poetry of the bhakti movement, composed in other Indic languages, such as Hindi, Bengali, Tamil, Gujarati, and Marathi, to name just a few of the most prominent ones. And there is, of course, the Hindu writing of the modern period, much of which is in English, though the vernacular languages of India continue to be rich loci of Hindu literary and philosophical activity, as does Sanskrit (though for a small audience, despite periodic resurgences of interest).

Secondary sources on Hinduism also abound. With a history beginning in the late 18th century, with such pioneers as Sir William Jones, the scholarly discipline of Indology (often termed, in the United States, South Asian Studies) has produced a great abundance of historical, philological, anthropological, sociological, and philosophical writing—a process that continues unabated today.

What follows is therefore not comprehensive but seeks to give a broad overview of at least the major works in this field, both primary and secondary. The major division this bibliography makes is between primary and secondary sources. The primary sources have been divided into original works composed in Sanskrit and other Indic languages, translations of Sanskrit and other original works, and primary sources written in English. The original works in Sanskrit and other Indic languages are often anonymous and have been listed alphabetically by title. In cases where the name of an author is known (or is traditionally attributed), this has been indicated with the phrase "of so-and-so" after the title (e.g., *The Rāmāyaṇa of Vālmīki*). The translations have been listed alphabetically by the last name of the translator.

The modern primary sources in English include writings by Western authors who have identified with or been deeply influenced by Hindu traditions, as well as sources by major Hindu figures or representatives of modern Hindu movements.

The secondary sources are divided by their subject matter and approach into: (a) broad surveys of and introductions to Hinduism; (b) historical studies; (c) textual studies; (d) studies of practice (primarily ritual and ethics); (e) studies of particular deities; (f) studies of the arts; (g) studies of Hindu society; (h) constructive studies of Hinduism—that is, studies that reflect philosophical or theological methodologies, or that have philosophy or theology as their subject matter; (i) studies of particular Hindu traditions; (j) studies of Hinduism outside South Asia; (k) works that focus on broad theoretical concerns; and (l) studies of other religious traditions that are closely related to Hinduism.

The first category—broad surveys and introductions—also includes reference works and other materials useful to beginners in the field of Hindu studies. Historical studies range from histories of the Indian subcontinent, to studies of the history of particular regions or movements, to biographies of individuals.

Textual studies often have relevance to other areas but are focused primarily on understanding a specific text or use a specific text or set of texts as the chief lens through which an issue is viewed. Studies of practice include ethnographic works and other primarily descriptive works on ritual and ethics.

Studies of deities are distinguished from textual studies and studies of particular Hindu subtraditions by the fact that their primary subject matter is the deity in question, rather than the texts or traditions centered on that deity. Studies of the arts include art histories, works on iconography, and works on both drama and dance. Studies of Hindu society include both theoretical and ethnographic studies of phenomena such as caste, Hindu nationalism, and women's issues.

Studies of philosophies and theologies include both descriptive works—histories of Indian philosophy—and normative, constructive works, in which the author identifies with and seeks to advance a philosophical or religious point of view. It is sometimes difficult to distinguish between the latter type of work and modern primary sources in English. Generally, works by figures who have come to be seen as major founders of movements or as exemplars of such movements (such as Sita Ram Goel as a representative of Hindu nationalism) have gone into the category of primary sources. Works by professional scholars of religion or philosophy, however, have also gone into this category.

Studies of particular Hindu traditions include works on Vaiṣṇavism, Śaivism, Tantra, and so forth, as distinct from broader surveys of Hinduism as a whole.

Studies of Hinduism outside of South Asia include works on Hinduism in areas such as Southeast Asia, where Hindu traditions have been practiced for many centuries, as well as in the Western world, where such traditions are a more recent phenomenon, as a result of both Hindu immigration and Westerners being drawn to particular Hindu ideas and practices.

Works that focus on broad theoretical concerns include works that engage with issues such as the validity of the category of Hinduism and the relationship between the study of India and issues of colonization and power.

The studies of traditions related to Hinduism include work on such traditions as Jainism, Buddhism, and Sikhism, which emerged either from or in close dialogue with Hindu traditions, as well as works on both Hindu–Christian and Hindu–Muslim relations.

Finally, I have included a section on Internet materials for the study of Hinduism, which can themselves be divided into primary and secondary sources, depending on the point of view that a given website takes. Avowedly Hindu websites that seek to advance a particular Hindu perspective are primary sources, in contrast with purely scholarly sites, which strive to present information in a more or less objective manner.

Among the many libraries with excellent collections relating to Hinduism, one of the most renowned is that of the Bhandarkar Oriental Research Institute in Poona, a city famous for its centers of language and textual study. Another is the Indian Institute of the Bodleian library at Oxford University and the University of Chicago's Regenstein library, both of which have proven invaluable in my own research.

The University of Chicago also provides an exceptionally useful Internet resource in the form of its *Digital South Asia Library* (http://dsal.uchicago.edu/reference/), which includes a vast collection of online materials, such as audio samples from the Linguistic Survey of India and digital versions of many journals and reference works that are listed in this bibliography, such as Schwartzberg's *Historical Atlas of India*. And as a primary source, *The Hindu Universe* (http://www.hindunet.org/) is especially rich.

Clearly, not all works fit neatly or obviously into any of these categories. It is not unlikely that some readers will take issue with the placement of certain works. (Indeed, I have argued with myself about some of these placements and am open to persuasion that some should be located in categories other than where they are currently.) The categories themselves are also less than perfect, but they are the ones that emerged organically as I compiled these titles, and most works do seem to lend themselves to placement in one of these categories.

At the beginning of each section, beginning with English translations of primary sources, I have included a brief paragraph in which I recommend texts from within that section that may be particularly useful or accessible to beginners in this field.

I. PRIMARY SOURCES

A. Sources in Sanskrit and Other Indic Languages

Abhijñānaśakuntala of Kālidāsa. Bombay: Nirnaya Sagara Press, 1958.

Adhyātma Rāmāyaṇa. Calcutta: Metropolitan Printing and Publishing House, 1935.

Agni Purāṇa. Poona: Anandasrama Sanskrit Series, 1957.

Aitareya Brāhmaṇa. Calcutta: Bibliotheca Indica, 1895.

Apastamba Dharma Sūtra. G. Bühler, ed. Bombay: Bombay Sanskrit Series 44 and 50, 1892, 1894.

Arthaśāstra of Kauṭilya. R. P. Kangle, ed. Bombay: University of Bombay, 1960.

Atharva Veda. Hoshiarpur: Vishveshvaranand Vedic Research Institute, 1960.

Baudhayana Dharma Sūtra. C. Sastri, ed. Benares: Kashi Sanskrit Series 104, 1934.

Bhagavad Gītā. (See *Mahābhārata*.)

Bhāgavata Purāṇa. Benares: Pandita Pustakalaya, 1972.

Brahma Sūtra Bhāṣya of Madhva. Tirupati: Tirumala-Tirupati-Devasthanena, 1893.

Brahma Sūtra Bhāṣya of Rāmāṇuja (Śrī Bhāṣya). Swami Vireswarananda and Swami Adidevananda, eds. Calcutta: Advaita Ashrama, 2008.
Brahma Sūtra Bhāṣya of Śaṅkara. Bombay: Nirnaya Sagara Press, 1948.
Brahmāṇḍa Purāṇa. Bombay: Venkateshvara Steam Press, 1857.
Brahmavaivarta Purāṇa. Poona: Anandasrama Sanskrit Series, 1935.
Bṛhaddevatā of Śaunaka. Cambridge, Mass.: Harvard University Press, 1904.
Buddhacarita of Aśvaghoṣa. E. H. Johnston, ed. Calcutta: Panjab University Oriental Publications, 1935–1936.
Daśāvatāracarita of Kṣemendra. Bombay: Kavyamala Series, 1891.
Devībhāgavata Purāṇa. Benares: Pandita Pustakalaya, 1960.
Garuḍa Purāṇa. Benares: Pandita Pustakalaya, 1969.
Gautama Dharmaśāstra. New Delhi: Veda Mitra, 1969.
Gītā Govinda of Jayadeva. Hyderabad: Sanskrit Academy Series, 1969.
Harivāṃśa. Poona: Bhandarkar Oriental Research Institute, 1969.
Harṣacarita of Baṇa. Bombay: Bombay Sanskrit and Prakrit Series, 1909.
Jaiminīya Brāhmaṇa. Nagpur: Sarasvati-vihara Series, 1954.
Jātakamāla of Āryaśura. Delhi: Motilal Banarsidass, 1971.
Kālika Purāṇa. Sri Biswanarayan Sastri, ed. Varanasi: Chowkhamba Sanskrit Series Office, 1972.
Kalki Purāṇa. Mathura: Jai Nitai Press, 2006.
Kāmasūtra of Vatsyayana. Varanasi: Kashi Sanskrit Series, 1964.
Kaṭhasaritsāgara. Bombay: Nirnara Sagara Press, 1930.
Kauṣītaki Brāhmaṇa. Calcutta: Bibliotheca Indica, 1903.
Kurma Purāṇa. Varanasi: All-India Kashiraj Trust, 1972.
Liṅga Purāṇa. Calcutta: Sri Arunodaraya, 1812.
Madhvavijaya of Nārāyaṇa Paṇḍitācārya. Vishakhapatnam: Shrimadananda Tirtha Publications, 1983.
Mahābhāgavata Purāṇa. Bombay: Venkateshvara Steam Press, 1913.
Mahābhārata. Poona: Bhandarkar Oriental Research Institute, 1933–1969.
Mahānirvāṇa Tantra. Madras: Tantrik Texts, 1929.
Maitrayaṇi Saṃhitā. Wiesbaden, Germany: R. Steiner, 1970–1972.
Manusmṛti. Bombay: Bharatiya Vidya Series, 1972–1978.
Naiṣadīyacarita of Śrī Harṣa. Bombay: Nirnaya Sagara Press, 1896.
Nirukta of Yaska. Lakshman Sarup, ed. London: Oxford University Press, 1920–1927.
Priyadarśika of Harṣa. M. R. Kale, ed. Bombay: Motilal Banarsidass, 1928.
Pūrvamīmāṃsā Sūtra of Śabarasvāmin. Hirayana: Ramlal Kapar, 1986.
Rāmacaritamānasa of Tulsīdās. Delhi: Motilal Banarsidass, 1990.
Rāmāyaṇa of Valmīki. Baroda: Oriental Institute, 1960–1975.
Ṛg Veda. London: Oxford University Press, 1890–1892.
Sarvadarśanasaṃgraha of Madhava. London: Trübner, 1914.
Śaṅkaradigvijaya of Madhava. Poona: Bhandarkar Oriental Research Institute, 1915.
Śatapatha Brāhmaṇa. Benares: Chowkhamba Sanskrit Series, 1964.
Satyārth Prakāś of Swāmī Dayānanda Sarasvatī (Reprint). Delhi: Manoj Publications, 2009.
Saura Purāṇa. Poona: Anandashrama Sanskrit Series, 1923.

Śiva Purāṇa. Benares: Pandita Pustakalaya, 1964.
Skanda Purāṇa. Bombay: Shree Venkateshvara Steam Press, 1867.
Śrī Rāmāṇuja Gītā Bhāṣya. Chennai: Sri Ramakrishna Math, 1992.
Taittiriya Brāhmaṇa. Rajendralal Mitra, ed. Calcutta: Bibliotheca Indica, 1859.
Taittiriya Saṃhitā. Poona: Anandashrama Sanskrit Series, 1979.
Upadeśasahasrī of Śaṅkarācārya. Mylapore, Madras: Sri Ramakrishna Math, 1961.
Upaniṣads. Bombay: Nirnaya Sagara Press, 1913.
Vajasaneyi Saṃhitā. Varanasi: Chowkhamba Sanskrit Series, 1972.
Vāmana Purāna. Benares: All-India Kashiraj, 1968.
Vāyu Purāṇa. Poona: Anandashrama Sanskrit Series, 1860.
Viṣṇu Purāṇa. Calcutta: Sanatana Shastra, 1972.

B. English Translations of Primary Sources (Including Compendia)

George Thompson's translation of the *Bhagavad Gītā* is excellent—a translation of this important text that has the exceptionally rare virtue of being both true to the original Sanskrit and highly readable for the native speaker of English. The same is true of Barbara Stoler Miller's translations of both the *Bhagavad Gītā* and the *Yoga Sūtras* of Patañjali (*Yoga: Discipline of Freedom*). Patrick Olivelle's translations of the *Upaniṣads* and the *Dharma Sūtras* are also both scholarly and readable. Wendy Doniger's *Hindu Myths* provides a good sampling of Hindu narrative literature from the epics and *Purāṇas*. Dominic Goodall's *Hindu Scriptures* is a nice compendium for beginners.

William Buck's novelized translations of the *Rāmāyaṇa* and *Mahābhārata* both provide highly accessible points of entry into these two epic poems.

All of these "high" Sanskritic sources are nicely balanced by R. K. Ramanujan's *Folk Tales of India*, which often give a twist to the better-known, dominant Brahmanical conceptions of Hindu belief and practice.

Ambikananda Saraswati, Swami. *The Uddhava Gītā: The Final Teaching of Krishna*. London: Frances Lincoln, 2000.
Avalon, Arthur, trans. *Tantra of the Great Liberation (Mahānirvāṇa Tantra)*. New York: Dover, 1972.
Bailly, Constantina Rhodes. *Shaiva Devotional Songs of Kashmir: A Translation and Study of Utpaladeva's Śivastotrāvali*. Albany: State University of New York Press, 1987.
Bhattacharya, Deben. *Love Songs of Chandidas*. London: Allen and Unwin, 1967.
Bloomfield, Maurice. *Hymns of the Atharvaveda*. London: Sacred Books of the East, 1897.
Buck, William. *Mahābhārata*. Berkeley: University of California Press, 1973.
———. *Rāmāyaṇa*. Berkeley: University of California Press, 2000.
Chatterji, Bankimcandra. *Ānandamath, or The Sacred Brotherhood*. Julius J. Lipner, trans. New York: Oxford University Press, 2005.

Cowell, E. B., trans. *Jataka Stories*. London: Pali Text Society, 1973.
Dimock, Edward C., and Tony K. Stewart, trans. *Caitanyacaritāmṛta of Krishnadasa Kaviraja*. Cambridge, Mass.: Harvard University Press, 1999.
Doniger, Wendy. *Hindu Myths*. New York: Penguin, 1975.
———. *The Rig Veda*. New York: Penguin, 1981.
———. *Textual Sources for the Study of Hinduism*. Chicago: University of Chicago Press, 1990.
Doniger, Wendy, and Brian K. Smith, trans. *Laws of Manu*. New York: Penguin, 1991.
Embree, Ainslie T. *The Hindu Tradition*. New York: Random House, 1966.
———. *Sources of Indian Tradition, Vol. 1: From the Beginning to 1800*. 2nd ed. New York: Columbia University Press, 1988.
Futehally, Shama, trans. *In the Dark of the Heart: The Songs of Meera*. San Francisco: HarperCollins, 1995.
Goldman, Robert P., trans. *The Rāmāyaṇa of Vālmīki*. Princeton, N.J.: Princeton University Press, 1984.
Goodall, Dominic, ed. and trans. *Hindu Scriptures*. Berkeley: University of California Press, 1996.
Griffith, Ralph T. H., trans. *Hymns of the Ṛg Veda*. Delhi: Motilal Banarsidass, 1973.
———, trans. *Hymns of the Sāmaveda*. Banaras: Chowkhamba, 1963.
———, trans. *Hymns of the Yajurveda*. Banaras: Chowkhamba, 1957.
Hawley, John Stratton, and Mark Juergensmeyer. *Songs of the Saints of India*. Oxford: Oxford University Press, 1988.
Hay, Stephen, ed. *Sources of Indian Tradition, Vol. 2: Modern India and Pakistan*. 2nd ed. New York: Columbia University Press, 1988.
Hess, Linda, and Shukdev Singh, trans. *A Touch of Grace: Songs of Kabir*. Boston: Shambhala, 1994.
Hume, Robert Ernest, trans. *The Thirteen Principal Upanishads*. Oxford: Oxford University Press, 1968.
Ingalls, Daniel H. H. *An Anthology of Sanskrit Court Poetry: Vidyākara's Subhāṣitaratnakośa*. Cambridge, Mass.: Harvard University Press, 1965.
Johnson, Clive, ed. *Vedānta: An Anthology of Hindu Scripture, Commentary, and Poetry*. New York: Harper and Row, 1971.
Johnson, Willard J. *The Bhagavad Gītā*. Oxford: Oxford University Press, 1994.
Layne, Gwendolyn, trans. *Kadambari of Baṇabhaṭṭa: A Classic Story of Magical Transformations*. New York: Garland, 1991.
Mayeda, Sengaku, trans. *A Thousand Teachings: The Upadeśasahasrī of Śaṅkara*. Albany: State University of New York Press, 1991.
Miller, Barbara Stoler, trans. *The Bhagavad Gītā: Krishna's Counsel in Time of War*. New York: Bantam Books, 1986.
———, trans. *Yoga: Discipline of Freedom*. New York: Bantam Books, 1998.
Müller, Friedrich Max. *Rig Veda*. London: W. H. Allen, 1874.
Nikhilananda, Swami, trans. *The Gospel of Sri Ramakrishna*. New York: Ramakrishna-Vivekananda Center, 1942.
Olivelle, Patrick, trans. *Dharmasūtras*. New York: Oxford University Press, 1999.
———, trans. *Upaniṣads*. New York: Oxford University Press, 2008.

Onians, Isabelle, trans. *Daśakumāracarita of Daṇḍin (What Ten Young Men Did)*. New York: New York University Press, 2005.
Panikkar, Raimundo. *The Vedic Experience: Mantramañjarī*. Delhi: Motilal Banarsidass, 1977.
Pereira, J., ed. *Hindu Theology: A Reader*. Garden City, N.J.: Doubleday, 1976.
Peterson, Indira V., trans. *Poems to Śiva: The Hymns of the Tamil Saints*. Princeton, N.J.: Princeton University Press, 1989.
Pope, G. U. *The Tiruvācagam or "Sacred Utterances" of the Tamil Poet, Saint, and Sage Manikkavacakar*. Oxford: Oxford University Press, 1900.
Prabhavananda, Swami, and Christopher Isherwood, trans. *How to Know God: The Yoga Aphorisms of Patanjali*. Hollywood: Vedanta Society of Southern California, 1953.
Radhakrishnan, Sarvepalli, and Charles A. Moore. *A Sourcebook in Indian Philosophy*. Princeton, N.J.: Princeton University Press, 1975.
Ramanujan, A. K. *Folktales from India: A Selection of Oral Tales from Twenty-two Languages*. New York: Pantheon Books, 1991.
———. *Hymns for the Drowning: Hymns for Vishnu by Nammalvar*. Princeton, N.J.: Princeton University Press, 1981.
———. *The Interior Landscape: Love Poems from a Classical Tamil Anthology*. Bloomington: Indiana University Press, 1967.
———. *Speaking of Śiva*. New York: Penguin, 1973.
Śarma, Viṣṇu. *The Pancatantra*. Chandra Rajan, trans. New York: Penguin, 2007.
Schweig, Graham. *Bhagavad Gītā: The Beloved Lord's Secret Song*. San Francisco: HarperOne, 2010.
Thompson, George. *The Bhagavad Gita: A New Translation*. New York: North Point Press, 2008.
Venkatesananda, Swami. *The Concise Rāmāyaṇa of Vālmīki*. Albany: State University of New York Press, 1988.
———. *The Concise Yoga Vāsiṣṭha*. Albany: State University of New York Press, 1984.

C. Modern Primary Sources in English

Some of these primary sources have become something akin to classics among contemporary spiritual seekers. They include Gandhi's autobiography (*The Story of My Experiments with Truth*), Aurobindo Ghose's *Essays on the Gita*, Huxley's *The Perennial Philosophy*, Thoreau's *Walden*, and Yogananda's *Autobiography of a Yogi*. As a source on the life of Ramakrishna that is at once a work of scholarship and devotion, Christopher Isherwood's *Ramakrishna and His Disciples* is particularly accessible.

Ambedkar, B. R. *The Buddha and His Dharma*. Bombay: Peoples Education Society, 1957.
———. *Towards an Enlightened India*. New Delhi: Penguin Books, 2004.

———. *What Congress and Gandhi Have Done to the Untouchables*. Bombay: Thacker, 1948.
———. *Why Go for Conversion?* Bangalore: Pariah Sahitya Akademy, 1981.
———. *The Untouchables*. Bombay: Thacker, 1948.
Besant, Annie. *Hindu Ideals*. Adyar, Madras: Theosophical Publishing House, 1904.
Blavatsky, Helena Petrovna. *The Secret Doctrine*. London: Theosophical Publishing, 1888.
Chowgule, Ashok V. *Christianity in India: The Hindutva Perspective*. Mumbai: Hindu Vivek Kendra, 1999.
Gandhi, Mohandas K. *An Autobiography: The Story of My Experiments with Truth*. Boston: Beacon Press, 1958.
———. *The Bhagavad Gita According to Gāndhī*. Berkeley, Calif.: Berkeley Hills Books, 2000.
———. *Selected Works of Mahatma Gandhi: A Complete Representative Set of Gandhian Literature in Six Volumes*. Ahmedabad: Navajivan Publishing, 1993.
Ghose, Aurobindo. *Essays on the Gita*. Pondicherry: Sri Aurobindo Ashram, 1983.
———. *The Life Divine*. Pondicherry: Sri Aurobindo Ashram, 2010.
———. *Secret of the Veda*. Pondicherry: Sri Aurobindo Ashram, 1953.
———. *The Upanishads*. Pondicherry: Sri Aurobindo Ashram, 1996.
Goel, Sita Ram. *Catholic Ashrams: Sannyasins or Swindlers?* New Delhi: Voice of India, 1994.
———. *Hindu Temples: What Happened to Them?* New Delhi: Voice of India, 1998.
———. *History of Hindu-Christian Encounters*. New Delhi: Voice of India, 1989.
Huxley, Aldous. *The Perennial Philosophy*. New York: Harper and Row, 1944.
Isherwood, Christopher. *My Guru and His Disciple*. Minneapolis: University of Minnesota Press, 2001.
———. *Ramakrishna and His Disciples*. Hollywood, Calif.: Vedanta Press, 1965.
Maharishi Mahesh Yogi. *Maharishi Mahesh Yogi on the Bhagavad Gītā, Chapters 1–6*. New York: Penguin, 1990.
———. *Science of Being and Art of Living*. New York: Plume, 2001.
Muktananda, Swami. *Play of Consciousness: A Spiritual Autobiography*. South Fallsburg, N.Y.: Siddha Yoga Publications, 2000.
Pandit, Bansi. *The Hindu Mind: Fundamentals of Hindu Religion and Philosophy for All Ages*. Glen Ellyn, Ill.: B and V Enterprises, 1998.
Prabhupāda, A. C. Bhaktivedānta Swāmī. *Bhagavad Gītā: As It Is* (Reprint). Los Angeles: Bhaktivedānta Book Trust, 1997.
Radhakrishnan, Sarvepalli. *The Hindu View of Life*. London: Macmillan, 1927.
Rama, Swami. *Living with the Himalayan Masters*. Blue Mountain, Pa.: Himalayan Institute Press, 2007.
Richards, Glyn. *A Source-Book of Modern Hinduism*. Richmond, U.K.: Curzon, 1985.
Satchidananda, Swami. *The Living Gita*. New York: Henry Holt, 1988.
Subramuniyaswami, Satguru Sivaya. *Dancing with Śiva: Hinduism's Contemporary Catechism*. Kauai, Hawaii: Himalayan Academy, 1997.
———. *How to Become a Hindu: A Guide for Seekers and Born Hindus*. Kauai, Hawaii: Himalayan Academy, 2000.

———. *Merging with Śiva: Hinduism's Contemporary Metaphysics*. Kauai, Hawaii: Himalayan Academy, 1999.

Thoreau, Henry David. *Walden*. New York: W. W. Norton, 1966.

Vivekananda, Swami. *The Complete Works of Swami Vivekananda*. Vols. 1–8. Kolkata: Advaita Ashrama, 1989.

Yogananda, Paramahamsa. *Autobiography of a Yogi*. Los Angeles: Self-Realization Fellowship, 1999.

II. SECONDARY SOURCES

A. Broad Surveys and Introductory Works

Among the titles listed in this bibliography, beginners will probably find the broad surveys and introductory works listed in this section especially helpful. But even some of these presuppose a measure of specialized knowledge. I especially recommend David Knipe's *Hinduism*, K. M. Sen's *Hinduism*, and Vasudha Narayanan's *Hinduism: Origins, Beliefs, Practices, Holy Texts, Sacred Places*, all of which I have used effectively in introductory-level college courses on Hinduism or Indic religions.

For the more ambitious reader, I would recommend Klaus K. Klostermaier's *A Survey of Hinduism* (for a view of Hinduism that many practitioners find authentic), as well as Wendy Doniger's *The Hindus: An Alternative History*, which many practitioners have found problematic but which presents an interpretation of the tradition by a scholar who has had a profound impact upon the ways in which the contemporary academy views Hinduism.

Aiyar, C. P. Ramaswamy. *Fundamentals of Hindu Faith and Culture*. Trivandrum: Government Press, 1944.

Brockington, J. L. *The Sacred Thread: Hinduism in its Continuity and Diversity*. Edinburgh, U.K.: Edinburgh University Press, 1996.

Dallapiccola, Anna L. *Dictionary of Hindu Lore and Legend*. London: Thames and Hudson, 2002.

Doniger, Wendy. *The Hindus: An Alternative History*. New York: Penguin, 2009.

Flood, Gavin. *The Blackwell Companion to Hinduism*. Oxford: Blackwell, 2003.

———. *An Introduction to Hinduism*. Cambridge: Cambridge University Press, 2004.

Fuller, Chris. *The Camphor Flame: Popular Hinduism and Society in India*. Princeton, N.J.: Princeton University Press, 2004.

Grimes, John. *A Concise Dictionary of Indian Philosophy: Sanskrit Terms Defined in English*. Albany: State University of New York Press, 1996.

Hopkins, Thomas. *The Hindu Religious Tradition*. Encino, Calif.: Dickenson, 1971.

Jacobs, Stephen. *Hinduism Today*. London: Continuum, 2010.

Jagannathan, Shakuntala. *Hinduism: An Introduction*. Mumbai: Vakils, Feffer and Simons, 1984.

Klostermaier, Klaus K. *A Survey of Hinduism*. 3rd ed. Albany: State University of New York Press, 2007.

Knipe, David. *Hinduism*. San Francisco: Harper, 1991.

Knott, Kim. *Hinduism: A Very Short Introduction*. Oxford: Oxford University Press, 1998.

Johnsen, Linda. *The Complete Idiot's Guide to Hinduism*. Indianapolis, Ind.: Alpha Books, 2002.

Kinsley, David. *Hinduism: A Cultural Perspective*. 2nd ed. Englewood Cliffs, N.J.: Prentice Hall, 1993.

Lal, Vinay, and Borin van Loon. *Introducing Hinduism*. Thriplow, U.K.: Icon Books, 2005.

Lipner, Julius. *Hindus: Their Religious Beliefs and Practices*. London: Routledge, 1994.

Lopez, Donald S. *Religions of India in Practice*. Princeton, N.J.: Princeton University Press, 1995.

Mittal, Sushil, and Gene Thursby, eds. *The Hindu World*. London: Routledge, 2004.

Monier-Williams, Monier. *Religious Thought and Life in India*. London: John Murray, 1885.

Narayanan, Vasudha. *Hinduism: Origins, Beliefs, Practices, Holy Texts, Sacred Places*. New York: Oxford University Press, 2004.

Sen, Kshiti Mohan. *Hinduism*. New York: Penguin, 1961.

Stutley, Margaret, and James Stutley. *A Dictionary of Hinduism: Its Mythology, Folklore, and Development, 1500 B.C.–A.D. 1500*. New York: Harper and Row, 1977.

Sullivan, Bruce M. *The Historical Dictionary of Hinduism*. Lanham, Md.: Scarecrow Press, 1997.

B. Historical Studies

As noted earlier, the works that are contained in this section range from histories of the Indian subcontinent, to studies of the history of particular regions or movements, to biographies of individuals.

In the first category, I recommend John Keay's *India: A History* and Romila Thapar's *Ancient Indian Social History*. Though a bit dated, A. L. Basham's *The Wonder That Was India* is a classic and creates a rich and vivid picture of ancient India in the mind of the reader. For the Indus Valley civilization, Jane R. McIntosh's *A Peaceful Realm: The Rise and Fall of the Indus Civilization* is especially good for beginners.

For the modern period, Collins and Lapierre's *Freedom at Midnight*, on the Indian independence movement, is a classic, as is Louis Fischer's *The Life of Mahatma Gandhi*. William Dalrymple's *White Moghuls: Love and Betrayal in 18th Century India* is accessible and entertaining as an introduction to the early colonial period.

Abbot, J. E. *The Poet Saints of Maharastra*. 12 vols. Poona: Scottish Mission Industries, 1926–1941.

Adcock, Catherine. *Religious Freedom and Political Culture: The Ārya Samāj in Colonial North India*. PhD diss., University of Chicago, 2007.

Agrawala, V. S. *India as Known to Pāṇini*. Varanasi: Prithvi Prakasan, 1963.

Aiyangar, S. K. *Some Contributions of South India to Indian Culture*. Calcutta: Calcutta University, 1942.

Aiyer, A. Nataraja, and S. Lakshminarasimha Shastri. *The Traditional Age of Śrī Śaṅkarāchārya and the Maths*. Madras: Private publication, 1962.

Allchin, B., and R. Allchin. *The Rise of Civilization in India and Pakistan*. Cambridge: Cambridge University Press, 1982.

Altekar, A. D. *The Position of Women in Hindu Civilization from Prehistoric Times to the Present Day*. Banares: Motilal Banarsidass, 1956.

———. *State and Government in Ancient India*. New Delhi: Motilal Banarsidass, 1962.

Ashby, Philip H. *Modern Trends in Hinduism*. New York: Columbia University Press, 1974.

Bakker, Hans T. *Ayodhya: The History of Ayodhya from the 7th Century BC to the Middle of the 18th Century*. Amsterdam: John Benjamins, 1986.

Ball, Charles. *The History of the Indian Mutiny, Giving a Detailed Account of the Sepoy Insurrection*. New Delhi: Master Publishers, 1859.

Basham, A. L. *The Origins and Development of Classical Hinduism*. Boston: Beacon Press, 1975.

———. *The Wonder That Was India*. London: Sidgwick and Jackson, 1954.

Beal, Samuel, trans. *Si-yu-ki: Buddhist Records of the Western World*. New York: Paragon, 1968.

Bryan, Edwin F. *The Quest for the Origins of Vedic Culture: The Indo-Āryan Migration Debate*. New York: Oxford University Press, 2004.

Chakrabarti, Dilip K. *The Archaeology of Ancient Indian Cities*. Delhi: Oxford University Press, 1995.

———. *India: An Archaeological History*. New Delhi: Oxford University Press, 1999.

Chakrabarti, Kunal. *Themes in Indian History*. Oxford Readings in Sociology. Delhi: Oxford University Press, 2006.

Chattopadhyaya, S. *The Evolution of Theistic Sects in Ancient India*. Calcutta: Progressive Publishers, 1963.

———. *Reflections on the Tantras*. Delhi: Motilal Banarsidass, 1978.

———. *Some Early Dynasties of South India*. Delhi: Motilal Banarsidass, 1974.

Chaudhuri, N. *That Compassionate Touch of Ma Anandamayee*. Reprint. Delhi: Motilal Banarsidass, 2006.

Clothey, Fred. *Images of Man: Religion and Historical Process in South Asia*. Madras: Blackie and Son, 1983.

Collins, L., and D. Lapierre. *Freedom at Midnight*. New York: Simon and Schuster, 1975.

Crawford, S. Cromwell. *Ram Mohan Roy: Social, Political and Religious Reform in Nineteenth Century India*. New York: Paragon House, 1987.

Dalrymple, William. *White Moghuls: Love and Betrayal in 18th Century India*. Hammersmith, U.K.: HarperCollins, Flamingo, 2003.
Dandekar, R. N. *Some Aspects of the History of Hinduism*. Poona: University of Poona, 1967.
Daniélou, Alain. *A Brief History of India*. Rochester, Vt.: Inner Traditions, 2003.
David, Saul. *The Indian Mutiny*. New York: Penguin Books, 2003.
Devahuti, D. *Harsha: A Political Study*. Oxford: Clarendon, 1970.
Eaton, Richard M. *Temple Desecration and Indo-Muslim States*. New York: Oxford University Press, 1990.
Eban, M., ed. *Maharishi the Guru: The Story of Maharishi Mahesh Yogi*. Bombay: Pear Publications, 1968.
Erikson, Erik H. *Gandhi's Truth*. New York: W. W. Norton, 1970.
Feuerstein, Georg, Subhash Kak, and David Frawley. *In Search of the Cradle of Civilization*. Wheaton, Ill.: Theosophical Publishing House, 1995.
Fischer, Louis. *The Life of Mahatma Gandhi*. Bombay: Bharatiya Vidya Bhavan, 1959.
Glucklich, Ariel. *The Strides of Vishnu: Hindu Culture in Historical Perspective*. New York: Oxford University Press, 2008.
Hardy, Friedhelm. *Viraha Bhakti: The Early History of Krishna Devotion in South India*. Delhi: Oxford University Press, 1983.
Hawley, John Stratton. *Three Bhakti Voices: Mirabai, Surdas and Kabir in Their Times and Ours*. Delhi: Oxford University Press, 2005.
James, Lawrence. *Raj*. New York: Little, Brown, 1997.
Keay, John. *India: A History*. New York: Grove Press, 2000.
Keer, Dhananjay. *Dr. Ambedkar: Life and Mission*. Bombay: India Printing Works, 1962.
Kenoyer, Jonathan Mark. *Ancient Cities of the Indus Valley Civilization*. Oxford: Oxford University Press, 1998.
Kulke, Hermann, and Dietmar Rothermund. *A History of India*. London: Routledge, 1986.
Lorenzen, David N. *Kabir Legends and Anantadas's Kabir Parachay*. Albany: State University of New York Press, 1991.
Ludden, David E. *India and South Asia: A Short History*. Oxford: One World, 2002.
Majumdar, R. C., ed. *The Vedic Age*. London: George Allen and Unwin, 1952.
McCrindle, J. W. *Ancient India as Described in Classical Literature*. Amsterdam: Philo Press, 1975.
McIntosh, Jane R. *A Peaceful Realm: The Rise and Fall of the Indus Civilization*. Boulder, Colo.: Westview Press, 2002.
McLean, Malcolm. *Devoted to the Goddess: The Life and Work of Ramprasad*. Albany: State University of New York Press, 1998.
Mishra, Pankaj. "Exit Wounds: The Legacy of Indian Partition." *New Yorker* (August 13, 2007): 80–84.
Moon, Penderel. *British Conquest and Dominion of India*. London: Duckworth, 1989.
Mukherjee, Ramkrishna. *The Rise and Fall of the East India Company: A Sociological Appraisal*. New York: Monthly Review Press, 1974.

Mukhia, Harbans. *The Mughals of India*. Malden, Mass.: Blackwell, 2004.
Neumayer, E. *Prehistoric Indian Rock Paintings*. Delhi: Oxford University Press, 1983.
Nikam, N. A., and Richard McKeon. *The Edicts of Aśoka*. Chicago: University of Chicago Press, 1978.
Nilakantha Shastri, K. A. *A Comprehensive History of India*. Delhi: People's Publishing House, 1957.
Olivelle, Patrick, ed. *Between the Empires: Society in India 300 BCE to 400 CE*. New York: Oxford University Press, 2006.
Parashar, Aloka. *Mlecchas in Early India: A Study in Attitudes toward Outsiders Up to AD 600*. Delhi: Munshiram Manoharlal, 1991.
Parpola, Asko. *Deciphering the Indus Script*. New York: Cambridge University Press, 1994.
Pollock, Sheldon. *The Language of the Gods in the World of Men: Sanskrit, Culture, and Power in Premodern India*. Berkeley: University of California Press, 2006.
Possehl, Gregory L. *The Indus Age: The Writing System*. Philadelphia: University of Pennsylvania Press, 1997.
———. *The Indus Civilization: A Contemporary Perspective*. Walnut Creek, Calif.: Altamira Press, 2002.
Renou, Louis. *Religions of Ancient India*. New York: Schocken, 1968.
Schwartzberg, J. E., ed. *Historical Atlas of India*. 2nd ed. Chicago: University of Chicago Press, 1990.
Seal, Anil. *The Emergence of Indian Nationalism: Competition and Collaboration in the Later Nineteenth Century*. Cambridge: Cambridge University Press, 1971.
Sen, Amitya. *Hindu Revivalism in Bengal, 1872–1905: Some Essays in Interpretation*. Delhi: Oxford University Press, 1993.
Sethna, K. D. *Ancient India in a New Light*. Delhi: Aditya Prakashan, 1989.
Singh, S. D. *Ancient Indian Warfare, with Special Reference to the Vedic Period*. Leiden: E. J. Brill, 1965.
Smith, Bardwell L., ed. *Essays on Gupta Culture*. Delhi: Motilal Banarsidass, 1983.
Suddhatmaprana, Pravrajika. *Indian Saints and Mystics*. Kolkata: Ramakrishna Mission Institute of Culture, 2009.
Thapar, Romila. *Ancient Indian Social History*. New Delhi: Orient Longman, 1978.
———. *Aśoka and the Decline of the Mauryas*. Oxford: Oxford University Press, 1961.
White, David Gordon. *The Alchemical Body: Siddha Traditions in Medieval India*. Chicago: University of Chicago Press, 1997.

C. Textual Studies

Ananda K. Coomaraswamy and Sister Nivedita's compendium of the *Myths of the Hindus and Buddhists* is an excellent introduction to the narrative traditions of Hinduism and Buddhism, as is Edward C. Dimock's *The Literatures of India: An Introduction*. Iravati Karve's *Yuganta: The End of an Epoch* is an intriguing guide to the *Mahābhārata*, as is Alf Hiltebeitel's *The Ritual of Battle* and his more recent work, *Rethinking the Mahābhārata: A Reader's Guide to the Education of the Dharma King*. Romila Thapar's *Exile and the Kingdom: Some Thoughts on the Rāmāyaṇa* is a similarly good entry into the *Rāmāyaṇa*.

Ali, S. M. *The Geography of the Purāṇas*. New Delhi: People's Publishing House, 1966.

Amore, R. C., and L. D. Shinn. *Lustful Maidens and Ascetic Kings: Buddhist and Hindu Stories of Life*. New York: Oxford University Press, 1981.

Apte, V. M. *Ṛgvedic Mantras in Their Ritual Setting in the Gṛhyasūtras*. Poona: Deccan College Research Institute, 1950.

Bakker, Hans T., ed. *Origin and Growth of the Puranic Text Corpus with Special Reference to the Skanda Purana*. Groningen, Netherlands: E. Forsten, 1986.

Balasundaram, T. S. *The Golden Anthology of Ancient Tamil Literature*. 3 vols. Madras: South India Śaiva Siddhānta Book Publishing Society, 1959–1960.

Banerjea, S. C. *Dharma Śāstras: A Study of Their Origin and Development*. Calcutta: Punthi Pustak, 1962.

Banerji, S. C. *Studies in the Mahāpurāṇas*. Calcutta: Punthi Pustak, 1991.

Bhattacharya, Asutosh. *Folklore of Bengal*. New Delhi: National Book Trust, 1978.

Bloomfield, Maurice. *Hymns of the Atharva Veda*. New York: Greenwood Press, 1969.

Brockington, John L. *The Sanskrit Epics*. Leiden: Brill, 1998.

Chakravarti, C. *Tantras: Studies on Their Religion and Literature*. Calcutta: Punthi Pustak, 1963.

Coburn, Thomas. *Devī Māhātmya: The Crystallization of the Goddess Tradition*. Delhi: Motilal Banarsidass, 1984.

Coomaraswamy, Ananda K., and Sister Nivedita. *Myths of the Hindus and Buddhists*. Reprint. New York: Dover, 1967.

Dandekar, R. N., ed. *Vedic Bibliography*. Poona: Bhandarkar Oriental Research Institute, 1961–1973.

———. *Vedic Mythological Tracts*. Delhi: Ajanta, 1977.

Derrett, J. Duncan M. *Dharmaśāstra and Juridical Literature*. Weisbaden, Germany: Otto Harrassowitz, 1973.

Devasthali, G. V. *Religion and Mythology of the Brāhmaṇas*. Poona: University of Poona, 1965.

Dimock, Edward C., ed. *The Literatures of India: An Introduction*. Chicago: University of Chicago Press, 1974.

Doniger, Wendy, ed. *Purāṇa Perennis: Reciprocity and Transformation in Hindu and Jaina Texts*. Albany: State University of New York Press, 1993.

Faddegon, Barend. *Studies in the Sāmaveda*. Amsterdam: North-Holland, 1951.

Goldman, Robert P. *Gods, Priests, and Warriors: The Bhṛgus of the Mahābhārata*. New York: Columbia University Press, 1977.

Gonda, Jan. *Dual Deities in the Religion of the Veda*. Amsterdam: North-Holland, 1974.

———. *The Indra Hymns of the Ṛgveda*. Leiden: E. J. Brill, 1989.
———. *Loka: World and Heaven in the Veda*. Amsterdam: North-Holland, 1966.
———. *Mantra Interpretation in the Śatapatha Brāhmaṇa*. Leiden: E. J. Brill, 1988.
———. *The Ritual Sūtras*. Wiesbaden, Germany: Otto Harassowitz, 1977.
———. *The Vision of the Vedic Poets*. The Hague: Mouton, 1963.
Gonzalez-Riemann, Luis. *The Mahabharata and the Yugas*. New York: Peter Lang, 2002.
Goudriaan, Teun. *Māyā Divine and Human: A Study of Magic and Its Religious Foundations in Sanskrit Texts*. Delhi: Motilal Banarsidass, 1978.
Hiltebeitel, Alf. *Rethinking the Mahābhārata: A Reader's Guide to the Education of the Dharma King*. Chicago: University of Chicago Press, 2001.
———. *The Ritual of Battle*. Ithaca, N.Y.: Cornell University Press, 1976.
Hopkins, E. W. *The Great Epic of India: Its Character and Origin*. New York: Charles Scribner's Sons, 1901.
Johnson, Willard J. *Poetry and Speculation of the Ṛg Veda*. Berkeley: University of California Press, 1980.
Kailasapathy, K. *Tamil Heroic Poetry*. Oxford: Clarendon, 1968.
Kane, P. V. *History of Dharmaśāstra*. Poona: Bhandarkar Oriental Research Institute, 1962.
Karve, Iravati. *Yuganta: The End of an Epoch*. Poona: Deshmukh Prakashan, 1969.
Katz, Ruth C. *Arjuna in the Mahābhārata: Where Krishna Is, There Is Victory*. Columbia: University of South Carolina Press, 1989.
Knipe, David M. *In the Image of Fire: Vedic Experiences of Heat*. Delhi: Motilal Banarsidass, 1975.
Lutgendorf, Philip. *The Life of a Text: Performing the Rāmcaritmānas of Tulsīdās*. Berkeley: University of California Press, 1991.
Mani, Vettam. *Purāṇic Encyclopaedia: A Comprehensive Dictionary of Epic and Purāṇic Literature*. Delhi: Motilal Banarsidass, 1975.
Minor, Robert, ed. *Modern Indian Interpretation of the Bhagavad Gītā*. Albany: State University of New York Press, 1986.
Narayan, Vasudha. *The Vernacular Veda: Revelation, Recitation, and Ritual*. Columbia: University of South Carolina Press, 1994.
Nath, Vijay. *Puranas and Acculturation: A Historico-Anthropological Perspective*. Delhi: Munshiram Manoharlal, 2001.
Patton, Laurie L., ed. *Authority, Anxiety, and Canon: Essays in Vedic Interpretation*. Albany: State University of New York Press, 1994.
Powell, Barbara. *Windows into the Infinite: A Guide to the Hindu Scriptures*. Fremont, Calif.: Asian Humanities Press, 1996.
Renou, Louis. *The Destiny of the Veda in India*. Delhi: Motilal Banarsidass, 1965.
Santucci, James A. *An Outline of Vedic Literature*. Missoula, Mont.: Scholars Press, 1967.
Sharma, Arvind, ed. *Essays on the Mahābhārata*. Leiden: E. J. Brill, 1991.
Thapar, Romila. *Exile and the Kingdom: Some Thoughts on the Rāmāyaṇa*. Bangalore: Mythic Society, 1978.

D. Practice: Ritual and Ethics

Lawrence Babb's *The Divine Hierarchy* and *Redemptive Encounters* are both fine examples of the genre of ethnographic writing: clear and accessible, and giving the reader a strong sense of lived Hinduism.

In the area of ethics, Christopher Chapple's *Nonviolence to Animals, Earth, and Self in Asian Traditions* is both clear and concise and has a considerable section devoted to Hinduism. For another perspective, D. N. Jha's *The Myth of the Holy Cow* reveals how recent the practice of cow protection as a defining feature of Hinduism really is.

On the philosophy and practice of yoga, Mircea Eliade's *Yoga: Immortality and Freedom* is a classic, while Chapple's recent *Yoga and the Luminous* is an excellent entry point to the practice of yoga by a scholar-practitioner.

Julia Leslie's *Roles and Rituals for Hindu Women* and Anne Mackenzie Pearson's *Because It Gives Me Peace of Mind: Ritual Fasts in the Religious Lives of Hindu Women* are especially good introductions to the rituals specific to Hindu women.

Arvind Sharma's *Hinduism and Human Rights* is a groundbreaking work that brings the discourse of dharma into conversation with the modern concept of human rights.

Alper, Harvey, ed. *Understanding Mantras*. Albany: State University of New York Press, 1989.

Babb, Lawrence A. *The Divine Hierarchy: Popular Hinduism in Central India*. New York: Columbia University Press, 1975.

———. *Redemptive Encounters: Three Modern Styles in the Hindu Tradition*. Berkeley: University of California Press, 1986.

Bahadur, Om Lata. *Book of Hindu Festivals and Ceremonies*. New Delhi: UBS, 1994.

Chapple, Christopher Key. *Nonviolence to Animals, Earth, and Self in Asian Traditions*. Albany: State University of New York Press, 1993.

———. *Yoga and the Luminous: Patañjali's Spiritual Path to Freedom*. Albany: State University of New York Press, 2009.

Chapple, Christopher Key, and Mary Evelyn Tucker, eds. *Hinduism and Ecology: The Intersection of Earth, Sky, and Water*. Cambridge, Mass.: Center for the Study of World Religions, 2000.

Clooney, Francis X. *Thinking Ritually: Rediscovering the Pūrva Mīmāṃsā of Jaimini*. Vienna: Institut für Indologie, 1990.

Creel, A. B. *Dharma in Hindu Ethics*. Columbia, Mo.: South Asia Books, 1977.

Cutler, Norman. *Songs of Experience: The Poetics of Tamil Devotion*. Bloomington: Indiana University Press, 1987.

Daniélou, Alain. *Virtue, Success, Pleasure, Liberation: The Four Aims of Life in the Traditions of Ancient India*. Rochester, Vt.: Inner Traditions International, 1993.

———. *Yoga: The Method of Reintegration*. New York: University Books, 1956.

Datta, V. N. *Sati: A Historical, Social, and Philosophical Enquiry into the Hindu Rite of Widow Burning*. New Delhi: Manohar, 1987.
Eliade, Mircea. *Yoga: Immortality and Freedom*. Princeton, N.J.: Princeton University Press, 1958.
Gold, Ann Grodzins. *Fruitful Journeys: The Ways of Rajasthani Pilgrims*. Berkeley: University of California Press, 1988.
Harman, William. *The Sacred Marriage of a Hindu Goddess*. Bloomington: Indiana University Press, 1989.
Hazra, R. C. *Studies in the Puranic Records of Hindu Rites and Customs*. Dacca: University of Dacca, 1940.
Heesterman, Jan C. *The Broken World of Sacrifice*. Chicago: University of Chicago Press, 1992.
———. *The Inner Conflict of Tradition: Essays in Indian Ritual, Kingship, and Society*. Chicago: University of Chicago Press, 1985.
Hocart, A. M. *Caste: A Comparative Study*. London: Methuen, 1950.
Houben, Jan E. M., and K. R. van Kooij, eds. *Violence Denied: Violence, Non-Violence, and the Rationalization of Violence in South Asian Cultural History*. Leiden: Brill, 1999.
Huffer, Amanda. *Guru Movements in a Globalized Framework: Amritanandamayi Ma's (Amma's) Community of Devotees in the United States*. PhD diss., University of Chicago, 2010.
Jha, D. N. *The Myth of the Holy Cow*. London: Verso, 2002.
Jordens, J. T. F. "Reconversion to Hinduism, the Shuddhi of the Ārya Samāj." In *Religion in South Asia: Religious Conversion and Revival Movements in South Asia in Medieval and Modern Times*, ed. G. Oddie, 144–53. London: Curzon Press, 1977.
Kakar, Sudhir. *Shamans, Mystics, and Doctors: A Psychological Inquiry into India and Its Healing Traditions*. New York: Knopf, 1982.
Leslie, Julia, ed. *Roles and Rituals for Hindu Women*. Rutherford, N.J.: Farleigh Dickinson University Press, 1991.
Pearson, Ane Mackenzie. *Because It Gives Me Peace of Mind: Ritual Fasts in the Religious Lives of Hindu Women*. Albany: State University of New York Press, 1996.
Sharma, Arvind. *Hinduism and Human Rights: A Conceptual Approach*. New Delhi: Oxford University Press, 2003.

E. Deities

As a broad overview of the Hindu pantheon, Alain Daniélou's *The Myths and Gods of India* is both accessible and very widely encompassing. Thomas Coburn's *Devī Mahātmya: The Crystallization of the Goddess Tradition* is an excellent guide to goddess traditions, as is David Kinsley's *Hindu Goddesses*. Philip Lutgendorf's *Hanuman's Tale* is a clear and comprehensive guide to the lore surrounding Hanuman. John Stratton Hawley's *Krishna, The But-*

ter Thief is a very good introduction to the devotional tradition surrounding Krishna, and Wendy Doniger's *Śiva: The Erotic Ascetic* is, despite its racy title, a fine guide to the primary source literature on Śiva and the ways in which this deity transforms over time.

Beck, Guy L., ed. *Alternative Krishnas: Regional and Vernacular Variations on a Hindu Deity*. Albany: State University of New York Press, 2005.
Bryant, Edwin F., ed. *Krishna, a Sourcebook*. New York: Oxford University Press, 2001.
Clothey, F. W. *The Many Faces of Murukan: The History and Meaning of a South Indian God*. The Hague: Mouton, 1978.
Coburn, Thomas B. *Devī Mahātmya: The Crystallization of the Goddess Tradition*. Delhi: Motilal Banarsidass, 1984.
Daniélou, Alain. *Hindu Polytheism*. London: Routledge and Kegan Paul, 1963.
———. *The Myths and Gods of India*. Rochester, Vt.: Inner Traditions International, 1985.
Das, B. *Kṛṣṇa: A Study in the Theory of Avatāras*. Bombay: Bharatiya Vidya Bhavan, 1962.
Doniger, Wendy. *Śiva: The Erotic Ascetic*. Oxford: Oxford University Press, 1973.
Erndl, Kathleen M. *Victory to the Mother: The Hindu Goddess of Northwest India in Myth, Ritual, and Symbol*. New York: Oxford University Press, 1993.
Handelman, Don, and David Shulman. *God Inside Out: Śiva's Game of Dice*. New York: Oxford University Press, 1997.
Hawley, John Stratton. *Krishna, The Butter Thief*. Princeton, N.J.: Princeton University Press, 1983.
Kinsley, David. *Hindu Goddesses*. Delhi: Motilal Banarsidass, 1998.
———. *The Sword and the Flute: Kali and Krishna*. Berkeley: University of California Press, 2000.
Lutgendorf, Philip. *Hanuman's Tale*. New York: Oxford University Press, 2007.
Nathan, Leonard, and Clinton Seely. *Grace and Mercy in Her Wild Hair*. Boulder, Colo.: Great Easter, 1982.

F. The Arts

For the beginner, T. Richard Blurton's *Hindu Art* is indispensable, as is Partha Mitter's *Indian Art*. Diana L. Eck's *Darśan: Seeing the Divine Image in India* is a fine introduction to the theology that underlies that use of images in Hindu worship. I then recommend Richard Davis's *Lives of Indian Images* as a follow-up.

On dance and drama, David L. Haberman's *Acting as a Way of Salvation: A Study of Raganuga Bhakti Sadhana* explores the religious significance of acting in Hinduism. Stella Kramrisch's *The Hindu Temple* is a good guide to the meaning of Hindu temple art and architecture.

Acharya, Prasanna K. *A Dictionary of Hindu Architecture*. London: Oxford University Press, 1946.

Anand, Mulk Raj. *The Hindu View of Art*. Bombay: Popular, 1957.

Archer, W. G. *Indian Miniatures*. Greenwich: New York Calligraphic Society, 1960.

———. *The Loves of Krishna in Indian Painting and Poetry*. London: Allen and Unwin, 1957.

Banerjea, Jitendra Nath. *The Development of Hindu Iconography*. Calcutta: University of Calcutta, 1956.

Blurton, T. Richard. *Hindu Art*. London: British Museum Press, 1992.

Coomaraswamy, Ananda K. *The Dance of Śiva*. Bombay: Asia Publishing House, 1956.

Davis, Richard. *Lives of Indian Images*. Princeton, N.J.: Princeton University Press, 1997.

Desai, Devangana. *The Religious Imagery of Khajuraho*. Mumbai: Franco-Indian Research, 1996.

Eck, Diana L. *Darśan: Seeing the Divine Image in India*. New York: Columbia University Press, 1996.

Gaston, Anne Marie. *Śiva in Dance, Myth and Iconography*. Delhi: Oxford University Press, 1982.

Goetz, Hermann. *Studies in the History and Art of Kashmir and the Indian Himalaya*. Weisbaden, Germany: Otto Harassowitz, 1969.

Gopinatha Rao, T. *Elements of Hindu Iconography*. Madras: Law Printing House, 1916.

Gupta, Chandra Bhan. *The Indian Theatre*. 2nd ed. New Delhi: Munshiram Manoharlal, 1991.

Haberman, David L. *Acting as a Way of Salvation: A Study of Raganuga Bhakti Sadhana*. Delhi: Motilal Banarsidass, 2001.

———. *Journey through the Twelve Forests: An Encounter with Krishna*. New York: Oxford University Press, 1994.

Hawley, John Stratton. *At Play with Krishna: Pilgrimage Dramas from Brindāban*. Princeton, N.J.: Princeton University Press, 1981.

Iyer, K. Bharata. *Kathakali: The Sacred Dance-Drama of Malabar*. London: Luzac, 1995.

Kramrisch, Stella. *The Hindu Temple*. Columbia, Mo.: South Asia Books, 1991.

———. *Unknown India: Ritual Art in Tribe and Village*. Philadelphia: Philadelphia Museum of Art, 1968.

Kuiper, F. B. J. *Varuṇa and Vidūṣaka: On the Origin of Sanskrit Drama*. Amsterdam: North-Holland, 1979.

Lidova, Natalia. *Drama and Ritual of Early Hinduism*. Delhi: Motilal Banarsidass, 1994.

Mehta, Tarla. *Sanskrit Play Production in Ancient India*. Delhi: Motilal Banarsidass, 1995.

Michell, George. *Hindu Art and Architecture*. London: Thames and Hudson, 2000.

———. *The Hindu Temple: An Introduction to Its Meaning and Forms*. Chicago: University of Chicago Press, 1988.

Mitter, Partha. *Indian Art*. Oxford: Oxford University Press, 2001.

Mookerjee, Ajit. *Tantra Art: Its Philosophy and Physics*. Basel: Ravi Kumar, 1971.

Rao, T. A. G. *Elements of Hindu Iconography*. New York: Paragon, 1968.

Stutley, Margaret. *The Illustrated Dictionary of Hindu Iconography*. London: Routledge and Kegan Paul, 1985.
Vaidyanathan, K. R. *Śrī Krishna, the Lord of Guruvayūr*. Bombay: Bhāratīya Vidyā Bhavan, 1977.
Varadpande, M. L. *Mahābhārata in Performance*. New Delhi: Clarion Books, 1990.
Waghorne, Joanne P., and Norman Cutler, eds. *Gods of Flesh/Gods of Stone: The Embodiment of Divinity in India*. Chambersberg, Pa.: Anima, 1985.
Wulff, Donna M. *Drama as a Mode of Religious Realization: The Vidagdhamādhava of Rūpa Gosvāmī*. Atlanta: American Academy of Religion, 1984.

G. Hindu Society

As introductions to the overall structure of Hindu society, two classics in the field remain Madeleine Biardeau's *Hinduism: The Anthropology of a Civilization* and Louis Dumont's *Homo Heirarchicus*. I also recommend Bernard S. Cohn's *India: The Social Anthropology of a Civilization*. A fine example of ethnographic writing that focuses on Hindu social structures in southern India is E. Valentine Daniel's *Fluid Signs: Being a Person the Tamil Way*. Nicholas Dirks's *Castes of Mind: Colonialism and the Making of Modern India* explores the reification of the caste system under the influence of colonial rule. Also excellent on the issue of caste is Ramdas Lamb's *The Ramnamis, Ramnam, and Untouchable Religion in Central India*, as is Brian K. Smith's work, *Classifying the Universe: The Ancient Indian Varna System and the Origins of Caste*.

Finally, Christophe Jaffrelot's *The Hindu Nationalist Movement in India* is, in my judgment, the best introduction available to the militant political wing of Hinduism.

Aiyar, S. P. *The Politics of Mass Violence in India*. Bombay: Manaktalas, 1967.
Aiyer, V. G. R. *The Economy of a South Indian Temple*. Annamalai, Tamil Nadu: Annamalai University, 1946.
Ali, S. *The Congress Ideology and Programme*. New Delhi: People's Publishing House, 1958.
Allen, Douglas, ed. *Religion and Political Conflict in South Asia: India, Pakistan, and Sri Lanka*. Westport, Conn.: Greenwood Press, 1992.
Altekar, A. D. *Sources of Hindu Dharma in Its Socio-Religious Aspect*. Sholapur, Maharashtra: Institute of Public Administration, 1952.
Altekar, A. S. *The Position of Women in Hindu Civilisation from Prehistoric Times to the Present Day*. Benares: Motilal Banarsidass, 1956.
Anand, Mulk Raj. *Coolie*. Bombay: Kutub, 1957.
———. *Untouchable*. Bombay: Jaico, 1956.
Anderson, W. K., and S. D. Dhamle. *The Brotherhood in Saffron: The Rāṣṭrīya Swayam-sevak Sangh and Hindu Revivalism*. Boulder, Colo.: Westview Press, 1987.

Baden-Powell, B. H. *The Indian Village Community*. New Haven, Conn.: Yale University Press, 1958.

Biardeau, Madeleine. *Hinduism: The Anthropology of a Civilization*. Delhi: Oxford University Press, 1994.

Bronkhorst, Johannes, and M. M. Deshpande, eds. *Āryan and Non-Āryan in South Asia: Evidence, Interpretation and Ideology*. Columbia, Mo.: South Asia Books, 1999.

Carstairs, G. M. *The Twice-Born*. London: Hogarth Press, 1957.

Cenkner, W. *A Tradition of Teachers: Śaṅkara and the Jagadgurus Today*. Delhi: Motilal Banarsidass, 1983.

Cohn, Bernard S. *India: The Social Anthropology of a Civilization*. Englewood Cliffs, N.Y.: Prentice Hall, 1971.

Daniel, E. Valentine. *Fluid Signs: Being a Person the Tamil Way*. Berkeley: University of California Press, 1984.

Daniélou, Alain. *India, a Civilization of Differences: The Ancient Tradition of Universal Tolerance*. Rochester, Vt.: Inner Traditions International, 2003.

Das, Veena. *Critical Events: An Anthropological Perspective on Contemporary India*. Delhi: Oxford University Press, 1995.

———. *Mirrors of Violence: Communities, Riots and Survivors in South Asia*. Delhi: Oxford University Press, 1990.

Deliege, Robert. *The Untouchables of India*. Oxford: Berg, 2001.

Dirks, Nicholas. *Castes of Mind: Colonialism and the Making of Modern India*. Princeton, N.J.: Princeton University Press, 2001.

Dumézil, Georges. *The Destiny of a King*. Alf Hiltebeitel, trans. Chicago: University of Chicago Press, 1973.

Dumont, Louis. *Homo Hierarchicus*. London: Weidenfeld and Nicolson, 1966.

———. *Religion, Politics and History in India: Collected Papers in Indian Sociology*. The Hague: Mouton, 1970.

Forbes, G. *Women in Modern India*. Cambridge: Cambridge University Press, 1996.

Ghurye, G. S. *The Scheduled Tribes*. Bombay: Popular Prakashan, 1963.

Glucklich, Ariel. *Religious Jurisprudence in the Dharmaśāstra*. New York: Macmillan, 1988.

———. *The Sense of Adharma*. Oxford: Oxford University Press, 1994.

Gopal, Sarvepalli, ed. *Anatomy of a Confrontation: Ayodhya and the Rise of Communal Politics in India*. Delhi: Penguin India, 1991.

Hardiman, David. *The Coming of the Devi: Adivasi Assertion in Western India*. Delhi: Oxford University Press, 1995.

Hardy, Friedhelm. *The Religious Culture of India: Power, Love, and Wisdom*. Cambridge: Cambridge University Press, 1994.

Hawley, John Stratton, ed. *Sati, the Blessing and the Curse: The Burning of Wives in India*. New York: Oxford University Press, 1994.

Huyler, Stephen P. *Village India*. New York: Harry Abrams, 1985.

Isaacs, Harold. *India's Ex-Untouchables*. New York: John Day, 1964.

Jaffrelot, Christophe, ed. *Hindu Nationalism: A Reader*. Delhi: Permanent Black, 2007.

———. *The Hindu Nationalist Movement in India*. New York: Columbia University Press, 1996.

———, ed. *Hindu Nationalism: A Reader*. Delhi: Permanent Black, 2007.

Juergensmeyer, Mark. *Religion as Social Vision: The Movement against Untouchability in 20th Century Punjab*. Berkeley: University of California Press, 1982.

Kulke, Hermann, and Burkhard Schnepel. *Jagannatha Revisited: Studying Society, Religion, and the State in Orissa*. New Delhi: Manohar, 2001.

Kuruvachira, J. *Roots of Hindutva: A Critical Study of Hindu Fundamentalism and Nationalism*. Delhi: Media House, 2005.

Lamb, Ramdas. *The Ramnamis, Ramnam, and Untouchable Religion in Central India*. Albany: State University of New York Press, 2002.

Marriott, McKim, ed. *India through Hindu Categories*. Newbury Park, N.J.: Sage, 1990.

Olivelle, Patrick. *The Ashrama System: The History and Hermeneutics of a Religious Institution*. New Delhi: Munshiram Manoharlal, 1993.

Omvedt, Gail. *Dalit Visions: The Anti-Caste Movement and the Construction of an Indian Identity*. New Delhi: Orient Longman, 1995.

Sharma, Jyotirmaya. *Hindutva: Exploring the Idea of Hindu Nationalism*. New Delhi: Penguin, Viking, 2003.

Smith, Brian K. *Classifying the Universe: The Ancient Indian Varna System and the Origins of Caste*. Oxford: Oxford University Press, 1994.

Weber, Max. *The Religion of India: The Sociology of Hinduism and Buddhism*. New York: Free Press, 1958.

H. Constructive Thought: Philosophy and Theology

The clearest introduction to Hindu theology available, to my knowledge—and one to which my students have responded very positively for years—is Pravrajika Vrajaprana's *Vedanta: A Simple Introduction*. Also clear and scholarly is Anantanand Rambachan's *The Advaita Worldview* (for the non-dualist stream of Hindu thought), as well as Deepak Sarma's *An Introduction to Mādhva Vedānta* (for a dualist counterpoint). Stephen Phillips, in his *Yoga, Karma, and Rebirth: A Brief History and Philosophy*, presents a very clear and cogent defense of the classical Hindu doctrines of karma and rebirth. Though it may be heavy going for a beginner, Debiprasad Chattopadhyaya's *Lokayata: A Study in Ancient Indian Materialism* is an intriguing exposition and defense of the relatively little-known materialist system of Indian philosophy.

The works of Wilhelm Halbfass listed here—*India and Europe: An Essay in Understanding*, *On Being and What There Is: Classical Vaiśeṣika and the History of Indian Ontology*, and *Tradition and Reflection: Explorations in Indian Thought* all give excellent overviews of various dimensions of Hindu intellectual history. The main focus of *India and Europe* is the interactions between India and the West. *On Being and What There Is* is probably the best exposition of the Vaiśeṣika system of Indian philosophy that is available in the English language. *Tradition and Reflection* is a wide-ranging, but quite accessible, collection of essays on a variety of topics relating to Hindu thought.

The articles in Rita Sherma and Arvind Sharma's edited volume, *Hermeneutics and Hindu Thought: Toward a Fusion of Horizons*, are excellent examples of constructive thought in contemporary Hinduism.

Arapura, J. G. *Hermeneutical Essays on Vedāntic Topics*. Delhi: Motilal Banarsidass, 1986.

Balasubramanian, R. *Advaita Vedānta*. Madras: University of Madras, 1976.

Banerjea, A. K. *Philosophy of Gorakhnāth*. Gorakhpur, Uttar Pradesh: Mahant Dig Vijai Nath Trust, Gorakhnath Temple, 1962.

Brown, W. Norman. *Man in the Universe: Some Continuities in Indian Thought*. Berkeley: University of California Press, 1966.

Carman, John Braisted. *The Theology of Rāmāṇuja: An Essay in Interreligious Understanding*. New Haven, Conn.: Yale University Press, 1974.

Carpenter, J. E. *Theism in Mediaeval India*. London: Constable, 1921.

Chakravarti, S. C. *The Philosophy of the Upaniṣads*. Calcutta: University of Calcutta, 1935.

Chapple, Christopher Key. *Karma and Creativity*. Albany: State University of New York Press, 1986.

Chatterjee, Margaret. *Gandhi's Religious Thought*. South Bend, Ind.: Notre Dame University Press, 1983.

Chatterji, Jagadish Chandra. *The Wisdom of the Vedas*. Wheaton, Ill.: Quest Books, 1992.

Chattopadhyaya, Debiprasad. *Lokayata: A Study in Ancient Indian Materialism*. New Delhi: People's Publishing House, 1959.

Clooney, Francis X. *Divine Mother, Blessed Mother: Hindu Goddesses and the Virgin Mary*. New York: Oxford University Press, 2005.

———. *Theology after Vedānta*. Albany: State University of New York Press, 1993.

Coward, H. G. *Bhartṛhari*. Boston: Twayne, 1976.

Dandekar, R. N. *Universe in Hindu Thought*. Bangalore: University of Bangalore, 1972.

Das, R. V. *Introduction to Śaṅkara*. Calcutta: Punthi Pustak, 1968.

Dasgupta, Surendranath. *History of Indian Philosophy*. 5 vols. Reprint. Cambridge: Cambridge University Press, 2009.

Deutsch, Eliot. *Advaita Vedānta: A Philosophical Reconstruction*. Honolulu: University of Hawaii Press, 1969.

Doniger, Wendy. "Do Many Heads Necessarily Have Many Minds? Hindu Polytheism and Religious Diversity" *Parabola* 30, no. 4 (2005): 10–19.

———, ed. *Karma and Rebirth in Classical Hindu Traditions*. Berkeley: University of California Press, 1980.

———. *The Origins of Evil in Hindu Mythology*. Berkeley: University of California Press, 1976.

Eck, Diana L. *Banaras: City of Light*. New York: Penguin, 1983.

Feuerstein, Georg. *The Philosophy of Classical Yoga*. Manchester, U.K.: University of Manchester Press, 1982.

———. *Tantra: The Path of Ecstasy*. Boston: Shambhala, 1998.

Halbfass, Wilhelm. *India and Europe: An Essay in Understanding*. Albany: State University of New York Press, 1988.

———. *On Being and What There Is: Classical Vaiśeṣika and the History of Indian Ontology*. Albany: State University of New York Press, 1992.

———. *Tradition and Reflection: Explorations in Indian Thought*. Albany: State University of New York Press, 1991.

Isayeva, Natalia. *Shankara and Indian Philosophy*. Albany: State University of New York Press, 1992.

Larson, Gerald James. *Classical Samkhya: An Interpretation of Its History and Meaning*. Santa Barbara, Calif.: Ross/Erikson, 1979.

Long, Jeffery D. *A Vision for Hinduism: Beyond Hindu Nationalism*. London: I. B. Tauris, 2007.

Marcaurelle, Roger. *Freedom through Inner Renunciation: Śaṅkara's Philosophy in a New Light*. Albany: State University of New York Press, 2000.

Matilal, Bimal Krishna. *The Character of Logic in India*. Albany: State University of New York Press, 1998.

Muller-Ortega, Paul Eduardo. *The Triadic Heart of Śiva: Kaula Tantricism of Abhinavagupta in the Non-Dual Shaivism of Kashmir*. Albany: State University of New York Press, 1989.

Obeyesekere, Gananath. *Imagining Karma*. Berkeley: University of California Press, 2002.

Phillips, Stephen. *Yoga, Karma, and Rebirth: A Brief History and Philosophy*. New York: Columbia University Press, 2009.

Rambachan, Anantanand. *Accomplishing the Accomplished: The Vedas as a Source of Valid Knowledge in Śaṅkara*. Honolulu: University of Hawaii Press, 1991.

———. *The Advaita Worldview: God, World, and Humanity*. Albany: State University of New York Press, 2006.

———. *The Limits of Scripture: Vivekananda's Reinterpretation of the Vedas*. Honolulu: University of Hawaii Press, 1994.

Sarma, Deepak. *An Introduction to Mādhva Vedānta*. Surrey, U.K.: Ashgate, 2003.

Sherma, Rita, and Arvind Sharma, eds. *Hermeneutics and Hindu Thought: Toward a Fusion of Horizons*. New York: Springer, 2010.

Tapasyananda, Swami. *Bhakti Schools of Vedanta*. Madras (Chennai): Sri Ramakrishna Math, 1990.

Vrajaprana, Pravrajika. *Vedanta: A Simple Introduction*. Hollywood, Calif.: Vedanta Press, 1999.

Whicher, Ian. *The Integrity of the Yoga Darśana: A Reconsideration of Classical Yoga*. Albany: State University of New York Press, 1999.

I. Hindu Traditions

Among the excellent works listed in this section, I would suggest, as particularly accessible to beginners, Vasudha Narayanan's *The Way and the Goal: Expressions of Devotion in the Early Śrīvaiṣṇava Community*, Douglas R. Brooks's *The Secret of the Three Cities: An Introduction to Hindu Śākta Tantrism*, and David N. Lorenzen's *Kapalikas and Kalamukhas: Two Lost Śaivite Sects*.

Ayyar, C. V. N. *Origin and Early History of Śaivism in South India*. Madras: University of Madras, 1936.

Bhandarkar, R. G. *Vaiṣṇavism, Śaivism and Minor Religious Systems*. Varanasi: Indological Book House, 1965.

Bhattacharya, Nagendranath. *History of the Tantric Religion*. Delhi: Munshiram Manoharlal, 1982.

Brooks, Douglas R. *The Secret of the Three Cities: An Introduction to Hindu Śākta Tantrism*. Chicago: University of Chicago Press, 1990.

Burghart, Richard. "The Founding of the Rāmanandī Sect." *Ethnohistory* 225 (1978): 121–39.

Dimock, Edward C. *The Place of the Hidden Moon: Erotic Mysticism in the Vaiṣṇava-sahajiya Cult of Bengal*. Chicago: University of Chicago Press, 1989.

Lorenzen, David N. *Kapalikas and Kalamukhas: Two Lost Śaivite Sects*. Berkeley: University of California Press, 1972.

Narayanan, Vasudha. *The Way and the Goal: Expressions of Devotion in the Early Śrīvaiṣṇava Community*. Cambridge, Mass.: Center for the Study of World Religions, 1987.

Openshaw, Jeanne. *Seeking Bauls of Bengal*. Cambridge: Cambridge University Press, 2002.

J. Hinduism Outside of South Asia

By far the most accessible book in this section is the enlightening and entertaining *American Veda*, by Phil Goldberg, which chronicles the influence of Hindu thought in the United States. Somewhat more theoretical and "academic," but nevertheless accessible and engaging, is Lola Williamson's *Transcendent in America: Hindu-Inspired Meditation Movements as New Religion*. Less wide-ranging, but also more in-depth than Goldberg's work, Williamson's book focuses on three specific Hindu-based traditions: Siddha Yoga, Transcendental Meditation (TM), and Self-Realization Fellowship (SRF).

Bakker, F. L. *The Struggle of the Hindu Balinese Intellectuals: Developments in Modern Hindu Thinking in Independent Indonesia*. Amsterdam: VU University Press, 1993.

Bilimoria, Purushottama. *Hinduism in Australia: Mandala for the Gods*. Melbourne: Spectrum Publications, 1989.
Bromley, David G., and Larry Shinn, eds. *Krishna Consciousness in the West*. Lewisburg, Pa.: Bucknell University Press, 1989.
Burghart, Richard, ed. *Hinduism in Great Britain*. London: Tavistock, 1987.
French, Harold. *The Swan's Wide Waters: Ramakrishna and Western Culture*. Port Washington, N.Y.: Kennikat Press, 1974.
Goldberg, Phil. *American Veda: From Emerson and the Beatles to Yoga and Meditation—How Indian Spirituality Changed the West*. Bourbon, Ind.: Harmony, 2010.
Jackson, Carl. *Vedānta for the West: The Ramakrishna Movement in the United States*. Bloomington: Indiana University Press, 1994.
Judah, J. Stillson. *Hare Krishna and the Counterculture*. New York: Wiley, 1974.
Klass, Morton. *Singing with Sai Baba: The Politics of Revitalization in Trinidad*. Boulder, Colo.: Westview, 1991.
Shankarananda, Swami. "Confessions of a Western Hindu" *Hinduism Today* (October–December 2005).
Vertovec, Steven. *Hindu Trinidad*. London: Macmillan, 1992.
Williamson, Lola. *Transcendent in America: Hindu-Inspired Meditation Movements as New Religion*. New York: New York University Press, 2010.

K. Theoretical Issues

A little more challenging for beginners, the works in this field are focused upon a range of theoretical concerns that are of great importance for the representation of Hindu traditions but are largely of interest to teachers and professional scholars. Works from this list that are particularly clear and powerful in making their argument, having become practically required reading for scholars in this field, are Ronald Inden's *Imagining India* and Sharada Sugirtharajah's *Imagining Hinduism: A Postcolonial Perspective*. But for those who are new to this field and to these issues, I would recommend starting with J. E. Llewellyn's edited volume of essays by various authors, *Defining Hinduism: A Reader*.

Breckenridge, Carol A., and Peter van der Veer, eds. *Orientalism and the Postcolonial Predicament*. Philadelphia: University of Pennsylvania Press, 1993.
Brown, W. Norman. *India and Indology*. Delhi: Motilal Banarsidass, 1978.
Dalmia, Vasudha, and Heinrich von Stietencron, eds. *Representing Hinduism: The Construction of Religious Traditions and National Identity*. Thousand Oaks, Calif.: Sage, 1995.
Inden, Ronald. *Imagining India*. Cambridge: Blackwell, 1990.
Jha, D. N. *Rethinking Hindu Identity*. London: Equinox, 2009.
Llewellyn, J. E. *Defining Hinduism: A Reader*. New York: Routledge, 2005.
Lorenzen, David N. "Who Invented Hinduism?" *Comparative Studies in Society and History* 41, no. 4 (October 1999): 630–59.

Nicholson, Andrew J. *Unifying Hinduism: Philosophy and Identity in Indian Intellectual History*. New York: Columbia University Press, 2010.
Pennington, Brian K. *Was Hinduism Invented? Britons, Indians, and the Colonial Construction of Religion*. New York: Oxford University Press, 2005.
Ramaswamy, Krishnan, Antonio de Nicolas, and Aditi Banerjee, eds. *Invading the Sacred: An Analysis of Hinduism Studies in America*. Delhi: Rupa, 2007.
Sen, Amartya. *The Argumentative Indian: Writings on Indian History, Culture, and Identity*. New York: Farrar, Straus, and Giroux, 2005.
Sontheimer, Günther-Dietz, and Hermann Kulke, eds. *Hinduism Reconsidered*. New Delhi: Manohar, 2001.
Sugirtharajah, Sharada. *Imagining Hinduism: A Postcolonial Perspective*. London: Routledge, 2003.
Trautmann, Thomas R. *The Aryans and British India*. Berkeley: University of California Press, 1997.
Tyagananda, Swami, and Pravrajika Vrajaprana. *Interpreting Ramakrishna*. New Delhi: Motilal Banarsidass, 2010.

L. Other Religious Traditions Related to Hinduism

For beginners, some of the clearest and most accessible works on traditions that are closely related to Hinduism are those published in the I. B. Tauris series of introducing the world's religions: Nikky-Guninder Kaur Singh's *Sikhism: An Introduction*, Jenny Rose's *Zoroastrianism: An Introduction*, and my own *Jainism: An Introduction*. Richard F. Gombrich's *Theravāda Buddhism*, recently revised, has become something of a classic in the field of Buddhist studies. Peter Gottschalk's *Beyond Hindu and Muslim: Multiple Identity in Narratives from Village India* is outstanding on Islam in India.

Ariarajah, S. W. *Hindus and Christians: A Century of Protestant Ecumenical Thought*. Grand Rapids, Mich.: Eerdmans, 1991.
Chand, T. *Influence of Islam on Indian Culture*. Allahabad: Indian Press, 1963.
Chattopadhyaya, Brajadulal. *Representing the Other? Sanskrit Sources and the Muslims*. Delhi: Manohar, 1998.
Coward, H. G. *Hindu-Christian Dialogue*. Maryknoll, N.Y.: Orbis Books, 1990.
Frykenberg, Robert Erik, ed. *Christians and Missionaries in India*. London: Routledge, 2003.
Gascoigne, Bamber. *The Great Moguls*. New York: Carroll and Graf, 2002.
Gilmartin, David, and Bruce B. Lawrence. *Beyond Turk and Hindu: Rethinking Religious Identities in Islamicate South Asia*. Gainesville: University Press of Florida, 2000.
Gombrich, Richard F. *Theravāda Buddhism: A Social History*. New York: Routledge, 2006.

Gottschalk, Peter. *Beyond Hindu and Muslim: Multiple Identity in Narratives from Village India*. New York: Oxford University Press, 2005.
Herman, Arthur. *Influences: How Ancient Hinduism Dramatically Changed Early Christianity*. Stevens Point, Wis.: Cornerstone Press, 2004.
Kaur Singh, Nikky-Guninder. *Sikhism: An Introduction*. London: I. B. Tauris, 2011.
Long, Jeffery D. *Jainism: An Introduction*. London: I. B. Tauris, 2009.
Monius, Anne E. *Imagining a Place for Buddhism*. New York: Oxford University Press, 2001.
Pangborn, Cyrus R. *Zoroastrianism: A Beleaguered Faith*. New York: Advent Books, 1983.
Rose, Jenny. *Zoroastrianism: An Introduction*. London: I. B. Tauris, 2011.

III. INTERNET SOURCES

A. Primary Sources

Complete Works of Swami Vivekananda:
http://www.ramakrishnavivekananda.info/vivekananda/complete_works.htm
The Hindu Universe:
http://www.hindunet.org/
Hinduism Today:
http://www.hinduismtoday.com/
Vedanta Spiritual Library:
http://www.celextel.org/

B. Secondary Sources—Popular

Adherents.com:
http://www.adherents.com/
Beliefnet.com:
http://www.beliefnet.com/

C. Secondary Sources—Academic

Digital South Asia Library (University of Chicago):
http://dsal.uchicago.edu/reference/
Hinduism Home Page (University of Wyoming):
http://uwacadweb.uwyo.edu/religionet/er/hinduism/index.htm
Sanskrit, Tamil, and Pahlavi Dictionaries (University of Cologne, Germany):
http://webapps.uni-koeln.de/tamil/

About the Author

Jeffery D. Long received a PhD in the philosophy of religions from the University of Chicago's Divinity School in the year 2000. His dissertation was entitled *Plurality and Relativity: Whitehead, Jainism, and the Reconstruction of Religious Pluralism*. In it, he attempts to re-articulate the religious pluralism of the modern or Neo-Vedanta tradition of Sri Ramakrishna in a way that draws upon both the process philosophy of Alfred North Whitehead and the Jain philosophy of relativity. Since completing his degree at Chicago, he has been teaching in the Department of Religious Studies at Elizabethtown College in Elizabethtown, Pennsylvania, where he is currently an associate professor and department chair. He is also a cofounder and codirector of Elizabethtown's Asian Studies program. He has published two books—*A Vision for Hinduism: Beyond Hindu Nationalism* (2007) and *Jainism: An Introduction* (2009). His other publications include three dozen articles and reviews in various edited volumes and scholarly journals. Ongoing projects include an introduction to Indian philosophy and a theology of divine incarnation for the Ramakrishna tradition, as well as a science fiction/fantasy epic that some of his students have dubbed "the Hindu *Lord of the Rings*." Raised Catholic, Long was drawn to Hinduism at an early age and formally embraced the tradition as an adult, at the age of 26. Both he and his wife, Dr. Mahua Bhattacharya (who teaches Japanese at Elizabethtown College), are active members of their local Hindu temple, as well as of the Ramakrishna Vedanta Society. He is also a regular consultant to the Hindu American Foundation. He has served as chair of the steering committee of the Dharma Academy of North America (DANAM) and he is currently cochair of the North American Hinduism consultation of the American Academy of Religion.